Philip W. Smith

THE FISHES OF ILLINOIS

Published for the Illinois State Natural History Survey by the

UNIVERSITY OF ILLINOIS PRESS

Urbana and Chicago

Publication of the original cloth edition of this book was
made possible with funds from the Illinois Department of
Conservation and grants from Illinois Power Company,
NALCO Foundation, Commonwealth Edition Company,
and Samuel G. Dennison.

First paperback edition, 2002
© 1979 by the Board of Trustees
of the University of Illinois
Manufactured in the United States of America
P 5 4 3 2 1
∞ This book is printed on acid-free paper.

Library of Congress Cataloging-in-Publication Data
Smith, Philip Wayne, 1921–
The fishes of Illinois. / Philip W. Smith
Includes bibliography and index.
ISBN 0-252-07084-4 (alk. paper)
1. Fishes—Illinois. 2. Fishes—Illinois—Identification.
I. Illinois. Natural History Survey. II. Title.
QL628.I3S58   2002
5970920773   78-12741

Important Contributors to the Knowledge of Illinois Fishes

LOUIS AGASSIZ
1807–1873

ROBERT KENNICOTT
1835–1866

STEPHEN A. FORBES
1844–1930

DAVID S. JORDAN
1851–1931

EDWARD W. NELSON
1855–1934

CARL L. HUBBS
1894–

FOREWORD

Among the responsbilities of the Illinois Natural History Survey are "to conduct a natural history survey" and "to publish, from time to time, reports covering the entire field of zoology and botany of the state." During the Survey's 117-year history, its published reports on groups of animals and plants in the state have brought great credit to the agency and have served as models for faunistic and floristic publications by many other institutions. The present contribution regarding Illinois fishes is a worthy continuation of that tradition.

In the early 1870's, the first Chief of the Survey, Stephen A. Forbes, began to study Illinois fishes and build a reference collection. Among the many reports that resulted from these efforts was the classic, *Fishes of Illinois,* written by Chief Forbes and Robert Earl Richardson and published by the Survey in 1908. Recognized as the finest publication on fishes of its time, it has been out of print for many years. It is now outmoded because of vast increases in our knowledge of ichthyology over the years. Moreover, aquatic environments have been enormously modified in the interim, as Illinois has become a major agricultural and industrial state and one of the most populous states of the nation.

Another of the Survey's responsibilities is the maintenance of the official state collections of flora and fauna. Fortunately, much of the fish collection assembled by Professor Forbes and his associates is still extant. This is an extremely valuable resource, for it not only provides a record of the species which occurred in the various waters of Illinois around the turn of the century, but in addition provides an indication of their abundance. It also makes possible reidentification of specimens of several species then recognized that are now known to be composites of as many as three and four species as we presently understand them.

With the Forbes and Richardson state report and collection as points of reference, a new survey of the fishes of the state was begun in the early 1960's. After more than 10 years of intensive field work throughout Illinois and the adjacent areas of bordering states, this investigation produced some of the finest, most concerted distributional data ever assembled for a geographic area the size of Illinois. Judicious analysis of the data from the two surveys documents and provides a lucid picture of the many changes that have occurred in fish populations and the aquatic ecosystems of Illinois during the 75-year interim. Fishes as a group are sensitive indicators of long-term changes in the quality of the environment. Changes similar to those described for fishes are likely to have occurred in other aquatic populations.

Dr. Smith's report is the culmination of the new survey. In addition to making available excellent base-line data, it will serve as an identification manual and a definitive reference book for those interested in the earlier and present status of fishes and aquatic habitats within the state.

GEORGE SPRUGEL, JR., *Chief*
Illinois Natural History Survey

CONTENTS

ACKNOWLEDGMENTS

Over the past 16 years so many persons have contributed to building the fish collection upon which this report is based that some may be forgotten. Present and former associates in the Section of Faunistic Surveys and Insect Identification include M. E. Braasch, B. M. Burr, Ralph Downer, Greg Hahn, Paul Martorano, L. M. Page, and M. R. Weber. Other Illinois Natural History Survey staff members aiding in field work from time to time include Warren Andrews, R. E. Bass, G. W. Bennett, J. A. Boyd, D. W. Bridges, D. H. Buck, W. U. Brigham, W. C. Childers, Dennis Dooley, Ed Doyle, Michael Duever, D. F. Hansen, R. W. Larimore, D. W. McGinty, M. A. Morris. H. H. Ross, R. E. Sparks, L. J. Stannard, W. C. Starrett, Sue Tevebaugh, D. L. Thomas, and J. A. Tranquilli. Frequent collecting partners over the years include Dorothy M. Smith, R. L. Hass, and M. M. Hensley. Several collections were made specifically at my request by Don Buth, Francis Collins, Don Daleske, Ron DeHollander, M. S. Goldman, H. R. Hungerford, R. McCann, Guy McConnell, Larry Moehn, Paul Parmalee, William Schmitz, John Schwegman, H. H. Shoemaker, Mike Sule, J. E. Thomerson, Robert von Neumann, H. D. Walley, John Wanamaker, and K. L. Williams.

The Department of Conservation's Division of Fisheries has provided enormous help with its stream inventories since 1963. Largely as a result of the Department's interest in this report, its staff of fishery biologists, under the direction of former Chief Fisheries Biologist A. C. Lopinot, collected throughout Illinois. They include Jim Allen, Ken Brummett, Joe Bystry, Mike Conlin, Larry Dunham, Bob Dunn, Ray Fisher, Bill Fritz, Don Garver, Tom Groutage, Rod Horner, Jim LaBuy, Jim Langbein, Roy Lockart, Al Lopinot, Dick Lutz, Thixton Miller, Bruce Muench, Jack Newton, Pete Paladino, Ed Pickering, Merle Price, Al Pulley, Leo Rock, Dick Rogers, Dick Rompasky, Ken Russell, Rudy Stinauer, Jim Sublett, Greg Tichacek, Paul Vidal, Harry Wight, and George Zebrun. W. J. Harth, Mike Conlin, and John Schwegman of the Conservation Department have also been helpful.

Present and former Illinois Natural History Survey staff members, whose services have been invaluable in the preparation of the manuscript, include these persons. Mrs. Bernice Sweeney, Miss Charlene Miles, and Miss Connie Kyse typed various drafts. Mrs. Doris Sublette and Brooks Burr made special efforts to locate pertinent literature and to help check references in the text. Larry Farlow and Wilmer Zehr provided the enormous amount of photographic services required. The new artwork and drafting were done by Mrs. Alice Ann Prickett, Craig Ronto, and Lloyd LeMere; the paintings, by Mrs. Prickett. The older illustrations, from Forbes & Richardson (1908), were copied photographically from the original paintings of Mrs. Lydia M. Green and Miss Charlotte Pinkerton. Technical Editor Robert M. Zewadski and Larry M. Page edited the manuscript, and William L. Pflieger of the Missouri Department of Conservation served as guest reviewer.

The Illinois Natural History Survey subsidized the entire project from its inception to the completion of the manuscript. Dr. H. H. Ross, in particular, encouraged me to undertake the study and saw to it that technical help was available as needed. The National Museum of Natural History of the Smithsonian Institution supplied photographs of L. Agassiz and D. S. Jordan. The Chicago Academy of Sciences provided that of R. Kennicott, and the American Society of Mammalogists, that of E. W. Nelson from its historical file.

George C. Becker of Wisconsin State University supplied fish distributional data for adjacent Wisconsin and William L. Pflieger of the Missouri Department of Conservation for adjacent Missouri. W. B. Scott of the Royal Ontario Museum supplied Canadian sculpins as models for illustrations, and E. J. Crossman of the same institution advised me on problems dealing with the esocid literature. Over the years Reeve M. Bailey of the University of Michigan and Carl L. Hubbs have provided counsel on various matters, and Dr. Bailey has confirmed identifications of specimens on several occasions. In recent years, Larry M. Page, Brooks M. Burr, and Marvin E. Braasch have advised me on a myriad of ichthyological details.

Charles T. Flora, Supervisor of Graphic Design of the University of Illinois Office of Campus Publications, designed the book and dust jacket.

PREFACE

When one writes a state report on an animal group over a long period, the objectives change with the passage of time. Aware that the incomparable *Fishes of Illinois* by S. A. Forbes and R. E. Richardson was an act impossible to follow, I ambitiously planned an identification manual that would also include variation analyses, summaries of available ecological data, and a thorough study of the distribution of each species with emphasis on the changes that have occurred over the years in a highly agricultural and industrial Illinois.

Since the inception of the original plan, dozens of excellent reports on fishes of other states and geographic regions have been published. Much of the material I planned to include in the Illinois report is no longer needed. As recently as a decade ago competent identifications could be made by relatively few ichthyologists; now there are dozens of workers with a good knowledge of the North American freshwater ichthyofauna. At that time there were only a handful of the modern taxonomic revisions of subgenera and species groups; now there are many more. Ecological information has also increased substantially and, while it is of enormous value, that which is available is repeated in virtually all of the recent state and regional reports. Even some of the distributional data are no longer new, because our Illinois records have been published in recent taxonomic revisions.

Consequently, I have revised my objectives and aimed at two specific audiences. One, of course, consists of academic and professional ichthyologists; the other consists of environmental consultants and aquatic biologists in Illinois agencies and students taking courses in ichthyology, the natural history of the vertebrates, and environmental biology in Illinois schools and universities. The latter audience needs an identification manual, but one that also contains carefully selected pieces of information so that it can be used as a reference book on the Illinois ichthyofauna.

Brief History of Ichthyological Investigations in Illinois. Illinois fishes have received a great deal of attention. Probably the first references to them were made in the latter half of the 17th century in the narratives of such early French explorers as Marquette, Jolliet, Hennepin, and La Salle, all of whom commented on the strange paddlefish and

also mentioned giant catfish and sturgeon. These references predate the formal descriptions of these species by more than 100 years. During the 18th and early 19th centuries many American species from various parts of the continent were described by Linnaeus, Rafinesque, Mitchill, Lacépède, Walbaum, Lesueur, Girard, Cope, and other early ichthyologists. Prior to 1850 C. A. Lesueur had described *Catharus nigro-maculatus* and *Esox vermiculatus* from the Wabash River in adjacent Indiana, but the first species to be described from Illinois waters was *Etheostoma caeruleum* by D. H. Storer in 1845. Louis Agassiz in 1854 described *Zygonectes dispar, Hybopsis dorsalis,* and *Catonotus lineolatus* (= *Etheostoma flabellare*) from waters either within or bordering Illinois, and in 1855, *Hybognathus nuchalis* from Quincy.

The first regional list of Illinois fishes was published by Robert Kennicott in 1855 and cited for Cook County 30 species, nearly all of which can be identified with the species as we know them today. From Illinois specimens, C. F. Girard described *Ichthyomyzon castaneus* in 1858, and F. W. Putnam described *Catonotus kennicotti* in 1863. E. D. Cope in 1870 described *Placopharynx carinatus* from the Wabash River in adjacent Indiana.

The first catalogue of fishes for all of Illinois was that of E. W. Nelson, who in 1876 described *Cottopsis ricei, Etheostoma phoxocephalum, Ichthyobus cyanellus* (= *Ictiobus bubalus*), *Noturus exilis,* and *Sternotremia isolepis* (= *Aphredoderus sayanus*). Jordan & Nelson collaborated in 1877 in describing *Lepiopomus ischyrus* (= *Lepomis cyanellus* X *Lepomis macrochirus* hybrid). Jordan & Eigenmann also in 1877 proposed *Morone mississippiensis* for the preoccupied *Morone interrupta,* described from St. Louis and New Orleans.

In 1878 D. S. Jordan prepared the second catalogue of Illinois fishes and described *Episema jejuna* (= *Notropis blennius*), *Cyprinella forbesi* (= *Notropis lutrensis*), *Lythrurus atripes* (= *Notropis umbratilis*), and *Pleurolepis asprellus.* In the same paper S. A. Forbes supplied the original descriptions of *Alburnops nubilus, Poecilichthys asprigenis,* and *Boleosoma camura* (= *Etheostoma chlorosomum*). In 1878 Nelson vividly recounted the fishes of Lake Michigan in the Chicago area. In 1880 Jordan described *Nanostoma vinctipes* (= *Etheostoma zonale*). Forbes in 1882 described *Chologaster papilliferus* (= *Chologaster agassizi*) and in 1883, *Platygobio pallidus* (= *Hybopsis meeki*), *Trycherodon megalops* (= *Notropis emiliae*), and *Lepomis symmetricus*. Also in 1883 Swain & Kalb proposed *Noturus elassochir* (= *Noturus exilis*).

The third catalogue of Illinois fishes was produced in 1884 by Forbes, who in a period of conservatism lumped under the oldest names available within the groups many of the species previously recognized. In 1885 Forbes published original descriptions of *Lepomis garmani* (= *Lepomis punctatus*), *Oxygeneum pulverulentum* (= *Campostoma anomalum* X *Phoxinus erythrogaster* hybrid), *Notropis phenacobius* (= *Notropis stramineus*), *Notropis macrolepidotus* (= *Notropis umbratilis* or *Notropis fumeus*), and *Notropis anogenus*.

A fourth catalogue of Illinois fishes was published in 1903 by Thomas Large, who established the nomenclature later to be used by Forbes and R. E. Richardson and who exhibited a remarkable insight for that time into the relationships of the Illinois species. Forbes & Richardson in 1905 described *Parascaphirhyncus album*. These authors published their magnificent *Fishes of Illinois* in 1908 although no publication date is given in the volume. It was accompanied by a separate atlas of distribution maps. Most of the copies of the initial edition were destroyed in a warehouse fire, and a second edition was produced in 1920 that has almost identical pagination. Both editions are long out of print and quite rare.

Throughout the period that Forbes was studying Illinois fishes, he was much interested in food habits of both adults and young and published countless papers on the subject. Forbes was greatly influenced and materially aided by his close friend, D. S. Jordan, in nearby Indiana.

In the period following publication of *The Fishes of Illinois*, S. E. Meek worked on fishes at the Field Museum, but he was never especially interested in Illinois species. T. L. Hankinson at Eastern Illinois University was doing life-history studies, and personnel at the Illinois Natural History Survey were beginning to develop fisheries programs. The luminary of the period was Carl L. Hubbs, who over the years either personally or with students and associates at the University of Michigan clarified the status of dozens of previously little-known groups of fishes. The present state of our knowledge of American fishes is due to the work of Dr. Hubbs more than to that of any other individual. Two other lists of Illinois fishes have been published, one by D. J. O'Donnell in 1935 and one by P. W. Smith in 1965. Both of these brief lists added a few species to the known fauna of the state.

In recent years students of Reeve M. Bailey at the University of Michigan and those of Edward C. Raney at Cornell University have conducted many excellent revisionary studies of fishes that occur in Illinois and elsewhere. Important centers for studies of Illinois fishes at present are, in addition to the Illinois Natural History Survey, several of the universities within the state and the Field Museum of Natural History in Chicago.

Setting the Scene. Illinois, bordered by large rivers and Lake Michigan, also has many interior streams, a few glacial lakes in the northeastern corner, and some cypress-tupelo swamps in the southern tip. For an excellent description of the hydrography and topography of Illinois, the reader is referred to C. W. Rolfe's detailed accounts of drainage systems in Forbes & Richardson (1908 and 1920). Although well watered, Illinois has lost many aquatic habitats to agriculture, stream impoundments, industrial and domestic pollution, and other human modification of watersheds.

Illinois is one of the most productive grain areas in the world. For more than a century, the state has undergone great changes in landscape, farming methods, industrial development, and human population expansion. The changes related to landscape and farming methods include the draining of extensive marshes and forested floodplain lakes; the tiling and plowing of the vast prairies to convert them to productive farmland; the use of large, heavy machinery; the widespread use of commercial fertilizers, insecticides, and herbicides; and the introduction of new and improved plant varieties. Farming practices of the early settlers were largely restricted to cattle raising and cultivating small crops on high areas or along stream sources where drainage was naturally good. With the development of large farm machinery, small farms were merged to form fewer, larger farms, and crops became less diversified. Corn and soybeans became the leading crops. Cattle and hog raising followed a similar trend toward larger acreages.

With the increased farming intensity, erosion became a serious problem. When the native vegetation was removed, the soil was directly exposed to rain and wind and became compact and less absorbent. The result was rapid runoff, flooding, and the transfer of topsoil from fields to streams. Farm animals grazing along stream banks further contributed to erosion and siltation. When the soil could no longer store water, droughts began to occur with regularity, and once relatively stable streams vacillated greatly in size during the year,

Map of Illinois, showing counties

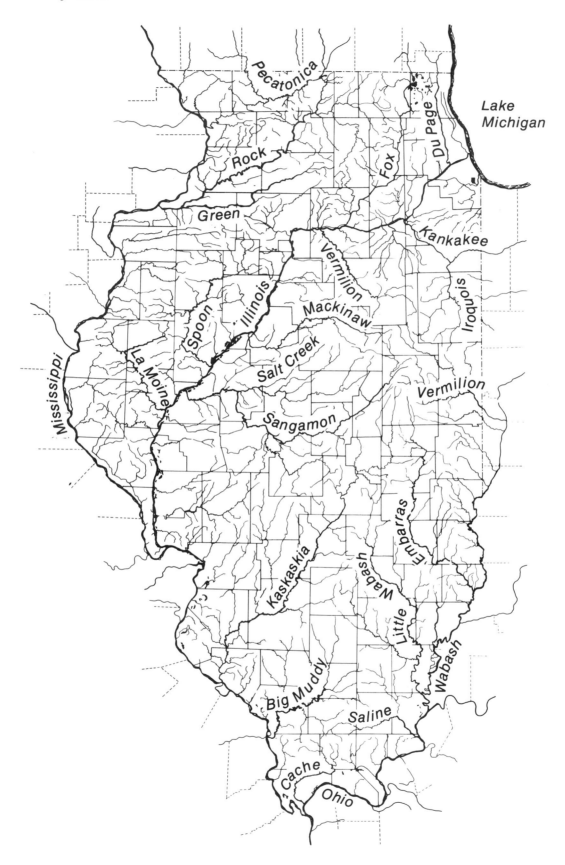

Map of Illinois, showing major rivers

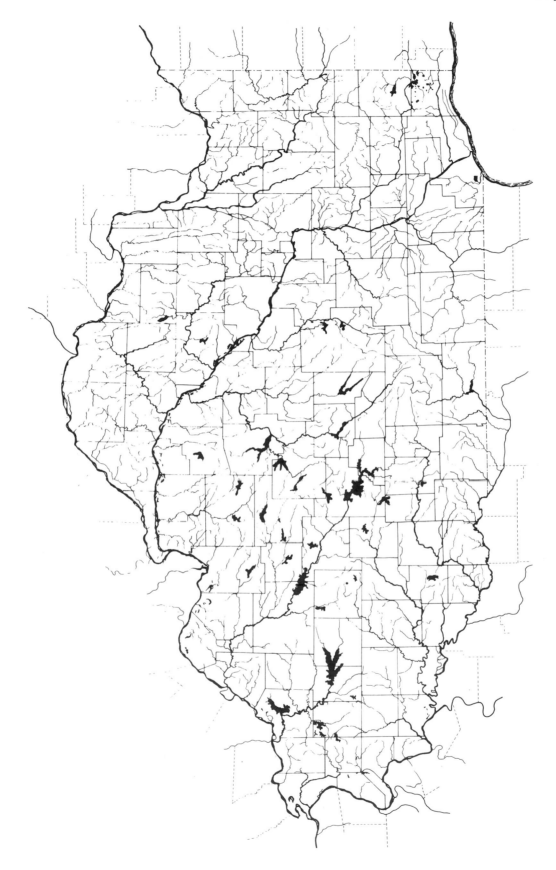

Map of Illinois, showing natural lakes and reservoirs as of 1978

some drying up completely in late summer and fall but creating great flood damage during wet seasons.

The gradually expanding human population resulted in the loss of much forest in hilly parts of the state and along watercourses. By the beginning of the 20th century, most of Illinois had been denuded of native vegetation. The increase in numbers and sizes of cities and villages required a similar increase in transportation facilities, with the result that vast acreages were devoted to urban and suburban properties and networks of roads. Domestic and industrial pollution was most easily disposed of by releasing it into streams. Water quality deteriorated rapidly. To supply sources of water for recreational and other essential needs of a large society, reservoirs were constructed by damming streams of various sizes in all parts of the state. Many square miles of streams and their floodplains lost the variety of aquatic habitats provided by the meandering stream and became reservoirs with essentially only one aquatic habitat. Deliberate and accidental releases of non-native fishes resulted in some unexpected interactions between species, particularly in habitats that had been much modified by human activities.

The cumulative effects of such environmental alteration have been enormous. Yet I have been surprised on several occasions to discover that an unusual fish species at an unexpected locality had also been found there by Forbes and Richardson's collectors some 75 years earlier. Evidently some fish populations are remarkably persistent in some of the more pristine streams and springs. For a detailed analysis of the effects of human modifications on fishes and aquatic habitats in Illinois, the reader is referred to Smith (1971). In the past the most damaging factors to the fish fauna have been siltation, drainage, a fluctuating water table (in recent decades), and interactions between fish species following habitat alteration. In the future the most damaging factors foreseeable are excessive siltation, additional stream impoundments, and conversion of more large rivers into barge canals.

Non-native, Extirpated, Decimated, Rare, and/or Restricted Species. This report on the fishes of Illinois contains accounts for 199 species. Thirteen of them are not native but now occur in the state through introduction or through natural dispersal after human modification of watersheds. They are the sea lamprey, alewife, threadfin shad, rainbow trout, brown trout, coho salmon, chinook salmon, American smelt, goldfish, carp, grass carp or white amur, white catfish, and striped bass. The remaining 186 are native species, but nine of them have been extirpated in Illinois. They are the Ohio lamprey, blackfin cisco, muskellunge, rosefin shiner, cypress minnow, greater redhorse, gilt darter, stargazing darter, and crystal darter. Three other species have not been collected in the state during the last 15 years and may also now be extirpated although too few data are available to be certain of their present status. They are the round whitefish, bigeye chub, and spoonhead sculpin.

Of the remaining 173 native species, a few have expanded their ranges and are now more abundant and more generally distributed than formerly, but many more are decimated to some degree by the widespread modification of habitats and deterioration of water quality. Prior to the passage of the Endangered Species Act of 1973, a few attempts had been made to list fish species as rare and endangered on the basis of their rarity, restricted distributions, and paucity of habitat as well as immediate or potential threats to their existence within Illinois (Lopinot & Smith 1973 and others). After implementation of the act, terminology was revised to include the categories endangered (actively threatened with extinction) and threatened (likely to become endangered in the near future). At this time none of the Illinois species qualifies as endangered and only one (lake sturgeon) as threatened in this context.

The new and still subjective definitions demote the importance of rarity and restricted distribution and eliminate a third category of "status uncertain because data are inadequate." The problem then becomes, How decimated must a species be to be regarded as endangered or threatened? Many species known from only a few localities have large localized populations, and the future of many of them seems secure because of protective measures, such as the designation of natural areas or ecological areas. Accordingly, a new attempt is made herein to list the seriously decimated and rare and/ or restricted fishes in Illinois. It is inevitable that changes in status of any one species can occur quickly at any time. For example, a proposed reservoir could immediately place an unlisted species on the vulnerable list; conversely, deactivation of the reservoir project could result in the removal of the species from the list.

Species now seriously decimated in Illinois are the lake sturgeon (also on national list of threatened species), alligator gar, cisco, pallid shiner, bluenose shiner, and bluebreast darter. Species presently decimated to a somewhat lesser degree are the lake trout, pugnose shiner, blacknose shiner, blackchin shiner, blacktail shiner, large-scale stoneroller, river redhorse, northern madtom, banded killifish, bantam sunfish, western sand darter, eastern sand darter, and harlequin darter. Species that presently are and, in many cases, have long been either rare or extremely restricted in distribution (so that their populations could become decimated quickly) are the least brook lamprey, northern brook lamprey, pallid sturgeon, lake chub, Alabama shad, lake whitefish, sturgeon chub, sicklefin chub, bigeye shiner, ironcolor shiner, weed shiner, river chub, longnose sucker, spring cavefish, northern studfish, slimy sculpin, fourhorn sculpin, spotted sunfish, banded pygmy sunfish, starhead topminnow, and cypress darter. Species such as the spotted sunfish and banded pygmy sunfish, regarded as in jeopardy only 3 or 4 years ago, have recently received protection through the designation of additional acreages as wildlife preserves by the National Forest Service and the Illinois Nature Conservancy and are presently out of danger.

ORGANIZATION

Each family and genus is introduced by a short paragraph that includes statements about the content and distribution of the group and, in some cases, remarks designed to give a better understanding of it. This paragraph is followed by a key of the conventional type. The species accounts are headed by the common and scientific names recommended in the official checklist (Bailey 1970). The families and genera are arranged phylogenetically rather than alphabetically and, for the most part, in the order most present-day ichthyologists follow. However, the species within each genus are in alphabetical order so that a specific account can be found quickly. Extirpated species are treated in the same fashion as species still present in the state, except that they are noted as extirpated by means of an asterisk. Introduced species are included only if there is evidence available that the populations are likely to be reproducing and surviving over more than 1 year. Nor is the bull shark from the Mississippi River near Alton (Thomerson et al. 1977) included, because the record, if valid, represents a highly unusual straggler.

The skeleton synonymy includes a reference to the original description, one to the first report of the species in the state, one for each synonym based on Illinois material, and one for one or more of the previous reports on Illinois species (Kennicott 1855, Nelson 1876, Jordan 1878, Forbes 1884, Large 1903, Forbes & Richardson 1908, O'Donnell

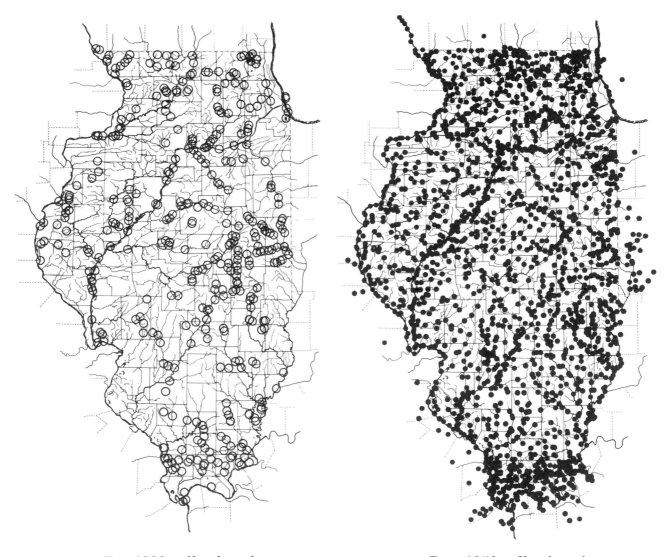

Pre-1908 collecting sites   **Post-1950 collecting sites**

1935, and Smith 1965). The first edition of Forbes & Richardson (1908) is cited rather than the 1920 reprint merely for historical reasons. The pagination is almost identical in the two printings.

The diagnosis gives only enough characters to enable the user to distinguish that species from all other Illinois fishes. It is presented merely to supplement the key and allow the user to confirm that he has keyed his specimens properly. It is therefore variable in length, the more difficult species obviously requiring a longer list of diagnostic characters. The length of the fish is total length and is given in both the metric and English systems.

The section entitled "Variation" cites pertinent literature on geographic variation and indicates which, if any, subspecies are recognized. For the most part, it merely lists the subspecies occurring in Illinois and refers the reader to published studies on geographic variation and to taxonomic revisions.

The section on ecology gives the preferred habitat of the species in Illinois waters and tersely outlines the information available on food and reproductive habits. It also refers the reader to the pertinent literature, where more detailed information can be found, or notes the absence of published life-history information.

The distribution section presents in general terms where the species occurs, how common and generally distributed it is, and what changes, if any, are discernible when comparison is made between its current distribution and its pre-1908 range (based on the Forbes & Richardson 1908 atlas of maps and the Forbes and Richardson collection housed at the Illinois Natural History Survey).

Forbes and Richardson's collecting spanned the years 1876 to 1908, more than 30 years, but the bulk of their work occurred between 1880 and 1905. The year 1950 was chosen as a starting date for the present survey because extensive lamprey censusing was done in the early 1950's, but the bulk of the recent collections were made between 1962 and 1972, a period of 11 years.

A distribution map accompanies most of the species accounts. Post-1950 records are plotted with solid dots; pre-1908 records with large open circles. Many of the latter are taken from the atlas of maps that is a companion volume to Forbes & Richardson (1908 and 1920), but some are based on Forbes and Richardson's specimens still extant in the Illinois Natural History Survey collection. Most of the collections were made before the several downstate reservoirs were constructed. Hence, the large, recent impoundments shown on the map on page xvii do not appear on the individual species' distribution maps, where they would obscure the dots and circles.

The Literature Cited includes references cited in the text and consists mostly of taxonomic and ecological studies. Many papers on the fishes of specific streams, drainages, counties, and portions of Illinois, as well as on the fishes of adjacent states, have been published in the last 25 years. All of them have been helpful, but because of their great number, they are not cited unless they reported particularly significant distributional records or extensive life-history information. A few references were not available to me for examination, and this fact is indicated parenthetically in the Literature Cited.

GLOSSARY

The following terms will be encountered in the keys and diagnoses:

Acuminate. Sharply pointed.

Acute. Sharp.

Adipose eyelid. Translucent fatty tissue overlying and partially obscuring margins of the eye.

Adipose fin. Fleshy unrayed fin on midline of back between dorsal and caudal fins.

Adpressed fin length. Length of fin when rays or spines are pressed against body.

Air bladder. Gas-filled sac in upper body cavity of many fishes.

Ammocoete. Larva of lamprey.

Anadromous. Returning from the ocean to fresh water to spawn.

Anal fin. Median ventral fin between anus and caudal fin.

Anal plate. Bony plate surrounding anus of gar.

Attenuate. Thin and lengthened.

Axial stripe. Thin longitudinal stripe along side of body of madtom.

Axillary process. Thin free flap of membrane at origin of pectoral or pelvic fin.

Barbel. Slender flexible process on chin and head of catfishes or on or near rear of maxilla in some cyprinids.

Basioccipital process. Posteriormost bone on underside of skull. Its dorsal surface is of diagnostic value in *Hybognathus* species. To examine, cut isthmus cleanly and bend head sharply backward until a posterior projection is visible.

Belly. Ventral surface of body between origin of anal fin and base of pelvic fins.

Bicuspid. Having two points.

Body depth. Depth of body at deepest part.

Body width. Width of body at widest part.

Branched ray. Fin ray that is both septate and branched.

Branchiostegal. Bone supporting gill membranes on underside of operculum.

Breast. Ventral surface of body between isthmus and base of pelvic fins.

Buccal funnel or *disc.* Entire mouth of a lamprey, including disc-like lips.

Bulbous. Bulging.

Caecum. Sac-like pouch between stomach and intestine.

Canine teeth. Conical teeth near front of upper jaw that project beyond other teeth.

Catadromous. Returning from fresh water to the sea to spawn.

Caudal fin. Tail fin.

Caudal peduncle. Slender part of body between bases of anal and caudal fins.

Cheek. Area between eye and preopercle.

Circumferential scale rows. The number of scale rows around body at the point of greatest body depth.

Circumoral teeth. "Teeth" within buccal funnel that surround the throat in a lamprey.

Compressed. Flattened laterally, slab sided.

Conjoined. Joined at least in part as opposed to separate.

Ctenoid scale. A scale with spinules (ctenii) near posterior tip and thus rough to the touch.

Cycloid scale. A scale that has a smooth posterior surface.

Depressed fin length. Length of fin when rays or spines are pressed against body.

Dentary nipple. A protuberance at tip of lower jaw in some carpsuckers.

Depressed. Flattened from top to bottom.

Distal. Point most remote from place of attachment.

Dorsal. Pertaining to the back.

Dorsal fin(s). Median unpaired fin or fins on back.

Dorsal ridge. Row of plates along midback in gars.

Elevated scale. Scale on side that is much higher than it is long from front to rear.

Emarginate. Having distal portion notched.

Entire. Smooth.

Eye diameter. Length of eye from front to rear.

Falcate. Concave and pointed; sickle shaped.

Filament. One or more fin rays that are appreciably longer than others.

Fimbriae. Fringe or numerous small processes.

Fin base. Area where fin is attached to body.

Fin insertion. Beginning or anteriormost point of attachment of fin to body.

Fin membrane. Thin tissue between rays or spines.

Fin origin. Beginning or anteriormost point of attachment of fin to body.

Frenum. Bridge of tissue between snout and premaxillary.

Fig. 1. External morphology of a fish, showing structures used in identification.

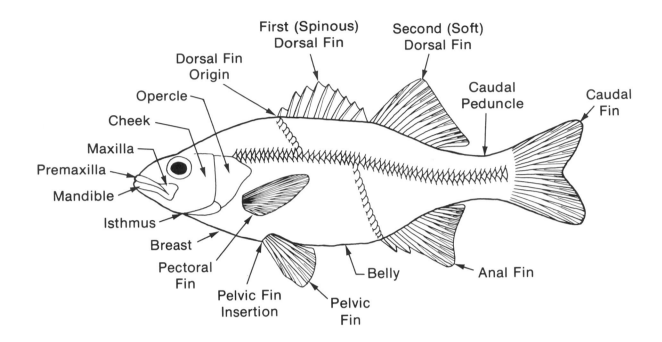

Ganoid scale. Thick heavy scale of ganoin in gars.

Gill membrane. Tissue supported by branchiostegals that encloses bottom and lower sides of gill chamber.

Gill rakers. Series of projections along anterior and upper part of gill arches.

Gill slit. Opening into gill chamber in a lamprey.

Gonopodium. Modified anterior rays of anal fin that serve as a sex organ in male poeciliid fish.

Gular. Pertaining to the throat.

Halo. Ring of another color surrounding a spot on bodies of some trouts.

Head length. Length from tip of snout to rear edge of opercle.

Heterocercal. Having the vertebral column flexed upward into the larger, upper lobe of tail fin.

Homocercal. Having the vertebral column terminating medially into a hypural plate to support tail fin and thus not invading either lobe of tail fin.

Horn. Strongly developed spine in a catfish.

Humeral. Pertaining to area just behind gill opening and above pectoral fin.

Hypural plate. Posteriormost vertebrae that are modified to support the homocercal tail fin.

Immaculate. Without pattern.

Inferior mouth. Mouth on bottom of head.

Infraorbital. Pertaining to area immediately below eye.

Interorbital. Space between the eyes on top of head.

Interradial. Space between rays or spines in a fin that is usually occupied by a membrane.

Intromittent organ. A structure serving as a penis.

Isthmus. Place of attachment of gill membranes to breast.

Jugular. Pertaining to throat.

Juxtaposed. Abutting and not overlapping.

Keel. Ridge.

Lateral. Pertaining to sides.

Lateral field. The space within a lamprey buccal funnel to either side of throat.

Lateral line. A row of tubules that is sensory in function along side of body.

Lateral series. Scales along side of body approximately in position of a lateral line, when lateral line is absent.

Leptocephalus. Larval stage of eel.

Lingual lamina. Horny ridge on "tongue" of a lamprey.

Mandible. Lower jaw bone.

Mandibular pore. Small opening to surface from a tube along each side of lower jaw. The tube is part of the cephalic lateral-line system.

Fig. 2. External morphology of a fish, showing measurements frequently used.

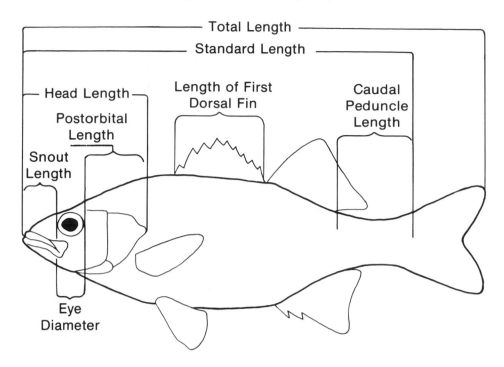

Maxilla or *maxillary*. Skin-covered bone behind premaxilla in upper jaw.

Median fin. A fin that is not paired and is located dorsally, ventrally, or caudally.

Melanophore. Black pigment cell.

Modal. Usual number.

Molariform. Having cusps and a flattened surface.

Myomere. Body or muscle segment.

Nape. Region behind head on dorsal surface of body.

Nares. External nostrils.

Nuptial tubercle. Hornlike protuberance on skin of many fishes in spawning condition.

Oblique. Angle between horizontal and vertical.

Occipital. Pertaining to back of head.

Opercle. Bony cover of gill chamber just behind cheek.

Opercular flap. Membranous or bony flap at rear edge of opercle.

Oral disc. Expanded mouth of a lamprey.

Paired fin. Either pectoral or pelvic fin, both of which occur in pairs.

Papilla. Nipplelike projection.

Papillary fringe. Rows of nipplelike projections around the mouth of a lamprey.

Papillose. Having many nipplelike projections, usu-ally referring to lips.

Paravertebral. Pertaining to either side of midline of back.

Parietal. Pertaining to top of head.

Pearl organ. Cavernous chamber in jaw of silverjaw minnow that resembles mother-of-pearl; also nuptial tubercle.

Pectoral fin. The anterior or uppermost of two paired fins; located just behind head.

Pellucid. Somewhat translucent; not opaque.

Pelvic fin. The posterior or lowermost of two paired fins; located behind and below the pectoral fin in most fishes.

Peripheral field. Distal area within buccal funnel of a lamprey.

Peritoneum. Inside lining of the abdominal cavity.

Pharyngeal arch. Fifth gill arch, which is not respiratory in function and is attached to muscles; not a part of the gill system.

Pharyngeal teeth. Teeth on the pharyngeal arch of certain fishes.

Plicate. Having parallel ridges of soft tissue.

Posterior field. The hind or bottom quarter of sucking disc of a lamprey.

Predorsum. The back between head and the anteriormost point of the dorsal fin.

Predorsal scales. Scales on the back between the back of the head and dorsal fin origin.

Premaxilla or *premaxillary.* Skin-covered anterior-most bone of upper jaw.

Preopercle. L-shaped bone bounding cheek below and behind.

Preorbital. Bone extending from anterior edge of eye onto snout.

Principal ray. A fin ray that extends to distal edge of fin and is approximately the length of other rays.

Process. Unusually elongated structure as certain rays of a fin.

Protractile. Capable of being thrust forward.

Pustule. Blisterlike protuberance.

Ray. Cartilaginous rod supporting fin membrane; distinguished from spine in being flexible and septate.

Rudimentary ray. A poorly developed ray or one appreciably shorter than most other rays in fin.

Scute. An enlarged and bony plate.

Second dorsal fin. Soft dorsal fin; the posteriormost when two dorsal fins are present.

Septate. Having thin partitions.

Serrate. Saw toothed.

Snout length. Length from anterior edge of eye to end of snout.

Soft ray. Cartilaginous flexible ray as opposed to spine.

Scale base. Anterior portion of scale which is attached to underlying flesh.

Spatulate. Spoon shaped.

Spine. Bony support of fin membrane; distinguished from ray in being stiff and without septa.

Spinous dorsal fin. First dorsal fin when it contains spines rather than soft rays.

Spiracle. Breathing orifice on top of head of lampreys and some fishes.

Standard length. Straight-line length from tip of snout to end of hypural plate; total length minus length of caudal fin.

Striate. Having minute grooves or raised lines.

Subequal. Almost the same length.

Subdistal. Almost marginal but not quite.

Subopercle. Small bone below opercle.

Suborbital. Pertaining to the area beneath eye.

Subterminal mouth. Mouth on bottom of head.

Superior mouth. Mouth on top of head.

Supraoral teeth. Paired teeth in a lamprey that are just above throat.

Supraorbital. Pertaining to area above eye.

Symphyseal. Pertaining to tip of lower jaw where mandibles end.

Synonym. Another scientific name for the same organism.

Syntopic. Occurring together in a habitat.

Teardrop. Dark bar below eye.

Terete. Cylindrical or slightly conical and rounded in cross section.

Terminal mouth. Jaws at front end of snout.

Thoracic. Pertaining to breast region.

Total length. Straight-line length from tip of snout to end of longest lobe of caudal fin.

Unicuspid. Having only one point.

Ventral. Belly or bottom side.

Vermiculate. Having worm-like markings.

Viviparous. Bearing young instead of laying eggs.

USE OF KEYS

The keys that follow are of the conventional type with numbered couplets consisting of contrasting statements. The user must select the statement that best fits the specimen he is identifying and then proceed to the couplet number indicated in the right-hand margin. The use of keys requires some familiarity with the morphological terminology of fishes and the methods of making counts and measurements. For this reason, outline drawings (Figs. 1, 2) and a glossary have been included.

For making counts and measurements, virtually all ichthyologists follow Hubbs & Lagler (1941 and subsequent editions). The most important instructions are that the last two rays in the anal and dorsal fins are counted as one, if they are united at their bases, and that only principal rays are counted. However, in fishes with fin rays that are graduated in size (as in some catfishes) rudimentary rays must also be counted. Circumferential counts are made at the deepest part of the body, starting at the scale in front of the dorsal fin origin and counting scale rows all the way around the body to the middorsal row again. Caudal peduncle counts are made in a similar fashion around the narrowest portion of the peduncle. Lateral-line scale counts are made to the end of the hypural plate. If the lateral line is not present, scales are counted in an imaginary lateral line.

Proportions are usually expressed as the number of times the length of a structure will go into the length of another and larger structure. A set of dividers is essential for "stepping" one distance into another. Sometimes proportions are expressed as percentages.

Greatest success will be obtained if fishes are first sorted into groups of individuals that look alike, and then one or two of the largest specimens are examined for key characters. Color is not essential but provides valuable clues. A dissecting microscope, forceps, sharply pointed scissors, and a millimeter ruler are essential for the identification of small fishes.

KEY TO FAMILIES

1. Mouth without jaws; paired fins absent; nostril single and median; seven gill openings on each side of body; body snakelike (lampreys) .... Petromyzontidae
   Mouth with jaws; at least one pair of fins present; nostrils paired, one on each side of snout; one gill opening on each side of head; body shape variable 2
2. Dorsal fin single, extending much over half of body length; anterior nostrils tubular (Fig. 3a) 3
   Dorsal fin single or double, and if single, extending much less than half of body length; anterior nostrils not tubular 4
3. Dorsal, caudal, and anal fins continuous; scales tiny, deeply imbedded; bony gular (chin) plate absent; body snakelike (eels) .... Anguillidae
   Dorsal, caudal, and anal fins not continuous; scales large, cycloid; bony gular (chin) plate present; body stoutly terete (bowfins) .... Amiidae
4. Caudal fin heterocercal (vertebral column flexed upward into tail fin) (Fig. 3b) 5
   Caudal fin homocercal (vertebral column not flexed upward into tail fin) (Fig. 3c) 7
5. Caudal fin rounded; vertebral column not continued into upper lobe an appreciable distance; snout a bony, strongly toothed beak; body completely covered with juxtaposed scales (gars) .... Lepisosteidae
   Caudal fin forked; vertebral column continued well into upper lobe; snout not a bony, strongly toothed beak; body not completely scaled 6
6. Snout very long and paddle-shaped; body naked; two small barbels on underside of snout (paddlefishes) ...... Polyodontidae
   Snout conical or shovel-shaped; body with rows of bony plates; four conspicuous barbels on underside of snout (sturgeons) ... . Acipenseridae
7. One set of paired fins (pectorals); head and jaws with rows of sensory papillae; eyes re-

Fig. 3. Key characters: a) head of *Amia calva*, showing tubular nostrils; b) heterocercal tail; c) homocercal tail; d) head, showing gill membranes free from isthmus; e) head, showing gill membranes united to isthmus.

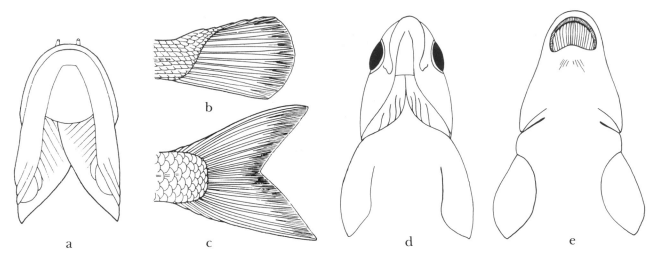

duced in size (cavefishes) ... Amblyopsidae

Two sets of paired fins (pectorals and pelvics); head and jaws without rows of sensory papillae; eyes variable 8

8. Adipose (unrayed fatty) fin present 9

   No adipose fin 12

9. Body naked; more than one pair of barbels present; first ray of dorsal and pectoral fins a heavy, bony spine or horn (catfishes and bullheads) .... Ictaluridae

   Body scaled; barbels absent or no more than two; first ray of dorsal and pectoral fins soft or at best a weak splintlike spiny ray .. 10

10. First one or two rays of dorsal and anal fins spiny; scales strongly ctenoid and rough to the touch; small, rather translucent fishes (trout-perches) .... Percopsidae

    All fin rays soft; scales cycloid; usually large, normally pigmented fishes 11

11. No pelvic axillary process; lower jaw strongly projecting; usually 70 or fewer scales in lateral line; conspicuously enlarged teeth on jaws and tongue (smelts) ..... Osmeridae

    Pelvic axillary process present; jaws equal or lower jaw slightly projecting; usually more than 70 scales in lateral line; teeth not conspicuously enlarged on jaws and tongue (trouts and whitefishes) ...... Salmonidae

12. Conspicuous median barbel near tip of chin; base of first dorsal fin less than one-fifth length of base of second dorsal; dorsal and anal fins each with 60 or more rays (codfishes) .... Gadidae

No median barbel near tip of chin; if two dorsal fins are present, base of first dorsal fin more than one-fifth length of base of second; dorsal and anal fins each with fewer than 35 rays 13

13. Anus situated just behind gill cleft (except in small young, which have anus farther back but well in advance of anal fin) (pirate perches) .... Aphredoderidae

    Anus situated just in front of anal fin ... 14

14. Anterior dorsal fin represented by four to nine spines, not connected by membrane (sticklebacks) .... Gasterosteidae

    Anterior dorsal fin single or, if double, without isolated, unconnected spine 15

15. Dorsal fin single and with one or no spiny ray 16

    Dorsal fin double or, if single, anterior portion with more than one spiny ray 24

16. Dorsal fin with one stout spine (the introduced *Carassius* and *Cyprinus*) .... Cyprinidae

    Dorsal fin without stout spine 17

17. Head and cheeks scaleless 18

    Head and cheeks partly or entirely scaled 21

18. Pelvic axillary process at base of each pelvic fin; gill membranes free from isthmus and gill slits extending far forward below (Fig. 3d) 19

    No pelvic axillary process; gill membranes united to isthmus and gill slits not extending forward an appreciable distance (Fig. 3e), or gill membranes free from isthmus and gill

slits extending far forward 20
19. Midline of belly with strong spiny scutes; dorsal fin base situated well anterior to anal fin base; lateral line absent; many long, slender gill rakers (herrings, shads, skipjacks) .....
.... Clupeidae
Midline of belly without strong spiny scutes; dorsal fin base situated partly or entirely over anal fin base; lateral line present; a few short, knobby gill rakers (mooneyes) .....
.... Hiodontidae
20. Lips thickened, striate, and papillose (except in buffalos); anal fin usually situated posteriorly, its adpressed rays reaching, or almost reaching, caudal base and its origin usually closer to caudal base than to pelvic insertion (except in *Cycleptus,* which has sucking mouth); 10 or more dorsal rays (except in *Erimyzon,* which has a sucking mouth and almost no lateral line); pharyngeal arch with one row of 15 or more teeth (suckers) .... Catostomidae
Lips thin (except in suckermouth minnow); anal fin situated farther forward, its adpressed rays far short of caudal base and its origin distinctly closer to pelvic origins than to caudal base; nine or fewer dorsal rays; pharyngeal arch with one to three rows of teeth, never more than seven in longest row (minnows) .... Cyprinidae
21. Caudal fin forked; snout a ducklike beak; jaws with large canine teeth; scales small, more than 90 in lateral series (pikes) .. Esocidae
Caudal fin rounded; snout not a ducklike beak; jaws without canine teeth; scales large, fewer than 50 in lateral series 22
22. Mouth terminal; premaxillaries not protractile, lacking transverse groove between snout and upper lip; origin of pelvic fins closer to caudal base than to tip of snout (mudminnows) .... Umbridae
Mouth superior; premaxillaries protractile, separated from snout by deep transverse groove; origin of pelvic fins closer to tip of snout than to caudal base 23
23. Anal fin of male without elongated anterior rays and ornamentations and not modified as an intromittent organ; body with dark vertical bars, a complete dark lateral band, or with numerous thin longitudinal lines (topminnows) .... Cyprinodontidae

Anal fin of male with elongated anterior rays and modified as an intromittent organ; body without vertical bars, a lateral band, or thin longitudinal lines (livebearers) ....
.... Poeciliidae
24. Body naked, sometimes prickly; four or fewer pelvic rays; pectoral fin very large, nearly twice the length and depth of the pelvic fin (sculpins) .... Cottidae
Body scaled; five or more pelvic rays; pectoral fin not very large, less than twice the length and width of the pelvic fin 25
25. Small anterior and large posterior dorsal fins both situated over elongate anal fin; first dorsal fin usually with fewer than six spines; body very slender (silversides) ....
.... Atherinidae
Anterior dorsal fin situated well in advance of anal fin origin; first dorsal with six or more spines (except in pygmy sunfish); body not extremely slender 26
26. Lateral line continued posteriorly to end of caudal fin; base of first dorsal fin approximately half as long as base of second; two anal spines, the second much longer than the first; pharyngeal teeth molarlike (drums)
.... Sciaenidae
Lateral line, if present, not continued to tip of caudal fin; if dorsal fins are separate, first more than half length of second; one or more anal spines; if two, the second not greatly longer than first; pharyngeal teeth not molarlike 27
27. Three or more anal spines; dorsal and anal spines very stiff and sharp; body slab-sided
.... 28
One or two anal spines; dorsal and anal spines flexible; body usually more or less terete (perches and darters) .... Percidae
28. A spine on opercular flap; dorsal fins separate or only slightly joined; ground color of body pale with thin, dark longitudinal lines (temperate basses) .... Percichthyidae
No spine on opercular flap (except in rock bass); dorsal fins distinctly joined by membrane even in species with deep notch between fins; body pattern variable but usually not consisting of pale ground color and thin, dark longitudinal lines in most species (sunfishes) .... Centrarchidae

Lampreys—Petromyzontidae

The lamprey family includes three genera represented in Illinois. Lampreys spawn in gravelly riffles in early spring. The egg hatches into an eel-like larva called an ammocoete, which is carried by the current into a quiet pool where it burrows into the mud bottom. The ammocoete has sievelike mouthparts (Fig. 4a) for extracting plankton from the water. After several years the ammocoete transforms into a sexually mature adult. Adults of some lampreys are parasitic on fishes; adults of others spawn and die without feeding. The sea lamprey is believed to have contributed heavily to the decline of commercial fishing in Lake Michigan, but the native species probably have a negligible effect, if any at all, on fish populations in Illinois rivers. At the peak of the sea lamprey's abundance in Lake Michigan, some Chicago restaurants reportedly served them under the misleading name of "lampfries." Lampreys are of great evolutionary interest because they are extremely primitive vertebrates with simple organ systems. They are members of an animal class distinct from, and predating, the fishes. Most adults are found either clinging to, or recently detached from, host fish or in clear gravelly streams when they are migrating to their spawning grounds. The family name Petromyzonidae is used by some specialists.

KEY TO GENERA

1. Oral disc hoodlike without a papillary fringe but with numerous fimbriae within buccal funnel; teeth and tongue absent (Fig. 4a); eyes small and partly covered with skin . . . . Ammocoetes
    Oral disc round or oval with papillary fringe and with teeth and tongue in buccal funnel; eyes well developed 2
2. A pair of widely separated supraoral teeth (Figs. 4b, c); peripheral teeth, if present, abruptly smaller than lateral circumorals, those on lateral and posterior fields visible only with magnification; anterior and posterior dorsal fins highly lobed and separated by deep notch . . . . Lampetra
    Supraorals, if present, close together; teeth gradually diminishing in size peripherally or all teeth minute and located on rows of mounds radiating out from mouth; dorsal fins either widely separated or a continuous fin without high lobes 3

Fig. 4. Mouth parts of lampreys: a) ammocoete; b) *Lampetra lamottei;* c) *L. aepyptera;* d) *I. bdellium;* (cont.)

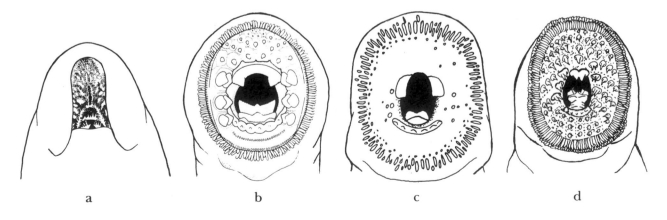

a   b   c   d

Fig. 4 (cont.) Mouth parts of lampreys: e) *Petromyzon marinus;* f) *Ichthyomyzon fossor;* g) *I. unicuspis;* h) *I. castaneus.*

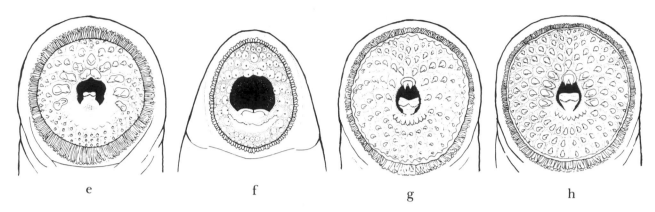

e   f   g   h

3. Two well-developed and widely separated dorsal fins; all teeth well developed but those in posterior field appreciably smaller and more widely separated than those in lateral and anterior fields (Fig. 4e); myomeres between last gill slit and anus usually more than 65; body usually mottled or marbled with black .... *Petromyzon*
   One dorsal fin, sometimes shallowly notched but always continuous, without high lobes; peripheral teeth subequal in all fields; myomeres fewer than 62; body not mottled or marbled with black .... *Ichthyomyzon*

Ichthyomyzon Girard

This eastern North American genus includes seven species, four of which have been recorded in Illinois, but only three now occur in the state. Two of these are parasites on such large fishes as carp, buffalos, and paddlefish; one is not a parasite.

KEY TO SPECIES

1. Sucking disc small, its diameter less than greatest body width; all teeth minute and barely visible on mounds that radiate from mouth opening (Fig. 4f) .... *fossor*
   Sucking disc large, its diameter at least equalling greatest body width; teeth large and conspicuous, the supraoral and lateral circumorals particularly prominent 2
2. Circumoral teeth almost all unicuspid (Fig. 4g); usually one or two supraoral cusps; usually three teeth in anterior row; usually six or seven teeth in lateral rows; usually 49–52 myomeres between last gill slit and anus; transverse lingual lamina proportionately large and moderately to strongly bilobed .... *unicuspis*
   Some circumoral teeth (usually four to eight) bicuspid (Figs. 4d, h); two or three supraoral cusps; usually four or five teeth in anterior row; usually eight or nine teeth in lateral rows; 51–60 myomeres; transverse lingual lamina proportionately small, linear or bilobed 3
3. Usually 51–56 myomeres; transverse lingual lamina linear to weakly bilobed; disc large, its length usually contained fewer than 13.3 times in total length .... *castaneus*
   Usually 55–59 myomeres; transverse lingual lamina moderately to strongly bilobed; disc relatively small, its length usually contained more than 13.3 times in total length .... *bdellium**

Ohio lamprey*
Ichthyomyzon bdellium (Jordan)

Petromyzon bdellium Jordan 1885b:4 (substitute name for preoccupied *P. argenteus*).
Ichthyomyzon bdellium: Hubbs & Trautman 1937:86 (resurrection of name, recorded from Illinois); Smith 1965:11 (extirpated in Illinois).

Diagnosis.—The adult Ohio lamprey has radiating rows of strongly developed teeth, several of which are bicuspid; a low, continuous, shallowly notched dorsal fin; transverse lingual lamina moderately to strongly bilobed; and 55–59 myomeres between the last gill slit and the anus (Fig. 4d). The ammocoete can be distinguished from that of other lampreys by the combination of a continuous dorsal fin and 55–59 myomeres. The adult attains a length of 259 mm (10 inches).

Variation.—Evidently the species is rather uniform throughout its range, and no subspecies have been proposed. The only comprehensive study of variation is in the formal description (Hubbs & Trautman 1937).

Ecology.—The Ohio lamprey occurs in medium-sized to large rivers. As an adult, it parasitizes fish. Like other parasitic lampreys, the Ohio lamprey

Distribution of the Ohio lamprey in Illinois.

leaves its large river habitat early in the spring to ascend small, gravelly tributaries to spawn. Nests are constructed in gravel-bottomed riffles, and the spawning adults die soon after egg deposition. The larval or ammocoete stage lives for several years, feeding on plankton near the mouths of their burrows. When large enough to transform, the lampreys return to the quiet waters of large rivers.

Distribution.—Extirpated in Illinois. Hubbs & Trautman (1937) examined specimens taken prior to 1918 from two localities in the Wabash River and two in the Embarras River. Starrett et al. (1960) reexamined the specimens and concurred that one of them was *bdellium* but noted that the others were unidentifiable because of their poor state of preservation and the intermediate nature of their characters. Recent collections from the Wabash valley of Illinois and Indiana contain *castaneus* but no *bdellium* and thus indicate that in Illinois *bdellium* has been supplanted by *castaneus*.

Chestnut lamprey
Ichthyomyzon castaneus Girard

Ichthyomyzon castaneus Girard 1858:381 (type-locality: Galena, Minnesota); Suckley 1860:368 (type-locality corrected to "Galena, Illinois?"); Large 1903:7; Hubbs & Trautman 1937:71 (resurrection of *castaneus*); Smith 1965:5.
Ichthyomyzon hirudo: Nelson 1876:52 (part.).
Ammocoetes hirudo: Jordan 1878:70 (part.).
Ichthyomyzon argenteus: Nelson 1876:52 (part.).
Ammocoetes argenteus: Jordan 1878:70 (part.).
Ichthyomyzon concolor: Forbes & Richardson 1908:9 (part.); O'Donnell 1935:475 (part.).

Diagnosis.—The chestnut lamprey is closely related and similar to the Ohio lamprey, from which it differs by having fewer myomeres (usually 52–56); the transverse lingual lamina linear to weakly bilobed; a slightly larger oral disc; and a greater maximum size (to 345 mm, or 13.5 inches, in total length). The adult can be distinguished from all other Illinois lampreys by the combination of a low, continuous dorsal fin; strong teeth in radiating rows; the presence of several bicuspid circumorals (Fig. 4h); and a myomere count of 52–56. The ammocoete cannot be distinguished with certainty from that of other species in the genus.

Variation.—Starrett et al. (1960) studied individual variation in the species and found that the largest specimens came from the Wabash River.

Other trends in geographic variation were not evident. A specimen from the Mississippi River, Rock Island County, was interpreted as a *castaneus* X *unicuspis* hybrid on the basis of its having a myomere count and lingual lamina shape of *unicuspis* but dentition of *castaneus*.

Ecology.—The chestnut lamprey occurs in medium-sized and large rivers. Adults are taken in greatest numbers by commercial fishermen in late winter and early spring on several species of commercial fishes. Specimens are occasionally taken in minnow seines at other seasons. The life history is similar to that of the Ohio lamprey.

Distribution.—Evaluation of the former occurrence and abundance of the chestnut lamprey is difficult in view of the conflicting statements of Jordan (1878), who noted that the species was abundant in the Ohio and Mississippi rivers, and those of Nelson (1876) and Large (1903), each of whom cited only one locality. Forbes & Richardson (1908) regarded the species as "rather rare" (their species was a composite of *castaneus* and *unicuspis*), presumably because of the scarcity of suitable spawning sites in Illinois streams. However, they noted that it was sufficiently common in the Mississippi River at Alton and Grafton that most paddlefish taken at these localities bore lamprey scars. O'Donnell (1935:475) stated that the lamprey (he did not distinguish *castaneus* from *unicuspis*) was commonly found in the winter months in streams having a drainage of 1,000 square miles or more. Starrett et al. (1960:341–344) reported that the species was "fairly common" in the Mississippi River below Hancock County. They noted that its range had withdrawn to the south, for their northernmost record was more than 100 miles south of the species' type-locality (Galena, Jo Daviess County). They also called attention to the spread of the species into the Ohio and Wabash basins, both of which had previously been inhabited only by *bdellium,* according to Hubbs & Trautman (1937).

Northern brook lamprey
Ichthyomyzon fossor Reighard & Cummins

Ichthyomyzon fossor Reighard & Cummins 1916:1 (type-locality: Mill Creek, Washtenaw County, Michigan); Smith 1965:5 (recorded from Illinois).

Diagnosis.—The northern brook lamprey is a small *Ichthyomyzon* that differs from other Illinois species by its weakly developed teeth, including the supraoral and lateral circumorals, and by its smaller oral disc (Fig. 4f). Many of the small blunt teeth are covered by skin. The width of the expanded disc is less than the greatest width of the body. Myomeres are usually 49–55. The ammocoete cannot be distinguished with certainty from that of other species. Adults may attain a total length of 180 mm (7 inches).

Variation.—In the five Illinois specimens known (three adults and two ammocoetes) the myomere count ranges from 51 to 54. The adults range from 115 to 151 mm in total length; the ammocoetes,

Distribution of the chestnut lamprey in Illinois.

140–154 mm. The adults have well-developed eyes, minute teeth, and very small oral discs.

Ecology.—The northern brook lamprey, a dwarfed derivative of *I. unicuspis* (Hubbs & Trautman 1937:9), is nonparasitic. Its alimentary tract is degenerate. Its life cycle is presumably similar to that of other species of *Ichthyomyzon*, except that after transformation it ascends gravelly creeks to spawn and die instead of descending to large rivers to parasitize fish.

Distribution.—Despite the inclusion of northeastern Illinois in the range of the species (Hubbs & Lagler 1958:36), the only Illinois records are rather recent collections from three localities in the Kankakee River in Kankakee County.

Distribution of the northern brook lamprey in Illinois.

Silver lamprey
Ichthyomyzon unicuspis Hubbs & Trautman

Ichthyomyzon unicuspis Hubbs & Trautman 1937:53 (type-locality: Swan Creek, Toledo, Lucas County, Ohio); Smith 1965:6.
Ichthyomyzon argenteus: Nelson 1876:52 (recorded from Illinois; part.); Forbes 1884:86 (part.).
Ammocoetes argenteus: Jordan 1878:70 (part.).
Ichthyomyzon hirudo: Nelson 1876:52 (part.).
Ammocoetes hirudo: Jordan 1878:70 (part.).
Ichthyomyzon concolor: Large 1903:7; Forbes & Richardson 1908:9 (part.); O'Donnell 1935:475 (part.).

Diagnosis.—The adult silver lamprey has radiating rows of strongly developed teeth, almost invariably all unicuspid (Fig. 4g). Supraoral cusps are one to four, usually one or two; teeth in anterior rows two to four, usually three. The proportionately large transverse lingual lamina is moderately to strongly bilobed. The oral disc is proportionately large. The dorsal fin is relatively low and continuous. Myomeres are usually 49 to 52 between the last gill slit and the anus. The ammocoete cannot be distinguished from that of the northern brook lamprey. The species attains a total length of 356 mm (14 inches).

Variation.—In 313 Illinois specimens studied by Starrett et al. (1960), no trends in geographic variation were evident. A natural hybrid between this species and *I. castaneus* has already been noted.

Ecology.—The life history and habits are presumably similar to those of other parasitic species of *Ichthyomyzon*. In Illinois the silver lamprey occurs in medium-sized as well as large rivers. As an adult, it parasitizes fish.

Distribution.—Starrett et al. (1960) reported this species as most common in the Mississippi River in extreme northwestern Illinois, the Wabash River, and the Ohio River near the mouth of the Wabash. Evaluation of its former occurrence and abundance is difficult, since the limited observations on parasitic lampreys prior to the description of this species in 1937 were based on a composite of *I. castaneus* and *I. unicuspis*. Like *I. castaneus*, this species has probably lost many of its breeding sites due to human alteration of the watersheds, but it is the most widely distributed and most common species of *Ichthyomyzon* in the state. It evidently no longer occurs in Lake Michigan.

Distribution of the silver lamprey in Illinois.

Lampetra Gray

This Holarctic genus of small nonparasitic lampreys contains several species, only two of which are known from Illinois, one of them recently discovered in the state. The latter species is placed in the genus *Okkelbergia* by some recent authors.

KEY TO SPECIES

1. Myomeres, fewer than 62, usually under 60; a pair of widely separated supraoral teeth and row of infraoral teeth, all other teeth much reduced to absent; oral disc distinctly smaller than body width .... *aepyptera*
   Myomeres, more than 62; some teeth in marginal fields of funnel well developed, usually three pairs of lateral bicuspids; oral disc almost as wide as body .... *lamottei*

Least brook lamprey
Lampetra aepyptera (Abbott)

Ammocoetes aepyptera Abbott 1860:327 (type-locality: Ohio River).
Okkelbergia aepyptera: Rohde 1977:313–314 (recorded from Illinois).

Diagnosis.—The adult of the least brook lamprey has a pair of prominent, widely separated supraoral teeth and a row of infraorbital teeth, but all other teeth in the oral disc are so reduced that they are barely visible or completely absent (Fig. 4c). The dorsal fin is bilobed with a wide notch between the lobes. Myomeres are usually 55 to 60 between the last gill slit and the anus. The eye is prominent. The oral disc is 4–7 mm in outside diameter and the encircling papillary fringe is somewhat constricted so that the funnel is much narrower than the body. The color is silvery gray to almost black above, lighter gray below. The species differs from all species of *Ichthyomyzon* in having a distinctly bilobed dorsal fin; from the sea lamprey by its smaller size, proportionately smaller disc, and lack of peripheral teeth; and from the American brook lamprey in having fewer than 62 myomeres and lacking some well-developed teeth in the lateral fields. The adult attains a length of 155 mm (6 inches).

Variation.—Rohde et al. (1976:105) summarized the published information available on variation and noted little other than in maximum size attained in different parts of the species' range.

Ecology.—The least brook lamprey occurs in clean gravelly riffles of creeks. In Delaware where Rohde et al. (1976) conducted an intensive life-history study the species occurs in slow-moving coastal streams with predominantly sand bottoms. Spawning occurs in late March, and nests of small stones are constructed by both sexes using their sucking discs and vigorous body movements to sweep away sand. The eggs average 874 per female and hatch in 24 to 26 days at 5 to 16° C. Each one averages 1.02 mm in diameter. The larvae, which feed on plankton, live for an average of 5.4 years and transform in late summer.

Distribution. — The least brook lamprey was recently discovered to occur in southeastern Illinois by F. C. Rohde, who found a specimen in our own collection from Big Creek in Hardin County. A 26-mm ammocoete, almost certainly the same species, is available from Big Grand Pierre Creek in Pope County. The specimens reported as *Entosphenus lamottenii* by Gunning & Lewis (1956*b*) from Sugar Creek in Williamson County are also available and reidentified herein as the least brook lamprey. It probably occurs throughout the eastern portion of the Shawnee Hills of southern Illinois but is evidently rare.

Distribution of the least brook lamprey in Illinois.

American brook lamprey
Lampetra lamottei (Lesueur)

Petromyzon lamottenii Lesueur 1827:9 (type-locality: cave near Mine Lamotte, Missouri).
Petromyzon niger: Nelson 1876:52 (recorded from Illinois).
Ammocoetes niger: Jordan 1878:70; Forbes 1884:86.
Lampetra wilderi: Large 1903:7; Forbes & Richardson 1908:11.
Lethenteron appendix: O'Donnell 1935:475.
Lampetra lamottei: Smith 1965:6.

Diagnosis. — The adult of the American brook lamprey has a pair of prominent supraoral teeth, usually three pairs of bicuspid lateral teeth, and a row of infraoral teeth; peripheral teeth are present but abruptly smaller, those on the posterior field often hidden (Fig. 4b). The dorsal fin is distinctly bilobed with a wide notch between the lobes. Myomeres are 66–73 between the posterior gill slit and the anus. The eye is prominent. The oral disc is 5–7 mm in outside diameter (to 10 mm in breeding adults). Color is tawny gray to almost black above, tan to grayish white below. This species differs from all species of *Ichthyomyzon* in having a distinctly bilobed dorsal fin; from the sea lamprey by its smaller size and different tooth arrangement; and from the least brook lamprey in its lower myomere count, smaller disc, and number of teeth. The adult reaches a total length of 200 mm (8 inches).

Variation. — Individual variation in 40 specimens from six localities in northern and central Illinois is slight. The most notable exception, a breeding male from Boone Creek in McHenry County, has only 58 myomeres and is rather boldly marbled with black on the back and upper sides. In all other characters it is identical with specimens of *lamottei* in the same series and is therefore assumed to be merely an aberrant specimen. Rohde et al. (1976: 108) found slight geographic variation in body size and proportions in different parts of the species range.

Ecology. — Both ammocoetes and adults are found in rather fast riffles and clean gravelly raceways of large creeks and small rivers. Spawning in northern Illinois occurs in late April and early May. Ammocoetes and newly transformed adults of the American brook lamprey have been found in the Kankakee River along with comparable stages of the northern brook lamprey and silver lamprey, suggesting that several lamprey species utilize the same spawning sites. Rohde et al. (1976) found that spawning in Delaware occurs in late March and early April and that the life history is similar to that of the least brook lamprey. The mean number of eggs per female is 1,691, and each egg averages 1.06 mm in diameter. Hatching at 5 to 17° C requires 20 to 22 days.

Distribution.— References to *L. lamottei,* prior to Forbes & Richardson (1908), gave the impression that it was abundant in streams in northern Illinois and that it was widely distributed in all parts of the state. Forbes & Richardson (1908) noted the almost complete absence of *L. lamottei* in their collections but assumed that the species had been missed because of its small size and nonparasitic habits. O'Donnell (1935) regarded it as "very rare" and reported an additional collection made in 1931 from a small creek near Danville, Vermilion County. The species is now rare and erratic in distribution but probably more generally distributed than available records indicate. Although pollution and drought may have eliminated some populations, the species was probably never common in central Illinois, where many of the streams lack suitable spawning sites.

Distribution of the American brook lamprey in Illinois.

Petromyzon Linnaeus

This North Atlantic genus contains one species, a landlocked form which spread into lower Lake Michigan in the 1930's.

Sea lamprey
Petromyzon marinus Linnaeus

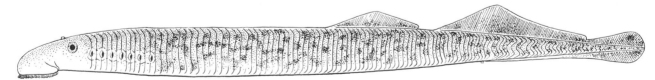

Petromyzon marinus Linnaeus 1758:230 (type-locality: European seas); Smith 1965:6 (recorded from Illinois).

Diagnosis.— The adult of the sea lamprey has radiating rows of strongly developed teeth, several of which (the circumorals) are bicuspid; teeth in anterior and lateral fields are well developed, those in the posterior field are abruptly smaller (Fig. 4e). It has 65 or more myomeres, widely separated dorsal fins, a large buccal funnel, and dark spotting or mottling on the body and fin bases. It can be distinguished from other Illinois lampreys by its mottling and larger size and by the combination of separate dorsal fins, radiating rows of well-developed teeth, and high myomere count. It attains a length of 510 mm (20 inches).

Variation.—A series of 17 adults from lower Lake Michigan ranges from 323 to 490 mm in total length and from 68 to 75 (mean 71.7) in myomere count. Blotching or mottling is present on all specimens but rather subdued on most of them.

Ecology.—The destructive sea lamprey is a marine species that has become landlocked in the Great Lakes. Its life history has been studied by Applegate (1950) and Wigley (1959). The remarks that follow have been extracted from these studies. Adults perform mass migrations, usually at night, into tributary streams when water temperatures are between 10° and 18° C. They may ascend streams as far as 80 km (50 miles) to spawn, after which they die. Nests consisting of craters 460 mm (1½ feet) in diameter are constructed in the gravel-rubble riffles, and 10,000–100,000 eggs are deposited by the female. Hatching occurs in two weeks at 15–16° C. A few days later the ammocoete leaves the nest and is carried by the current into a quiet pool, where it burrows into the bottom. After a larval life of 7 years, the lamprey transforms and moves into the lake, where it parasitizes salmonids, coregonids, catostomids, and other large fish for approximately 1½ years.

Distribution.—Native to the Atlantic Ocean and Lake Ontario (as a landlocked form), the sea lamprey was unable to surmount Niagara Falls until an avenue was provided in the way of the Welland Canal in the 1820's. Inexplicably, almost 100 years elapsed before the lamprey appeared in Lake Erie, but then it spread inexorably throughout the Great Lakes basin. By the middle 1940's it was a source of alarm because of its threat to the Great Lakes fishery. The first specimen reported in lower Lake Michigan was found on a lake trout in March 1936 (Hubbs & Pope 1937). By the 1950's it was abundant and was believed responsible for the decimation of the lake trout and other important commercial species in Lake Michigan. In the early 1960's a selective sea lamprey larvicide was found

that was effective (Applegate et al. 1961). Wide use of this chemical, referred to as TFM, in tributaries apparently brought the lamprey population under control but not until the native predatory fishes of Lake Michigan were severely decimated. Specimens from two sites in the Illinois waters of Lake Michigan are available. The only stream record (Du Page River, near Lombard, Du Page County) was regarded as highly questionable by Starrett et al. (1960).

Distribution of the sea lamprey in Illinois.

Sturgeons—Acipenseridae

The Holarctic sturgeon family includes two genera represented in Illinois. Sturgeons are of evolutionary interest because of their great age. They were once of considerable economic importance because of the demand for their eggs for caviar, flesh for smoked steaks, swim bladders for the manufacture of isinglass (a corruption of *huizenblas*, meaning sturgeon bladder), and for their oil. At an earlier period, they were extremely common in the northern United States and Canada and scorned by fishermen. However, one species (lake sturgeon) is said to have been a food source as important to the eastern forest Indian tribes as the bison was to the western plains tribes (Harkness & Dymond 1961). Although sturgeons are occasionally caught on baited hook or snagged, most of them are taken by commercial fishermen in nets of one kind or another. They are recognized by almost everyone because of their distinctive snouts, bizarre caudal fins, and partially plated bodies.

KEY TO GENERA

1. Snout pointed (Fig. 5a); caudal peduncle short, origin of anal fin closer to origin of caudal than to pelvic fins; peduncle round in cross section, with a few well-separated bony plates; barbels smooth; caudal fin not produced into a filament; spiracles present; lower lip with two smooth lobes .... *Acipenser*
   Snout flattened and shovel-like (Figs. 5b, c); caudal peduncle long, origin of anal fin closer to pelvics than to caudal origin; peduncle depressed in cross section, completely encased in bony plates; barbels fringed; caudal fin often produced into a long filament; spiracles absent; lower lip with four papillose lobes .... *Scaphirhynchus*

Fig. 5. Undersides of heads of sturgeons: a) *Acipenser fulvescens;* b) *Scaphirhynchus albus;* c) *S. platorynchus.*

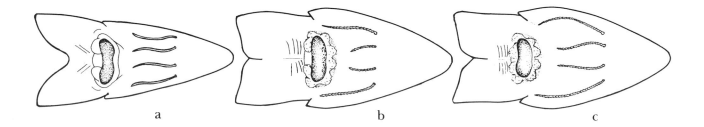

a   b   c

Acipenser Linnaeus

This Holarctic genus includes one Illinois species, which is tied with the alligator gar as being the largest fish species known in the state.

Lake sturgeon
Acipenser fulvescens Rafinesque

Acipenser fulvescens Rafinesque 1817b:288 (type-locality: Great Lakes); O'Donnell 1935:475; Smith 1965:6.

Acipenser rubicundus: Kennicott 1855:595 (recorded from Illinois); Nelson 1876:51; Jordan 1878:69; Forbes 1884:85; Large 1903:7; Forbes & Richardson 1908:24–26.

Acipenser maculosus: Nelson 1876:51; Jordan 1878:69.

Diagnosis.—The lake sturgeon differs most obviously from other species of sturgeons by its pointed, rather conical snout; robust body; par-

Lake sturgeon

tially plated and almost terete caudal peduncle; smooth and subequal barbels; and the two smooth lobes on the lower lip. Young specimens are prominently marked with one or two large dark blotches and numerous small flecks. The highly sculptured plates are sharp and relatively prominent. Old specimens tend to be unicolor gray, olive, or reddish, and the plates are smooth and partially overgrown with skin. One of the two largest specimens known (almost 2.5 meters and 682 kg (7 feet, 11 inches and 310 pounds) was taken in Lake Michigan in 1943.

Variation.—The most complete account of variation in the species is that of Harkness & Dymond (1961).

Ecology.—According to Harkness & Dymond (1961), the lake sturgeon lives on the bottom of large rivers and in the shallow waters of large lakes. The adult migrates to areas of rocky rapids or shoals with strong wave action to spawn in the spring. Large females lay hundreds of thousands of adhesive eggs, which require 5 days to hatch at water temperatures of 15°–18° C. Growth is comparatively slow, and sexual maturity is reached in 15–20 years, when the fish is about 760 mm (30 inches) long. Spawning occurs every 4–7 years thereafter. Harkness & Dymond (1961) reported that spawning adults make spectacular leaps and may leave the water, but that for most of the year the sturgeon lives on the bottom, sucking up caddisfly larvae and immatures of other aquatic insects, mollusks, crustaceans, fish and their eggs, and some detritus.

Distribution.—The lake sturgeon was reportedly "very abundant" in Lake Michigan and present in large rivers of the state before 1880 (Nelson 1876; Jordan 1878). It was recorded by Large (1903) as rarely taken in Lake Michigan and as rare in Lake Michigan and in rivers by Forbes & Richardson (1908). The initial decimation is believed to have been due to deliberate elimination of a large nuisance fish by man. Later the sturgeon found its

migration routes to spawning beds blocked by man-made dams. It is likely that siltation also destroyed some habitats of the species. The species is now so rare in Illinois that it is a novelty. A small specimen from the Rock River at Sterling, Whiteside County, collected in October 1934 is in the

Distribution of the lake sturgeon in Illinois.

Illinois Natural History Survey collection, and specimens from the Rock River are still reported with some regularity. In 1966 fishermen in the Mississippi River caught two specimens with a combined weight of 25 kg (56 pounds) at Quincy, Illinois, and a 14-kg (32-pound) specimen at Elsbery, Missouri, and a fisherman caught a specimen estimated at 9–13 kg in the Illinois River near Bath, Illinois. Published records for the Mississippi River by navigation pools are listed in Smith et al. (1971). No specimens are available from the Wabash River, but a commercial fisherman at Darwin reported he once caught a "rubbernose sturgeon" locally. Although the species has become rare in Lake Michigan, it is probably more common there than in Illinois rivers.

Scaphirhynchus Heckel

This North American genus includes two species, both of which occur in the large rivers of Illinois.

KEY TO SPECIES

1. Inner pair of barbels approximately half the length of outer pair, not reaching anterior edge of mouth (Fig. 5b); snout long, acuminate; mouth wide, outer barbel extending backward to anterior edge of lower lip; dorsal rays, 37 or more; anal rays, 24 or more; head and body attenuate; color pallid ..... *albus*
   Inner pair of barbels about three-quarters length of outer pair, reaching edge of upper lip; snout short, proportionately wide (Fig. 5c); mouth less wide, outer barbel not extending backward to anterior edge of lower lip; dorsal rays, 36 or fewer; anal rays, 23 or fewer; head and body stout; color brownish
   .... *platorynchus*

Pallid sturgeon
Scaphirhynchus albus (Forbes & Richardson)

Parascaphirhynchus albus Forbes & Richardson 1905:34 (type-locality: Mississippi River, Grafton, Illinois) and 1908:28–29; O'Donnell 1935: 475.
Scaphirhynchus albus: Smith 1965:6.

Diagnosis.—The pallid sturgeon differs from the lake sturgeon by its much flattened and shov-el-shaped snout; long, slender, depressed, and completely armored caudal peduncle; prolonged upper lobe of the caudal fin; and by the absence of a spiracle. It differs from the shovelnose sturgeon by its proportionately larger head and wider mouth, shorter inner barbel (about half the length of the outer), smaller eye, absence of scutes on the belly, more numerous dorsal rays (37 or more) and anal rays (24 or more), paler color, and larger maximum size. Forbes & Richardson (1908) noted that commercial fishermen believed the species attained a weight of 15 to 25 pounds (5–11 kg). A specimen weighing 30 kg (68 pounds) was reported from North Dakota (Bailey & Allum 1962).

Variation.—An excellent account of variation in the species was published by Bailey & Cross (1954).

Distribution of the pallid sturgeon in Illinois.

Ecology.—The pallid sturgeon is a large-river species. Spawning occurs in June and July (Forbes & Richardson 1908). Little else is known about its life history. Its food, according to Cross (1967:37), consists of small fishes and immatures of aquatic insects.

Distribution.—The species occurs in Illinois in the Mississippi River between the mouths of the Missouri and Ohio rivers and is rare. Forbes & Richardson (1905) reported nine specimens from fish markets in Grafton and Alton in their description of the species, and Barnickol & Starrett (1951) reported a small specimen taken near the mouth of the Missouri River. Since 1970 commercial fisherman Paul Kimmel has secured a few specimens in the Mississippi River at two sites in Jackson County. A published record for the Mississippi River at Keokuk, Iowa (Coker 1930), was rejected as probably in error by Smith et al. (1971). The evidence available suggests that this silt-tolerant species enters the Mississippi River from the Missouri River and that the specimens Forbes & Richardson reported from fish markets of Grafton and Alton were captured below the mouth of the Missouri River. The type-locality of the species is herein restricted to the Mississippi River at the mouth of the Missouri. The pallid sturgeon has probably always been rare in Illinois waters, and it may be threatened by man-made modification of the channel of the Mississippi River.

Shovelnose sturgeon
Scaphirhynchus platorynchus
(Rafinesque)

Acipenser platorynchus Rafinesque 1820a:80 (type-locality: Ohio River).
Scaphirhynchus platyrhynchus: Nelson 1876:51 (recorded from Illinois); Jordan 1878:69; Forbes 1884:85.
Scaphirhynchus platorynchus: Large 1903:8; Smith 1965:6.
Scaphirhynchus platorhynchus: Forbes & Richardson 1908:27–28; O'Donnell 1935:475.

Diagnosis.—The shovelnose sturgeon differs from the lake sturgeon by the same characters that distinguish the pallid and lake sturgeons. It differs from the pallid sturgeon most obviously in its inner barbel that is much more than half the length of the outer, the presence of scutes on the belly, its fewer dorsal rays (36 or fewer) and anal rays (23 or

fewer), its darker color, and its smaller maximum size. According to Forbes & Richardson (1908:27), the species rarely reaches 3 feet (1 meter) in length. Most of the recent specimens available are much smaller.

Variation.—An excellent account of variation in the species was presented by Bailey & Cross (1954).

Ecology.—This species is much more common than the pallid sturgeon, but its life history is almost as poorly known. According to Forbes & Richardson (1908:27), adults ascend tributaries and spawn from April to June. Males become sexually mature at about 20 inches (510 mm) and females at about 25 inches (630 mm) (Cross 1967:

Distribution of the shovelnose sturgeon in Illinois.

35). Spawning is believed by commercial fishermen to take place in swift chutes such as boulder riffles and old dam sites. Helms (1974) studied age and growth in 110 Mississippi River specimens. The food consists primarily of immatures of aquatic insects sucked from the bottom of the channel (Cross 1967:35). Specimens are caught on baited hooks and in nets by commercial fishermen, and those too small to sell are often thrown up on sand and gravel bars to die.

Distribution.—The shovelnose sturgeon is taken with regularity by commercial fishermen in the Mississippi River down the entire length of Illinois but evidently in only a fraction of the former numbers caught. Records are also available for such large tributaries as the Illinois, Kaskaskia, Vermilion, and Big Muddy rivers. It is apparently more abundant in the Wabash River, where flood-control dams and other modifications of the river have been less severe than in other rivers. It occurs in the lower Ohio River, but no information is available on its present abundance. The species was thought to be extirpated in the Illinois River, where it had not been collected in this century until 1970. In June of that year, a commercial fisherman caught a small specimen in Lake Chautauqua and delivered it to the late Dr. W. C. Starrett.

Paddlefishes—Polyodontidae

This North American and Asiatic family contains one monotypic genus in the United States and another in the Yangtze River of China. Like other primitive fishes, paddlefishes are of great interest in studies of embryology and evolution. Although primitive, they are at the same time highly specialized and regarded as curiosities. The North American species is erroneously believed by many fishermen to be a kind of catfish and usually called spoonbill cat. It was formerly of great commercial importance in the large rivers and adjacent overflow lakes, where they were seined and taken in other kinds of nets. It seldom takes a baited hook but can sometimes be snagged in spillways below impoundments. Formerly Illinois fishermen prized the species more for its roe in making caviar than for its flesh, although it was and still is eaten.

Polyodon Lacépède

This genus contains one species that occurs in the large rivers and lakes of the state. One of the first species of fish to be reported from Illinois, it was alluded to in journal logs of early explorers more than 100 years before the formal description of the species.

Paddlefish
Polyodon spathula (Walbaum)

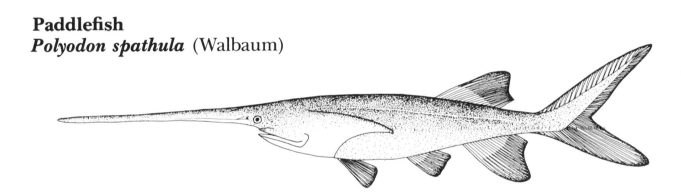

Squalus spathula Walbaum 1792:522 (type-locality not stated).
Polyodon folium: Nelson 1876:51; Jordan 1878:69.
Polyodon spathula: Forbes 1884:86; Large 1903:7; Forbes & Richardson 1908:16; O'Donnell 1935: 475; Smith 1965:6.

Diagnosis.—The unique paddlefish cannot be confused with any other American fish. Its enormous spatulate snout, smooth skin, and heterocercal tail make it immediately recognizable. According to Forbes & Richardson (1908:17), the species attains a weight of more than 150 pounds (67 kg) but at present most adults are less than 50 pounds (22 kg) and 39 inches (1 meter) in length.

Variation.—No studies on geographic variation of the species have been published.

Ecology.—The paddlefish, believed by early workers to be a species of freshwater shark, occurs in channels of large rivers, marginal lakes, and bayous. It is evidently strongly migratory, specimens on rare occasions ascending rivers of small to moderate size. According to Forbes & Richardson (1908:17), it prefers pools in the river and backwater areas, where it swims with mouth wide open for a time, moving its head and snout alternately to right and left while engulfing an enormous quantity of water. The spatulate snout is believed to serve as a stabilizer to prevent the nose diving that would otherwise occur because of the drag created by water entering the gaping mouth. The extensive food studies of Forbes, summarized in Forbes & Richardson (1908), reveal that planktonic organisms comprise virtually the entire diet of the paddlefish. Until recently the life history of the species

15

Distribution of the paddlefish in Illinois.

was almost unknown, and very small specimens were much sought after. The smallest specimen known was 17 mm long (Thompson 1933). Information on reproduction was reported by Purkett (1961), who noted that the species assembles in fast water over submerged gravel bars and spawns in the spring when the water levels are high. The adhesive eggs settle to the gravel. Development is rapid, and the prolarvae are soon swept into downstream pools. While early development is fast, growth is presumably slow, and several years are required for the fish to attain sexual maturity.

Distribution.—The paddlefish is regularly taken in large rivers of the state but is much less common than formerly. Forbes & Richardson (1908:17) noted that it was "sparingly" represented in their collections and that it had already become rare in the Illinois River. Older commercial fishermen on the Mississippi and Wabash rivers can recall vast numbers of paddlefish in their seines. They report that they rarely see specimens at present. In addition to occurring in large rivers, the species lives in the lower reaches of major tributaries and sometimes ascends small rivers for considerable distances until a dam blocks upstream movement. The record for the Calumet River in extreme northeastern Illinois was believed by Forbes (1884: 86) to have been a stray from the Illinois River by way of the canal.

Gars—Lepisosteidae

Although known as fossils from other continents this family, with only one genus, is now believed to be restricted to North and Central America including Cuba. *Lepisosteus sinensis* Bleeker, described from China in 1873, is unknown except from the original description and its identity as a gar needs verification. Gars take bait from hooks but are rarely caught by fishermen because a hook usually cannot penetrate the bony jaws. Most individuals caught are taken by commercial fishermen and either killed or thrown on the bank to die. In some waters gars are rather easy to catch by seine. Gars are fearsome in appearance, and in handling them it is easy to be accidentally snagged by the sharp teeth. It is difficult to hold a struggling specimen in the bare hands without having the skin lacerated by the sharp body scales.

Lepisosteus Lacépède

Four species of this genus occur in Illinois. Highly predaceous and considered nuisances by most fishermen, gars are valuable natural predators. All are readily recognized by the prolonged and well-toothed beak; diamond-shaped ganoid scales that encase the body in a kind of armor; the short and posteriorly placed dorsal fin; and the abbreviate heterocercal, paddle-shaped caudal fin. The alligator gar attains an enormous size and is one of the two largest species of Illinois fishes.

Fig. 6. Tops of heads of gars: a) *Lepisosteus osseus;* b) *L. spatula;* c) *L. oculatus;* d) *L. platostomus.*

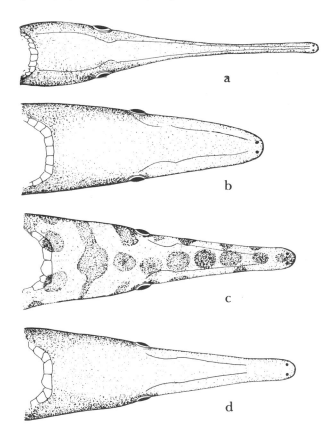

KEY TO SPECIES

1. Snout a long narrow beak, its width at nostrils less than eye diameter (Fig. 6a); distance from rear edge of eye to back edge of opercular membrane contained more than 3.5 times in head length; caudal peduncle length at least twice its height .... *osseus*

   Snout short and broad, its width at nostrils greater than eye diameter; distance from rear edge of eye to back edge of opercular membrane contained fewer than 3.5 times in head length; caudal peduncle length less than twice its height 2

2. Snout short and very broad, its width at nostrils 1.5 or more times eye diameter (Fig. 6b); distance from rear edge of eye to back edge of opercular membrane contained 2.5–3.0 times in head length; scales number 23–25 from anal plate scale diagonally to middorsum .... *spatula*

   Snout moderate in length and breadth, its width at nostrils 1.0–1.5 times eye diameter; distance from rear edge of eye to back edge of opercular membrane contained 3.0–3.5 times in head length; scales number 17–23 from anal plate to middorsum 3

3. Beak and head distinctly spotted (Fig. 6c); 54–58 scales in lateral series; scales from anal plate diagonally to middorsum, 17–20; scales

along dorsal ridge are fewer than 50; adult with bony plates on ventral surface of isthmus under gill membrane .... *oculatus*
Beak and head, and usually anterior half of body, unspotted (Fig. 6d); 59–63 scales in lateral series; scales from anal plate to mid-dorsum, 20–23; scales along dorsal ridge, more than 50; adult without bony plates on ventral side of isthmus .... *platostomus*

Spotted gar
Lepisosteus oculatus Winchell

Lepidosteus (Cylindrosteus) oculatus Winchell 1864: 183 (type-locality: Duck Lake, Michigan).
Lepisosteus platostomus: Forbes & Richardson 1908: 34–35 (part.).
Lepisosteus productus: Hubbs & Lagler 1941:26 (recorded from Illinois).
Lepisosteus oculatus: Smith 1965:6.

Diagnosis.—The spotted gar differs from the longnose gar by its shorter and wider beak; from the alligator gar by its more slender body, longer snout, and fewer scale rows. It differs from the rather similar shortnose gar in having head and beak distinctly spotted, fewer than 50 scales along the dorsal ridge, 54–58 lateral-line scales, and 17–20 scales from anal plate diagonally to mid-dorsum, and in the absence of bony plates on the ventral surface of the isthmus under the gill membranes. The adult is readily distinguished by pigmentation and by meristic and proportional characters. The juvenile, which (like other gar species) has a caudal filament above the caudal fin, is more difficult to distinguish because proportional and pigmentation characters vary with size, and incomplete squamation makes scale counting unreliable. The largest known specimen from Illinois is 840 mm (33 inches) long.

Variation.—The most thorough account of variation in the species is that of Suttkus (*in* Bigelow 1963), who noted that the female attains a greater size than does the male.

Ecology.—The spotted gar differs most markedly from other Illinois species in the genus in its preference for clear pools with luxuriant vegetation. It occurs in streams, lakes, and swamps. Presumably its life history is similar to those of other gars, except that the pattern features may develop at a smaller size (Suttkus *in* Bigelow 1963:74). Eggs are probably deposited over vegetation or

gravel when one female and several males assemble to spawn in late spring and early summer. The larva has an attachment organ on the head for a short time. Growth is rapid in young held in aquaria. Captives often wait until food is alongside the body and then snap it up with a sideways thrust of the head and work it into position for swallowing. Very small young may feed on arthropods, but the food of this species, and others in the genus, consists predominantly of other fish.

Distribution.—The spotted gar was not recognized by early workers but is represented in some of the extant Forbes and Richardson collections of shortnose gars. Their poor state of preservation

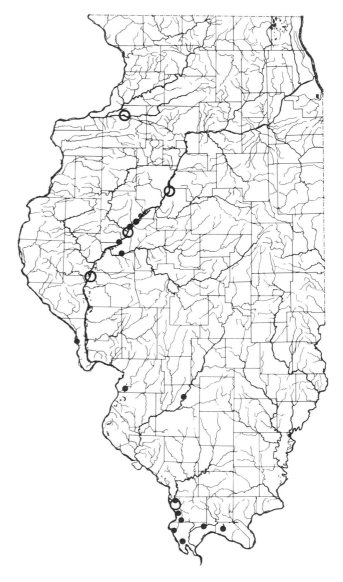

Distribution of the spotted gar in Illinois.

and small size make positive identification difficult, but specimens are available from the Green and Illinois rivers and from swamps in Union County. The present distribution of the species is extremely sporadic, but in some localities the spotted gar is as common as other gars. Because its preferred habitat of clear pools with vegetation has greatly diminished in Illinois, it is likely that the species is less common than formerly, but it may never have been widely distributed in the state.

Longnose gar
Lepisosteus osseus (Linnaeus)

Esox osseus Linnaeus 1758:313 (type-locality: Virginia).
Lepidosteus osseus: Nelson 1876:51 (recorded from Illinois); Jordan 1878:68; Forbes 1884:85.
Lepisosteus osseus: Large 1903:8; Forbes & Richardson 1908:31–34; O'Donnell 1935:477; Smith 1965:6.

Diagnosis.—The adult longnose gar is easily recognized by its extremely long and slender snout, its width at the nostrils being less than the eye diameter, and the distance from the rear edge of the orbit to the back of the operculum going more than 3.5 times into the head length. The juvenile, if 100 mm or more (4+ inches) in total length, can be distinguished from other gars by its longer and more slender caudal peduncle and pattern details of the body. A dark lateral band is either scalloped occasionally on its upper margin or fused with some of the spots in a dorsolateral row. A silvery or creamy white stripe above the lateral dark band is narrow and irregular. The young of the shortnose and spotted gar have a straight upper margin to the lateral dark band, bordered above by a broad, regular, white or silver stripe. According to Forbes & Richardson (1908:31), the species attains a length of more than 3 feet (1 m).

Variation.—The most comprehensive study of variation in the species is that of Suttkus (*in* Bigelow 1963). Subspecies are no longer recognized.

Ecology.—The longnose gar occurs in lakes and streams and is the common gar of small rivers and large creeks. Adults are most often found in deep quiet pools; juveniles, in shallow, weedy shoreline areas. Reproductive habits and life history are similar to those described for the spotted gar, but the

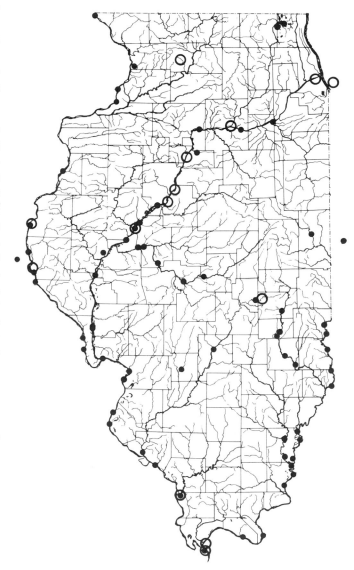

Distribution of the longnose gar in Illinois.

longnose gar has been studied in more detail than have other species of the genus. According to Netsch & Witt (1962), sexual maturity is attained by males in 3 or 4 years and by females in about 6 years, and the life span may exceed 20 years.

Distribution.—The longnose gar is distributed statewide and is relatively common. It is the only gar in the glacial lakes of northeastern Illinois. Large (1903:8) indicated that it did not occur in Lake Michigan; Forbes & Richardson (1908:32) indicated that it did. It is not known in Lake Michigan at present but once was common there (Nelson 1878). The species is much less common in the Mississippi River and most of the Illinois River than is the shortnose gar, but it occurs in more of the smaller rivers. Except in northeastern Illinois, there is no evidence that the longnose gar is less common than formerly.

Shortnose gar
Lepisosteus platostomus Rafinesque

Lepisosteus platostomus Rafinesque 1820*a*:72 (type-locality: Ohio River); Large 1903:8; Forbes & Richardson 1908:34–35; Smith 1965:6.
Lepidosteus platystomus: Nelson 1876:51 (recorded from Illinois); Jordan 1878:69.
Lepidosteus platostomus: Forbes 1884:85.
Cylindrosteus platostomus: O'Donnell 1935:477.

Diagnosis.—The adult shortnose gar is readily separable from the longnose gar by its much shorter and wider beak, but it has a body shape and proportions similar to those of the spotted gar. It differs from the spotted gar in lacking discrete dark spots on the head, beak, and front half of the body; having 59–63 lateral-line scales; having 20–23 scales from the anal plate diagonally to the middorsum; having more than 50 scales along the dorsal ridge; and in the presence of bony plates on the ventral surface of the isthmus under the gill membrane. Occasional specimens are caught that have healed after having the ends of their beaks chopped or broken off, and they at first glance resemble alligator gars. The shortnose gar can be distinguished with certainty from that species by the number of scales from the anal plate to the middorsum and the usually more slender body. The young can be distinguished from young longnose gars by the deeper and shorter caudal peduncle and pattern details, but is almost indistinguishable from the young spotted gar. The species is usually less than 610 mm (2 feet) in length.

Variation.—No subspecies have been proposed for the shortnose gar. Considerable individual variation occurs in snout length and shape, relative body depth, and pigmentation, sometimes so much that it is difficult to believe that extreme variants are of the same species.

Ecology.—The shortnose gar is presumably similar to the longnose gar in life history and behavioral aspects but differs somewhat in habitat. It is the common species of very large rivers and lowland lakes, and, though it can tolerate silty water, it is taken commonly over a sand bottom as well as over mud.

Distribution of the shortnose gar in Illinois.

Distribution.—The species is extremely abundant in the Mississippi, Ohio, and middle Illinois rivers. It does not occur in the glacial lakes nor anywhere in the northeastern part of Illinois. It is restricted to the major rivers, their marginal lakes, and lower reaches of larger tributaries.

Alligator gar
Lepisosteus spatula Lacépède

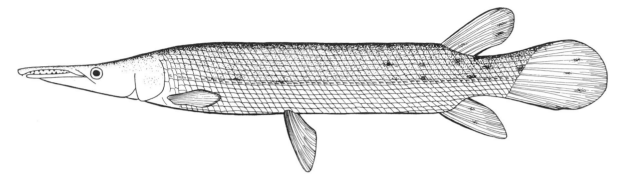

Lepisosteus spatula Lacépède 1803:333 (type-locality not stated); Smith 1965:6.
Litholepis adamanteus: Nelson 1876:51 (recorded from Illinois).
Litholepis spatula: Jordan 1878:69.
Litholepis tristoechus: Forbes 1884:84.
Lepisosteus tristoechus: Large 1903:8; Forbes & Richardson 1908:35–36.
Atractosteus tristoechus: O'Donnell 1935:477.

Diagnosis.—The alligator gar has a short broad snout, its width at the nostrils being much greater than the eye diameter; the distance from the rear edge of the orbit to the back of the opercle is contained 2½–3 times in the head length. It has 23–25 scales from the anal plate diagonally to the middorsum and a heavier and deeper body than have other gars. It can be separated from shortnose gars with mutilated and shortened beaks by the scale counts and the presence of nostrils, for the shortnose with part of the beak missing will lack nostrils. The young can be distinguished from those of other gars by the stout body, ducklike beak, and presence of a light middorsal stripe. The largest Illinois specimen known was more than 2 meters (6′8″) long, but much larger specimens have been found in the southern states.

Variation.—The most thorough study of variation is that of Suttkus (*in* Bigelow 1963).

Ecology.—Very little is known about the life history and behavior of the species. Suttkus (*in* Bigelow 1963:85–86) noted that in Louisiana spawning occurs in April, May, and June; he believed that

Distribution of the alligator gar in Illinois.

stories of the ferocity and destructiveness of the alligator gar were exaggerated.

Distribution.—The alligator gar, apparently always rare in Illinois waters, has been taken only a few times, but commercial fishermen claim that they occasionally see specimens too large to be any other species. Forbes (1884:84) reported the species from the Big Muddy River near Carbondale, and Forbes & Richardson (1908:35) from the Mississippi River above St. Louis and from the lower Illinois River. Other reports in our files, mostly personal communications, record the species from the Kaskaskia River near Baldwin, the Big Muddy River near Murphysboro, and Horseshoe Lake near Cairo. Photographs of a 58-kg (130-pound) specimen and a 49-kg (110-pound) specimen from the Mississippi River at Cairo and Chester, respectively, are also available (Smith et al. 1971). The only specimen available in the Illinois Natural History Survey collection is a juvenile bearing a label "Illinois River, locality unknown, October 23, 1935."

Bowfins—Amiidae

This North American family contains one genus and one recent species. Bowfins are ancient fishes extinct except for the one easily recognized species. They are much like gars except in appearance, and they are of much interest to persons studying evolution and embryology. Occasionally caught on baited hooks, they are said to provide good sport and are taken also in various kinds of nets. The flesh is practically inedible. Adults are so well armored that they probably have few natural enemies other than man. While generally disliked by fishermen, they are regarded as curiosities.

Amia Linnaeus

The only modern species in this genus occurs in most parts of Illinois and is easily recognized by its extremely long dorsal fin, heterocercal and rounded tail, well-armored head, large mouth and strongly developed teeth, bony gular plate, and tubular nostrils.

Bowfin
Amia calva Linnaeus

Amia calva Linnaeus 1766:500 (type-locality: Charleston, South Carolina); Kennicott 1855: 595 (recorded from Illinois); Nelson 1876:51; Jordan 1878:68; Forbes 1884:84; Large 1903:8; Forbes & Richardson 1908:38–41; O'Donnell 1935:477; Smith 1965:6.

Diagnosis.—The bowfin is so distinctive in its generic characters that it can hardly be confused with other Illinois fish. The young superficially resembles the adult mudminnow but differs from it in having a long dorsal fin; heterocercal tail; and a different pattern, the most conspicuous field characters being the large black caudal spot and thin dark stripes through the face. The bowfin does not resemble the American eel but shares with it a long dorsal fin and tubular nostrils. According to Forbes & Richardson (1908:38), the female, which is larger than the male, attains a length of 2 feet (600 mm).

Variation.—No studies of geographic variation in the species have been published and no subspecies have been proposed.

Ecology.—The bowfin occurs in oxbows and backwater pools of rivers, lakes, and swamps. It prefers relatively shallow, clear, well-vegetated waters and can often be seen at night foraging along the shoreline. Forbes & Richardson (1908) summarized observations of their own and others on the bowfin's general breeding habits. Spawning occurs in the late spring and early summer, depending on the latitude. Males construct nests close together in weedy bays and backwater areas and guard them for several weeks. Eggs hatch in 8–10 days, depending upon the water temperature. The young, which has an adhesive organ and a lance-shaped, upper caudal process like that of the young gar, feeds on plankton and presumably grows rapidly. The young school until about 90

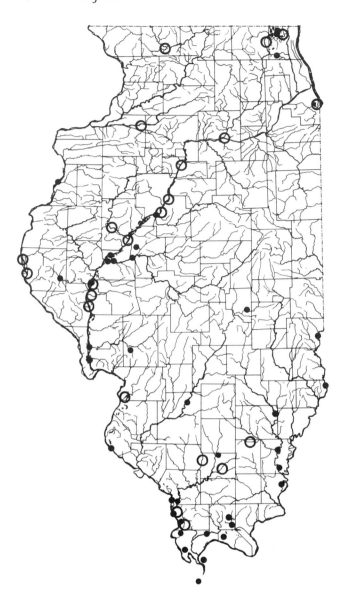

Distribution of the bowfin in Illinois.

mm (3½ inches) in length. The food of the adult consists of other fish, crayfish, mollusks, and almost any animal small enough to be ingested.

Distribution.—Although still locally abundant, the bowfin is less generally distributed than formerly, primarily because of the drainage of natural lakes and swamps marginal to large rivers and the loss of clear, well-vegetated aquatic habitats. The species is still rather general in swampy areas in the southern third of the state, in sloughs adjacent to large and medium-sized rivers throughout the state, and in some of the glacial lakes in northeastern Illinois.

Freshwater eels—Anguillidae

This family contains one genus in eastern North America. Eels are occasionally caught on hooks baited with earthworms or minnows but more often captured in nets of commercial fishermen or in seines. The flesh is reputedly rich in flavor and in demand in some areas, and the hide is sometimes used as a novelty or for binding books. In Illinois they are too rarely encountered to be of importance as a sport or commercial fish, and they are disliked by many people because of their superficial resemblance to snakes.

Anguilla Shaw

The only American species in the genus occurs as an adult in freshwaters of the eastern United States and Canada and the Caribbean islands. After several years, the adult migrates to a delimited area in the Atlantic Ocean south of Bermuda to spawn and die. The floating egg hatches into a planktonic leptocephalous larva, which grows rapidly and eventually makes its way into mainland streams. The remarkable life history of this species and that of the related *Anguilla anguilla* of Europe and North Africa are now comparatively well known.

American eel
Anguilla rostrata (Lesueur)

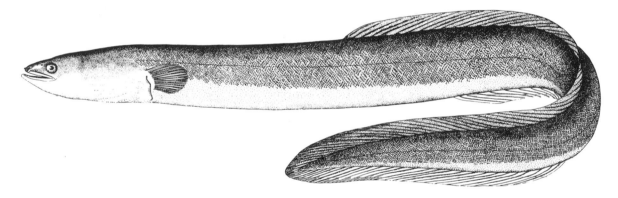

Muraena rostrata Lesueur 1817a:81 (type-locality: Cayuga Lake, New York).

Anguilla lutea: Kennicott 1855:595 (recorded from Illinois).

Anguilla vulgaris var. *rostrata:* Nelson 1876:51.

Anguilla rostrata: Jordan 1878:68; Forbes 1884:71; Smith 1965:6.

Anguilla chrysypa: Large 1903:20; Forbes & Richardson 1908:59–60.

Anguilla bostoniensis: O'Donnell 1935:478.

Diagnosis.—The American eel with its snakelike body is sufficiently distinctive that it cannot be confused with other Illinois fishes. It differs most conspicuously from lampreys in having jaws, paired pectoral fins, two nostrils, and only one gill slit on each side. It superficially resembles the salamander *Siren*, but can be readily distinguished from it by the minute imbedded scales, presence of a pair of pectoral fins rather than legs, and absence of external gills. Since the leptocephalous stage is marine and the young adult, or elver, stage lives in coastal waters, there is no problem of identifying young specimens. The smallest Illinois specimen known is almost 300 mm long, and most of the specimens are much larger, some more than a meter in length.

Variation.—The most comprehensive study of geographic variation is that of Jordan & Evermann (1896:347–348), who, without elaborating, synonymized many of the earlier names that had been

Distribution of the American eel in Illinois.

proposed for the species in different parts of the range. Many other names applied to the species were based on early developmental stages and were reduced to the synonymy when the life history was understood. In fact, the larval stage was for a time assigned to another genus *(Leptocephalus)*.

Ecology.—The American eel is said to prefer deep pools with mud bottoms (Forbes & Richardson 1908:59), but it is occasionally found in large creeks, lakes, ponds, and even on land when migrating back to the sea. The eel is most active at night. It is a voracious predator and also a scavenger. The belief is prevalent that all adult eels in freshwaters are females and that the smaller males remain in the ocean. However, the adult has sex organs in such a state of atrophy that sex determination is not possible. Once the adult enters the ocean, the gonads begin developing. According to Forbes & Richardson (1908:60), the female produces several million eggs. Spawning occurs in the fall. The journey of the young eel back to fresh water requires more than a year.

Distribution.—The American eel occurs throughout Illinois where water quality is such that fish can survive, except in the Lake Michigan drainage. It is extremely sporadic and now most often taken in large rivers, but it can appear almost anywhere upon occasion. The construction of dams has undoubtedly greatly decreased the number of eels, but occasional individuals are able to surmount such barriers.

Herrings—Clupeidae

This wide-ranging marine and freshwater family contains two genera in Illinois. Herrings are enormously abundant and diverse in species in the shallow seas, and they are of great importance as forage fishes. Some marine and anadromous species are economically important and netted in great numbers for marketing. Not only are they used for human consumption but also for pet food, fertilizer, and as a source of oil. Their economic importance stems from their extreme abundance and schooling behavior which together allow them to be captured in large quantities. In Illinois only the skipjack is regarded as a food fish. It is too rarely encountered to be of importance but is taken occasionally on baited hook or in nets. The shads provide food for many larger predatory fishes and are sometimes stocked in reservoirs for this purpose.

KEY TO GENERA

1. Last ray of dorsal fin of the adult elongated into a filament; mouth small, upper jaw length contained more than 3.2 times in head length; pectoral fins extending posteriorly to or beyond pelvic insertion; anal rays, 19 or more .... *Dorosoma*
   Last ray of dorsal fin not elongated; mouth large, upper jaw length contained fewer than 3.2 times in head length; pectoral fins not extending to pelvic insertion; anal rays, 18 or fewer .... *Alosa*

Alosa Linck

This Holarctic genus contains three Illinois species, one of which is a relatively recent arrival in the state. All are thin-bodied silvery fishes with terminal mouths.

KEY TO SPECIES

1. Posterior end of maxillary beneath the front of pupil; mouth small, nearly vertical; pelvic axillary process less than half the length of pelvic rays; dorsal rays, 14–16; body depth in adult greater than head length .... *pseudoharengus*
   Posterior end of maxillary beneath pupil or farther back; mouth moderate in size, oblique; pelvic axillary process more than half the length of pelvic rays; dorsal rays, usually 17 or 18; body depth in adult usually less than head length 2
2. Tip of lower jaw protruding well beyond upper jaw; eye diameter distinctly less than snout length; jaws with teeth .... *chrysochloris*
   Tip of lower jaw barely projecting beyond upper or jaws subequal; horizontal eye diameter about equal to snout length; jaws without teeth .... *alabamae*

Alabama shad
Alosa alabamae Jordan & Evermann

Alosa alabamae Jordan & Evermann *in* Evermann 1896:203 (type-locality: Black Warrior River, Tuscaloosa, Alabama); Smith 1965:6.
Alosa ohiensis: Forbes & Richardson 1908:49–50 (said to occur in Mississippi River to St. Louis); Coker 1930:169 (Illinois locality cited); O'Donnell 1935:477.

Diagnosis.—The Alabama shad differs from the skipjack herring, which also occurs in the Mississippi River, in lacking a noticeably protruding lower jaw and possessing a relatively larger eye. Since it does not occur in Lake Michigan, no problem exists in separating it from the superficially similar alewife. According to Coker (1930:170), the anadromous Alabama shad reaches a weight of 2¾ pounds (1 kg), but Illinois specimens will likely be young of the year weighing a few grams and measuring less than 150 mm (6 inches) long.

Variation.—Hildebrand (*in* Bigelow 1964:310) synonymized *ohiensis* under *alabamae* and noted that while *ohiensis* was supposed to be more elon-

Alabama shad

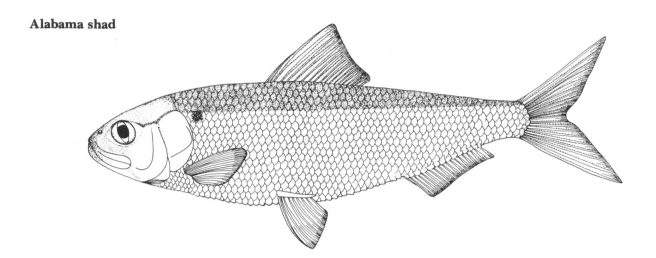

gate and to have more gill rakers, considerable individual variation occurs in both characters. He also noted that young individuals are more slender and have fewer gill rakers than adults have. Coker (1930:169) noted that specimens from the Mississippi River were elongate; hence his referral of his specimens to *ohiensis* rather than *alabamae*.

Ecology.—According to Hildebrand (*in* Bigelow 1964), the Alabama shad appears in inland rivers in May and June and ascends streams until locks and dams block farther upstream migration. Many thousand eggs are scattered over the river bottom by each female. By fall young specimens approximately 100 mm in total length are presumably making their way back to the sea. Spawning adults in fresh water do not feed; adults not in spawning condition feed on such items as aquatic insects, crustaceans, small fish, and vegetation. Laurence & Yerger (1967) conducted a thorough life-history study of the species in the Apalachicola River of Florida.

Distribution.—Knowledge of the occurrence of this species in Illinois waters is limited to the excellent published account (Coker 1930:170) of spawning adults in the Keokuk region of the Mississippi River and to a juvenile collected 21 August 1962 in the Mississippi River near Harrisonville in Monroe County. On the basis of Missouri collections, Pflieger (1971:321) concurred with Coker (1930) that the species migrates into inland rivers only to spawn. Coker (1930) and Hildebrand (*in* Bigelow 1964) commented that the Alabama shad has decreased in abundance because dams prevent migration up many rivers.

Distribution of the Alabama shad in Illinois.

Skipjack herring
Alosa chrysochloris (Rafinesque)

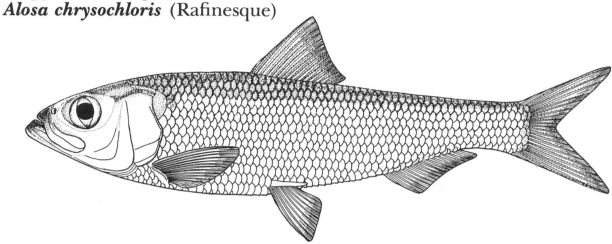

Pomolobus chrysochloris Rafinesque 1820*a*:39 (type-locality: Ohio River); Jordan 1878:55; Large 1903:20; Forbes & Richardson 1908:48–49; O'Donnell 1935:477.
Pomolobus chrysochrous: Nelson 1876:44 (recorded from Illinois).
Clupea chrysochloris: Forbes 1884:73.
Alosa chrysochloris: Smith 1965:6.

Diagnosis.—The skipjack herring is readily distinguished from other clupeids by its elongate and much compressed body, silvery coloration, the prominently protruding lower jaw, and the presence of teeth in both jaws. Small individuals are recognizable by the thin body shape and the upper jaw which partly overrides the lower jaw. The adult attains a length of 380 mm (15 inches) in Illinois (Forbes & Richardson 1908:48).

Variation.—Hildebrand (*in* Bigelow 1964) has presented the most complete study of variation in the species.

Ecology.—The skipjack herring occurs in clear, fast water over sand and gravel in large rivers. It is a schooling fish and derives its common name from its habit of leaping out of the water. Coker (1930: 166–168) noted this species in spawning condition at Keokuk from late April until mid-June. Actual spawning was not observed. Each egg is 0.8 mm in diameter. The young grow rapidly and attain lengths of 130–150 mm (5–6 inches) by the end of the first growing season. Since the skipjack also occurs in the ocean and belongs to a group of strongly anadromous species, it was once believed to be present in rivers only during the summer months. However, its return to the ocean is prevented in some places by downstream locks and

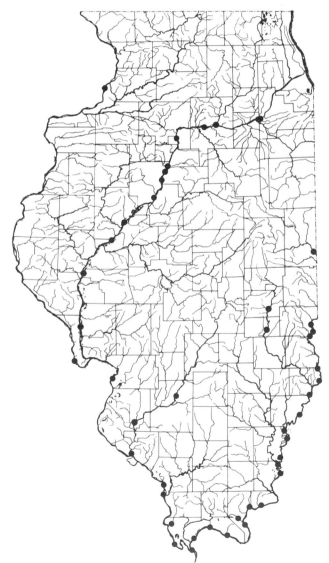

Distribution of the skipjack herring in Illinois.

dams. It is somewhat migratory and assembles below dams in the spring of the year.

Distribution.—The skipjack herring is taken occasionally throughout the length of the Illinois River and in the Mississippi River downstream from pool 25, but it is much more common in the Wabash and Ohio rivers. Too few early collections are available to assess the extent of changes in the distribution of the species, although Forbes & Richardson (1908:49) reported it from the Rock River, where it evidently no longer occurs. Coker (1930:167) noted that the skipjack was once "enormously abundant" at Keokuk and that a decided decline in abundance followed the construction of the Keokuk dam. The species still occurred in the Mississippi River above pool 25 in the 1950's but had become rare. It was not found above pool 25 during the intensive field studies of the Mississippi River in the 1960's (Smith et al. 1971).

Alewife
Alosa pseudoharengus (Wilson)

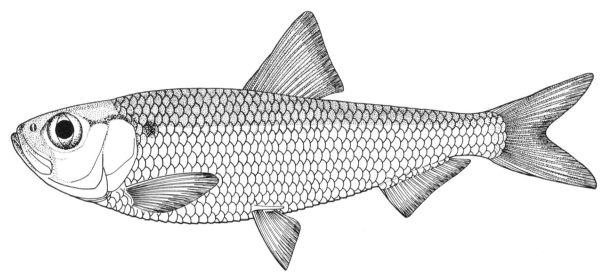

Clupea pseudoharengus Wilson *ca.* 1811:no page number given (type-locality: not given but traditionally indicated as "probably Philadelphia, Pa.").

Alosa pseudoharengus: Smith 1965:6 (recorded from Illinois).

Diagnosis.—The alewife is a thin silvery fish abounding in Lake Michigan and is unlikely to be confused with other species. It differs from the Alabama shad and skipjack herring in its smaller size, smaller and more upturned mouth, deeper body, and shorter maxilla. Most specimens are less than 310 mm (12 inches) long.

Variation.—Hildebrand (*in* Bigelow 1964:338) noted that specimens from the northern part of the range of the species and populations landlocked in freshwater lakes tend to be more slender and larger headed and to have an emaciated look.

Ecology.—Since 1960, the alewife has been so abundant in Lake Michigan that it is a serious problem. Crews of men have scooped up the windrows of alewife carcasses on beaches following massive die-offs and transported the fish elsewhere, and several vessels have been contracted with to catch and remove live fish from the lake. Water intake valves have had to be screened to keep alewives from entering them, and beaches have had to be closed during several summers. Tons of alewives have been used for fertilizer and pet food. The alewife is extremely prolific. According to Hildebrand (*in* Bigelow 1964), many spawning pairs aggregate and produce millions of eggs which float to the bottom in quiet waters. The strongly adherent, 1.25-mm egg hatches in 6 days at 15.5° C. An adult female contains over 100,000 eggs at the time of spawning. The dramatic die-offs occur in late spring and early summer. The young attains a length of about 10 mm at the end of its first growing season. Sexual maturity is reached at about 20 mm and 3 or 4 years of age. While the species is strongly anadromous, no Illinois streams that are fit for spawning runs enter

Distribution of the alewife in Illinois.

Canal in the 1820's, the Niagara escarpment was no longer a barrier to upstream migration by the alewife and other marine species, but the alewife did not appear in Lake Michigan until 1949 after the sea lamprey had severely decimated the populations of large fishes in the lake. Without effective predators and competition from coregonid fishes, the alewife exploded in numbers in the unfilled niche and quickly spread throughout the lake. The die-offs may have resulted in part from the warmer temperatures in shallow water. At the present writing the alewife problem is much less serious than it was in the late 1960's.

Dorosoma Rafinesque

This North American genus contains five species, two of which occur in Illinois. One of them is statewide in distribution; the other has recently extended its range northward in the Mississippi River to the southern part of the state. The genus includes both marine and freshwater species.

KEY TO SPECIES

1. Mouth terminal; snout pointed; head large, length contained 3.5 times in standard length; lateral-line scales, about 42; anal rays, 20–23; anterior dorsal fin insertion over pelvic insertion; upper sides with rows of dark spots .... *petenense*
   Mouth inferior; snout blunt; head small, length contained 4.3 times in standard length; lateral-line scales, about 56; anal rays, about 31; anterior dorsal fin insertion behind pelvic insertion; upper sides usually without rows of dark spots .... *cepedianum*

Gizzard shad
Dorosoma cepedianum (Lesueur)

Megalops cepediana Lesueur 1818:361 (type-locality: Delaware and Chesapeake Bay).
Dorosoma notatum: Nelson 1876:44 (recorded from Illinois).
Dorosoma cepedianum: Jordan 1878:55; Forbes 1884: 73; Large 1903:20; Forbes & Richardson 1908: 45–47; O'Donnell 1935:477; Smith 1965:6.

Diagnosis.—The gizzard shad is a compressed white or silvery fish with a saw-toothed midventer,

Lake Michigan. Hence, the species is restricted in Illinois to Lake Michigan proper. In the late 1960's conservation agencies introduced the salmons *Oncorhynchus kisutch* and *O. tshawytscha* and restocked lake and rainbow trouts in the hope that the alewife would provide an ample food supply for these sport fishes and be brought under control by their predation.

Distribution.—The alewife is native to the Atlantic Ocean and coastal streams of eastern North America. There is some question whether the landlocked population in Lake Ontario is native, but there is no doubt that the spread of the species into other Great Lakes has occurred since 1930 (Miller 1957). With completion of the Welland

Gizzard shad

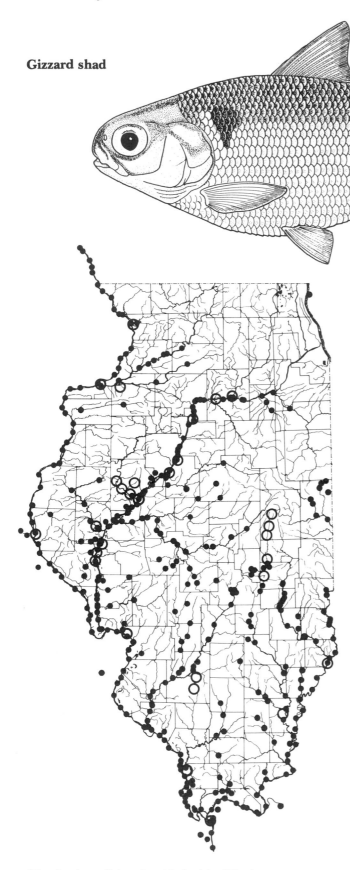

Distribution of the gizzard shad in Illinois.

a dorsal fin with the last ray prolonged into a long filament, and an inferior or subterminal mouth. It can be distinguished from the threadfin shad by the position of its mouth, its smaller scales, and its higher anal ray count. According to Forbes & Richardson (1908:45), it attains a length of 15–18 inches (380 mm or more) in the Mississippi River, but specimens over 200 mm (10 inches) long are unusual.

Variation.—Miller (1950, 1960, and *in* Bigelow 1964) described ontogenetic and geographic variation in the species. No subspecies are recognized.

Ecology.—Miller (1960) has summarized the published information on the biology of the species. Spawning occurs in April, May, and June. Breeding adults aggregate and eject quantities of eggs and sperm while swimming close together. A female contains many thousand eggs. Each egg is 0.75 mm in diameter and adhesive. Hatching requires 3 days at 25° C. The newly hatched shad is long and cylindrical with a terminal mouth and teeth in both jaws. The young fish feeds on zoo-plankton until it is about 25 mm long, when it becomes slab-sided, loses its teeth, and becomes a mud feeder. Growth is rapid, and the young is about 100 mm (4 inches) by the end of its first growing season. The shad is sexually mature in its 2nd year and may live 6 or 7 years. The gizzard shad is often the most abundant fish in reservoirs and oxbows and may make up most of the biomass. In streams it is usually found in deep, quiet pools with silt and debris on the bottom, but migrating schools may be seen in shallow and fast waters. Shad often leap out of the water, especially when being pursued by predacious fishes. The species is highly specialized for mud feeding with a muscular, gizzard-like stomach; a long and much-coiled intestine; and numerous long, fine gill rakers for straining plankton from the mud that is ingested.

Distribution.—The gizzard shad is statewide in distribution and abundant everywhere except in extreme northeastern Illinois. It is more common and general in occurrence over most of the state than is indicated on the distribution map, and it has probably expanded its range and increased in abundance because of the construction of reservoirs and ponds and the increase in silt in many streams.

Threadfin shad
Dorosoma petenense (Günther)

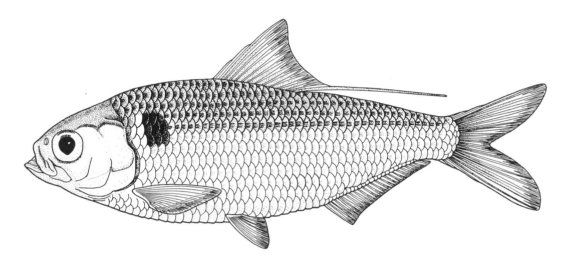

Meletta petenensis Günther 1866:603 (type-locality: Lake Peten, Guatemala).
Signalosa petenensis: Minckley & Krumholz 1960: 172 (recorded from Illinois).
Dorosoma petensense: Smith 1965:6.

Diagnosis.—The threadfin shad is a delicate silvery fish similar to the gizzard shad but differing from it most obviously in having a terminal mouth. If one drags a finger over the snout of the threadfin shad, the lower lip will be forced open, but a finger will slide over the recessed lower jaw of the gizzard shad without catching on the lower lip. The threadfin shad is usually less than 130 mm (5 inches) long in Illinois waters.

Variation.—Weed (1925) studied variation in this species and described some subspecies no longer recognized. Miller (*in* Bigelow 1964) summarized the available information on variation and biology of the threadfin shad. Minckley & Krumholz (1960) reported hybridization between the gizzard shad and the threadfin shad in the lower Ohio River. Some of the hybrids were collected at Illinois localities.

Ecology.—Although pools over soft bottoms are preferred, the threadfin is also common over sand bottoms. According to Miller (*in* Bigelow 1964), the threadfin shad is a midwater species that feeds in large schools often made up of one age class. The species occurs in lakes, oxbows, and quiet pools of large rivers. The adult is sexually mature in less than 1 year. Spawning occurs at two peaks, one in the spring and one in the fall. The eggs are deposited over vegetation or debris in quiet waters. The young and adult fish feed on plankton. The species is sensitive to rapid temperature changes and subject to large-scale die-offs. Since it is extremely prolific and a good forage fish, it has been introduced into artificial lakes in many places throughout this country, including Hawaii.

Distribution.—Prior to 1945 the threadfin shad was known from tropical waters from Florida to Central America. Somewhat later it appeared in some of the TVA impoundments in the southeastern states. Evidently the species acclimated itself at that latitude and spread rapidly. The first Illinois specimens were collected in 1957 (Minckley & Krumholz 1960) from tributaries of the Ohio

River. It has since been found in abundance at all stations along the Ohio River and a few miles upstream in both the Mississippi and Wabash rivers. It presumably disperses northward into southern Illinois from the lower Mississippi River each summer.

Distribution of the threadfin shad in Illinois.

Mooneyes—Hiodontidae

This family of rather primitive fishes occurs only in eastern and central North America and contains only one genus. Mooneyes differ from herrings most obviously in that they lack the sawtooth midline of the belly. They are sometimes caught on dry flies or artificial bait but are more often taken in nets or by seining. The flesh is not highly esteemed as food. In most of Illinois they are not numerous enough to be of much importance, but in the Mississippi River the young must be of some value as a forage fish. Because they are primitive fishes rather restricted in distribution, they are of considerable interest in evolutionary studies and greatly desired as museum specimens. They are the only temperate representatives of the order Osteoglossiformes; all other members are tropical.

Hiodon Lesueur

This genus of herringlike fishes contains two species, both of which occur in large rivers of Illinois.

KEY TO SPECIES

1. Origin of dorsal fin ahead of origin of anal fin; dorsal rays, 11 or 12; iris silvery; fleshy mid-ventral keel not extending forward of pelvic bases; pectoral fins usually not extending posteriorly to origin of pelvics .... *tergisus*
   Origin of dorsal fin behind origin of anal fin; dorsal rays, 9 or 10; iris golden; fleshy midventral keel extending forward almost to pectoral bases; pectoral fins usually extending posteriorly to origin of pelvics .... *alosoides*

Goldeye
Hiodon alosoides (Rafinesque)

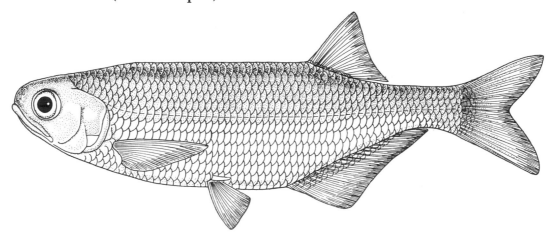

Amphiodon alveoides (*=alosoides*): Rafinesque 1819: 421 (type-locality: Ohio River).
Hyodon tergisus: Nelson 1876:44 (?part., recorded from Illinois); Jordan 1878:54 (?part.).
Hyodon alosoides: Forbes 1884:74.
Hiodon alosoides: Large 1903:20; Forbes & Richardson 1908:43–44; Smith 1965:6.
Amphiodon alosoides: O'Donnell 1935:477.

Diagnosis. — The goldeye is a compressed, white or silvery, soft-rayed fish with pelvic axillary processes, a single short dorsal fin located far behind the pelvic fin insertion, short and knoblike gill rakers, teeth in the jaws and on the tongue, and a gold-colored eye, but it is without a saw-toothed midventer and a prolonged dorsal fin ray. It differs from the related mooneye in having only 9 or

Distribution of the goldeye in Illinois.

firm sandy bottom. The species spawns in the early spring. By the end of the first growing season, the young are 100 mm or more (4 or 5 inches) long in Illinois. In Canadian waters, according to McPhail & Lindsey (1970), the species ascends tributary streams and spawns over gravel shoals, perhaps at night. A large female may produce 25,000 eggs. The 4-mm egg is semibuoyant, as is the newly hatched larva for a time. In Illinois the goldeye probably reaches sexual maturity in its 3rd year. The species is said to feed mostly on insects, but fish and crustaceans are also taken (Coker 1930: 162).

Distribution.—Forbes & Richardson (1908:43) noted that the goldeye had once been abundant in the Mississippi and Ohio rivers but was quite rare at the time of their field work. It still occurs over all of Illinois, except the northeastern part of the state, but it is limited to rather large rivers. The species is moderately common in the turbid Mississippi below the mouth of the Missouri River, but it appears to be uncommon in the Ohio and Wabash rivers.

Mooneye
Hiodon tergisus Lesueur

Hiodon tergisus Lesueur 1818:366 (type-locality: Ohio River); Large 1903:20; Forbes & Richardson 1908:44–45; O'Donnell 1935:477; Smith 1965:6.
Hyodon tergisus: Nelson 1876:44 (part., recorded from Illinois); Jordan 1878:54 (part.); Forbes 1884:74.

Diagnosis.—The mooneye is similar to the goldeye but differs in having 11 or 12 dorsal rays, the dorsal fin origin ahead of the anal fin origin, a silvery eye, a fleshy midventral keel that does not reach the front of the pelvic fin bases, and pectoral fins that do not extend posteriorly as far as the origin of the pelvic fins. The mooneye is also deeper bodied with a comparatively larger eye, and it has an area of various-sized scales just above the anal fin interrupting the regularity of the scale rows along the lower sides. The mooneye is a smaller species, attaining a length of 310 mm (12 inches) in the Mississippi River (Coker 1930:163).

Variation.—Several synonyms exist because the species was described as new more than once, but no detailed analysis of geographic variation in the species has been published.

10 dorsal rays, the dorsal fin origin behind the anal fin origin, and a midventral keel extending forward almost to the base of the pectoral fins. In most specimens the pectoral fins extend backward as far as the origin of the pelvic fin base. The adult attains a length of more than 460 mm (18 inches) in the Mississippi River (Coker 1930:162).

Variation.—Apparently no studies of geographic variation in this wide-ranging species have been published, and the species has had a remarkably stable nomenclatural history.

Ecology.—The goldeye occurs in large and medium-sized rivers. It is quite tolerant of turbid water but prefers a moderate to fast current over a

Mooneye

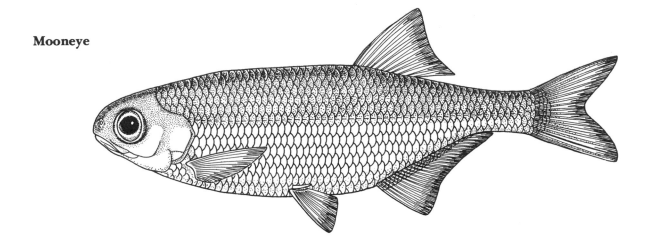

Ecology.—The mooneye occurs in large and medium-sized rivers that are clear. Although it is found in quiet water occasionally, it is more often taken in swift current over a firm bottom and in deep water. Coker (1930:163) found the mooneye in spawning condition in mid-March and mature adults as small as 240 mm (9½ inches). The unfertilized egg was slightly over 2 mm in diameter. Little else is known about the life history of the species in Illinois waters, but its habits are presumably similar to those of the related goldeye. The mooneye feeds on aquatic insects, small fish, and mollusks (Forbes & Richardson 1908:44).

Distribution.—The mooneye was said to have been once abundant in the Ohio River by Forbes & Richardson (1908), who found it only in the Rock and Illinois rivers and regarded it as rare at that time. The species still occurs in the Mississippi River and its direct tributaries throughout the length of Illinois, but it is much more common in the clear pools well above the mouth of the Missouri River. It has withdrawn from most of the Illinois River, presumably because of its intolerance for silty water. It is now uncommon in both the Ohio and Wabash rivers.

Distribution of the mooneye in Illinois.

Trouts—Salmonidae

This Holarctic family of cold-adapted fishes contains the whitefishes, trouts, and salmons and is represented in Illinois by five genera in Lake Michigan. Some ichthyologists place the whitefishes, including the ciscos, bloater, and "chubs," in the family Coregonidae; others regard the whitefishes as a subfamily. Whitefishes include many poorly defined species that can be identified only by a specialist because of the amount of variation and great overlap of characters. Only a few of them have been recorded from the Illinois waters of Lake Michigan, but conceivably other species that occur in deep water could appear along the Illinois shoreline. Some of the described species have been extirpated from the lake. Salmonids are of great economic importance. Whitefishes were once extremely important commercial species in Lake Michigan, where they were caught in trawls and other nets. Trouts and salmons are popular sport fishes since they take artificial lures readily, attain large size, and are good tasting.

KEY TO GENERA

1. Mouth relatively small, maxillary not extending to below middle of eye; fewer than 100 scales along lateral line; ground color silvery, without pattern of dark markings; jaws and tongue with minute teeth or toothless; adipose eyelids (Fig. 7a) conspicuous 2
   Mouth large, maxillary reaching behind eye; more than 100 scales along lateral line; ground color not silvery, definite pattern of dark markings; jaws and tongue with large strong teeth; eyelids normal 3
2. One flap between nostrils (Fig. 7b); body terete .... *Prosopium*
   Two flaps between nostrils (Fig. 7c); body usually somewhat compressed ...... *Coregonus*
3. Anal fin base longer than height of fin, with more than 12 principal rays ... *Oncorhynchus*
   Anal fin base less than height of fin, with fewer than 12 principal rays 4
4. Back with discrete black and brown spots; less than 140 scales in lateral line; mouth small, maxillary barely extending behind eye; shaft of vomer with teeth .... *Salmo*
   Back vermiculate; more than 190 scales along lateral line; mouth large, maxillary extending well behind eye; shaft of vomer toothless .... *Salvelinus*

Fig. 7. Key characters: a) adipose eyelid of *Coregonus artedii;* b) nostril of *Prosopium cylindraceum,* showing single flap; c) nostril of *Coregonus artedii,* showing double flap.

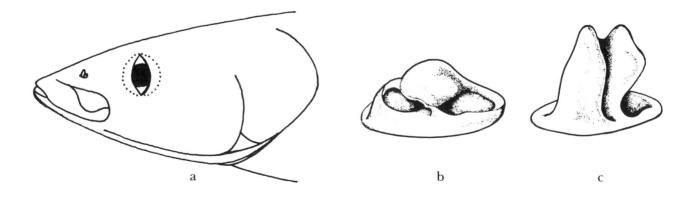

Coregonus Linnaeus

This Holarctic genus includes four species definitely reported from the Illinois waters of Lake Michigan, but one of them is presumably extirpated. Five others *(reighardi, zenithicus, alpenae, johannae,* and *kiyi)* were cited for Lake Michigan by O'Donnell (1935:478) but without any indication that they occur in Illinois. Three of them *(reighardi, alpenae,* and *kiyi)* have been taken recently in southeastern Lake Michigan (Wells 1968) but not in the Illinois portion of the lake. The species of *Coregonus* are extremely difficult to identify.

KEY TO SPECIES

1. Tip of snout projecting beyond tip of lower jaw (Fig. 8a); mouth subterminal; gill rakers fewer than 32; premaxillary length contained in head length about three times .... *clupeaformis*

   Snout not projecting; mouth terminal; gill rakers usually more than 32; premaxillary length contained in head length more than three times 2
2. Body ovate (Fig. 8b), deeper anteriorly than at midbody; body compressed; mandible heavy; lower jaw not protruding when mouth is closed; fins entirely blue-black ... *nigripinnis**

   Body elliptical, deepest at midbody; body more or less terete, slightly compressed; mandible thin; lower jaw usually projecting when mouth is closed; fins plain or with black margins 3

3. Mouth large, lower jaw distinctly protruding when mouth is closed (Fig. 8c); gill rakers usually fewer than 45; body rather terete; premaxillary lightly pigmented, upper parts of body quite dark; total length less than 200 mm (8 inches) .... *hoyi*

   Mouth moderate in size, lower jaw at most slightly protruding when mouth is closed (Fig. 8d); gill rakers usually more than 45; body somewhat compressed; premaxillary darkly pigmented, upper parts of body moderately dark; total length up to 450 mm (18 inches) .... *artedii*

Cisco
Coregonus artedii Lesueur

Coregonus artedi Lesueur 1818:231 (type-locality: Lake Erie [at Buffalo] and Niagara River [Lewiston]); Jordan 1878:54; Forbes 1884:73.

Coregonus: Kennicott 1855:595 (recorded from Illinois).

Argyrosomus clupeiformis: Nelson 1876:44.

Argyrosomus artedi: Large 1903:20; Forbes & Richardson 1908:54–55.

Leucichthys artedi: O'Donnell 1935:478.

Coregonus artedii: Smith 1965:6.

Diagnosis.—The cisco is a rather slender, slab-sided whitefish, dull bluish above and silvery below. Its fins are usually unpigmented. The lower jaw barely protrudes beyond the upper when the mouth is closed, and the premaxillary is usually darkly pigmented. The species attains a length of 400 mm (16 inches) or more.

Variation.—There are so many described populations that the cisco is sometimes referred to as the "*Coregonus artedii* complex," and there is disagreement whether the named taxa are species, subspecies, or phenotypic expressions to different environments. An excellent summary of the taxonomic confusion in the group is presented by McPhail & Lindsey (1970).

Ecology.—Until the late 1940's the cisco was evidently an important commercial species in Lake Michigan and was sold in large numbers in many lakeside fish markets. The species spawns in late fall and early winter (November) and scatters its

Fig. 8. Heads of whitefishes: a) *Coregonus clupeaformis;* b) *C. nigripinnis;* c) *C. hoyi;* d) *C. artedii.*

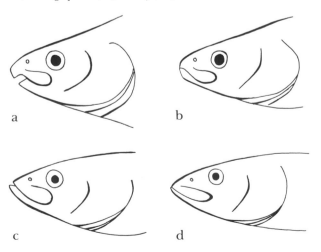

Cisco

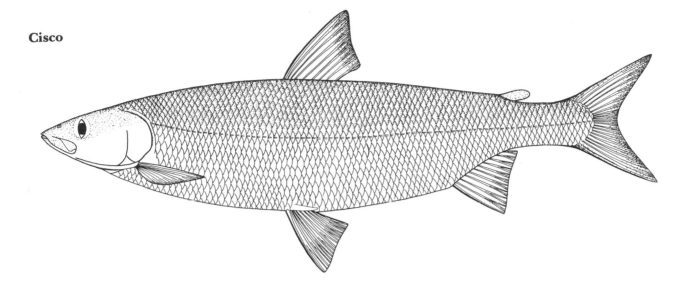

Distribution of the cisco in Illinois.

eggs, which hatch in 10–12 weeks, over the sandy or gravelly bottom. The adult feeds on plankton, especially large crustaceans, and occasionally on small fish (Cahn 1927:110–111; McPhail & Lindsey 1970). It was severely decimated in Lake Michigan by the sea lamprey, and when the lamprey was brought under control, it was seemingly unable to compete with other Lake Michigan fishes with similar feeding habits. Age and growth in the species were reported upon by Hile (1936). It may live for 10 years (Cahn 1927:110).

Distribution.—The cisco still occurs in Illinois waters but has become very rare. After completion of the canals connecting Lake Michigan and the Illinois River, the species occasionally descended the Illinois River for considerable distances. Large (1903:20) reported specimens from Ottawa and Meredosia. In the middle 1930's a specimen was captured in the Illinois River and was discarded after it had been identified, and another was taken in Lake Senachwine. The canals are presently too polluted for any fish to survive very long in them, and the population of ciscos in Lake Michigan is extremely low. One specimen recently collected off Waukegan is available in the Illinois Natural History Survey collection.

Lake whitefish
Coregonus clupeaformis (Mitchill)

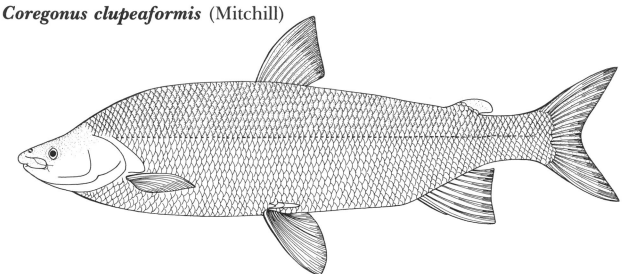

Salmo clupeaformis Mitchill 1818:321 (type-locality: Falls of St. Mary, northern Lake Huron [= Sault Ste. Marie?]).

Coregonus albus: Kennicott 1855:594 (recorded from Illinois); Nelson 1876:44.

Coregonus clupeiformis: Jordan 1878:54; Forbes 1884:73; Large 1903:20; Forbes & Richardson 1908:51–53.

Coregonus clupeaformis: O'Donnell 1935:477; Smith 1965:11 (status in Illinois uncertain).

Diagnosis.—The lake whitefish is a compressed, deep-bodied coregonine that differs from other species in the genus in having a snout which projects beyond the tip of the lower jaw so that the mouth is decidedly subterminal. It is dusky above and silvery beneath, and the fins are unpigmented or slightly dusky. It has fewer than 32 gill rakers, and the length of its downwardly curved premaxillary goes into the head length more than three times. The species attains a length of 610 mm (2 feet) or more (Forbes & Richardson 1908:51).

Variation.—Like the cisco, the lake whitefish is a complex of closely related species and subspecies, which differ from each other primarily in modal gill-raker counts and are difficult to identify because of the great amount of variation and overlap in most characters.

Ecology.—Forbes & Richardson (1908:52) stated that this species was the most important food fish in the Great Lakes but that it had been decimated from overfishing and was rare in the Illinois waters of Lake Michigan. They described it as a deepwater species that comes into shallow water to

Distribution of the lake whitefish in Illinois.

spawn in October through December. It spawns at night, and each female produces many thousands of eggs, which are merely scattered over the bottom. The young feeds on plankton; the adult, on benthos.

Distribution.—I have never seen Illinois specimens, but Harry L. Wight (personal communication) advises me that he has collected five specimens near Waukegan since 1972. Like other commercial fishes in Lake Michigan, the lake whitefish has been decimated severely by sea lamprey predation and the ecological imbalance that followed.

Bloater
Coregonus hoyi (Gill)

Argyrosomus hoyi Gill *in* Hoy 1872:100 (type-locality: Lake Michigan off Racine, Wisconsin); Nelson 1876:44 (recorded from Illinois); Large 1903: 21; Forbes & Richardson 1908:55.

Coregonus hoyi: Jordan 1878:54; Smith 1965:11 (status in Illinois uncertain).

Leucichthys hoyi: O'Donnell 1935:478.

Diagnosis.—This small and cylindrical, darkly pigmented whitefish has a large mouth and distinctly protruding lower jaw and 35–43 gill rakers. The premaxillary is rather lightly pigmented, but the upper parts of the body are quite dusky. The length of the species is less than 250 mm (10 inches).

Variation.—Although distinguishing specimens of the bloater from allied whitefish may be difficult, this wide-ranging species is relatively distinctive. No subspecies have been described.

Ecology.—The bloater is apparently the most common coregonine in Lake Michigan, but it is less common than a few years ago. Although it occurs infrequently in shallow water, it is taken in trawling operations in deep water. When overfishing and sea lamprey predation decimated the lake trout predator and the larger species of plankton-feeding coregonines in Lake Michigan, the bloater, which is too small to be attacked by the sea lamprey, became numerous and the object of heavy fishing pressure. As its numbers were depleted, an environmental niche became available for the alewife. The life history of the bloater is presumably similar to those of other whitefishes. Wells & Beeton (1963) found that its principal food is crustaceans of the genera *Mysis* and *Pontoporeia*.

Distribution.—The bloater is generally distributed in deep water throughout the Illinois portion of Lake Michigan, but is threatened by the vastly more numerous alewife, which has similar feeding habits. Two small series are available in the Illinois Natural History Survey collection from collections made off Waukegan.

Distribution of the bloater in Illinois.

Blackfin cisco*
Coregonus nigripinnis (Gill)

Argyrosomus nigripinnis Gill *in* Hoy 1872:100 (type-locality: Lake Michigan off Racine, Wisconsin); Nelson 1876:44 (recorded from Illinois); Forbes & Richardson 1908:55.
Argyrosomus nigripennis: Large 1903:21.
Coregonus nigripinnis: Jordan 1878:54; Smith 1965:11 (not known from Illinois waters).

Diagnosis. — The blackfin cisco is a deep-bodied, thick whitefish with a heavy mandible, darkly pigmented fins, and 46 or more gill rakers. It attains a length of 510 mm (20 inches).

Variation. — Several subspecies have been described, but the Lake Michigan population is the nominal subspecies (*C. n. nigripinnis*).

Ecology. — The blackfin cisco is a deepwater species that spawns in the winter months. Its life history and feeding habits are presumably similar to those of other members of the genus *Coregonus,* but it has not been studied as intensively as other species.

Distribution. — Extirpated in Illinois. The blackfin cisco was reportedly common in southern Lake Michigan in the early part of this century (Forbes & Richardson 1908:55). Because specimens have not been found since the middle 1950's (Moffett 1957), it is believed that the Lake Michigan form is now extinct. I have never seen an Illinois specimen.

Prosopium Milner

This North American genus of six cold-adapted species contains one species that is now problematic in the Illinois waters of Lake Michigan.

Round whitefish
Prosopium cylindraceum (Pallas)

Salmo cylindraceus Pallas *in* Pennant 1784:ciii (type-locality: Lena, Kowyma, and Indigirska rivers [Siberia]).
?Coregonus albus: Nelson 1876:44.
Coregonus quadrilateralis: Jordan 1878:54 (recorded from Illinois); Forbes & Richardson 1908:53; Large 1903:20.
Prosopium quadrilaterale: O'Donnell 1935:477.

Prosopium cylindraceum quadrilaterale: Smith 1965:11.

Diagnosis. — The round whitefish is a cigar-shaped coregonine with a short head, small mouth overhung by a snout, and a single flap between the nostrils. It is olive brown above and silvery below and attains a length of 500 mm (20 inches) (McPhail & Lindsey 1970:111).

Variation. — The round whitefish has an Old World and a New World subspecies. Variation in the species was studied by Dymond (1943) and McPhail & Lindsey (1970), who noted that the population in northeastern Canada differs from that in the Canadian northwest. They regarded the populations as different morphological types but not as subspecies even though their ranges are disjunct, and they did not recognize the subspecies *quadrilateralis.*

Ecology. — The round whitefish is a common northern fish. According to McPhail & Lindsey (1970), it occurs in lakes, streams, and brackish water. It feeds on aquatic insects, gastropods, crustaceans, and eggs of other fish. Spawning occurs in the fall, and the eggs are merely shed over gravel. A large female lays many thousand eggs.

Distribution. — The round whitefish has always been rare in Lake Michigan, according to early authors, and it has not been collected there in many years. The species may be extinct in the Illinois portion of the lake.

Salvelinus Richardson

This Holarctic genus is represented in Illinois by two species, both native to Lake Michigan.

KEY TO SPECIES

1. Caudal fin slightly forked, almost plain; first ray of pectoral, pelvic, and anal fins milky white; back and sides with discrete blue and red spots .... *fontinalis*
   Caudal fin deeply forked, heavily speckled and mottled; first ray of pectoral, pelvic, and anal fins not milky white; back and sides with fine greenish gray spots on a dark ground color .... *namaycush*

Brook trout
Salvelinus fontinalis (Mitchill)

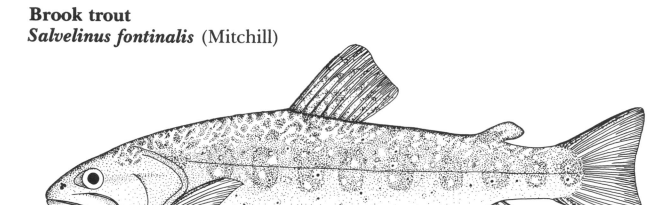

Salmo fontinalis Mitchill 1815:435 (type-locality: Long Island, New York).

Salvelinus fontinalis: Large 1903:21 (frequent introductions in Illinois unsuccessful); O'Donnell 1935:478 (Illinois localities cited); Smith 1965:11 (status in Illinois uncertain).

Diagnosis. — The brook trout has distinct vermiculations over its back, more than 210 scales along the lateral line, a slightly forked caudal fin, heavily speckled dorsal and caudal fins, and a milky white first ray of the ventral fin. Some of the spots on the sides are bright red and blue. The breeding male has a wash of red or orange along the lower sides. The young can be distinguished from that of the lake trout by the eight or nine decidedly rectangular parr marks along the sides and from the young of other trouts and salmons by the lack of small, round dark spots on the back and upper sides. The species attains a length of more than 800 mm (30 inches) in Canadian waters (McPhail & Lindsey 1970:155), but most adults are 100–380 mm (5–15 inches) long.

Variation. — Several synonyms, a few of which are subspecies names, exist, but the species has been so widely transplanted that studies of geographic variation would now be meaningless.

Ecology. — The brook trout occurs in cold lakes, rivers, and small streams in northeastern North America, and it is anadromous in streams near the ocean. The adult feeds on arthropods and small fishes; the young on plankton and insects. According to McPhail & Lindsey (1970:157), spawning occurs in late fall and early winter over gravel beds. The female excavates a redd by fanning her

Distribution of the brook trout in Illinois.

tail. The male darts in beside her and releases milt over the eggs in the nest. The 4- or 5-mm egg hatches into an alevin in early spring. A large female may lay 5,000 eggs and may spawn with different males in one season. In Canadian waters the young reach a length of 80 mm (3 inches) at the end of the 1st year and become sexually mature in the 2nd year.

Distribution.—The brook trout is native to Lake Michigan but not to Illinois streams. It has been stocked for many years in northern Illinois streams that appeared to have suitable habitat. The species reproduced at a few localities, but the populations failed to survive for long. After the alewife calamity in Lake Michigan, brook trout fingerlings were stocked along with other trouts and salmons. Presently, the species still occurs in southwestern Lake Michigan, where it may or may not become established. A recently collected specimen from Montrose Pier in Chicago is available in the Illinois Natural History Survey collection.

Lake trout
Salvelinus namaycush (Walbaum)

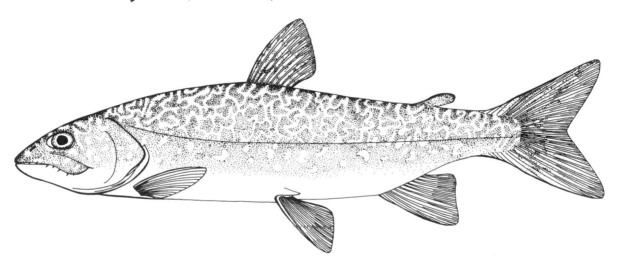

Salmo namaycush Walbaum 1792:68 (type-locality: lakes far inland from Hudson Bay); Nelson 1876:44.
Salmo amethystus: Kennicott 1855:544 (recorded from Illinois).
Salmo siskowit: Kennicott 1855:594.
Cristivomer namaycush: Jordan 1878:54; Large 1903: 21; Forbes & Richardson 1908:56–57; O'Donnell 1935:478.
Salvelinus namaycush: Forbes 1884:73; Smith 1965: 6.

Diagnosis.—The lake trout is a greenish-brown salmonid with many pale vermiculations and small spots crowded over the back and sides. It differs from the brook trout most obviously in lacking bright colors and having a deeply forked tail. It differs from other trouts and salmons in lacking dark brown or black spots over the back. The young has about seven dark, vertical parr marks along the sides and lacks small brown spots on the back. Its parr marks are less rectangular than those of the brook trout and they are separated by interspaces as wide as each mark. The species attains a length of a meter (3 or more feet) (Forbes & Richardson 1908:56) although larger specimens are said to occur in Canada.

Variation.—No detailed study of geographic variation has been made, and the wide-scale stocking of the species in western North America would now make such a study meaningless. Three subspecies have been described. If they are recognized, the typical subspecies inhabits Lake Michigan.

Ecology.—The lake trout occurs only in northern North America from the Atlantic to the Pacific. It inhabits cold deep lakes but comes into shallow water in October to spawn over rubble and gravel (Forbes & Richardson 1908:56). The male may sweep silt and sand away from the spawning site but does not construct a nest. The female is usually attended by more than one male. A large female

Distribution of the lake trout in Illinois.

lamprey predation in the 1940's and 1950's. Since the lamprey has been brought under control, young lake trout have been stocked at many sites in Lake Michigan, and it is hoped that the species will make a comeback. Recently collected specimens from three sites off Lake County are available at the Illinois Natural History Survey.

Salmo Linnaeus

This Holarctic genus is represented in Illinois by two introduced species. A third species, the Atlantic salmon (*Salmo salar*), has been introduced countless times as early as the late 19th century and as recently as the early 1970's. One or two specimens have been taken by fishermen, if indeed the fish were correctly identified, but there is little likelihood that the species will become established in Lake Michigan.

KEY TO SPECIES

1. Many small black spots scattered over back and sides; top of head and caudal fin with small dark spots; a red or orange band along each side; no red spots on body .... *gairdneri*
   Few small black spots on back and sides; top of head and caudal fin usually unspotted; no red or orange band along the side; red spots with blue halos scattered over sides ...... *trutta*

Rainbow trout
Salmo gairdneri Richardson

Salmo gairdnerii Richardson 1836:221 (type-locality: Columbia River at Fort Vancouver).
Salmo iridea: O'Donnell 1935:478.
Salmo gairdneri: Smith 1965:6.

Diagnosis.—The rainbow trout has many small black or brown spots scattered over the top of the head, back, sides, and caudal fins; usually a red or orange band along each side; an anal fin base greater than the height of the fin; and fewer than 12 principal rays in the anal fin. It differs from the brown trout in having many more dark spots on the body and a red or orange band along the side, and in lacking red spots with blue halos on the sides. The young has about eight distinct parr marks and many discrete brown or black dots on

contains many thousand eggs, each 4 or 5 mm in diameter (McPhail & Lindsey 1970:140). The young appears in late winter and early spring (Forbes & Richardson 1908:57). The young feeds on plankton and bottom organisms in competition with the alewife; the adult feeds on fish and is in competition with salmons and other trouts. The adult is extremely voracious and has been reported to ingest a variety of unlikely items by accident. The commercial fishery for lake trout was once extremely important, second only to that for whitefish (Forbes & Richardson 1908:57).

Distribution.—According to Forbes & Richardson (1908:56), the lake trout was less common in southern Lake Michigan than in the northern part of the lake. However, it was generally distributed in deep water until it was severely decimated by sea

Rainbow trout

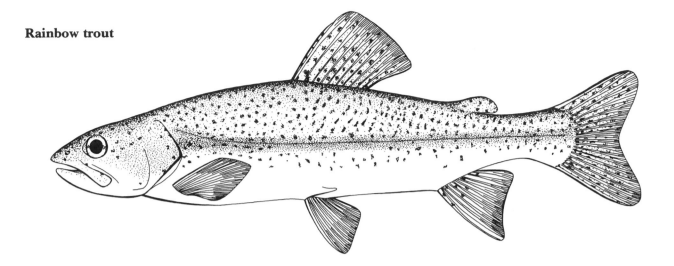

the back and sides, some below the parr marks. The species attains a length of 760 mm (30 inches).

Variation.—Several names have been applied to different populations of this species, but the genic exchange that has resulted from repeated stockings and wide-scale introductions obscures any trends in geographic variation that once may have existed.

Ecology.—Near the ocean the species is anadromous, and the sea-run adult, called a steelhead, is more nearly unicolorous. Elsewhere the species is not migratory. It occurs in lakes and streams with cold, highly oxygenated waters. It has been propagated artificially for many years, and an immense literature now exists concerning the rearing and stocking of this important sport fish. Its food consists of aquatic invertebrates and small fish. Spawning occurs early in the spring. The female constructs a redd by beating her tail fin against the gravel, and she is often attended by more than one male. The female deposits several hundred eggs in several different spawnings. The eggs, which average 3–5 mm in diameter, are covered with gravel by the female on completion of the spawning act. In northwestern Canada, the young reaches a length of about 100 mm (4 inches) at 1 year of age and is sexually mature in 3 or 4 years (McPhail & Lindsey 1970:162).

Distribution.—The rainbow trout is native to the Pacific Coast of North America. It has been introduced over most of the world. Although the species was not credited to Illinois by Forbes & Richardson (1908) and earlier workers, unsuccessful

Distribution of the rainbow trout in Illinois.

attempts to stock the rainbow trout, Atlantic salmon, and other salmonids were made before 1900. More recently the rainbow trout has been stocked in streams of northern Illinois, Iowa, and Wisconsin and in Lake Michigan. It now occurs sporadically in Lake Michigan and appears occasionally as a straggler in the Mississippi River. Recent records are available from Will, McHenry, Winnebago, Tazewell, and Rock Island counties. Some small and ephemeral populations are maintained in highly localized, rather artificial quarters by sporting clubs for the enjoyment of their members, but these stocks would quickly disappear without intensive care.

Brown trout
Salmo trutta Linnaeus

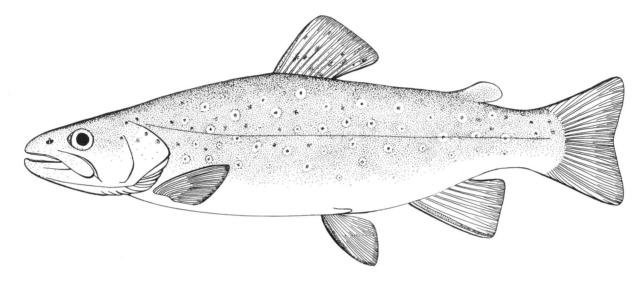

Salmo trutta Linnaeus 1758:309 (type-locality: European streams); O'Donnell 1935:478 (recorded from Illinois); Smith 1965:6.

Diagnosis.—The brown trout has relatively few small black or brown spots on the top of the head and on the back and sides, but it has some red spots with blue halos. It differs from the rainbow trout in lacking a red or orange band along the sides, from the salmons by having fewer than 12 principal rays in the anal fin, and from the brook trout in lacking light vermiform markings on the back and sides. The young has 10 or 11 dark, closely crowded but small parr marks and many small, discrete brown spots on the back and sides. The species attains a length of about 510 mm (20 inches).

Variation.—The brown trout is exotic in North America. In Newfoundland it is anadromous, as it is in Europe, and the sea-run adult is more silvery and unicolorous than is the landlocked adult. No clinal variation can be expected on this continent, since the species has been extensively introduced and transplanted.

Ecology.—According to Sigler & Miller (1963), the brown trout in Utah is more tolerant of turbid water and pollution than are other salmonids, but it prefers cool lakes and streams. The young feeds on aquatic invertebrates, the adult on fish. Spawning occurs in November and December. The female scoops out a redd and deposits 200–6,000 eggs, which are covered after being fertilized. The eggs hatch in approximately 50 days at a water temperature of about 10° C. Sexual maturity is reached in 2–4 years. The species has been artificially propagated in many hatcheries in this country but not as extensively as the related rainbow trout.

Distribution.—The brown trout was reported from tributaries of the Kishwaukee and Pecatonica rivers by O'Donnell (1935:478). It has more recently been taken in the Rock River at Rockton and at several sites along the Illinois shoreline of Lake Michigan. Although it may not reproduce successfully in Illinois streams, it probably will survive in Lake Michigan if pollution of the lake can be curtailed.

Distribution of the brown trout in Illinois.

Oncorhynchus Suckley

This North American and Asiatic genus of large and commercially important fishes contains several species, two of which have recently been introduced into Lake Michigan to provide a new sport fishery and to prey on the alewife. A third species, the sockeye salmon (*O. nerka,* kokanee stock), was repeatedly planted in Lake Michigan in the late 1960's, but none survived through 1970 (Parsons 1973:48). Because of the limited spawning grounds in Great Lakes tributaries, it is necessary to replace all salmons with hatchery-reared young each year to maintain a fishery.

KEY TO SPECIES

1. Fleshy gums of lower jaw black; small black spots on both lobes of caudal fin; intestinal caeca, 140 or more; anal fin usually with 14–17 principal rays .... *tshawytscha*
   Fleshy gums of lower jaw not black; small black spots, if present on caudal fin, only on upper lobe; intestinal caeca, fewer than 85; anal fin usually with 12–15 principal rays ... *kisutch*

Coho salmon
Oncorhynchus kisutch (Walbaum)

Salmo kisutch Walbaum 1792:70 (type-locality: rivers and lakes of Kamchatka).

Diagnosis. — The salmons can be distinguished from the trouts by their anal fins, which are longer than high and have 12 or more principal rays. The adults of the two species recently introduced into Lake Michigan, both of which are silvery fishes with small black or brown spots over the back, can be separated by characters given in the key to species. The young of the coho salmon has about nine brown vertical parr marks separated by interspaces as wide as or wider than each parr mark, and its adipose fin is uniformly pigmented with black. The species attains a length of about 510 mm (20 inches).

Variation. — The adult becomes dark blue during the spawning season, and the male is said to develop a bright red lateral stripe (McPhail & Lindsey 1970:171). No studies of geographic variation in the species have been published, and there are no generally used synonyms.

Ecology. — According to McPhail & Lindsey (1970:173), spawning in Canadian waters occurs in November. The female constructs a nest and is attended by more than one male. A large female may lay 5,000 red-orange eggs about 5–6 mm in diameter. The female may spawn several times with different males, after which she covers the eggs by beating the gravel with her caudal fin. The eggs hatch in 6–8 weeks, depending on water temperature. In Canada the young migrate to sea in the 2nd year and remain there 2 years before returning to fresh water to spawn and die. The young and the adult feed on aquatic invertebrates and small fish. In Lake Michigan the species does not

Coho salmon

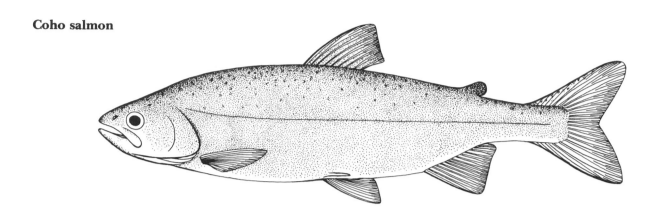

ascend the polluted Illinois streams but does "run" in several Michigan streams. Planted young in the Great Lakes drainage grow incredibly fast, reaching weights of 0.9–1.3 kg (2–3 pounds) within 1 year. When examined, the stomachs of a few Lake Michigan salmon contained smelt and alewives. Whether the coho will effectively control the number of alewives in the lake remains to be seen.

Distribution.—The coho salmon was initially introduced into Lake Michigan by personnel from the Michigan Department of Conservation in 1967. Many adult specimens have been taken by fishermen in spring and summer at various sites along the Illinois shoreline of Lake Michigan, but it is in the Michigan portion of the lake that the initial results of the introduction have been so spectacular. It is too soon to guess whether this population will be a permanent one.

Chinook salmon
Oncorhynchus tshawytscha
(Walbaum)

Salmo tshawytscha Walbaum 1792:71 (type-locality: rivers of Kamchatka).

Diagnosis.—The chinook salmon attains a larger size (up to 900 mm) than the coho, but it differs from that species most obviously in the characters cited in the key to species. The young has larger and more closely crowded parr marks than has the coho, and the young chinook has distal concentrations of dark pigment on the adipose fin that leave an unpigmented "window" in its center.

Distribution of the coho salmon in Illinois.

Variation.—No studies of geographic variation have been published, and there are no well established synonyms.

Ecology.—The chinook salmon has a life history and habits similar to those of the coho (McPhail & Lindsey 1970:176–177).

Distribution.—Although the chinook is one of the most important commercial species of salmons in western North America, it is insignificant in Illinois. It was stocked with the coho in Lake Michigan in 1967 and 1968, but to my knowledge the only specimen to be taken in Illinois waters was a 2-kg (4½-pound) fish caught offshore from Zion.

Smelts—Osmeridae

This circumpolar family includes marine and freshwater fishes and is represented in Illinois by one genus that has dispersed throughout Lake Michigan from an introduction into Crystal Lake, Michigan, in 1912 (Hubbs & Lagler 1958:57). Smelts are abundant fishes in the shallow seas and coastal areas. Some are anadromous. They are popular sport and commercial species, and many people enjoy eating the rich but oily meat. They are marketed both fresh and frozen. They are taken in various kinds of nets and seines, but in Illinois mostly by dipnetting while they are spawning. Smelts are also important forage fishes and were once condemned because they were taken so commonly that they fouled the trawling nets of commercial fishermen.

Osmerus Lacépède

This Holarctic genus occurs in northern Europe, Asia, and North America. Some authors believe it contains one species with several subspecies; others regard the European and American smelts as different species.

Rainbow smelt
Osmerus mordax (Mitchill)

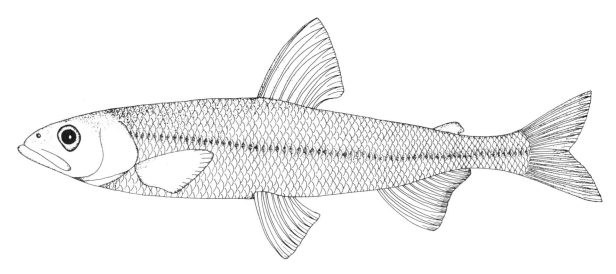

Atherina mordax Mitchill 1815:446 (type-locality: New York).

Osmerus mordax: Hubbs & Lagler 1941:28 (range includes Illinois by implication); Smith 1965:6.

Diagnosis.—The rainbow smelt is a cylindrical fish, greenish gray above and silvery beneath, with an adipose fin, a large mouth and long teeth, a projecting lower jaw, and short pectoral fins and without a pelvic axillary process. Illinois specimens are usually less than 250 mm (10 inches) in length.

The young is translucent and could be mistaken for a minnow except for its adipose fin and characteristic jaws.

Variation.—The smelt family was revised by McAllister (1963) and monographed by Bigelow & Schroeder (*in* Bigelow 1963), both studies referring the American populations of rainbow smelt to one polytypic species, *Osmerus eperlanus*. Recognizing the need for a critical study of geographic variation in the North American and Asiatic range

Distribution of the rainbow smelt in Illinois.

of the species, American authors currently have gone back to the species name *mordax,* which is firmly entrenched in the literature.

Ecology.—The smelt feeds primarily on crustaceans and small fishes but probably also eats various kinds of aquatic invertebrates. Populations near the ocean are anadromous; those in the Great Lakes are landlocked. Spawning occurs in the spring, when adults congregate in great numbers. The female produces many thousand eggs, which sink to the bottom and adhere to each other and to gravel. Hatching occurs in about 2 weeks, the time depending upon the water temperature. Sexual maturity is reached at 2 years of age and at a length of about 140 mm (5½ inches) (Bigelow & Schroeder *in* Bigelow 1963:562). According to Trautman (1957:203), the smelt has not been observed spawning in lakes, but the abundance of quite small young along the Illinois shore line of Lake Michigan suggests that spawning must have occurred along the pebbly shore. There are no Illinois tributaries of Lake Michigan in which spawning adults could long survive.

Distribution.—The introduced smelt is now generally distributed and common in the Illinois waters of Lake Michigan. The species evidently spread into southern Lake Michigan in the 1940's and 1950's, after which it became scarce for a period. It does not occur in the small glacial lakes of northeastern Illinois, but occasionally enters the Illinois River via the shipping canals connecting the river and Lake Michigan. Prior to the alewife problem in the late 1960's, the dipnetting of smelt was a popular sport on southern Lake Michigan. Population size has fluctuated. When the species was abundant, it probably competed with native species in Lake Michigan.

Mudminnows—Umbridae

This North American and Eurasian family of small primitive fishes consists of three genera, if the Alaska blackfish *Dallia* is included, or two, if *Dallia* is regarded as representing a family of its own. One genus is represented in Illinois. Mudminnows are small fishes that have been variously classified but are now considered to be close relatives of the pikes, to which they have little superficial resemblance. The species tend to be highly tolerant of waters of high acidity (sphagnum bogs), low dissolved oxygen, and those susceptible to heavy freezing. They are best known from minnow-seine collections and locally sold as bait minnows. They are important forage fishes in some waters and of interest to ichthyologists because of their phylogenetic position and wide physiological tolerances.

Umbra Müller

This genus contains a European species, an Atlantic Coast species, and one in the upper Mississippi River and Great Lakes drainages. A related genus with one species occurs in the Pacific Northwest.

Central mudminnow
Umbra limi (Kirtland)

Hydargira limi Kirtland 1841*a*:277 (type-locality: streams in northern Ohio).
Hydrargyra (Melanura) limi: Kennicott 1855:594 (recorded from Illinois).
Melanura limi: Nelson 1876:43; Jordan 1878:52.
Umbra limi: Forbes 1884:71; Large 1903:21; Forbes & Richardson 1908:203–205; O'Donnell 1935:484; Smith 1965:6.

Diagnosis.—The central mudminnow is a small, terete to slightly compressed, mottled fish with a short dorsal fin situated posteriorly, rather large scales over the head and body, a terminal mouth, a rounded caudal fin, and a dusky vertical bar on the caudal base. The species is distinctive but resembles the topminnows, from which it differs by lacking a superior mouth and a groove between the upper lip and snout tip. The small young resembles those of certain minnows but differs in having a rounded caudal fin and many brownish vertical markings on the sides. It superficially resembles the pirate perch young but lacks the prominent suborbital bar of that species and has larger scales that are cycloid rather than ctenoid. It differs most obviously from the young of the bowfin in having a short dorsal fin. The mudminnow attains a length of about 130 mm (5 inches).

Variation.—The central mudminnow evidently does not show trends in geographic variation, since subspecies have not been described and there are no synonyms.

Ecology.—The mudminnow occurs in bogs, well-vegetated streams, ponds, and mud-bottomed potholes where water temperatures do not become excessive in the summer months. In some shallow marshes in northern Illinois, it may be the only species of fish present. When marshes are drained, the species occupies drainage ditches. According to Forbes & Richardson (1908:204), it feeds on aquatic and terrestrial arthropods, snails, and such plant material as algae and duckweed. Gunning & Lewis (1955:554) found, in addition, aquatic beetles and young spring cavefish in the mudminnow's diet. It spawns in April, the female depositing eggs singly on aquatic vegetation. The eggs hatch in about a week, the length of time depending upon the water temperature. The scales do not show growth annuli; hence age must be estimated from total length. The species is probably sexually mature in its 2nd year. In the wild the mudminnow is said to be able to burrow rapidly into the bottom mud, a habit responsible for its common name. It tolerates the acid waters of bogs.

Distribution.—The central mudminnow is common in northeastern Illinois but rather sporadic over the rest of the state. It has evidently disappeared in the lower Wabash River valley, probably because the natural ponds and sloughs have been drained or polluted by the many oil fields in the area. It is less generally distributed in the northern half of Illinois than formerly because of the elimination of many marshes and sloughs.

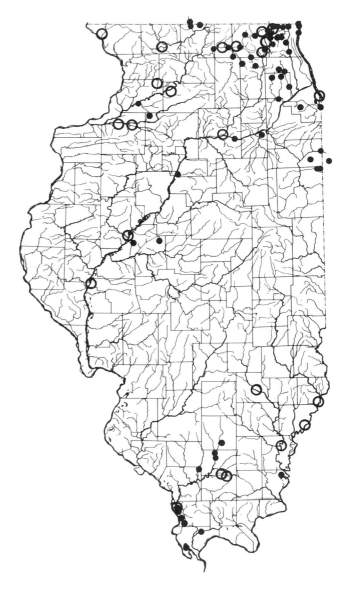

Distribution of the central mudminnow in Illinois.

Pikes—Esocidae

This Holarctic family contains only one genus. Members of the family are easily recognized by the duck bill, long teeth, short and posteriorly situated dorsal fin, and forked tail. Pikes are highly prized as sport and trophy fish and frequently stocked in new reservoirs. Although they are not highly regarded as food, they are extremely popular because of their large size, fighting ability, and the readiness with which they take artificial lures. In Illinois, the larger species are not common enough to be of great importance, and the grass pickerel is too small to be widely sought.

Esox Linnaeus

This genus consists of five species, three of which are confined to North America, one to eastern Asia, and one to northern Europe and North America. Two species now occur in Illinois and another is extirpated. A fourth species (*E. niger*) occurs in adjacent Kentucky but has not been found in this state.

KEY TO SPECIES

1. Cheeks and opercles fully scaled (Fig. 9a); prominent dark teardrop present . . . .
   . . . . *americanus*

Opercles scaleless on lower halves (Figs. 9b, c); teardrop absent or faint 2
2. Cheeks fully scaled; ground color olive, green, or brown with a pattern of whitish or yellowish bars and spots; fins of adults usually with light spots on dark ground color; branchiostegals, 14–16; sensory pores on lower jaw large, usually five . . . . *lucius*
   Cheeks, like opercles, scaleless on lower halves; ground color olive, brown, or greenish with pattern of dark spots; fins of adults with dark spots on lighter ground color; branchiostegals, 17–19; sensory pores on lower jaw small, usually six to nine . . . . *masquinongy**

Fig. 9. Heads of pikes: a) *Esox americanus;* b) *E. lucius;* c) *E. masquinongy.*

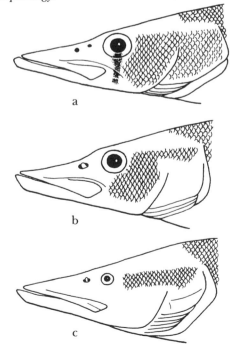

Grass pickerel
Esox americanus Gmelin

Esox lucius americanus Gmelin 1789:1390 (type-locality: Long Island, New York).
?*Esox reticulatus:* Kennicott 1855:594 (recorded from Illinois).
Lucius vermiculatus: Large 1903:21.
Esox salmoneus: Nelson 1876:43; Jordan 1878:53.
Esox cypho: Nelson 1876:43; Jordan 1878:53.
Esox umbrosus: Nelson 1876:43.
?*Esox ravenelli:* Forbes *in* Jordan 1878:53.
Esox vermiculatus: Forbes 1884:71; Forbes & Richardson 1908:206–207; O'Donnell 1935:485.
Esox americanus vermiculatus: Smith 1965:6.

Diagnosis.—The grass pickerel is at once recognizable as a pike by its ducklike beak. It can be distinguished from the muskellunge and northern pike by its fully scaled cheeks and opercles and prominent dark suborbital bar. It differs from the chain pickerel, which does not occur in Illinois, by having fewer than 14 branchiostegals, no chainlike reticulations in the adult, and fewer than 110 scales in the lateral line. The young differs from those of the northern pike and muskellunge by having unspotted dorsal, anal, and caudal fins and from the young of the chain pickerel by its branchiostegal count, the usual absence of light-centered lateral blotches, and its discrete, light-colored mid-lateral stripe. The adult grass pickerel attains a length of 310 mm (12 inches).

Variation.—The most complete studies of geographic variation are those of Crossman (1962 and 1966), who regarded the species as consisting of two well-marked subspecies: an Atlantic Coast form (*E. a. americanus*) and a Mississippi Valley subspecies (*E. a. vermiculatus*).

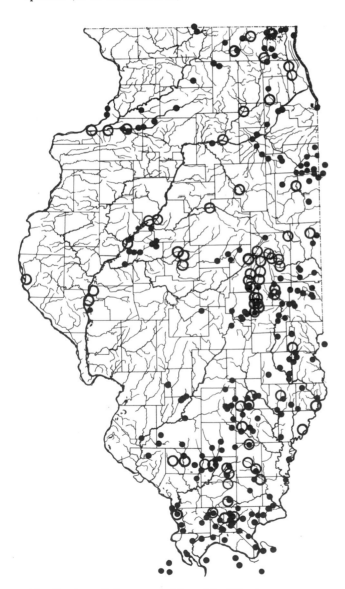

Distribution of the grass pickerel in Illinois.

Ecology.—The grass pickerel is most common in quiet pools of streams, especially those containing aquatic vegetation. It is also common in marshes, sloughs, and swamps and is tolerant of turbid water although it prefers clear water. Spawning occurs in March and April. According to Crossman (1962), the several hundred eggs produced by a female are broadcast, and the adhesive eggs, which average 1.4 mm in diameter, cling to vegetation or debris on the bottom. A hatching time of about 10 days was inferred by Crossman for the species in Ontario. Growth is quite rapid, the young being 50–80 mm (2–3 inches) long by June and 130–150 mm (5–6 inches) long by October. In Illinois the grass pickerel probably spawns at 1 year of age. The young feeds on plankton and other small invertebrates; the adult eats fish primarily but also takes crayfish, tadpoles, and immatures of aquatic insects.

Distribution.—The grass pickerel occurs in all parts of the state but is extremely sporadic in western Illinois. It is still common in the southern and eastern parts of the state but less generally distributed than formerly. The species was probably abundant in the prairie marshes and interconnecting waterways before the prairie was drained. In addition to drainage, the loss of aquatic vegetation because of siltation and desiccation of aquatic habitats during drought periods has adversely affected the species.

Northern pike
Esox lucius Linnaeus

Esox lucius Linnaeus 1758:314 (type-locality: Europe); Jordan 1878:53; Forbes 1884:71; Large 1903:21; Forbes & Richardson 1908:207–208; O'Donnell 1935:485; Smith 1965:6.
?*Esox estor:* Kennicott 1855:594 (recorded from Illinois).
Esox lucius var. *estor:* Nelson 1876:43.
Esox boreus: Nelson 1876:43.

Diagnosis.—The northern pike is distinctive because of its pattern of light-colored markings on a green or brown ground color. It also differs from other species in the genus in having fully scaled cheeks, but only the upper half of the opercle is scaled. The teardrop is usually weak. The young differs from that of the grass pickerel in having discrete black or brown spots on the dorsal, anal, and caudal fins and from the young of all other

Northern pike

species in lacking dark-colored markings on its back and sides. The species attains a length of about 790 mm (31 inches).

Variation.—The northern pike in Eurasia and North America is regarded as one species and, although synonyms exist, no subspecies have been described. McPhail & Lindsey (1970:208) noted that two morphological types occur in northern Canada but suggested that subspecies should not be recognized. In much of this country, pike have been widely introduced, and trends in geographic variation would likely be obscured.

Ecology.—This pike occurs in lakes, marshes, pools of creeks, and in large rivers. It spawns in March in clear, shallow backwaters and in flooded weedy bottomland. The female, attended by one or more males, scatters many thousand eggs that adhere to vegetation and debris over the bottom. Hatching requires about 2 weeks, the time depending on the water temperature. Growth is extremely rapid, the young reaching a length of about 200 mm (8 inches) by the end of its 1st year. According to Forbes & Richardson (1908:208), this piscivorous species also feeds on insects, crayfish, frogs, reptiles, and even small birds and mammals.

Distribution.—The northern pike was once abundant in the Illinois River but by 1900 had greatly decreased in numbers (Forbes & Richardson 1908:209). The species still occurs rather generally throughout the northern third of Illinois. It occurs in the Illinois River as far south as Havana and in the Mississippi River almost to the mouth of the Ohio River, but it is present in the Mississippi below the mouth of the Missouri River only as a straggler. The population that once occurred in the streams of western Union County was eliminated many years ago, probably because of its inability to withstand high water temperatures in the summer months. Except for the extirpation of the population in southern Illinois, the range of the

species in the state is much the same as it has always been, but the northern pike is decidedly less common and less general in occurrence than formerly.

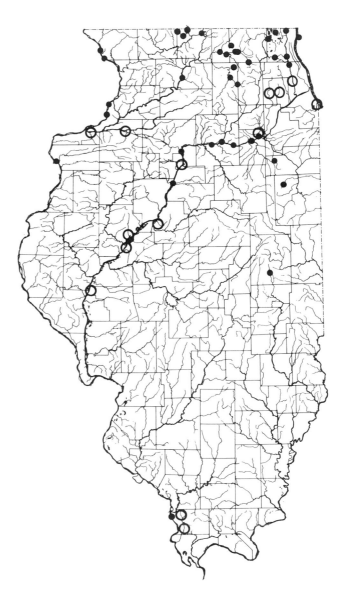

Distribution of the northern pike in Illinois.

Muskellunge*
Esox masquinongy Mitchill

Esox masquinongy Mitchill 1824:297, according to DeKay 1842:222 (type-locality: Lake Erie); Forbes & Richardson 1908:209; O'Donnell 1935:485; Smith 1965:11 (possibly still in southern Lake Michigan).

Esox nobilior: Nelson 1876:43 (recorded from Illinois); Jordan 1878:52; Forbes 1884:71.

Lucius masquinongy: Large 1903:21.

Diagnosis.—The muskellunge is a yellowish green or brownish olive pike with small dusky spots on the fins and on the sides of the body in oblique rows, a poorly developed teardrop (if present at all), cheeks and opercles scaled only on the upper halves, and 17–19 branchiostegals. The young is distinguished by the combination of distinctly spotted median fins and widely separated, oblique, dusky bars on the sides, in addition to the characters cited in the key. According to Forbes & Richardson (1908:209), the species attains a length of almost 2 meters (6 feet) and a weight of nearly 45 kg (100 pounds).

Variation.—For many years three subspecies were recognized, and the Lake Michigan form was said to be intermediate between *E. m. masquinongy* and *E. m. immaculatus* (Hubbs & Lagler 1958:94). However, so much genic mixing has occurred through transplantings of hatchery-cultured fish that it is doubtful that subspecies are recognizable.

Ecology.—The muskellunge is said to prefer medium-sized, rather cold lakes, and it spawns in shallow areas containing aquatic vegetation. It is a voracious species that feeds on a variety of live prey. Spawning occurs in early spring, and the many eggs are broadcast over the bottom. An enormous fishery literature exists for this highly prized trophy fish.

Distribution.—Extirpated in Illinois. The muskellunge was probably never common in Illinois and may have been present only in Lake Michigan, despite Nelson's (1876:43) statement that it had been reported to occur in smaller lakes. Natural populations have probably been extirpated from Illinois waters for many years, but the species is being stocked in many Illinois reservoirs.

Distribution of the muskellunge in Illinois.

Minnows and carps—Cyprinidae

The largest and most widely distributed family of present-day fishes, this group contains well over 200 North American described species and many more in the Old World. About a third of the Illinois fishes belong to this family. Some uncertainty exists about how many genera of minnows should be recognized. Three in Illinois are represented by introduced Eurasian species; the others are native. Like their close relatives, the suckers, minnows have toothless jaws but have uniquely toothed pharyngeal arches. The family occurs in fresh waters of all continents except South America, Australia, and Antarctica. The carps are important commercial fishes, and one of them (carp) is also a low-quality sport fish often caught on doughballs and other types of bait. The minnows are extremely diverse, and as a group make up a large portion of the midwater biomass in most streams. Minnows are valuable forage fishes and occupy virtually every aquatic habitat. Some species are valuable ecological indicators of water quality, and some help control mosquitoes and other aquatic insects.

KEY TO GENERA

1. Dorsal and anal fins with three spiny rays, the first two very small, the third large, strong, and serrated posteriorly; dorsal fin with more than 15 rays 2
   Dorsal and anal fins with soft rays only; dorsal fin with fewer than 15 rays 3
2. Upper jaw with two conspicuous barbels; lateral-line scales, more than 32 or lateral-line area unscaled .... *Cyprinus*
   Upper jaw without barbels; lateral-line scales, 32 or fewer .... *Carassius*
3. Anal fin situated far to the rear, the distance from anal fin origin to caudal base going three times or more into distance between tip of snout and anal fin origin; large, often exceeding 330 mm (15 inches) .... *Ctenopharyngodon*
   Anal fin situated in normal position, the distance from anal fin origin to caudal base going fewer than three times into distance between tip of snout and anal fin origin; small, seldom exceeding 300 mm (12 inches) 4
4. Terete barbel at posterior of maxillary (Fig. 10a) or small flaplike barbel partially hidden (and often difficult to discern) in groove above maxillary anterior to posterior end of maxillary on each side of head (Fig. 10b) 5
   No barbels, maxillary adorned with, at most, a tubercle at angle of jaws (in some breeding males of *Pimephales*) 9
5. Barbel at posterior of maxillary on each side of head (if not apparent on underside of head, extend premaxillary and examine rear end of maxillary) 6
   Small flaplike barbel (often difficult to discern) on upper side of maxillary anterior to angle of jaws (Fig. 10b); combination of robust body, very small scales, and large terminal mouth, the maxillary extending backward almost to a point beneath pupil of eye .... *Semotilus*
6. Premaxillary bound to snout by fleshy frenum (Fig. 10c); scales minute; ground color usually dark with irregular patches of darker pigment .... *Rhinichthys*
   Premaxillary protractile, separated from snout by groove; scales variable in size; ground color usually pale with variable pattern of dark markings 7
7. Mouth rather large, somewhat oblique, almost terminal, with barely protruding snout; dorsal fin convex; anal fin rounded 8

Fig. 10. Key characters: a) underside of head of *Nocomis,* showing barbel at end of maxillary; b) head of *Semotilus,* showing barbel near end of maxillary; c) head of *Rhinichthys,* showing frenum; d) ventral keel of *Notemigonus;* e) underside of head of *Phenacobius,* showing fleshy lobes on mandibles; f) underside of head of *Campostoma,* showing cutting edges of jaws; g) dorsal fin of *Pimephales,* showing thickened anterior ray; h) dorsal view of *Pimephales,* showing crowded predorsal scales.

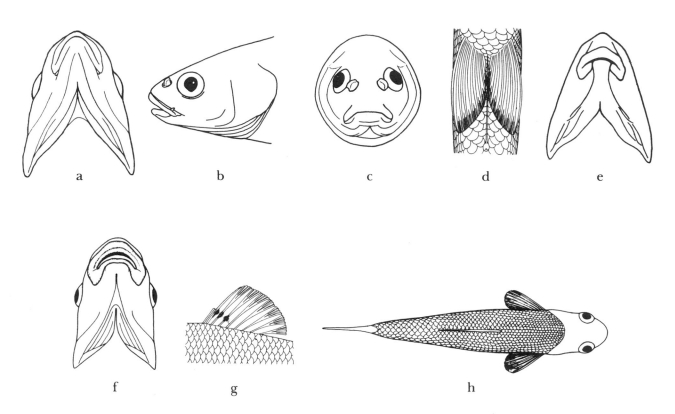

Mouth rather small, horizontal, subterminal, fleshy snout distinctly protruding well beyond upper lip; dorsal fin falcate or straight edged; anal fin falcate or straight edged, not rounded .... *Hybopsis*

8. Lateral-line scales, fewer than 45; eye small, its diameter much less than snout length; dorsal fin origin directly over pelvic fin insertions .... *Nocomis*

   Lateral-line scales, more than 50; eye large, its diameter almost equal to snout length; dorsal fin origin behind pelvic fin insertions .... *Couesius*

9. Abdomen between pelvic fin insertions and anus with a midventral fleshy keel, over which scales do not pass (Fig. 10d); anal fin strongly falcate; mouth rather large and sharply upturned; lateral line strongly flexed downward .... *Notemigonus*

   Abdomen without midventral fleshy keel; anal fin normal; mouth not sharply upturned if large; lateral line variable in position 10

10. Lip of lower jaw fleshy only on posterior halves, producing a fleshy lobe on either side superficially resembling the mouth of a sucker; anterior halves of each lower jaw covered only with skin (Fig. 10e) .... *Phenacobius*

    Lip of lower jaw without fleshy posterior halves and not suckerlike 11

11. A hard cartilaginous ridge (for scraping stones) margining lower lip and separated from lower jaw by a groove (Fig. 10f); extremely long intestine usually spirally coiled about swim bladder; ground color dark with darker scales and pigment patches irregularly arranged on back and sides .... *Campostoma*

Lower lip normal, without cartilaginous scraping rim; intestine variable in length, not coiled about swim bladder; ground color usually pale, patternless, or with a regular pattern of dark markings 12

12. Body scales minute, 60 or more in lateral line; a broad light-colored lateral band, bordered above and below by dark stripes .... *Phoxinus*

Body scales large, fewer than 60 in lateral line; one or no dark lateral stripe 13

13. Pearl organs (cavernous chambers separated by thin vertical septa) on lower cheeks and ventral surface of head, appearing as mother-of-pearl; snout long, flattened, overhanging small horizontal mouth; eyes directed upward; head flattened ventrally, roundly triangular in cross section .... *Ericymba*

Pearl organs absent; snout, eye position, and head shape variable (*Notropis dorsalis* is like *Ericymba* but it lacks pearl organs and has a larger, almost terminal mouth) 14

14. Dorsal fin with stout, blunt anterior splint, not closely bound to first developed soft ray (Fig. 10g); predorsal region thick, rather flattened and with small, crowded, irregularly arranged scales (Fig. 10h); anterior webbing of dorsal fin with one or several discrete black blotches .... *Pimephales*

Dorsal fin with anterior splint slender, pointed, and so closely associated with first developed soft ray that the two appear as one ray; predorsal region variable, not thick, flattened, and with small crowded scales; dorsal fin without discrete black blotch in anterior part 15

15. Intestine short, about equal to standard length; belly firm, white or silvery in preserved specimens .... *Notropis*

Intestine very long, at least twice standard length, much coiled; belly soft, either darkly discolored or transparent enough that coiled gut is visible through body wall of preserved specimens 16

16. Coloration rather pale, without distinctive pattern; large deciduous scales; hard protuberance on inside of lower jaw .... *Hybognathus*

Coloration olivaceous, with a dark lateral band that continues onto snout; scales small, slightly deciduous, those in predorsal area with peripheral concentration of dark pigment; mouth large, without hard protuberance on inside of lower jaw .... *Dionda*

Carassius Nilsson

This Palearctic genus contains two introduced species, one of which (the goldfish, *Carassius auratus*) is abundant in the upper Illinois River and sporadic in other parts of the state. The other, the crucian carp (*C. carassius*), was recorded from lagoons in Chicago parks by Meek & Hildebrand (1910:282–284) but evidently soon disappeared from the state. The Asiatic goldfish differs from the European crucian carp in having fewer than 32 lateral-line scales, more than 38 gill rakers on the first arch, and a deeper and more angulate body; it lacks a dusky caudal spot when young.

Goldfish
Carassius auratus (Linnaeus)

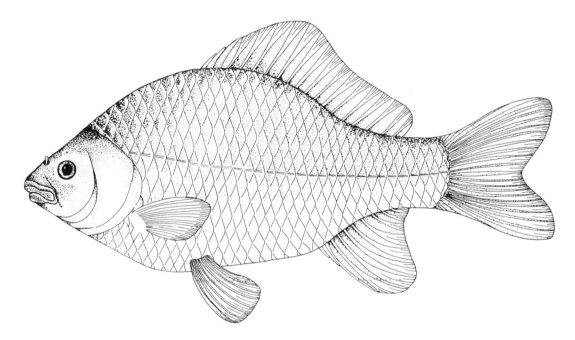

Cyprinus auratus Linnaeus 1758:323 (type-locality: China and streams of Japan).
Carassius auratus: Nelson 1876:48 (recorded from Illinois); Jordan 1878:63; O'Donnell 1935:480; Smith 1965:6.

Diagnosis.—The goldfish is a deep-bodied, red-orange, pink, gray, or black cyprinid fish with three dorsal spines and more than 12 soft dorsal rays, with fewer than 32 lateral-line scales, but without barbels and without dusky spots at the bases of the scales. It differs from the carp in lacking barbels and having fewer than 32 scales in the lateral line and from the grass carp or white amur in having more than 12 dorsal rays, dorsal fin spines, a deep body, and fewer lateral-line scales. The darkly pigmented young superficially resembles that of the largemouth buffalo but differs in having some dorsal fin and anal fin spines and larger scales. The goldfish attains a length of 360 mm (14 inches).

Variation.—Most goldfish found in Illinois are the so-called wild type and are dark gray in color, but occasional individuals may be uniform red, orange, bronze, black, or even mottled with two or more of these colors. In streams and canals in the greater Chicago area, goldfish-carp hybrids are common.

Ecology.—The goldfish prefers clear quiet pools with submerged vegetation, but it can tolerate considerable turbidity and high organic content in the water. In some badly polluted streams in Chicago, it is the predominant fish and one of the two or three species able to exist in such waters. The goldfish has a prolonged spawning season in the late spring and summer and is extremely prolific, a large female producing many thousand eggs each

Distribution of the goldfish in Illinois.

viduals for bait and at the end of the day released their remaining bait "minnows" into the stream or lake. The distribution of the species is sporadic over most of Illinois, but an occasional specimen may be seen almost anywhere in the state. The largest population is clearly that occupying the Illinois River and its headwaters in the Chicago area. At some sites on the upper Illinois River, dozens of goldfish can be taken in one seine haul. The increase in the population size is not because optimal habitat for the species has increased but rather because there are extensive areas where most other fishes have been eliminated, and the ecologically tolerant goldfish thus has little competition.

Cyprinus Linnaeus

This genus contains one species, native to China but introduced into Europe centuries ago, into the United States in 1877, and into Illinois in 1879 (Forbes & Richardson 1908:105).

Carp
Cyprinus carpio Linnaeus

Cyprinus carpio Linnaeus 1758:320 (type-locality: Europe); Large 1903:13 (recorded from Illinois); Forbes & Richardson 1908:104–110; O'Donnell 1935:480; Smith 1965:7.

Diagnosis.—The carp is a compressed, bronze- or olive-colored cyprinid with four long barbels, one principal and two small spinous rays in both the dorsal and the anal fin, and a long dorsal fin having at least 17 rays. The adult is familiar to almost everyone. The young superficially resembles small bigmouth buffalo and goldfish, but the young carp has a distinctive, dusky vertical bar on the caudal peduncle. The species attains a length of about 760 mm (30 inches) or more.

Variation.—Considerable individual variation exists in the species, but no geographic trends are discernible in this widely introduced fish. Individuals completely lacking scales are called leather carp; partially scaled individuals are called mirror carp. Most Illinois specimens are normally scaled. The color of the back and sides varies greatly, and many specimens have some red or orange on the

season. The adhesive eggs are scattered over the bottom. Sexual maturity is probably reached in 1 year by faster growing individuals and in 2 years by others. In Russia some populations are known that consist only of females. Egg cleavage is initiated by sperm from the carp (Berg 1964:389), a phenomenon termed gynogenesis. Sex ratios for Illinois populations have not been studied. Goldfish feed on both plant and animal matter and are also scavengers.

Distribution.—The first goldfish to be found in the state were presumably escapees from ponds where the species was kept for ornamental purposes. Subsequently, the goldfish was distributed over the state by fishermen, who used small indi-

Carp

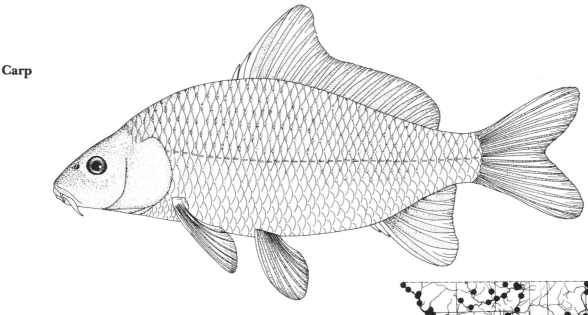

fins. The so-called Israeli carp, stocked to control aquatic vegetation, is indistinguishable morphologically from the ordinary carp.

Ecology.—The carp is most abundant in soft-bottomed pools of rivers, but it can be found in almost any aquatic habitat. It is especially common around brush piles and in weedy overflow areas. It feeds on both plant and animal matter and often congregates where sewage is discharged into streams or lakes. While blamed for feeding on fish eggs, the chief nuisance value of the carp, aside from competing for available food, is its habit of rooting in the bottom and keeping the water turbid. Spawning occurs throughout the spring and early summer. A female produces many thousand small eggs, which are scattered over debris and vegetation on the bottom. The eggs hatch in approximately 12 days, and the young carp averages about 130 mm (5 inches) by late fall of its 1st year. Sexual maturity is attained in the spring of its 3rd year of life (Forbes & Richardson 1908:107).

Distribution.—The carp is abundant in all parts of the state and in virtually all types of water. It is not especially common in the cold water of Lake Michigan, and it is rarely found in small brooks and in strong riffle areas. It hybridizes rather freely with the goldfish in the polluted streams of the Chicago area and the hybrid seems better adapted for life in these marginal habitats than is the pure carp.

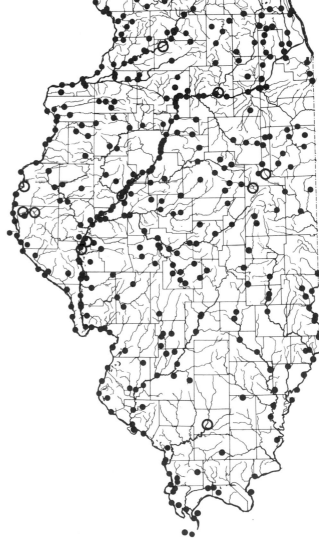

Distribution of the carp in Illinois.

Ctenopharyngodon Steindachner

This genus, native to eastern Asia, contains one species that is reared in ponds and propagated in many Asian countries and recently has been introduced into the southern United States. The species is the white amur or grass carp. Although it is an exotic species, it is not closely related to the European carp. Its closest relatives are the rudds of the Asiatic genus *Scardinius*.

Grass carp or White amur
Ctenopharyngodon idella (Valenciennes)

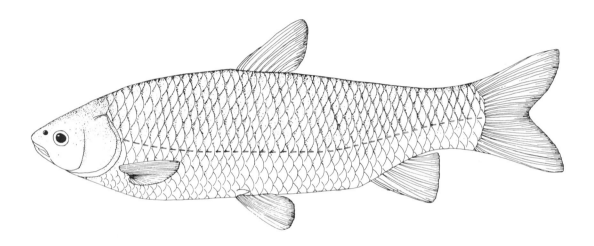

Leuciscus idella Valenciennes *in* Cuvier & Valenciennes 1844:360 (type-locality: China).
Ctenopharyngodon idella: Smith et al. 1971:6 (recorded from Illinois).

Diagnosis.—The white amur is an elongate, pale gray cyprinid with thin unspecialized lips, the anal fin located far posteriorly, seven soft dorsal rays, and a subterminal mouth. The short dorsal fin is situated over the pelvic fins. The species is sufficiently distinctive that it cannot be confused with other Illinois fishes. It attains a length of about a meter (39 inches).

Variation.—No studies of geographic variation have been published for the white amur.

Ecology.—This large minnow is well known as a vegetation feeder, but it probably also consumes animal matter and may be a partial scavenger. In China spawning occurs from April until mid-August. The hundreds of thousands of eggs produced by a female float until hatching (Berg 1964: 134). Although the species is typically a large-river fish, it can be propagated in ponds and rice paddies. In the southern United States, the species has been deliberately introduced to control unwanted aquatic vegetation and to provide another species of food fish.

Distribution.—In January 1971 an 860-mm (34-inch) specimen was caught in the Mississippi River at Chester by a commercial fisherman. Later in 1971 two more individuals were reportedly caught in the Mississippi and eaten by commercial fishermen. At this time commercial fishermen report that the grass carp is taken with regularity.

Distribution of the grass carp in Illinois. Data from Pflieger 1975:129.

Notemigonus Rafinesque

This eastern North American genus contains only one species, which is the only New World representative of the subfamily Abramadinae.

Golden shiner
Notemigonus crysoleucas (Mitchill)

Cyprinus crysoleucas Mitchill 1814:23 (type-locality: New York).

Leuciscus crysoleucus (Americanus): Kennicott 1855: 594 (recorded from Illinois)

Notemigonus americanus: Nelson 1876:48.

Notemigonus chrysoleucus: Jordan 1878:61; Forbes 1884:74.

Abramis crysoleucas: Large 1903:15; Forbes & Richardson 1908:126–128.

Notemigonus crysoleucas: O'Donnell 1935:480; Smith 1965:7.

Diagnosis.—The golden shiner is an extremely slab-sided golden, gray, or greenish cyprinid with a scaleless midventral keel extending from the bases of the pelvic fins to the anus, a strongly decurved lateral line, a falcate anal fin with 11–14 rays, and a small and sharply upturned mouth. The young superficially resembles small redfin and ribbon shiners but differs from them by having a sharper snout, a more upturned mouth, and a darker ground color. The young has a well-defined dusky lateral band. According to Forbes & Richardson (1908:126), it attains a length of 310 mm (12 inches); most individuals are much smaller.

Variation.—The golden shiner has been described under several different names, and for many years two subspecies were recognized. Studies of geographic variation in the species by Hubbs (1918) and Schultz (1926) revealed north-to-south clinal variation in the number of anal rays. Subspecies are not currently recognized.

Ecology.—The preferred habitat of the golden shiner is clear, well-vegetated waters of ponds and lakes and quiet pools of creeks and small rivers. The species has great ecological tolerance and can persist in badly polluted and highly turbid streams and in swamps where water temperatures are high in the summer months. It is a good indicator of pollution or modification of the habitat when it outnumbers other species at a site. The species is seldom found in riffles or in pools with current,

Golden shiner

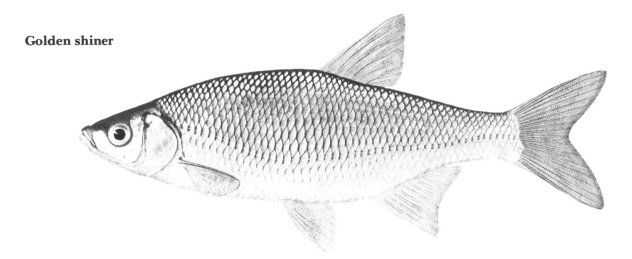

and it is uncommon in small temporary streams and in the channels of large rivers. It is usually common in oxbows, marginal sloughs, and bays with mud bottoms. According to Forbes & Richardson (1908:127), its food consists of mud, plankton, plant materials, mollusks, and terrestrial insects. It has an efficient pharyngeal tooth apparatus, numerous long and fine gill rakers, and a rather long gut. Spawning apparently extends from late spring until midsummer. Forbes & Richardson (1908:128) reported ripe females from early May until the end of July. The eggs are broadcast and adhere to vegetation and debris. The young attains a length of 75–100 mm (3–4 inches) at the end of its 1st year.

Distribution.—This minnow is found statewide and is very common in low-gradient streams and in standing bodies of water in eastern and southern Illinois. Despite its general occurrence in most parts of the state and its ability to thrive in farm ponds and artificial lakes, the evidence available suggests that it is less generally distributed now than it was before 1900. Its decline in western and northern Illinois is probably due to the draining of marshes and swales. It has also been affected by the draining of floodplain lakes and swamps along rivers.

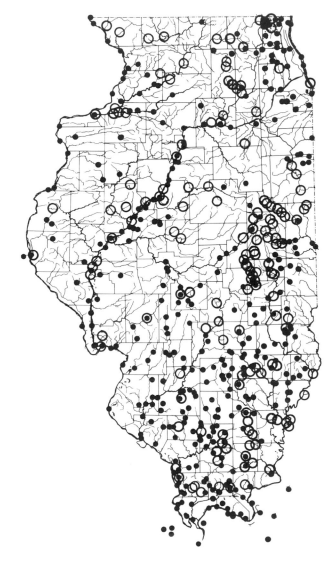

Distribution of the golden shiner in Illinois.

Semotilus Rafinesque

This eastern North American genus contains three well-marked species, only one of which occurs in Illinois. The genus is easily recognized by its overall appearance, but the uninitiated person must look closely for the principal generic character (a tiny flaplike barbel on the upper lip anterior to the angle of the jaws) when he is running an unknown minnow through a key. The species known in Illi-nois, the creek chub, is one of the most common and widely distributed fishes in the state. Another species, the pearl dace (*Semotilus margarita*), was recorded from adjacent Rock County, Wisconsin, by Greene (1935:84), but it has not been found in Illinois despite a systematic effort to collect it in Illinois border localities.

Creek chub
Semotilus atromaculatus (Mitchill)

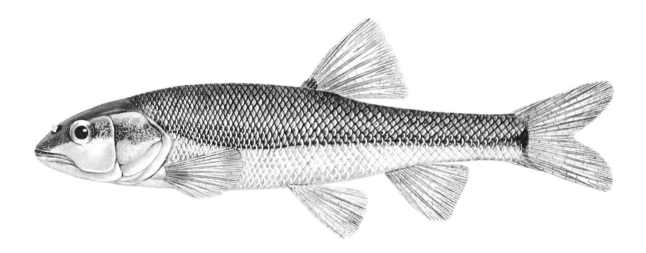

Cyprinus atromaculatus Mitchill 1818:324 (type-locality: Wallkill River, New York).
Leuciscus diplema: Kennicott 1855:594 (recorded from Illinois).
Semotilus corporalis: Nelson 1876:45; Jordan 1878: 62; Forbes 1884:75.
Semotilus atromaculatus: Large 1903:45; Forbes & Richardson 1908:121–123; O'Donnell 1935:480; Smith 1965:8.

Diagnosis.—The creek chub is a terete, stout-bodied minnow with a large head and very large mouth, a black spot on the anterior basal portion of the dorsal fin, 50–60 scales in the lateral line, and a small flaplike barbel on the upper lip anterior to the angle of the jaws. The young superficially resembles that of the hornyhead chub but has smaller scales, a larger mouth, a small wedge-shaped caudal spot rather than a large squarish blotch, a gray rather than a red caudal fin, and a barbel anterior to the angle of the jaws rather than at their juncture. The young usually has a dusky lateral band and sometimes herringbone lines on the upper sides like those of the fathead minnow, but it can be distinguished from that species by its large and nearly horizontal mouth. The species attains a length of 250 to 310 mm (10 to 12 inches).

Variation.—This species has been described by several early workers under different names, but no thorough study of geographic variation in the species has been published. For several years, a northern and a southern subspecies were recognized, but Bailey, Winn, & Smith (1954:124) pointed out that the number of scale rows varies clinally from north to south and that subspecies should not be recognized.

Ecology.—This minnow is well named, for it is abundant in creeks, especially in low-gradient streams with mud or clay substrates. It is some-times common in headwaters over sand or gravel and in the vicinity of bank cutouts and tree roots, but it occurs there because it is a pioneer species in newly available watercourses. It is rare in standing water and present only as a straggler in the channels of rivers. The creek chub feeds on a variety of plant and animal materials, ranging from algae to small fishes. It takes both aquatic and terrestrial invertebrates. Starrett (1950) found a variety of larger invertebrate animals in stomachs of the species and large numbers of small fishes in fall-collected chubs. The breeding male has several large and numerous small tubercles on the top of its head and snout and a wash of pale orange on the lower sides. The male excavates a nest in sand or gravel in quiet clear pools by picking up small pebbles with its mouth. After the female deposits eggs in the nest, the male presumably covers them with gravel and small stones. Tuberculate males are taken in April and May. According to Forbes & Richardson (1908:123), nests are abandoned after spawning, but Cross (1967:80) noted that the male guards the nest site. There is surprisingly little spawning detail available for such an abundant fish, and much of the information in the literature on reproduction is based on observations made many years ago. The young reaches a length of approximately 80 mm (3 inches) at the end of its 1st year, and most individuals are probably sexually mature at 2 years of age. The presence of many creek chubs in a collection often denotes excessive modification of the habitat by such factors as pollution or siltation although such an interpretation depends somewhat upon which associated species are represented in the collection.

Distribution.—The creek chub is common in suitable habitats throughout Illinois, except in the Lake Michigan drainage, and it has increased in abundance in virtually all parts of the state as a result of the increase in silt, the temporary decrease in the size of many streams, and the elimination of competing species by human modification of streams and watersheds. The number of available habitats for this species has increased in almost all parts of the state.

Distribution of the creek chub in Illinois.

Couesius Jordan

This genus has recently been resurrected from the synonymy of *Hybopsis* (Bailey 1970:68) for the species or species complex known as the lake chub, which occurs only in northern North America.

Although the genus shares with *Hybopsis* the presence of a well-developed barbel and with *Semotilus* an overall resemblance, its phylogenetic relationships are not yet understood.

Lake chub
Couesius plumbeus (Agassiz)

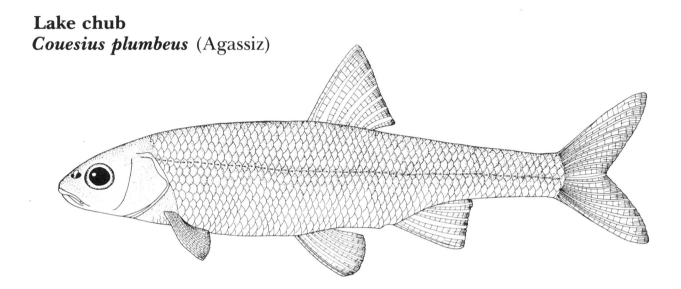

Gobio plumbeus Agassiz 1850:366 (type-locality: Lake Superior).
Couesius prosthemius: Jordan 1878:62 (recorded from Illinois); Forbes 1884:75.
Couesius plumbeus: Large 1903: 13 (may be occasionally found in Illinois).
Hybopsis plumbea: Smith 1965:7.

Diagnosis.—The lake chub is a terete, rather slender minnow with a well-developed barbel on each side of the head near the posterior meeting point of the jaws, a large eye approximately equal to the snout in length, 55 or more scales in the lateral line, the dorsal fin origin behind the pelvic fin insertions, and a groove separating the snout from the upper lip. The young, which has a prominent dusky lateral band that continues through the eye, superficially resembles the small creek chub or the adult fathead minnow but can be distinguished from those species by its much larger eye and prominent barbels. The somewhat similar longnose dace has a wide frenum, a small eye, and patches of dusky pigment scattered over the back and sides. A specimen from Lake County, Illinois, is 210 mm (8⅛ inches) long and is seemingly the largest known.

Variation.—Three subspecies have been recognized by several recent authors, but the subspecies are regarded as doubtful (Hubbs & Lagler 1958: 78). At least two allopatric morphological forms are said to occur in Canada (McPhail & Lindsey 1970:244), but these authors did not use subspecific names for them. If subspecies were to be recognized, the Lake Michigan population would be referable to the nominate race.

Ecology.—The food of the lake chub probably consists of algae, various invertebrates, and even small fishes. In Canadian waters the species spawns in May and June over rocky riffles; no nest is constructed or guarded, and the nonadhesive eggs are broadcast over the bottom, according to Brown et al. (1970). Breeding is communal. The breeding male has red pigment in the area of the pectoral fins. Growth is rather slow because of the cold water temperature; the species lives 5 or 6 years.

Distribution.—In Illinois the lake chub occurs rarely in the cold deep water and along the shore over pebbly and sand-gravel bottoms of Lake Michigan. Its distribution and abundance in the state may be unchanged since the 19th century.

Distribution of the lake chub in Illinois.

Although recorded from Illinois by Jordan (1878), the record was generally overlooked by subsequent authors until the 1960's, when additional collections of the species were made at two sites in the shallow waters of Lake Michigan near Zion and Deerfield in Lake County.

Nocomis Girard

This distinctive eastern North American genus was for a time included as a subgenus in the catchall *Hybopsis*. Intensive study of the group by Ernest A. Lachner & Robert M. Jenkins (1971) in the last few years has more than doubled the number of described species, most of which have quite restricted distributions. Two species, which have been recognized for many years, occur in Illinois.

KEY TO SPECIES

1. Caudal spot large, rounded, and prominent; tail of juvenile usually red-orange; distance from front margin of eye to tip of snout 1.3 or more times the distance from front of eye to posterior margin of opercle; teeth 1, 4—4, 1; breeding male with nuptial tubercles confined to top of head; a prominent red spot behind eye .... *biguttatus*
Caudal spot, if present, small, irregular, and pale; tail of juvenile usually slate-gray; distance from front margin of eye to tip of snout less than 1.3 times the distance from front of eye to posterior margin of opercle; teeth 4—4; breeding male with nuptial tubercles extending onto snout; no red spot behind eye .... *micropogon*

Hornyhead chub
Nocomis biguttatus (Kirtland)

Semotilus biguttatus Kirtland 1841*b*:344 (type-locality: Yellow Creek, a tributary of Mahoning River, Ohio); Forbes 1884:75.
Ceratichthys biguttatus: Nelson 1876:45 (recorded from Illinois); Jordan 1878:62.
Hybopsis kentuckiensis: Large 1903:19; Forbes & Richardson 1908:167–170.
Nocomis biguttatus: O'Donnell 1935:481.
Hybopsis biguttata: Smith 1965:7.

Diagnosis.—The hornyhead chub is a terete stout-bodied minnow with a large head, a moderately large mouth, terminal barbels, 40–43 scales in the lateral line, the dorsal fin origin slightly behind the pelvic insertions, a yellowish or bronzy ground color, and usually an evident caudal spot. It is much like the river chub, but the two can be distinguished by the characters in the key. It somewhat resembles the creek chub, but it has terminal barbels, a smaller mouth, and larger scales. It differs from the lake chub in being more robust and having much larger scales. The young has a discrete, dusky lateral band, a prominent black caudal spot, and a red caudal fin. Small specimens that have lost the red color in preservative slightly resemble young stonerollers but can be distinguished from that species by the fleshy lower lip, shorter gut, and lack of irregular pigment patches on the

Hornyhead chub

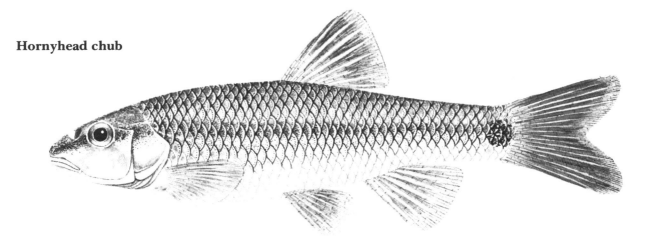

sides. The species attains a length of 200–230 mm (8 or 9 inches).

Variation.—The most thorough account of geographic variation is that of Lachner & Jenkins (1971). Their paper cites other published studies by themselves and others.

Ecology.—The hornyhead chub lives in clear, high-gradient creeks and small rivers with gravel or rubble bottoms. It avoids sluggish waters, silt bottoms, and large rivers. The young ascend vernal rivulets in early summer but return to the creek channel as water levels recede. The food, according to Forbes & Richardson (1908:169), includes both plant and animal materials and prey items as large as crayfishes. Reproduction in the species has been well described by Hankinson (1920, 1932) and Lachner (1952). The breeding male develops large white tubercles on top of its head, a swollen nape, and an ephemeral dusky lateral stripe, and the red spot behind the eye becomes bright crimson in contrast to the greenish cast of the rest of the head. In April and May the male constructs a large mound by picking up individual pebbles with its mouth and forming a dome-shaped nest of loose gravel, which the male guards. The female deposits several hundred eggs over the dome, as do females of several other species of minnows, thus providing an opportunity for hybridization between different species and even different genera. The young may attain a length of 75 mm (3 inches) at the end of the 1st year. Sexual maturity is reached at 2 or 3 years of age. Few individuals live longer than 3 years.

Distribution.—The hornyhead chub is a common species in clear, moderately fast, gravelly streams throughout the northern half of Illinois. It

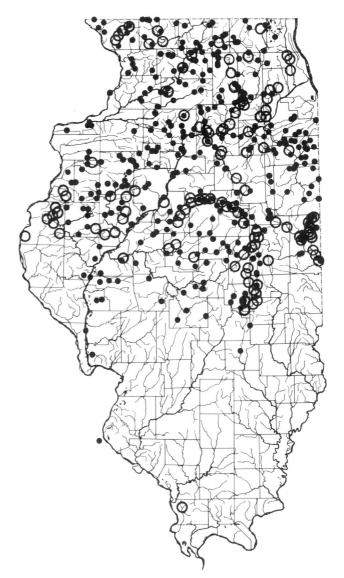

Distribution of the hornyhead chub in Illinois.

was reported from some glacial lakes in northeastern Illinois by Forbes & Richardson (1908:169) but now appears to be limited to streams and absent from the Great Lakes drainage of Illinois. It also once occurred in streams of Union County (Forbes & Richardson 1908 atlas of maps), but efforts to rediscover the species anywhere in the southern half of the state have been unsuccessful even though it is common in Ozark streams of Missouri. The species is still widely distributed and common, but it is less common than formerly because so many streams have deteriorated in quality.

River chub
Nocomis micropogon (Cope)

Ceratichthys micropogon Cope 1864:277 (type-locality: Conestoga River, near Lancaster, Pennsylvania).

Nocomis micropogon: O'Donnell 1935:481 (recorded from Illinois).

Hybopsis micropogon: Smith 1965:7.

Diagnosis.—The river chub is a terete, stout-bodied minnow much like the hornyhead chub but differing from it in lacking a red tail as a juvenile, the red spot behind the eye as an adult, and a well-defined round caudal spot, and in having 4—4 teeth and having tubercles on the side of the head and snout of the breeding male. Its snout is longer and its eye is situated higher on the head than in the hornyhead chub. The young superficially resembles that of the creek chub, but they can be distinguished by the same characters that separate the creek chub and the hornyhead chub. The species attains a length of 250 mm (10 inches) or more.

Variation.—Lachner & Jenkins (1971) studied geographic variation in this species and in other members of the genus and summarized the results of their earlier studies.

Ecology.—The river chub is similar to the hornyhead chub in habits but occurs in larger streams. It attains a slightly larger size. The breeding male develops swollen areas on the occipital and interorbital regions to produce a helmet-shaped head not found in the male hornyhead chub. The male does not develop the dark lateral band and light dorsal streak as does the hornyhead (Lachner 1952:440). The species may live as long as 5 years. Reproduction and growth in this species are similar to those of the hornyhead chub.

Distribution of the river chub in Illinois.

Distribution.—The river chub was first reported from streams of the Wabash River drainage (O'Donnell 1935:481). At present it is known to occur in fast water of the Wabash River proper at single localities in Clark and Lawrence counties, Illinois, but it is widely distributed and common in large creeks of adjacent Indiana. Its range in Illinois probably has not changed appreciably since the earliest fish catalogs were published. It was probably overlooked by earlier authors only because they failed to collect at sites where it occurred.

Hybopsis Agassiz

This genus of eastern North American minnows contains 16 described species, 7 of which occur in Illinois. Formerly this assemblage also included *Couesius* and *Nocomis,* both of which have recently been split off. There are cogent arguments for dividing *Hybopsis* still further, as the species remaining in the genus represent various degrees of relationship. However, because the generic status of the type-species (*amblops*) is in question, it seems best to keep the species together, pending the solution of the type-genus question. All of the species presently assigned to *Hybopsis* share the presence of a maxillary barbel and an anteriorly placed dorsal fin.

KEY TO SPECIES

1. Sides of body with scattered and irregular black dots or X-shaped markings 2
   Sides of body plain, without scattered dots or X markings 3
2. Body with scattered black dots; snout extremely bulbous and projecting far beyond mouth; barbel as long as eye diameter and situated below front edge of eye .... *aestivalis*
   Body with X-shaped markings; snout slightly projecting beyond mouth; barbel not as long as eye diameter, situated beneath nostril ... . *x-punctata*

3. Eye equal to or barely larger than nostril; gular region with central patch of papillae; breast mostly scaleless 4
   Eye distinctly larger than nostril; gular region without papillae; breast scaled 5
4. Dorsal and pectoral fins extremely falcate; pectorals extending well behind pelvic insertions; body scales smooth; snout rounded .. .. *meeki*
   Dorsal fin straight edged; pectoral fins rounded, not reaching pelvic insertions; many body scales keeled; head sturgeonlike with long flattened snout .... *gelida*
5. Scales small, more than 45 in lateral line; snout greatly flattened; eye small, contained about five times in head length; fins falcate .... *gracilis*
   Scales large, fewer than 45 in lateral line; snout rounded; eye large, contained fewer than four times in head length; pectoral and dorsal fins sharp but not very falcate 6
6. Black lateral stripe on head and body, usually extending onto snout; dorsal fin pointed, almost midway between tip of snout and end of caudal peduncle; snout bulbous ... *amblops*
   No black lateral stripe on head and body; dorsal fin rounded, nearer tip of snout than caudal peduncle; snout not bulbous .... *storeriana*

Speckled chub
Hybopsis aestivalis (Girard)

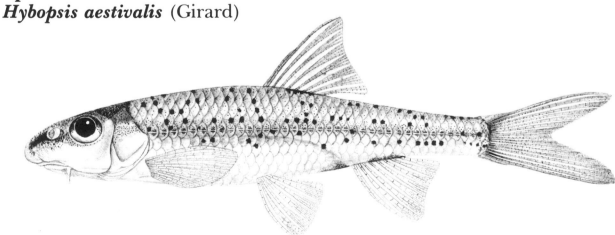

Gobio aestivalis Girard 1856:189 (type-locality: Rio San Juan, near Cadereyta, Nuevo Leon [Mexico]).
Hybopsis hyostomus: Large 1903:19 (recorded from Illinois); Forbes & Richardson 1908:163–164.
Extrarius hyostomus: O'Donnell 1935:480.
Hybopsis aestivalis (Girard) subspecies: Smith 1965: 7.

Diagnosis. — The speckled chub is a small terete minnow with barbels almost as long as the eye diameter, scattered black dots on the back and sides, dorsally directed eyes, and a bulbous snout. The barbel is beneath the front edge of the elongate eye. This combination of characters distinguishes the species from other Illinois fishes. The young resembles that of the sicklefin and sturgeon chubs, both of which lack the scattered black dots. The species attains a length of about 75 mm (3 inches) in the Wabash River but is much smaller elsewhere in Illinois.

Variation. — Most recent authors have casually recognized an eastern subspecies with two barbels and a western subspecies with four, but no thorough study of geographic variation throughout the range of the species has been undertaken. The Illinois subspecies is *H. a. hyostoma*.

Ecology. — The speckled chub is most abundant in fast clear riffles and chutes of large rivers. In the Mississippi and lower Illinois rivers, juveniles are found in shallow sand-bottomed riffles. In the Wabash River, where both juveniles and adults can be taken together, the species prefers very fast riffles over a firm gravel bottom. Starrett (1950) found that bottom-dwelling immatures of aquatic insects were the principal food of the species. Its reproductive habits are poorly known. Starrett (1951:18) described the species in the Des Moines River of Iowa as a short-lived, late-spawning fish that seldom exceeded 1½ years in age. He believed that its reproductive success was correlated with summer floods and that high water during the spawning period resulted in a dramatic decrease in the population in the following year. Bottrell et al. (1964) found that in Oklahoma egg laying occurred about noon from mid-May to late August. Hatching took only 24–28 hours in the field, and growth of the young was also quite rapid.

Distribution. — The species occurs in the Wabash, the lower half of the Illinois, and the Mississippi rivers and in the lower reaches of their principal tributaries. The species is never common and is a rather insignificant fish in the major rivers, but there is no evidence that its status has changed in Illinois since it was first recorded here.

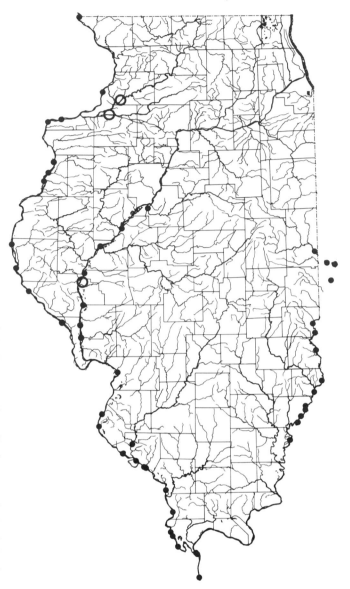

Distribution of the speckled chub in Illinois.

Bigeye chub
Hybopsis amblops (Rafinesque)

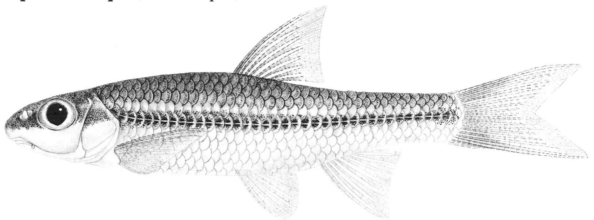

Rutilus amblops Rafinesque 1820*a*:51 (type-locality: Ohio River at the falls).

Ceratichthys amblops: Jordan 1878:62 (recorded from Illinois).

Semotilus amblops: Forbes 1884:75.

Hybopsis amblops: Large 1903:19; Forbes & Richardson 1908:165–166.

Erinemus hyalinus: O'Donnell 1935:481.

Hybopsis amblops amblops: Smith 1965:7.

Diagnosis.—The bigeye chub is a slender minnow with barbels and a pronounced black lateral stripe extending from the tip of the snout to the caudal peduncle. It is sharply set off from other members of the genus by the black lateral stripe and very large eye, which is directed both dorsally and laterally. The species resembles most closely the pallid shiner, *Notropis amnis,* from which it differs by possessing maxillary barbels. It superficially resembles the mimic shiner, *Notropis volucellus;* bigeye shiner, *Notropis boops;* and suckermouth minnow, *Phenacobius mirabilis,* all of which also lack maxillary barbels. The young is distinctive because of the eye shape and size and the black lateral stripe. The species attains a length of about 75 mm (3 inches).

Variation.—No detailed studies of geographic variation in the bigeye chub have been published, but Dr. Glenn Clemmer of Mississippi State University will presumably soon publish the results of his investigations. Bailey, Winn, & Smith (1954: 124) have questioned the validity of a southern subspecies long known as *H. a. winchelli.*

Ecology.—The bigeye chub occurs in clear well-vegetated pools of creeks and among beds of emer-

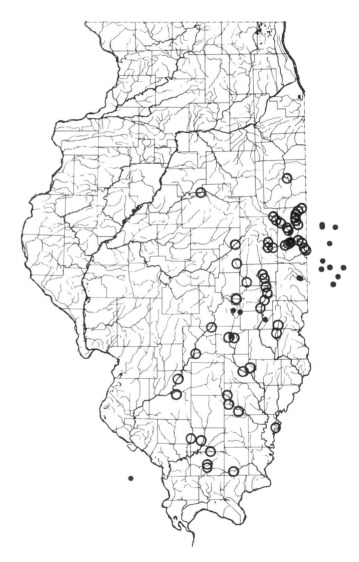

Distribution of the bigeye chub in Illinois.

gent water willow along gravelly raceways of small rivers. It requires extremely clear water, some current, a high dissolved oxygen content, and a bottom of sand and fine gravel. Little is known of its feeding and reproductive habits. It presumably feeds on small aquatic and terrestrial arthropods. According to Forbes & Richardson (1908:166), females distended with eggs are found by 1 June. The eggs are probably deposited on vegetation.

Distribution.—The bigeye chub was once an abundant fish in creeks and small rivers of southern and eastern Illinois, and its decimation from this state is a dramatic and classical example of the effects of human modification of aquatic ecosystems. The species occurred in southern Illinois until the 1930's and was still present in creeks in the Vermilion River drainage of eastern Illinois in the early 1950's. By 1960 it had disappeared from the state except for localized populations in the Salt Fork and Middle Fork in Vermilion County. It has not been taken anywhere in Illinois since June 1961 and may now be extirpated although it still occurs in clear streams of adjacent Indiana and in Ozark streams of Missouri. There is little doubt about the factor chiefly responsible for the disappearance of the bigeye chub in Illinois and other agricultural states. The increasing siltation of water courses made the pools too turbid for aquatic vegetation to survive, and deposits of fine silt over substrates that were once sand and gravel eliminated the habitat of the species. Other alterations of streams and their watersheds and local fish kills hastened the disappearance of this chub, and ultimately there were no sources for recruitment left even though the water quality of some streams has been partially restored.

Sturgeon chub
Hybopsis gelida (Girard)

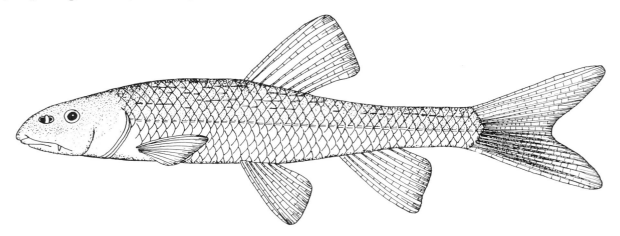

Gobio gelidus Girard 1856:188 (type-locality: Milk River [Montana]).

Hybopsis gelidus: Large 1903:19 (occurrence in Illinois uncertain).

Machrybopsis gelidus: O'Donnell 1935:480–481 (recorded from Illinois).

Hybopsis gelida: Smith 1965:7.

Diagnosis.—The sturgeon chub is a slender and plain-colored minnow with a long depressed snout, small eyes, barbels, longitudinal keels on some dorsal scales, a pustulose gular region, and rounded pectoral fins. The dorsal and anal fins are almost straight edged. The lower lobe of the caudal fin is darker than the upper lobe except along the ventral margin, which is milky white and reminiscent of those of the silver chub and of some unrelated species. The sturgeonlike head and dorsal keels distinguish this tiny minnow from all other Illinois cyprinids. The young superficially resembles that of the sicklefin chub but can be distinguished by its long depressed snout and rounded or straight-edged fins. It can be distinguished from the young of the flathead chub and from all shiners by the heavily pustulose gular region. The adult attains a length of about 75 mm (3 inches).

Variation.—Almost nothing is known of variation in this rare and elusive species.

Ecology.—The sturgeon chub is restricted to shallow fast riffles over fine gravel or coarse sand in large rivers. Cross (1967:98–99) described the morphological adaptations of this species for the fast and turbid shallow riffles of streams in the Great Plains. Branson (1963) discussed the highly developed olfactory sense, which helps it locate food in the turbid water. The feeding and reproductive habits of the sturgeon chub are virtually unknown. Cross (1967:99) surmised that breeding occurs in late June in Kansas.

Distribution.—This chub occurs in Illinois only in the Mississippi River below the mouth of the Missouri River. It is one of the rarest of Illinois fishes and is known from a very few specimens from single localities in Madison and Union counties. The reason for its rarity in the Illinois portion of the Mississippi River is probably that nearly all shallow riffles in this part of the river flow over fine sand rather than gravel. This highly specialized but relatively insignificant minnow has probably always been rare in Illinois waters.

Distribution of the sturgeon chub in Illinois.

Flathead chub
Hybopsis gracilis (Richardson)

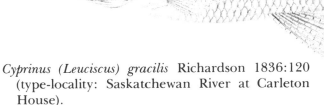

Cyprinus (Leuciscus) gracilis Richardson 1836:120 (type-locality: Saskatchewan River at Carleton House).
Platygobio pallidus Forbes *in* Jordan & Gilbert 1883:220 (type-locality: Ohio River at Cairo, Illinois); Forbes 1884:75; Large 1903:20.
Platygobio gracilis: Forbes & Richardson 1908:170–171; O'Donnell 1935:481.
Hybopsis gracilis: Smith 1965:7.

Distribution of the flathead chub in Illinois.

Diagnosis.—The flathead chub is a barbeled minnow with a broad flattened head, falcate pectoral fins, more than 45 scales in the lateral line, and rather small eyes. Its back is dusky brown, the sides silvery. The flathead chub and the silver chub are the largest species in the genus, but they are not apt to be confused. The flathead chub has smaller scales, smaller eyes, and a wide depressed head. The young of the flathead chub resembles that of the sicklefin chub but lacks the pustulose gular region and falcate dorsal fin of that species. The flathead chub attains a length of about 200 mm (8 inches).

Variation.—A thorough study of variation in the species by Olund & Cross (1961) revealed the presence of a northern subspecies with a high vertebral count (*gracilis*) and a southern subspecies with a lower count (*gulonella*). The nominate form occurs in Illinois.

Ecology.—The flathead chub is a species of the channels of large turbid rivers. It occurs in flowing water over a firm sand bottom. Cross (1967:86) assumed that tuberculate males taken in July and August indicated a late-summer spawning. No details on reproduction are available. Cross (1967) also noted that the food consisted of aquatic insects, many of which were terrestrial species that had fallen into the water.

Distribution.—This species is restricted in Illinois to the Mississippi River below the mouth of the Missouri River. It is common in flowing stretches of the river and is morphologically well adapted to live in the current of large turbid rivers.

Sicklefin chub
Hybopsis meeki Jordan & Evermann

Hybopsis meeki Jordan & Evermann 1896:317 (type-locality: Missouri River at St. Joseph, Missouri); Smith 1965:7.
Platygobio gracilis: Forbes & Richardson 1908:170 (specimen shown for *P. gracilis* is *H. meeki,* thus constituting first record for Illinois).

Diagnosis.—The sicklefin chub is a pallid barbeled minnow with extremely falcate fins, a pustulose gular region, a rounded snout, and small eyes. The lower lobe of the caudal fin is darkly pigmented except for its ventral margin, which is white. The species can be separated from similar chubs by the characters outlined in the preceding key. The young superficially resembles that of the speckled chub but lacks the black specks. It differs from the young flathead chub in having the distinctive pustulose gular region. The species attains a length of about 100 mm (4 inches).

Variation.—No studies on variation of this poorly known fish have been published.

Ecology.—The species occurs in fast water of large rivers over a bottom of firm sand or fine gravel. No information is available on its feeding and reproductive habits.

Sicklefin chub

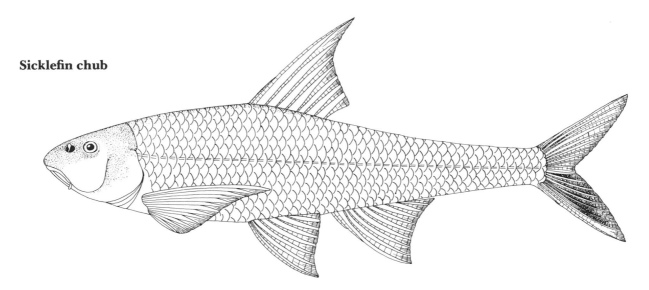

Distribution.—Restricted in Illinois to the Mississippi River below the mouth of the Missouri River, this chub is known from several sites, but it is, and probably always has been, quite rare. Its occurrence in the state will probably be secure unless locks and dams are constructed in the presently uncanalized river below the mouth of the Missouri.

Distribution of the sicklefin chub in Illinois.

Silver chub
Hybopsis storeriana (Kirtland)

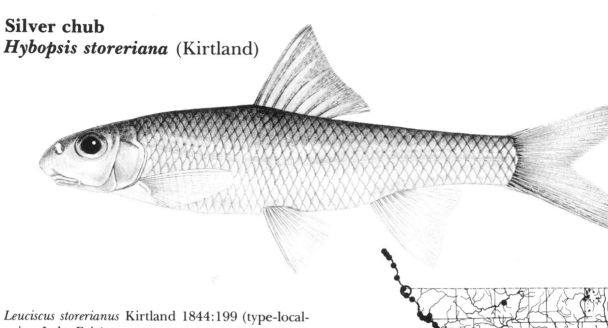

Leuciscus storerianus Kirtland 1844:199 (type-locality: Lake Erie).

Hybopsis storerianus: Nelson 1876:46 (recorded from Illinois); Large 1903:19; Forbes & Richardson 1908:166–167.

Alburnops storerianus: Jordan 1878:56.

Erinemus storerianus: O'Donnell 1935:481.

Hybopsis storeriana: Smith 1965:7.

Diagnosis.—The silver chub is a whitish or silvery barbeled minnow with rounded fin tips, a relatively large eye, a dorsal fin origin well in advance of the pelvic fin insertions, and 37–41 scales in the lateral line. It resembles some of the larger shiners more than it resembles other chubs, but its lack of markings, the presence of barbels, and the anteriorly placed dorsal fin make it easy to recognize. The young can be distinguished from the young of other fishes by the same characters that serve to distinguish the adults. The lower lobe of the caudal fin in the adult is darkly pigmented except for a ventral whitish margin. The species attains a length of about 200 mm (8 inches).

Variation.—This large chub is widely distributed, but no subspecies have been described, suggesting little geographic variation in the species.

Ecology.—The silver chub is a large-river fish that is poorly known. It also occurs in some lakes and some small rivers. It is usually found in pools or deep-flowing channels over sand or mixed silt-sand-gravel. No details are available on its food and reproductive habits. It is a bottom feeder.

Distribution.—Although primarily a fish of large rivers and lakes, the silver chub occurs commonly

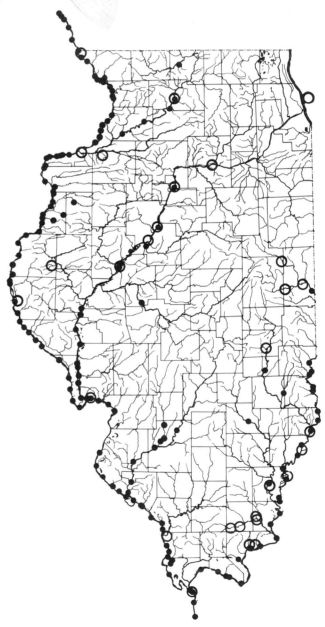

Distribution of the silver chub in Illinois.

in the lower reaches of their major tributaries. Jordan (1878:56) recorded it as rather frequent in Lake Michigan, but it evidently does not occur there at present nor anywhere in northeastern Illinois. The species is common in all of the large rivers except the polluted upper reaches of the Illinois River. However, it does not ascend as far upstream in tributaries as it did formerly, probably because of the low water levels during dry periods of the last several decades.

Gravel chub
Hybopsis x-punctata Hubbs & Crowe

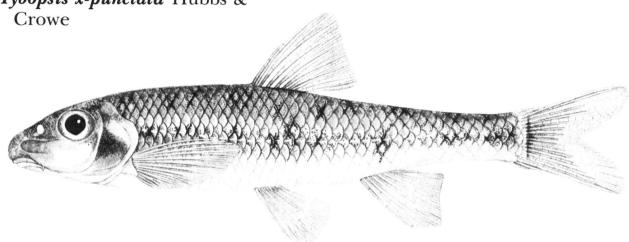

Ceratichthys dissimilis: Nelson 1876:45 (recorded from Illinois); Jordan 1878:62.
Semotilus dissimilis: Forbes 1884:74.
Hybopsis dissimilis: Large 1903:19; Forbes & Richardson 1908:164–165.
Erimystax dissimilis: O'Donnell 1935:481.
Hybopsis x-punctata x-punctata Hubbs & Crowe 1956: 7 (type-locality: Gasconade River at Starks Ford, 8 miles S of Richland, Pulaski County, Missouri).
Hybopsis x-punctata trautmani Hubbs & Crowe 1956: 7 (type-locality: Waldoning River, Newcastle Township, Coshocton County, Ohio).
Hybopsis x-punctata: Smith 1965:7.

Diagnosis.—The gravel chub is an olivaceous and barbeled minnow with rather large eyes: 40–43 scales in the lateral line; and scattered, dusky, X-shaped markings on the back and sides. Among Illinois species, only the speckled chub is likely to be confused with the gravel chub, but the speckled chub has round black dots on its body and much longer barbels. The young is as distinctive as the adult, but the X-markings are less distinct on the living fish than on preserved specimens. The species attains a length of 75 mm (3 inches) or more.

Variation.—The only published revisionary study of the gravel chub is the original description of the species (Hubbs & Crowe 1956). An eastern and a western subspecies were described (*trautmani* and *x-punctata,* respectively), and the authors noted the need of additional specimens from the Wabash drainage of Illinois, where intergrades should occur. Only a few specimens are available from the Wabash River and streams in adjacent Indiana. A few of them do indeed tend to have longer, more pointed snouts and more slender caudal peduncles than do specimens from the Ozarks of Missouri and from the Rock River drainage of northwestern Illinois. Most of the specimens are not assignable to subspecies because of the great amount of variation found in series from any one locality. Whether the Wabash drainage population is intergrade or not is still unresolved. Several recent authors have ignored subspecies in this chub.

Ecology.—This minnow occurs in rather deep riffles and channels of moderate to very fast current over a substrate of gravel or firm sand-gravel. It occupies medium-sized creeks in northern Illinois and is found in the Wabash and Mississippi rivers in southern Illinois. The habits of the species are poorly known. Cross (1967:90) found both sexes ready for spawning in Kansas in early April. The adults were concentrated in a swift raceway almost a meter deep adjacent to a gravel bar.

Distribution.—This species once occurred sporadically throughout central Illinois but was probably never common. It has now disappeared from most of the state but is still common in the Rock River system of northwestern Illinois. It occurs much less commonly in the Wabash and Mississippi rivers. The reason for its extensive decimation is almost certainly the increase in silt in streams over most of the state. The gravel chub can exist only in channels and raceways where the current keeps the gravel bottom swept clean of silt.

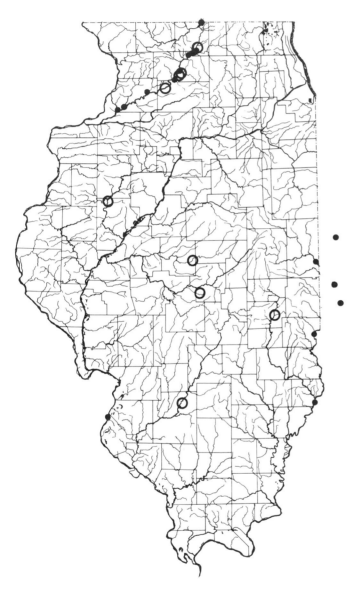

Distribution of the gravel chub in Illinois.

Rhinichthys Agassiz

This widespread North American genus of small-scaled, barbeled minnows with short intestines includes five currently recognized species, two of which occur in the northern half of Illinois.

KEY TO SPECIES

1. Upper jaw extending far beyond lower into a conspicuously elongated snout; mouth almost horizontal; lateral dark band poorly demarcated; snout length usually twice eye diameter .... *cataractae*
   Upper jaw extending slightly beyond lower, not forming a conspicuously elongated snout; mouth somewhat oblique; lateral dark band usually well demarcated below; snout length less than twice eye diameter ...... *atratulus*

Blacknose dace
Rhinichthys atratulus (Hermann)

Cyprinus atratulus Hermann 1804:320 (type-locality: North America).
Rhinichthys atronasus: Nelson 1876:45 (recorded from Illinois); Forbes 1884:75 (part.); Large 1903:18 (part.); Forbes & Richardson 1908:162–163; O'Donnell 1935:480.
Rhinichthys lunatus: Nelson 1876:46.
Rhinichthys meleagris: Nelson 1876:46; Jordan 1878: 63.
Rhinichthys obtusus: Jordan 1878:63.
Rhinichthys atratulus meleagris: Smith 1965:8.

Diagnosis.—The blacknose dace is a dusky-olive and barbeled minnow with a broad frenum; minute scales; and numerous, small, scattered patches of black pigment on the back and sides. It bears a superficial resemblance to the stoneroller but differs sharply in its possession of barbels, a firm belly, and much smaller scales. The blacknose and longnose dace are similar, but the blacknose has a much shorter snout and larger eye. The young of the blacknose dace resembles the young of the stoneroller and of the longnose dace but can be distinguished from them by the same characters that separate mature specimens. The species attains a length of a little more than 75 mm (3 inches).

Variation.—An intensive study of geographic variation in the blacknose dace has not been published, but for many years two distinctive subspecies have been recognized. *R. a. atratulus* occurs in

Blacknose dace

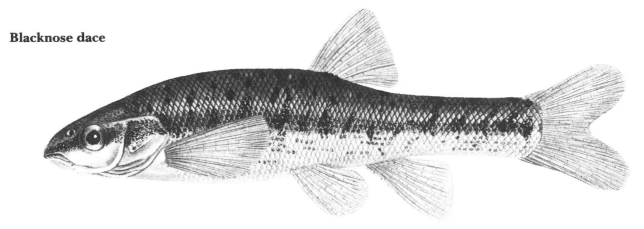

the Atlantic Coast drainage; *R. a. meleagris*, in the interior.

Ecology.—The blacknose dace is a characteristic species of clear, fast, gravelly brooks or runs, but it may also occur over mixed sand-gravel in pools overhung by tree roots or rock outcrops. Raney (1940) published a comparative study of the spawning habits of the two subspecies and found striking differences in breeding color and behavior. The western subspecies is strongly territorial and spawns with several females over a period of a few days. The tuberculate male has a brick-red lateral band. According to Forbes & Richardson (1908:163), spawning occurs in June in shallow fast water, but it is likely that spawning also occurs in May and perhaps late April. Small pebbles are carried in the mouth of the male and are deposited on top of the nest. By fall the young exceed 25 mm (1 inch) in length. The young often ascend into headwaters where there is seemingly too little water for fish to live. A thorough study (Tarter 1970) of the feeding habits of this dace in Kentucky revealed that feeding activity is greatest in the morning and that aquatic insect immatures and amphipods are the predominant foods although a variety of other aquatic invertebrates may also be taken.

Distribution.—In northern Illinois the blacknose dace is generally distributed; in central Illinois it is restricted to spring-fed streams that remain cool during the summer months. The species is abundant in fast gravelly creeks but cannot tolerate silt or high temperatures. Its range has not changed greatly, except that it once occurred in streams of western Union County in southern Illinois. Its disappearance there is probably the result of the fluctuating water table in recent years and the depositing of silt over the gravel in these streams.

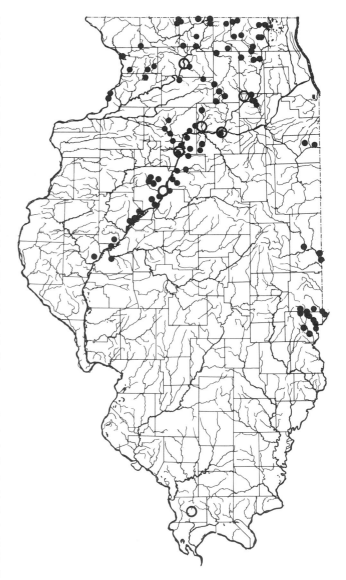

Distribution of the blacknose dace in Illinois.

Longnose dace
Rhinichthys cataractae
(Valenciennes)

Gobio cataractae Valenciennes *in* Cuvier & Valenciennes 1842:315 (type-locality: Niagara Falls).
Rhinichthys maxillosus: Nelson 1876:45 (recorded from Illinois).
Rhinichthys nasutus: Nelson 1876:45.
Rhinichthys cataractae: Jordan 1878:62; Forbes & Richardson 1908:160–161; O'Donnell 1935: 480; Smith 1965:8.
Rhinichthys atronasus: Forbes 1884:75 (part.); Large 1903:18 (part.).

Diagnosis.—The longnose dace is a dusky or olivaceous and barbeled minnow with a broad frenum, minute scales, scattered irregular patches of black pigment on the back and sides, and a conspicuously elongated snout. It most closely resembles the blacknose dace but can be distinguished by characters given in the key. Its young superficially resembles that of the stoneroller, from which it differs by its distinctive snout shape and by having barbels, a firm belly, and smaller scales. The species attains a length of more than 100 mm (4 inches).

Variation.—Despite the transcontinental range of this species, little geographic variation has been discerned. Hubbs (1926:31) noted that careful comparison of series of specimens from various parts of the range failed to support the presence of even an eastern and a western subspecies.

Ecology.—Two forms of the longnose dace inhabit Illinois. Along the turbulent pebble beaches of Lake Michigan, a pallid form of dace is abundant in the shallow water. In two streams in northwestern Illinois, a darkly pigmented form occurs in cascading stretches of gravelly, boulder-strewn

Distribution of the longnose dace in Illinois.

habitat. The Lake Michigan form is light olive with pale brown mottling on the body and yellowish pigment around the mouth and pectoral fin insertions. The stream form is heavily mottled with black and has crimson pigment around the mouth and fin insertions. Presumably the color difference is induced by the habitat, the lake form occurring in colder and more turbid waters. The longnose dace probably spawns in the spring over gravel in strong riffles and raceways or along the shallow pebble-bottomed shoreline of Lake Michigan. No details are available. Most of the published studies of this species are on western populations, but Reed (1959) studied age, growth, and food in a population in a stream in western Pennsylvania. He found that the species lives to be 5 years old and that each year class could be recognized by average total length and number of annuli on the scales. He found the principal food items to be adult and immature aquatic insects, but annelids and algae were present in some stomachs.

Distribution.—The longnose dace is common along the shoreline of Lake Michigan but extremely rare in inland streams. Like the blacknose dace, it once occurred in streams in western Union County but has since been extirpated, probably because of the siltation and fluctuating water levels of recent decades and the drying up of springs that prevented high water temperatures in summer. The species was likely never common in Illinois streams.

Phenacobius Cope

This North American genus contains four species in the southeastern states and one in the Mississippi Valley and Great Plains. The species are all terete, bottom-dwelling minnows with the highly specialized lower jaw responsible for the common name of suckermouth.

Suckermouth minnow
Phenacobius mirabilis (Girard)

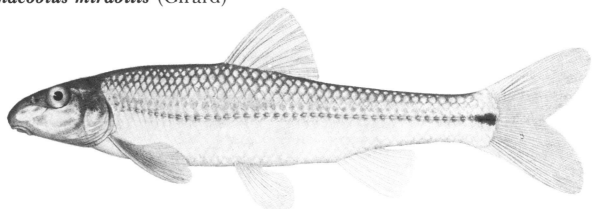

Exoglossum mirabile Girard 1856:191 (type-locality: Arkansas River near Fort Smith, Arkansas).
Phenacobius teretulus var. *liosternus* Nelson 1876:46 (type-locality: small streams in McLean County [Illinois]).
Phenacobius scopiferus: Jordan 1878:61.
Phenacobius mirabilis: Forbes 1884:76; Large 1903: 18; Forbes & Richardson 1908:158–160; O'Donnell 1935:483; Smith 1965:8.

Diagnosis.—The suckermouth minnow is a terete and olivaceous minnow with a horizontal mouth, fleshy lateral lobes on the lower jaw, 42–50 lateral-line scales, and a small and intense black spot on the caudal peduncle. It resembles some of the species in the chub genus *Hybopsis* but differs from them in lacking maxillary barbels. It bears a superficial resemblance to small redhorse suckers but differs from them in lacking the fleshy lips on the upper jaw and tip of the lower jaw and in having an intense, black caudal spot. The mouth structure, body shape, and caudal spot distinguish the young of this minnow from those of other Illinois fishes. The species attains a length of about 100 mm (4 inches).

Variation.—Geographic variation in this wide-ranging species has apparently not been investigated.

Ecology.—This minnow is a Great Plains species that is said by many authors to occur in relatively silt-free riffles and raceways that have turbid and organically rich water. It is also said to be most common in the absence of other riffle-inhabiting species and to be a pioneer species in streams of newly deforested areas. While its eastward spread after the removal of the Eastern Deciduous Forest is well documented, its habitat in Illinois appears always to have been clear fast riffles and raceways over gravel or sandy gravel in large creeks and small rivers. It does not seem to fluctuate greatly in numbers from year to year, and it occurs commonly with several other riffle-adapted species in most Illinois streams where it is present. Cross (1967:101) noted that the species has a long reproductive period in Kansas streams and that spawning occurs two or more times from April into August. The eggs are probably deposited over gravel in the riffles. The spawning site is the habitat utilized by the species all year. In fact, the suckermouth minnow is often one of the predominant riffle species in winter, when other riffle-inhabiting species are overwintering in quiet pools. In its quest for food, the suckermouth minnow behaves much like a darter except that the food is sucked up rather than seized. Forbes & Richardson (1908: 159–160) and Starrett (1950) described the food of this species as predominantly bottom-dwelling immature stages of aquatic insects.

Distribution.—The suckermouth minnow is statewide in distribution except for the extreme northeastern corner of Illinois. It is common in sandy and gravelly streams throughout the state except in extreme southeastern Illinois. The number of old records suggests that the species was once even more generally distributed. Thus, the speculation of several authors that turbid water and high nutrient content have benefitted this minnow is not supported. In Illinois siltation and the reduction of stream size during drought periods have probably been responsible for the observed decimation. The species was probably abundant in

flowing streams of the natural prairie but absent or scarce in heavily forested areas where the tree canopy shaded the streams.

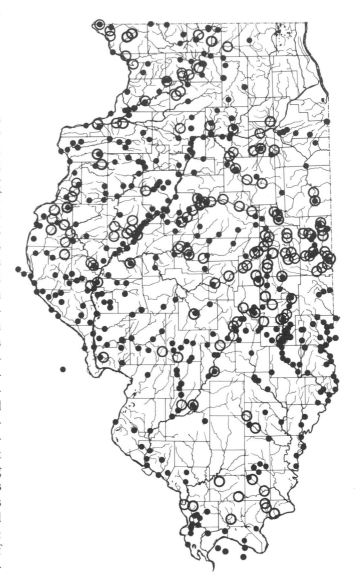

Distribution of the suckermouth minnow in Illinois.

Notropis Rafinesque

This eastern North American genus contains more than 100 described species in the United States, 25 of which presently occur in Illinois. One other is now extirpated. Several species occur up to the Illinois border in other states but cannot be found in Illinois, presumably because the large marginal rivers are barriers. They include *N. maculatus* in adjacent Kentucky and *N. zonatus, N. telescopus,* and *N. greenei* in adjacent Missouri. *Notropis* is the largest genus of freshwater fishes on this continent and one of the largest in the world. New species are still being discovered occasionally. All of the species in the genus are called shiners.

KEY TO SPECIES

1. Dorsal fin with a modal ray count of nine or more 2
   Dorsal fin with a modal ray count of eight 3
2. Body slab sided; anal rays, modally 9 or 10; lateral line absent .... *hubbsi*
   Body terete; anal rays, modally 8; lateral line present .... *emiliae*
3. Anal rays, usually 10 or more; origin of dorsal fin distinctly behind pelvic fin insertions 4
   Anal rays, usually fewer than 10; origin of dorsal fin slightly behind, over, or slightly in advance of pelvic fin insertions 8
4. Predorsal scales small and closely crowded, in 25 or more rows; lateral line strongly decurved; lateral-line scales, usually more than 38 6
   Predorsal scales not noticeably small and crowded, in fewer than 25 rows; lateral line gently decurved; lateral-line scales, 38 or fewer 5
5. Snout rather blunt, its length no greater than eye diameter; dorsal fin pointed at tip .... *atherinoides*
   Snout long and sharply pointed, its length greater than eye diameter; dorsal fin rounded .... *rubellus*
6. Black spot at origin of dorsal fin; body of adult deep, its greatest depth going fewer than four times into standard length; lateral band poorly developed; scales on upper sides uniformly pigmented 7
   No black spot at origin of dorsal fin; body of adult slender, its greatest depth four or more times standard length; an intense dusky lateral band extending onto snout; scales on upper sides outlined by peripheral melanophores .... *fumeus*
7. Body deep, its depth usually greater than head length; dark vertical bands on upper sides weakly developed or absent; breeding male with tubercles on cheeks; snout somewhat rounded; anal rays, usually 11 .. *umbratilis*

Body elongate, its depth usually less than head length; dark vertical bands on upper sides prominent; breeding male without tubercles on cheeks; snout rather sharp; anal rays, usually 10 .... *ardens**
8. Mouth very small, upturned almost to a vertical position .... *anogenus*
   Mouth large, horizontal or oblique, not upturned to nearly vertical position 9
9. Dorsal fin origin slightly behind pelvic insertions; dorsal fin either with a posterior black blotch or with some membranes sprinkled with melanophores; scales on anterior body diamond shaped 10
   Dorsal fin origin above or slightly in front of pelvic fin insertions; dorsal fin membranes clear with melanophores confined to margins of fin rays; scales on anterior body usually not diamond shaped 13
10. Caudal peduncle with a large, black squarish blotch .... *venustus*
    Caudal peduncle without a large black blotch 11
11. Body deep, its depth usually going 3.5 times or fewer into standard length; dorsal fin membranes uniformly pigmented without a posterior dusky spot .... *lutrensis*
    Body not markedly deep, its depth usually going more than 3.5 times into standard length; dorsal fin with posterior dusky spot 12
12. Anal rays, modally eight; anterior membranes of dorsal fin clear with melanophores confined to margins of fin rays (except in breeding males) .... *spilopterus*
    Anal rays, modally nine; anterior membranes of dorsal fin well speckled with melanophores .... *whipplei*
13. Anal rays, modally nine 14
    Anal rays, seven or eight 16
14. Lateral-line scales somewhat elevated, higher than long; predorsal stripe broad; dorsal fin rounded 15
    Lateral-line scales not elevated; predorsal stripe narrow; dorsal fin large and sharply pointed .... *shumardi*
15. Upper sides with many parallel dark lines that converge at midline, forming V-shaped markings on back; broad middorsal stripe without parallel paravertebral stripe; tip of chin densely pigmented; predorsal scales in 13–17 rows .... *chrysocephalus*
    Upper sides without dark lines that converge on midline; a broad dark middorsal stripe

and usually a paravertebral dark stripe on each side of it; chin with little or no pigment; predorsal scales in more than 17 rows . . . .
. . . . *cornutus*

16. A discrete black lateral band extending forward onto snout 17
Black lateral band absent or, if present, not extending forward onto snout 22

17. Anal rays, modally seven; last three or four anal rays frequently outlined with melanophores; several scales below black lateral band outlined with melanophores . . . .
. . . . *texanus*
Anal rays, modally eight; last three or four anal rays like preceding rays; scales below black lateral band not outlined with melanophores 18

18. Chin without pigment; snout overhanging lower jaw; mouth small, almost horizontal; mandible and premaxillary fused proximally for one-third of their lengths . . . 19
Chin with some pigment; mouth almost terminal, sharply oblique; mandible and premaxillary not extensively fused 20

19. Eye large, diameter contained about three times in head length, horizontally elliptical; black lateral band without prominent black crescents; predorsal scales diamond shaped
. . . . *amnis*
Eye small, diameter contained more than three times in head length, round in shape; black lateral band with prominent vertical black crescents; predorsal scales rounded
. . . . *heterolepis*

20. Eye rather small, its diameter going more than three times into head length; roof of mouth heavily pigmented with black; breast unscaled; lateral line poorly developed and incomplete . . . . *chalybaeus*
Eye large, its diameter going about three times into head length; roof of mouth not extensively pigmented with black; breast with some scales; lateral line strongly developed, complete or incomplete 21

21. Peritoneum black; pigment on chin restricted to margin of lower jaw; eye very large, its diameter going into head length fewer than three times . . . . *boops*

Peritoneum silvery; pigmented band traversing tip of lower jaw; eye moderate in size, its diameter going into head length about three times . . . . *heterodon*

22. Anal rays, modally seven 23
Anal rays, modally eight 24

23. Middorsal stripe expanded into wedge-shaped spot in front of dorsal fin and not surrounding fin base; lateral-line pores usually punctate; mouth rather small, its length less than eye diameter; body slender . . . .
. . . . *stramineus*
Middorsal stripe not expanded into wedge-shaped spot before dorsal fin and continuing along either side of fin base; lateral-line pores not punctate; mouth large, its length exceeding eye diameter; body robust . . . . .
. . . . *blennius*

24. Prominent black spot on caudal peduncle; both dorsal and anal fins rather falcate . . .
. . . . *hudsonius*
No black spot on caudal peduncle; dorsal and anal fins not both falcate 25

25. Head flattened ventrally, triangular in cross section; eyes directed laterally and upward; a pair of dark crescents between nostrils . .
. . . . *dorsalis*
Head not flattened ventrally, not triangular in cross section; eyes directed only laterally; no dark crescents between nostrils 26

26. Lateral-line scales not noticeably elevated; lateral-line pores not punctate; mouth terminal and sharply oblique . . . . *shumardi*
Lateral-line scales elevated, at least twice as high as long; lateral-line pores punctate; mouth subterminal and horizontal 27

27. Lateral-line scales extremely elevated, four times as high as long; body milky white and semi-translucent, melanophores restricted to anal fin base; snout sharp; dorsal fin pointed; middorsal row of scales not widened . . . . .
. . . . *buchanani*
Lateral-line scales somewhat elevated, about two times as high as long; body normally pigmented, not semi-translucent; snout bluntly rounded; dorsal fin rounded; middorsal row of scales wider than paravertebral scales . .
. . . . *volucellus*

Pallid shiner
Notropis amnis Hubbs & Greene

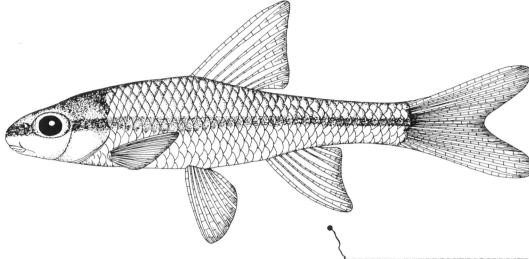

Notropis cayuga: Forbes & Richardson 1908:135 (part.; recorded from Illinois).

Notropis amnis Hubbs & Greene *in* Hubbs 1951:2 (type-locality of nominate subspecies given on page 14 as Mississippi River, 1 mile N of Prairie du Chien, Crawford County, Wisconsin); Smith 1965:7.

Diagnosis.—The pallid shiner is a small terete minnow with a black lateral stripe extending from the tip of the snout to the caudal peduncle; eight anal rays; 1, 4—4, 1 pharyngeal teeth; 34–37 lateral-line scales; a complete lateral line; a large horizontally elliptical eye; and very small mouth with the maxilla and mandible extensively fused proximally. The species is remarkably similar to the bigeye chub, from which it differs principally by lacking maxillary barbels. Both the young and adult can be distinguished from other black-striped shiners by the anteriorly placed dorsal fin and the distinctly chublike head and body. The species attains a length of 55 mm (slightly more than 2 inches).

Variation.—In the original description of the species (Hubbs 1951), geographic variation was analyzed, and two subspecies were described: *N. a. amnis* from the upper Mississippi River valley and *N. a. pinnosa* from east Texas, Oklahoma, and western Arkansas.

Ecology.—The pallid shiner is one of the rarest and least known American fishes. Even a description of its habitat has to be conjectural. In Illinois it is now confined to the Mississippi River, but it once occurred sparingly in inland streams. Its form sug-

Distribution of the pallid shiner in Illinois.

gests that it occupies clear vegetated pools with little flow.

Distribution.—Prior to 1950 the pallid shiner was confused with the blacknose shiner. Hence, old published records without voucher specimens for re-examination cannot be used. The only specimens among the pre-1950 collections of *"Notropis cayuga"* were from the Rock River, Oxbow Island, Rock Island County. Hubbs (1951:7) plotted eight other Mississippi River records, all above the mouth of the Missouri River, and one record for the Sangamon River in northwestern Champaign County. Most of these records were based on specimens collected between 1905 and 1950, and

their precise dates are not available to me. Since 1950 a few Mississippi River collections have been sent to the Illinois Natural History Survey, but only one specimen (from northern Carroll County) is an Illinois record, the few other recent collections being from Wisconsin. This inconspicuous minnow appears to be nearly extirpated throughout the Mississippi valley, and the reasons for its drastic recent decimation are unknown because the ecology of the species is not known. Pflieger (1971:353) noted a marked decline or perhaps complete disappearance of the species in Missouri since 1941 and suggested that turbidity and siltation might be implicated.

Pugnose shiner
Notropis anogenus Forbes

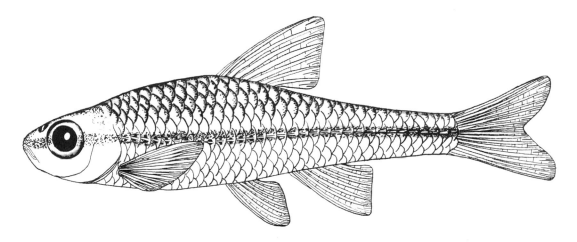

Notropis anogenus Forbes 1885:138 (type-locality: Fox River at McHenry, Illinois); Large 1903:16; Forbes & Richardson 1908:132–133; O'Donnell 1935:481; Smith 1965:7.

Diagnosis.—The pugnose shiner is a small straw-colored minnow with a mouth so sharply upturned as to be almost vertical, a black stripe from the tip of the snout to the caudal peduncle, a black peritoneum, 34–37 lateral-line scales, a complete lateral line, 4—4 pharyngeal teeth, and seven or eight anal rays. It can be distinguished from other black-striped shiners by the sharply upturned mouth, and from the pugnose minnow by the black peritoneum, the complete lateral line, and its eight rather than nine dorsal rays. The young differs from that of the golden shiner in having a nearly terete body shape and fewer anal rays, and from the blackchin shiner, with which it occurs, by the

distinctive mouth shape and black peritoneum. The species attains a length of 50 mm (almost 2 inches).

Variation.—Bailey (1959) summarized the existing knowledge of this little-known species and failed to find any well-marked variation.

Ecology.—The extremely rare pugnose shiner occurs in clear, well-vegetated, natural lakes and once occurred in low-gradient streams with aquatic vegetation. Forbes & Richardson (1908:133) noted ripe females in early May and early June. No details on reproductive or feeding habits of the species are available.

Distribution.—The pugnose shiner was described from the Fox River in McHenry County in 1885 and found in Fourth Lake, Lake County, in 1892 and in a floodplain lake in Mason County

Distribution of the pugnose shiner in Illinois.

in 1909. The species was believed to be extirpated in Illinois (Bailey 1959) until 1965, when it was collected in Channel Lake, Lake County. It has since been taken in nearby Loon and Grass lakes, also in Lake County, but only one or two specimens have been found at one time. Rare throughout most of its range, the species is believed to be disappearing because of increased turbidity in the natural lakes and streams.

Rosefin shiner*
Notropis ardens (Cope)

Hypsilepis ardens Cope 1867:163 (type-locality: headwaters of Roanoke River, Montgomery County, Virginia).

Notropis ardens lythrurus: Greene 1935:219 ("Specimens from Illinois found in the Museum of Comparative Zoology by Dr. Hubbs").

Notropis umbratilis fasciolaris?: Forbes & Richardson 1908:155.

Notropis ardens: Smith 1965:5 (said not to occur in Illinois, but subsequently specimens were found in an old collection of *N. umbratilis*).

Diagnosis.—The rosefin shiner is a slender but somewhat compressed minnow, dusky in color, with small, closely crowded scales in the predorsal region; a black spot on the basal portion of the anterior rays of the dorsal fin; numerous dusky saddle bands over the back and upper sides; usually 2, 4—4, 2 pharyngeal teeth; 9–11 anal rays; and red-orange fins on the male. The breeding male is without nuptial tubercles on the cheeks. It is most like the redfin shiner but differs in having pronounced vertical dusky bands over the back, a more slender body, a sharper snout, one or two fewer anal rays, and in lacking tubercles on the cheeks. It is similar to the ribbon shiner but differs in lacking an intense black lateral band and in possessing a dark spot at the dorsal fin base, a smaller eye, and rose-colored fins (in the live breeding male). The young so closely resembles the young of the redfin and ribbon shiners that associated adults are usually necessary for certain identification. The rosefin shiner does not occur with either the redfin or ribbon shiner. The young also superficially resembles the young of the emerald and rosyface shiners. The rosefin shiner attains a length of about 80 mm (3 inches).

Variation.—A thorough study of geographic variation, as yet unpublished, was conducted in 1969 by Dr. Franklin F. Snelson, Jr., then at Cornell University. He recognized three subspecies; the one formerly occurring in Illinois was *N. a. lythrurus*.

Ecology.—The rosefin shiner occupies pools usually below riffles in creeks and has strong schooling tendencies. Yokley (1974) studied the life history of the species in northern Alabama and found that its food consisted of both plant and animal material and that spawning occurred in association with that of the longear sunfish. The male shiner and male

Rosefin shiner

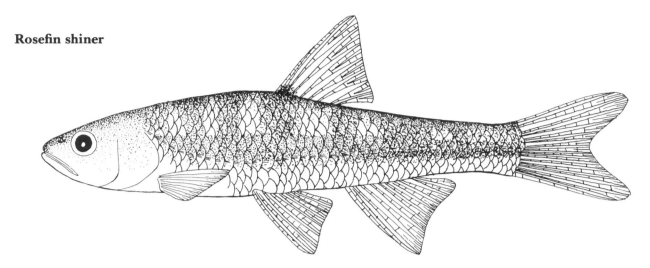

sunfish both guard the same saucer-shaped nest in sand or fine gravel. In Big Creek in Hardin County, where the rosefin shiner once occurred, spawning probably took place in May.

Distribution.—Extirpated in Illinois. The only extant specimens from Illinois are from Spring Branch, Wolrab Mills, Hardin County. These six specimens, collected in 1900, were found in the Forbes and Richardson series of *Notropis umbratilis.* Greene (1935:219) noted that Dr. C. L. Hubbs had found Illinois specimens in the Museum of Comparative Zoology at Harvard. The rosefin shiner and the redfin shiner apparently do not occur together anywhere in their ranges. The rosefin shiner has been replaced by the redfin shiner in southeastern Illinois.

Distribution of the rosefin shiner in Illinois.

Emerald shiner
Notropis atherinoides Rafinesque

Notropis atherinoides Rafinesque 1818c:204 (type-locality: Lake Erie); Jordan 1878:60; Forbes & Richardson 1908:151–153; O'Donnell 1935:482; Smith 1965:7.

Notropis amabilis: Nelson 1876:47 (recorded from Illinois).

Notropis dilectus: Nelson 1876:47; Large 1903:18.

Notropis dinemus: Nelson 1876:48; Forbes 1884:76.

Notropis rubellus: Nelson 1876:48.

Notropis arge: Large 1903:18.

Diagnosis.—The emerald shiner is a slender and slab-sided minnow, silvery in color, with 10–13 anal rays; the dorsal fin situated well behind the pelvic bases; 35–40 lateral-line scales; a sharply pointed dorsal fin; usually 2, 4–4, 2 pharyngeal teeth; and a rounded snout. It differs from the rosyface shiner in having a rounded snout, the length of which is equal to or less than the eye diameter, and a sharply pointed dorsal fin. It is superficially similar to the ribbon and redfin shiners but has fewer lateral-line scales, a relatively straight lateral line, and larger predorsal scales. The young of the emerald shiner can be confused with the young of the above-mentioned species but can be distinguished by the same characters that differentiate the adult. The young differs from the young of most other species of shiners by the posteriorly placed dorsal fin and slender body. The species attains a length of 90 mm (3½ inches).

Variation.—Hubbs (1945) recognized a widespread river subspecies and a lacustrine subspecies in Lake Michigan. For the latter, he resurrected the name *acutus.* The same author noted that the Great Plains were occupied by a distinctive species, for which he resurrected the name *percobromus.* At present neither *N. a. acutus* nor *N. percobromus* is

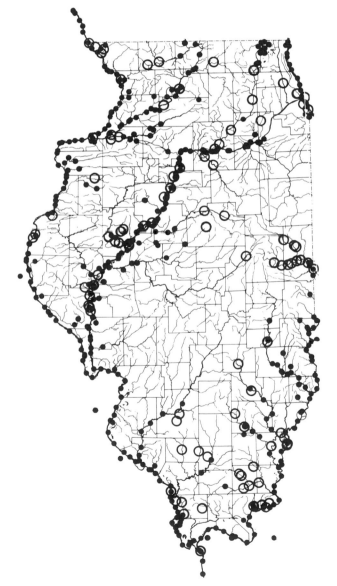

Distribution of the emerald shiner in Illinois.

recognized. The emerald shiner appears to attain a larger size in Lake Michigan and to be less variable than are river populations.

Ecology.—The emerald shiner is typically a large-river minnow and occurs in small streams only near their mouths. It is the most abundant fish species in large rivers. Preferring clear flowing water over a substrate of sand, it is, however, tolerant of such turbid water as that in the Mississippi River below the mouth of the Missouri. The species tends to aggregate in large schools in mid-water or near the surface. According to Forbes & Richardson (1908:153), its food consists mainly of terrestrial insects, but some crustaceans, algae, and immature stages of aquatic insects are taken. Spawning probably occurs during late spring and early summer. No details are available, but sexual maturity is al-most certainly reached at 1 year of age, and spawning is probably a communal affair with fertilized eggs being broadcast over a substrate of mixed sand, gravel, and silt.

Distribution.—The emerald shiner is common in all large and medium-sized rivers. Like many other large-river species, it occurs in small streams only in southern Illinois and there its numbers fluctuate widely from year to year. This shiner formerly abounded in the shallow water of Lake Michigan. LaRue Wells (personal communication) believed that it was virtually extirpated in that lake by the late 1960's, when the alewife reached the peak of its abundance, but it still occurs in Lake Michigan near the shore. Because of low water levels during dry periods, this large-river species no longer ascends tributaries as far as it once did.

River shiner
Notropis blennius (Girard)

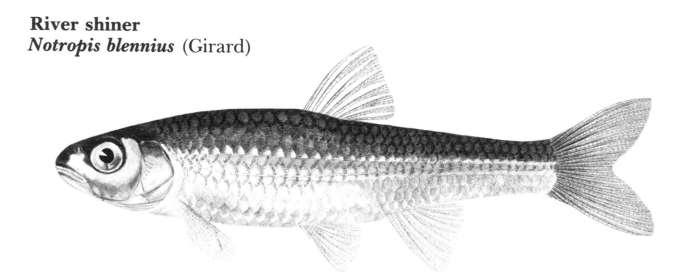

Alburnops blennius Girard 1856:194 (type-locality: Arkansas River near Fort Smith, Arkansas).
Episema jejuna Jordan 1878:60 (type-locality: Illinois River).
Notropis jejunus: Forbes 1884:77; Large 1903:18; Forbes & Richardson 1908:150–151.
Hybopsis blennius: O'Donnell 1935:482.
Notropis blennius: Smith 1965:7.

Diagnosis.—The river shiner is a robust and rather large-scaled (34–37 scales in the lateral line) minnow, straw colored above, with seven anal rays; a large oblique mouth; a rather broad middorsal stripe of uniform width, continuing along either side of the dorsal fin base; usually 1, 4—4, 1 pharyngeal teeth; a complete unpunctate lateral line; and a poorly defined plumbeous lateral band.

The species is superficially similar to the silvery minnows (*Hybognathus*) but differs in having a larger mouth, short intestine (and thus a firm belly), seven rather than eight anal rays, and a scaleless breast. It shares with the sand shiner a color similarity and seven anal rays but differs in having a larger and more oblique mouth and in lacking an expanded wedge-shaped spot in front of the dorsal fin origin and a punctate lateral line. It differs from the bigmouth shiner in having an oblique mouth, seven rather than eight anal rays, and the ventral surface of the head rounded instead of flattened. The young of the river shiner resembles young of these same species, especially of the silvery minnows, but young silvery minnows have a soft and discolored belly, a much smaller mouth, and eight anal rays. The river shiner attains a length of about 100 mm (4 inches).

Variation.—Hubbs & Bonham (1951:103) resurrected *jejunus* as a subspecific name for shiners in the eastern and northern parts of the range of the species. Most recent authors have not used subspecies names. Geographic variation in the species has not been extensively studied.

Ecology.—The river shiner is a large-river species that enters small streams of Illinois only in the south. It is extremely abundant in clear flowing water over a sand or gravelly bottom and is less tolerant of turbidity than the emerald shiner. For example, it is common in the Mississippi River

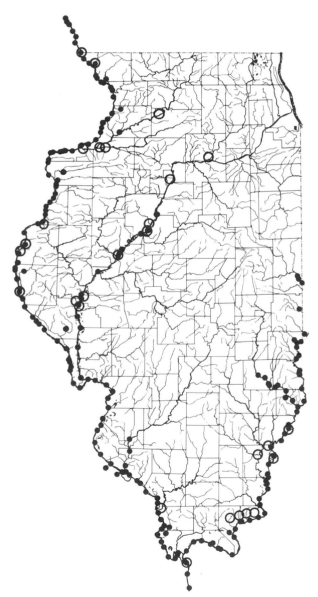

Distribution of the river shiner in Illinois.

along the entire length of the state, but it is more abundant in the clear portion above the mouth of the Missouri. It is common in other large rivers, except the sluggish Illinois River, where it is less frequent. Its feeding and reproductive habits are virtually unknown but are presumed to be similar to those of the emerald shiner, with which it usually occurs. It is a species of the mid-water with strong schooling tendencies. Forbes & Richardson (1908:151) inferred that spawning occurs in July and August. Sexual maturity is probably reached at 1 year of age, and spawning is likely communal over a sand and gravel substrate.

Distribution.—The river shiner is restricted to large and medium-sized rivers but does not ascend the Illinois River a great distance. The record for the Great Lakes drainage in northeastern Illinois (Forbes & Richardson 1908, atlas of maps) must have been either a cartographic error or a misidentification. There is little evidence of change in the distribution and abundance of the species although it may have been more widespread in the Illinois River before 1900.

Bigeye shiner
Notropis boops Gilbert

Notropis boops Gilbert 1884:201 (type-locality: Salt Creek, Brown County, and Flat Rock Creek, Rush County, Indiana); Smith 1965:7.

Notropis shumardi: Large 1903:17 (part.; recorded from Illinois).

Notropis illecebrosus: Forbes & Richardson 1908: 140–141.

Hybopsis boops: O'Donnell 1935:481.

Diagnosis.—The bigeye shiner is a terete, broadheaded, black-striped minnow with a very large eye (diameter contained less than three times in head length); a pronounced black band from the eye to the tip of upper jaw; a sharply pointed dorsal fin; eight anal rays; a black peritoneum; a complete lateral line; 1, 4—4, 1 pharyngeal teeth; and a light band above the black lateral stripe. The bigeye shiner closely resembles the blackchin shiner, from which it differs in having an eye diameter that goes into the head length fewer than three times, a black peritoneum, a complete lateral line, and pigment on the chin restricted to the sides of the lower jaw. From all other Illinois minnows this species is easily distinguished by its much larger eye and the combination of characters listed above. The young is as distinctive as the adult and could easily be confused

Bigeye shiner

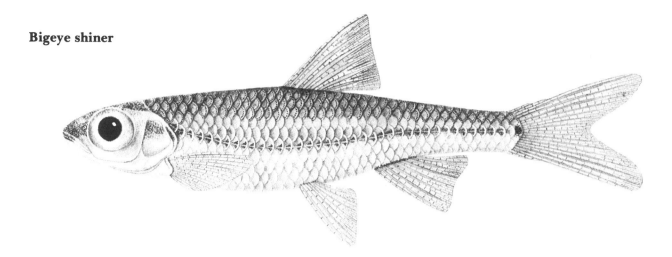

with the young blackchin shiner if they occurred together, which they do not. The young slightly resembles that of the sand shiner, but eye size distinguishes them. The species attains a length of about 90 mm (3½ inches).

Variation.—Apparently no study of geographic variation has been undertaken for this distinctive species.

Ecology.—The bigeye shiner occurs in clear, rather high-gradient streams over a substrate of clean gravel or mixed sand and gravel. It is often found at the stream margin in beds of emergent vegetation. Feeding and reproductive habits are poorly known. Spawning presumably occurs in late spring and summer. The species is sexually mature in 1 year.

Distribution.—The bigeye shiner is extremely sporadic in distribution and rare in Illinois. It was probably never abundant, except in the Vermilion and Little Vermilion systems, where Forbes and Richardson found it at virtually every station. Siltation, high-water turbidity, and impoundments are responsible for the severe decimation of the species.

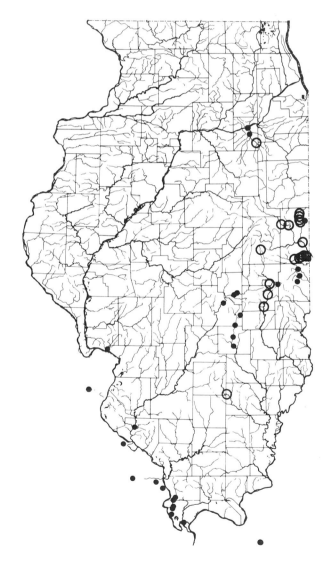

Distribution of the bigeye shiner in Illinois.

Ghost shiner
Notropis buchanani Meek

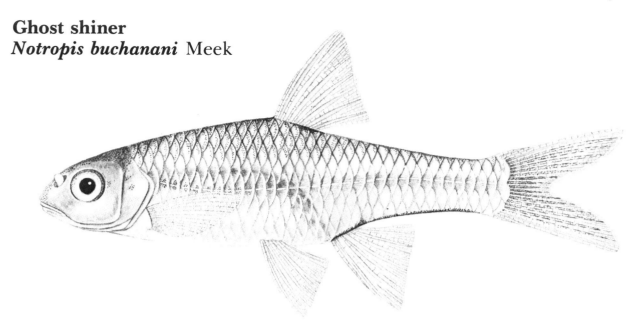

Notropis buchanani Meek 1896:342 (type-locality: small creek near Poteau, Indian Territory [Oklahoma]); Smith 1965:7.

Notropis blennius: Forbes & Richardson 1908:137–138 (part.; specimens of *N. buchanani* found in several of their old collections of *N. "blennius"* = *stramineus*).

Diagnosis.—The ghost shiner is a small and delicate minnow, milky white and somewhat translucent, with 4—4 pharyngeal teeth, a sharply pointed snout, pointed dorsal and anal fins, a slender caudal peduncle, eight anal rays, and highly elevated (four times as high as long) lateral-line scales. The compressed body is almost devoid of pigment except for melanophores at the base of the anal fin. The ghost shiner resembles closely the mimic and sand shiners but differs from them by having less pigment and highly elevated lateral-line scales. It is superficially similar to the poorly pigmented young of the silverband shiner, but it is deeper bodied, with eight rather than nine anal rays, and has more highly elevated lateral-line scales. The ghost shiner attains a length of slightly over 50 mm (2 inches).

Variation.—Although described in 1896, this species name was regarded as a synonym first of *blennius* and later of *deliciosus* until Hubbs & Greene (1928) resurrected *buchanani* as a subspecific name for the southern populations of *Notropis volucellus*. Bailey (*in* Harlan & Speaker 1951:193) elevated *buchanani* to full specific rank. Geographic variation in this shiner has probably not been investigated.

Distribution of the ghost shiner in Illinois.

Ecology.—The ghost shiner is a typical large-river species that is common at only a few localities in Illinois. Contrary to Trautman's (1957:387) statement that in Ohio the species prefers clear water and a bottom of clean sand and gravel, in Illinois the ghost shiner is often found in turbid water over a soft bottom of silt and detritus. Like other large-river species, it is poorly known, and its life history is presumed to be similar to that of other shiners occupying the same habitat.

Distribution.—The ghost shiner is common,

oddly enough, in the polluted upper Illinois River, the lower portion of the Kaskaskia River (or it was common there until that stretch was channelized for barge traffic), and in the lower portion of Clear Creek in Alexander and Union counties in southern Illinois. Elsewhere it is rather rare in large rivers, and there are no records at all from the Wabash River. Nor does it occur in small streams, except at the confluence with a large river. There is evidence that the species was once more widely distributed in the upper Mississippi River, but the reasons for its decimation there are unknown.

Ironcolor shiner
Notropis chalybaeus (Cope)

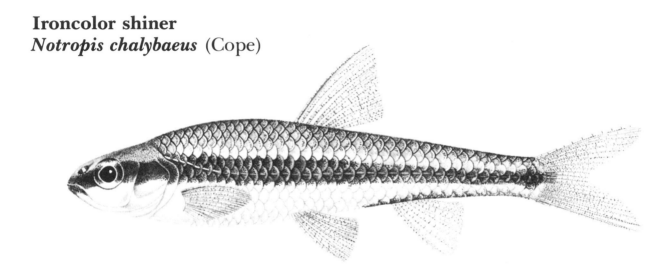

Hybopsis chalybaeus Cope 1866:383 (type-locality: Schuylkill River near Conshohockco, Pennsylvania).

Notropis heterodon: Forbes & Richardson 1908:134–136 (part.).

Notropis chalybaeus: Smith 1965:7 (recorded from Illinois).

Diagnosis.—The ironcolor shiner is a rather deep-bodied shiner, straw colored above, with an intense black lateral band from the caudal fin forward to the tip of the snout and lower jaw; eight anal rays; 2, 4—4, 2 pharyngeal teeth; the breast unscaled; a moderate-sized eye (diameter contained more than three times in head length); a broad dusky middorsal stripe; dorsal scales heavily outlined with melanophores; and intense black pigment around and inside the mouth. It resembles the weed shiner but differs from that species in having a modal anal ray count of eight rather than seven, black pigment on the roof of the mouth, and the black lateral band sharply and evenly demarcated below (the weed shiner has

some scales below the lateral band outlined with melanophores) and in lacking pigment in the anterior rays of the anal fin. The ironcolor shiner differs from the blackchin and bigeye shiners in having a smaller eye and an unscaled breast and from the pallid and blacknose shiners in having the lower jaw pigmented. No other Illinois shiner has so much black pigment inside the mouth. The species attains a length of 65 mm (2½ inches).

Variation.—No studies of variation in this species have yet been published, but Dr. Camm C. Swift of the Los Angeles County Museum has recently studied the ironcolor shiner and its allies intensively.

Ecology.—The ironcolor shiner occurs most frequently in clear well-vegetated creeks with sandy bottoms, but it is also found in soft-bottomed swamps adjacent to the Kankakee River. It sometimes schools with the weed shiner, a similar black-striped minnow characteristic of streams in extensive areas of sand prairie. In Illinois females distended with eggs have been taken in June and

July. According to Marshall (1947), spawning occurs from April to September in central Florida. No nest is prepared. During daylight hours the male pursues any female that is nearby, and if she is receptive, the two swim side by side with their vents close together. The adhesive eggs, averaging a little less than a millimeter in diameter, drop to the bottom. At a mean temperature of 15.5° C, the eggs hatch in 54 hours. Sexual maturity is almost certainly reached in 1 year.

Distribution.—One specimen of the ironcolor shiner, collected in the Des Plaines River of Cook County in 1901, was found by Dr. Camm C. Swift among the Forbes and Richardson collections of the blackchin shiner. Recent collections are all from the Kankakee sand area of Kankakee and

Iroquois counties and from the sand area of Mason and Tazewell counties. In these two areas it is common, but it has been found nowhere else in Illinois. The species is common in the sandy floodplain in the bootheel of Missouri and in the Kankakee sand area of northwestern Indiana. Some of the collections Forbes & Richardson (1908:134–136) referred to as *Notropis heterodon* may have been *Notropis chalybaeus* although most of the so-called *heterodon* from streams in western and central Illinois are reidentified herein as *Notropis texanus*.

Striped shiner
Notropis chrysocephalus
(Rafinesque)

Luxilus chrysocephalus Rafinesque 1820a:48 (type-locality: Kentucky).

Luxilus cornutus: Nelson 1876:47 (part., recorded from Illinois); Jordan 1878:57 (part.); O'Donnell 1935:482 (part.).

Notropis megalops: Forbes 1884:77 (part.).

Notropis cornutus: Large 1903:17 (part.); Forbes & Richardson 1908:147–148 (part.).

Notropis pilsbryi: Forbes & Richardson 1908:149; O'Donnell 1935:482 (said to have been based on *Notropis cornutus* [= *chrysocephalus*] X *Notropis rubrifrons* [= *rubellus*] hybrid).

Notropis chrysocephalus chrysocephalus: Smith 1965:7.

Diagnosis.—The striped shiner is a large and much compressed shiner, bluish or greenish on the sides, with its dorsal fin situated far forward (in advance of the pelvic fin insertions); distinctly elevated lateral-line scales; nine anal rays; 2, 4—4, 2 pharyngeal teeth; rounded fins; a broad dusky middorsal stripe; 37–40 lateral-line scales; sides frequently mottled with dark pigment; upper sides with many parallel dark lines that converge obliquely on the midline of the back; 13–17 rows of predorsal scales that are sharply outlined with melanophores; and the tip of the chin densely pigmented with black. It resembles the related common shiner but differs from that species in having larger predorsal scales (fewer than 17), the tip of the chin heavily pigmented, and numerous parallel dark lines converging at midback rather than a middorsal stripe and one or two paravertebral dark stripes (Fig. 11). The young striped shiner is readily distinguished from the red and steelcolor shiners, which also possess nine anal rays, by its larger head and eye and more anteriorly placed dorsal fin. The young differs from the silverband

Distribution of the ironcolor shiner in Illinois.

Striped shiner

shiner by its rounded dorsal fin and from the redfin shiner by its much larger scales and fewer anal rays. The species attains a length of more than 180 mm (7 inches).

Variation.—A thorough study of this species and other members of the subgenus *Luxilus* was made by Gilbert (1961 and 1964), who concluded that *Notropis chrysocephalus* was specifically distinct from *Notropis cornutus* and that the former consisted of two well-marked subspecies but that the latter lacked recognizable subspecies, *frontalis* thus being synonymized with *cornutus*. R. J. Miller (1968) disputed Gilbert's interpretation and argued that the data available supported recognition of one polytypic species with secondary intergradation between *cornutus* and *chrysocephalus* where their ranges came together. In northwestern Illinois these two fishes do not occur together, and their ranges complement each other precisely. In northeastern Illinois there are six counties in which both forms occur. Of the 68 extant recent collections from these counties, 61 contain one or the other but not

both fishes. Seven contain both *cornutus* and *chrysocephalus,* and at least three of these contain intermediates as well as the two parental types. If only Illinois collections are considered, hybridization between two species seems more plausible than intergradation between two subspecies. The evidence supports the contention of both Gilbert and Miller that differentiation between these fishes is at a level between that of well-marked subspecies and full species.

Ecology.—The striped shiner occurs in clear water of fast to moderately flowing small brooks and large creeks that have bottoms of gravel, rubble, or mixed sand and gravel. It avoids strong riffles and deep soft-bottomed pools, and it is sometimes present in large schools at the foot of riffles and in shallow hard-bottomed pools with some flow. Forbes & Richardson (1908:148) listed a variety of plant and animal food items and noted that the striped shiner will take a hook baited with an earthworm or grasshopper. Breeding occurs in May and June in Illinois. The tuberculate male develops bright pink on its fins and sides, and the body is suffused with iridescent steel blue. Several excellent studies have been published on the life history of this species and the common shiner, which until recently were believed to be subspecies of the same species. Hankinson (1932) described in detail the use of nests of hornyhead chubs by striped shiners. Raney (1940) summarized earlier studies and described many new aspects of the spawning behavior. He found that the nuptial tubercles were used in fighting off other males, in the spawning act, and in defending the nest from other fishes. Spawning occurred during daylight hours over a

Fig. 11. Dorsums of the striped shiner (upper) and common shiner (lower).

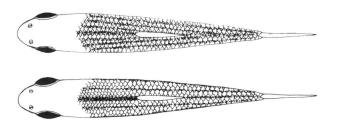

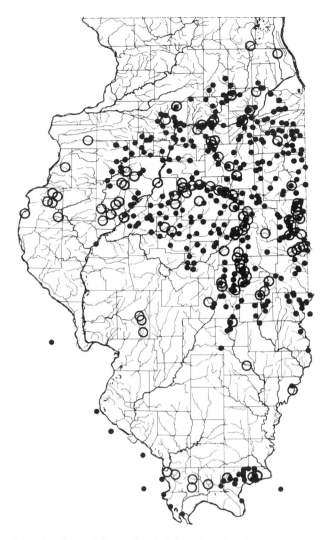

Distribution of the striped shiner in Illinois.

gravelly creeks of eastern and central Illinois, but its range is sharply bounded on the north, west, and south. An outlier population occurs in the extreme southeastern part of the state. Formerly the species occurred slightly farther north and much farther west, and it was distributed across the Shawnee Hills of southern Illinois. The range shrinkage is probably due to a combination of increasing siltation, turbidity, and the temporary drying up of small creeks during dry periods of late summer and fall. In western Illinois agricultural pollution may also have affected populations in creeks.

Common shiner
Notropis cornutus (Mitchill)

Cyprinus cornutus Mitchill 1817:289 (type-locality: Wallkill River, New York).

?*Leuciscus diplema:* Kennicott 1855:594 (recorded from Illinois).

Luxilus cornutus: Nelson 1876:47 (part.); Jordan 1878:57 (part.); O'Donnell 1935:482 (part.).

Notropis megalops: Forbes 1884:77 (part.).

Notropis cornutus: Large 1903:17 (part.); Forbes & Richardson 1908:147–148 (part.); Smith 1965:7.

Diagnosis.—The common shiner is closely related and exceedingly similar to the striped shiner (Fig. 11), differing from it in having smaller predorsal scales (more than 17 between the head and the origin of the dorsal fin) and the tip of the chin immaculate or with a few melanophores on the sides, and in lacking the parallel dark lines that converge obliquely at midback. Instead there are a conspicuous, broad, middorsal dusky predorsal stripe and one or two parallel paravertebral dusky stripes. The young is similar to those of the shiners cited as resembling the young of the striped shiner. It can be distinguished from the young striped shiner most readily by the zone of smaller, almost granular, predorsal scales; the more intense predorsal stripe; and the lack of pigment on the chin. The species attains a length of more than 150 mm (6 inches).

Variation.—See the account of variation under the striped shiner. The common shiner was long known as *Notropis cornutus frontalis.* Gilbert (1961 and 1964) analyzed variation in the species and synonymized *frontalis.*

Ecology.—See the account of the ecology of the striped shiner. Gilbert (1964) and others have com-

period of about 10 days in water temperatures of 15° to 18° C. Spawning occurred over gravel in riffles, in craterlike depressions excavated by the male in the gravel, and in depressions made by other nest-building species in both still and running water. The male embraced the female with his body, holding her on her side with the venter facing upstream. Fewer than 50 eggs were laid at a time. Each was orange and about 1½ mm in diameter. The communal use of nests by more than one species results in the frequent production of hybrids with other species and genera. One such hybrid, with a rosyface shiner as the other parent, was erroneously identified as *Notropis pilsbryi* by Forbes & Richardson (1908:149).

Distribution.—The striped shiner is an abundant and generally distributed species in clear,

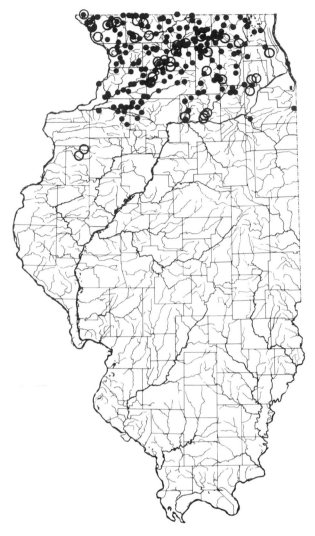

Distribution of the common shiner in Illinois.

mented on the similarity of reproductive habits of the two shiners, and Gilbert presented convincing evidence that the striped shiner is more tolerant of warmer and more turbid water and that it has supplanted the common shiner in several areas modified by agricultural practices. Such has happened in northern Illinois. Starrett (1950) noted the seasonal change in food habits. A variety of animal food and some plant material is taken.

Distribution.— Although the range of the common shiner has been encroached upon by the more southern striped shiner, the former is extremely abundant in gravelly creeks in northern Illinois. It is often the most abundant fish in such streams.

Bigmouth shiner
Notropis dorsalis (Agassiz)

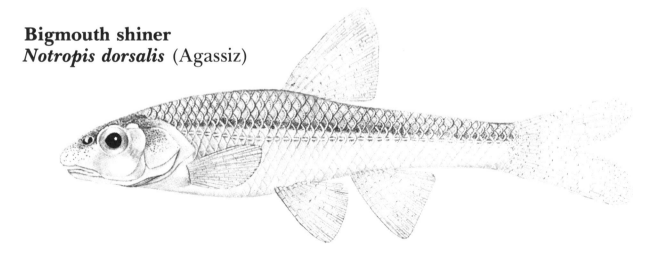

Hybopsis dorsalis Agassiz 1854:358 (type-locality: Burlington, Iowa); O'Donnell 1935:481.
Notropis gilberti: Large 1903:17 (recorded from Illinois); Forbes & Richardson 1908:139–140.
Notropis dorsalis: Smith 1965:7.

Diagnosis.—The bigmouth shiner is a terete silvery to plumbeous shiner with eight anal rays; 34–37 lateral-line scales; 1, 4—4, 1 pharyngeal teeth; unmarked fins; a large horizontal mouth; the dorsal fin origin almost over the pelvic fin insertions; a ventrally flattened head, triangular in cross section; eyes directed somewhat upward and forward as well as laterally; and a pair of distinct dusky crescents between the nostrils viewed from above. The species bears a remarkable resemblance to the silverjaw minnow, from which it differs in lacking the pearl organs on the upper lip and lower jaw and in having a much larger mouth (extending backward to the front of the eye). It also resembles the sand shiner but differs in having eight rather than seven anal rays and a discrete middorsal stripe of uniform width rather than a stripe that expands into a wedge-shaped spot at the dorsal fin origin. It differs from the mimic shiner in lacking elevated lateral-line scales and in having a ventrally flattened head and eyes directed upward. The young bigmouth shiner resembles the young of these same species but is distinguishable by the peculiar position of the eyes and the absence of pearl organs. The species attains a length of 65 mm (2½ inches).

Variation.—No thorough study of variation in this species has been published. Some authors recognize an upper Great Plains subspecies (*piptolepis*), and a few years ago a subspecies (*keimi*) was recognized in New York and Pennsylvania for a disjunct population. Both subspecific names were resurrected from the older literature for the localized populations.

Ecology.—The bigmouth shiner is a plains species that is gradually expanding its range eastward. Essentially a fish of shallow water in creeks and small rivers, it is occasionally found in large rivers but seldom in small temporary streams. During the course of the field work for this study, the species has entered the Wabash drainage in the Vermilion River system. It is one of the most abundant fishes in sandy creeks that lack shade from marginal trees. The food consists primarily of insects but also includes some bottom ooze and plant material (Starrett 1950:221). Spawning evidently occurs throughout May, June, and July, as indicated by the presence in collections of females distended with eggs.

Distribution.—The bigmouth shiner is found throughout the state, except for the southern and extreme eastern parts. It is probably more abun-dant and widespread now than it has ever been because human modification of streams has created many more areas of shallow habitat suitable for the bigmouth shiner but for few other fishes.

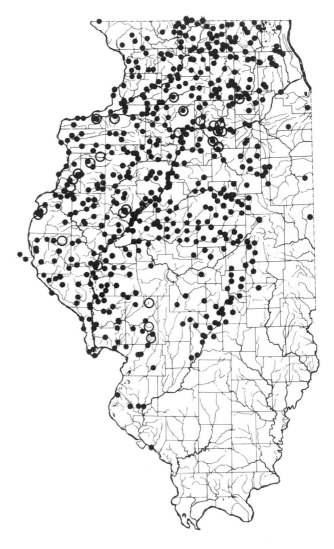

Distribution of the bigmouth shiner in Illinois.

Pugnose minnow
Notropis emiliae (Hay)

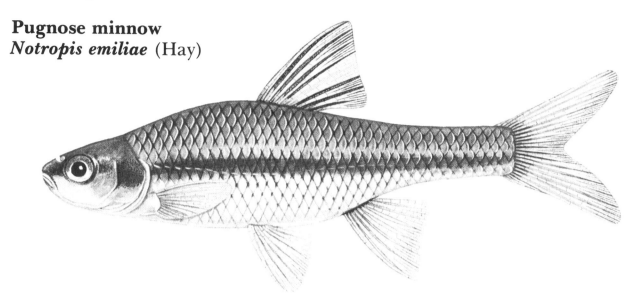

Opsopoeodus emiliae Hay 1881:507 (type-locality: Artesia, Macon, and Enterprise, Mississippi); Forbes 1884:74; Large 1903:15; Forbes & Richardson 1908:124–125; O'Donnell 1935:480; Smith 1965:8.

Trycherodon megalops Forbes *in* Jordan & Gilbert 1883:247 (type-locality: Illinois River at Pekin and Peoria and Mackinaw Creek [Tazewell County], Illinois).

Opsopoeodus megalops: Large 1903:15.

Diagnosis.—The pugnose minnow is a slender and delicate shiner, dusky above and silvery beneath, with nine dorsal rays, eight anal rays, 37–39 lateral-line scales, usually 5—5 pharyngeal teeth, a small terminal mouth upturned to an almost vertical position, and a silvery peritoneum. The breeding male has a large anterior and posterior black blotch in the dorsal fin with a clear area between them. Both sexes have scales on the back and sides distinctly outlined with melanophores, producing a cross-hatching. The young has a narrow but distinct black lateral band from the snout to the caudal peduncle. This species and the bluehead shiner are unique among shiners in having nine dorsal rays. It resembles the pugnose shiner but differs in having a silvery peritoneum and an incomplete lateral line in addition to the higher dorsal ray count. The young is readily identified by its sharply upturned mouth. The adult attains a length of a little more than 50 mm (2 inches).

Variation.—An excellent account of variation in this minnow was published by Gilbert & Bailey (1972), who found that the species consists of a wide-ranging nominate subspecies and one (*peninsularis*) restricted to the Florida peninsula. Some

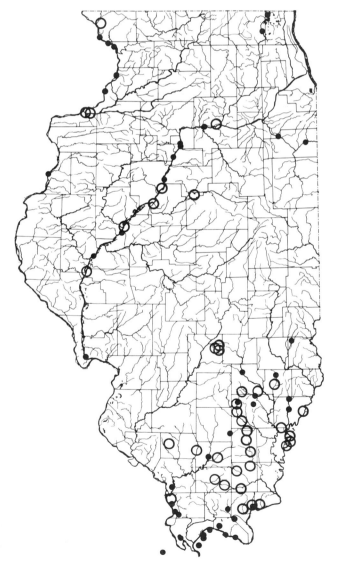

Distribution of the pugnose minnow in Illinois.

authors are reluctant to include this species in the genus *Notropis* and place it in *Opsopoeodus.*

Ecology.—The pugnose minnow occurs in streams ranging in size from creeks to the Mississippi River, but it is most abundant in clear, well-vegetated bottomland lakes and sloughs. In streams it prefers quiet clear pools over a bottom of muck or debris. According to Gilbert & Bailey (1972:19), the species feeds on chironomid larvae and minute crustaceans. Its highly specialized mouth seemingly offers no advantages for the type of food taken. The spawning male has closely crowded tubercles around the mouth. Forbes & Richardson (1908:125) suggested that spawning in the Meredosia region occurs in mid-June. No other details are available.

Distribution.—The pugnose minnow occurs in all parts of Illinois but is extremely sporadic in distribution and rare in most areas. It was formerly generally distributed and common in the southern third of the state, but it is now decimated as a result of excessive siltation in the streams and the drainage of lakes and swamps. The only places where it is still moderately common are a few lakes and swamps that have clear water and much aquatic vegetation.

Ribbon shiner
Notropis fumeus Evermann

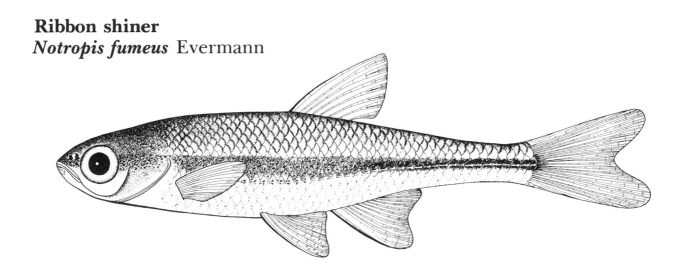

Notropis fumeus Evermann 1892:81 (type-locality: Hunter Creek, about 9 miles W of Houston, Texas); Smith 1965:7 (recorded from Illinois).
?*Notropis microlepidotus* Forbes 1884:76 (*nomen nudum*); Forbes 1885:138 (type-locality not stated).
Notropis umbratilis atripes: Forbes & Richardson 1908:154–156 (part., variety *microlepidotus* synonymized with *atripes*).

Diagnosis.—The ribbon shiner is a slender and somewhat slab-sided shiner, whitish with a black lateral band on the head and body (poorly developed in specimens from turbid waters); usually 11 or 12 anal rays; 39–41 lateral-line scales; usually 1, 4—4, 1 pharyngeal teeth; small and crowded predorsal scales usually outlined by peripheral melanophores; and a strongly decurved lateral line; and without a black spot at the origin of the dorsal fin and without herringbone lines on the upper sides. The species is extremely similar to immature specimens of the redfin shiner, differing in lacking the predorsal dusky spot and in having many predorsal scales outlined with melanophores, a shallower body, a bigger eye, a more intense lateral band, and yellow rather than red fins on the breeding male. The young is difficult to distinguish from the young redfin shiner, the absence of the predorsal spot being the most reliable character. The young also resembles that of the emerald shiner but has smaller scales and a deeper body. The species attains a length of about 50 mm (2 inches).

Variation.—An excellent account of variation in the species and its relationships to other members of the subgenus *Lythrurus* has been published by Snelson (1973), who found little clinal and racial variation in the range of the ribbon shiner.

Ecology.—The ribbon shiner occurs in low-gradient creeks flowing over substrates of sand, clay, or mud. Although its optimal habitat is probably clear vegetated pools over sand with little to mod-

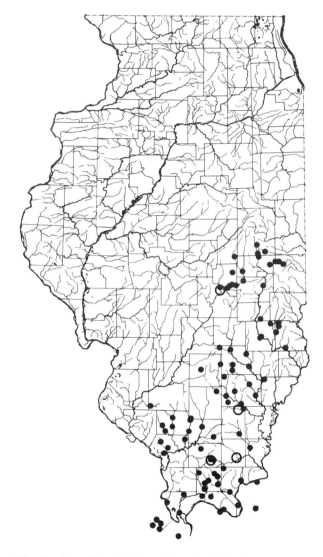

Distribution of the ribbon shiner in Illinois.

erate current, there are few such habitats available within the Illinois range of the species, and the ribbon shiner is usually found in turbid, clay- or mud-bottomed creeks, which often contain detritus and debris in pools. In such turbid waters, the fish is usually pale and lacks the well-developed, black lateral stripe that helps to distinguish this species from the redfin shiner, which occupies the same habitat. Almost nothing is known of the feeding and reproductive habits of this obscure but rather common lowland fish. The breeding male has yellow fins and shagreenlike tubercles on the pectoral fin. Females distended with eggs have been taken in early May, but many more such females are present in collections made in late June.

Distribution.—This species is widely distributed in eastern and southern Illinois but is usually outnumbered by specimens of the redfin shiner wher-

ever it is taken. It is tolerant of turbidity and of silt on the bottoms of streams. Thus, the ribbon shiner may be more abundant now than formerly because many other species, with which it otherwise might have to compete, are decimated in streams modified by increased turbidity and silting.

Blackchin shiner
Notropis heterodon (Cope)

Alburnops heterodon Cope 1864:281 (type-locality: Lansing and Grosse Isle, Michigan).
Hemitremia heterodon: Nelson 1876:47 (recorded from Illinois); Jordan 1878:62.
Notropis heterodon: Forbes 1884:78; Large 1903:16; Forbes & Richardson 1908:134–136 (part.); Smith 1965:7.
Hybopsis heterodon: O'Donnell 1935:481.

Diagnosis.—The blackchin shiner is a slender and terete shiner, straw colored above and silvery beneath, with a prominent black lateral band from the caudal fin to the tip of the snout and chin tip; eight anal rays; 34–38 lateral-line scales; 1, 4—4, 1 or 4—4 pharyngeal teeth; a scaled breast; a silvery peritoneum; a large eye (diameter contained about three times in head length); a sharply pointed dorsal fin situated above the pelvic fin insertions; and an oblique and rather large mouth. The species most closely resembles the bigeye shiner but differs in having a smaller eye, a silvery peritoneum, and a duskier chin tip. The two species do not occur together in Illinois. The blackchin shiner does occur with the blacknose shiner and pugnose shiner but can be distinguished from the former by the pigmented tip of the lower jaw and from the latter by having a silvery rather than black peritoneum and eight rather than seven anal rays. The species differs from the weed shiner and ironcolor shiner in having a larger eye and a sharply pointed dorsal fin. It does not occur with either of these species in Illinois. The young resembles the young of all of these species but can be distinguished by the same characters that separate the adults. The species attains a length of more than 50 mm (2 inches).

Variation.—No subspecies have been described for this distinctive shiner. Evidently there is little, if any, geographic variation. The references to an unnamed variety and to different forms by Forbes & Richardson (1908:136) probably refer to the superficially similar weed shiner and ironcolor shiner, and their illustration of *Notropis heterodon* is really of *Notropis texanus*.

Blackchin shiner

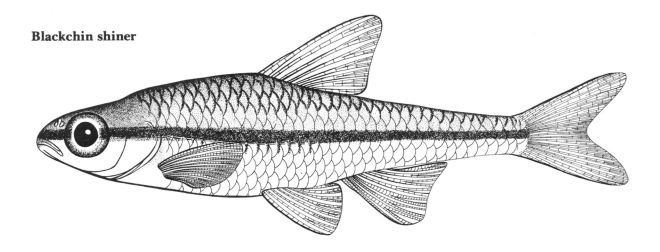

Ecology.—Schools of blackchin shiners abound in some of the clear, well-vegetated glacial lakes in northeastern Illinois. The species also occurs in streams entering or leaving these natural lakes. Forbes & Richardson (1908:136) reported that the food consisted primarily of minute crustaceans but that plant material and immatures of aquatic insects were also utilized. Their mention of May and June as the time of spawning in central Illinois refers to the weed shiner rather than the blackchin shiner. Hence, no details are available on the reproductive habits of this species.

Distribution.—This species occurs only in Cook and Lake counties and has probably never in historic times had a more extensive Illinois range. As noted under variation, the central and southern Illinois records of Forbes & Richardson were based on the weed shiner, and some of the stream records for northern Illinois may have been based on the ironcolor shiner. Although still common in a few of the glacial lakes, the blackchin shiner has disappeared from others, especially those highly modified by human disturbance.

Distribution of the blackchin shiner in Illinois.

Blacknose shiner
Notropis heterolepis Eigenmann & Eigenmann

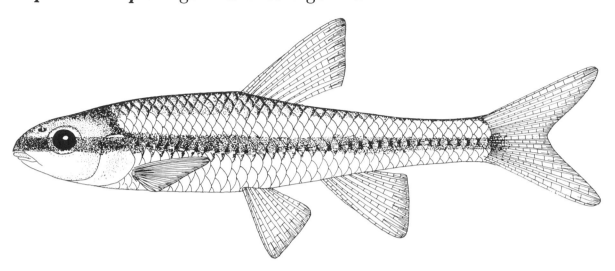

Notropis heterolepis Eigenmann & Eigenmann 1893:
    152 (type-locality: Fort Quappelle [= Qu'Ap-
    pelle], Saskatchewan); Smith 1965:7.
Notropis cayuga: Large 1903:16 (recorded from Illi-
    nois); Forbes & Richardson 1908:133.
Notropis cayuga atrocaudalis: Forbes & Richardson
    1908:134.
?Hybopsis atrocaudalis: O'Donnell 1935:482.
Hybopsis heterolepis: O'Donnell 1935:481.

Diagnosis. — The blacknose shiner is a slender
and terete shiner, grayish olive above and silvery
beneath, with a distinct black lateral band extending from the caudal peduncle to the tip of the
snout but not touching the tip of the chin, black
vertical crescents within the lateral band, eight anal
rays, 34–38 lateral-line scales, 4—4 pharyngeal
teeth, the eye rounded (diameter contained three
or more times in head length), the mouth small
and horizontal with the mandible and maxillary extensively fused proximally, the dorsal fin pointed
and situated over the pelvic fin insertions, and with
dorsal scales boldly edged with melanophores. The
species is most similar to the pallid shiner but differs from it in having a smaller and round eye,
rounded predorsal scales, and vertical black crescents within the lateral band. It does not occur with
the pallid shiner but does occur with the blackchin,
weed, and ironcolor shiners, from which the blacknose shiner can be distinguished by the lack of
black pigment on the tip of the chin. The young
blacknose shiner differs from young of other similar species in the same characters that distinguish
the adult. The species attains a length of 65 mm
(2½ inches).

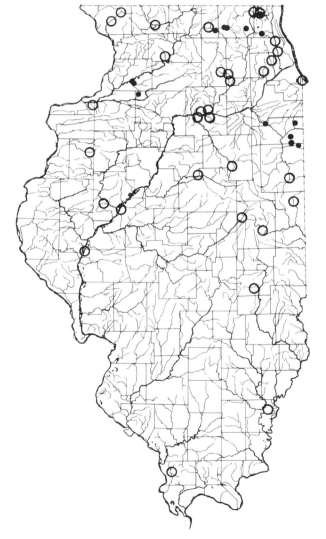

Distribution of the blacknose shiner in Illinois.

Variation.—Hubbs (1951:16 and elsewhere) has commented on an unnamed southern subspecies of the blacknose shiner that should occur in central Illinois, but the species has been extirpated in all but the northern part of the state and no such specimens are available. The only named subspecies other than the nominate form is a localized population on Isle Royale that is known as *N. h. regalis* Hubbs & Lagler.

Ecology.—The blacknose shiner is disappearing in many parts of its range. In Illinois it occurs in some of the clear, well-vegetated glacial lakes and in a few of the clear, sand-bottomed streams. Its decimation is due primarily to siltation, and it has been unable to exist in highly turbid waters with silty bottoms and in waters that lack aquatic vegeta-tion. Its feeding and reproductive habits are poorly known. The small horizontal mouth suggests that the species feeds on minute forms of benthos and minute arthropods that live in beds of aquatic vegetation. Forbes & Richardson (1908:133) reported that spawning in Illinois occurs between 5 June and 1 August.

Distribution.—The species formerly occurred throughout the northern two-thirds of the state and was probably common in the prairie swales and natural lakes before they were drained. It is still found in some of the glacial lakes of Lake County and in some of the clear streams in extensive sand areas. Elsewhere it is extremely sporadic and uncommon.

Bluehead shiner
Notropis hubbsi Bailey & Robison

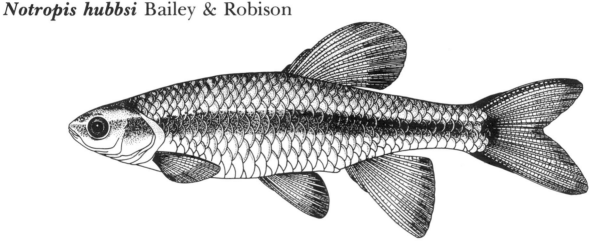

Notropis hubbsi Bailey & Robison 1978:1 (type-locality: Locust Bayou, tributary of Ouachita River, 1 km W of Locust Bayou, Calhoun County, Arkansas).

Diagnosis.—The bluehead shiner is a slab-sided shiner, olive above and white below with a distinct narrow black stripe extending from the tip of the snout and lower jaw backward to a prominent caudal spot; the dorsal fin rays and membranes closely stippled with melanophores; an extremely convex dorsal fin in the breeding male situated just behind the pelvic fin insertions; diamond-shaped scales and 34–36 scales in the lateral series (lateral line absent); dorsal rays, 9 or 10; pharyngeal teeth 2, 4—4, 2; a rather small and sharply upturned mouth; and a moderate-sized eye, the diameter of which is about equal to the length of the lower jaw.

The breeding male is amber above with bright blue on top of the head and orange on the fins. The species superficially resembles the young of the golden shiner but differs in many ways (larger scales, more dorsal rays, no lateral line, and no midventral keel). The bluehead shiner is unique among species of *Notropis* in having both the dorsal and anal fins with 9 or 10 rays. It attains a length of about 65 mm (2½ inches).

Variation.—The only account of variation in this newly described species is the original description (Bailey & Robison 1978). The fry tend to have longitudinal black stripes, two down the back and one along each side. Larger young have the pattern of the adult.

Ecology.—Known in Illinois only from an oxbow of the Big Muddy River in Union County, the first specimens of this species were found in lotus beds in rather deep water by William M. Lewis and Gerald E. Gunning of Southern Illinois University in the middle 1950's. The specimens were sent to Reeve M. Bailey of the University of Michigan for identification. Subsequently Dr. Bailey located additional specimens of the new species from Arkansas and a lake in Texas, and Henry W. Robison of Southern Arkansas University discovered several additional localities in the lowlands of Arkansas. In 1973, Larry M. Page and Brooks M. Burr of the Illinois Natural History Survey found two adults with some breeding color (red tails) and 21 fry ranging in total length from 14 to 20 mm in lotus beds near the shore. In late July they collected two more adults without breeding color and 19 fry ranging in length from 18 to 26 mm. In late August they found no adults but collected 144 young ranging from 22 to 38 mm in total length. In September and October no specimens could be found, but in late November a young specimen 44 mm long was taken by dip net from a lotus bed. Subsequently two railroad tank cars derailed into the lake, spilling toxic fluid that caused a massive fish and vegetation kill. No specimens of the bluehead shiner have been seen since.

Distribution.—This shiner is known in Illinois only from Wolf Lake in western Union County.

Distribution of the bluehead shiner in Illinois.

Spottail shiner
Notropis hudsonius (Clinton)

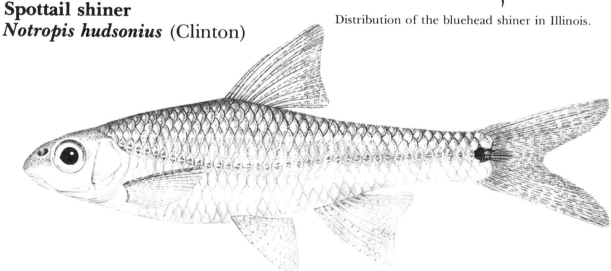

Clupea hudsonia Clinton 1824:49 (type-locality: Albany and Hudson River).
Hybopsis hudsonius: Nelson 1876:46 (recorded from Illinois); O'Donnell 1935:482.

Alburnops hudsonius: Jordan 1878:56.
Notropis hudsonius: Forbes 1884:77; Large 1903:17; Forbes & Richardson 1908:141–143; Smith 1965:7.

Diagnosis.—The spottail shiner is a somewhat slab-sided shiner, light olive above and silvery or white beneath, with a large black spot on the caudal peduncle, eight anal rays, 36–40 lateral-line scales, rather falcate dorsal and anal fins, the dorsal fin slightly in advance of the pelvic fin insertions, a nearly horizontal mouth, a rather large eye, the ventral edge of the caudal fin milky white, and variable pharyngeal teeth (most often 2, 4—4, 2). The species most closely resembles the blacktail shiner (but does not occur with it), differing in lacking black pigment in the dorsal fin rays and having an anteriorly placed dorsal fin. Occasional specimens of the spottail shiner have the caudal spot poorly developed and resemble the sympatric emerald shiner. The spottail shiner has a stouter body, fewer anal rays, and the dorsal fin ahead rather than behind the pelvic fin insertions. The young resembles that of the bluntnose and suckermouth minnows but differs from them in generic characters. The spottail shiner attains a length of more than 130 mm (5 inches).

Variation.—Hubbs & Lagler (1958:82) recognized four subspecies, one of which (an unnamed race) occurs in all of the Great Lakes except Superior. Most other recent authors do not recognize any subspecies. The spottail shiner in Lake Michigan averages generally larger than the river and small-lake form and frequently lacks the prominent black caudal spot. It appears otherwise inseparable from the spottail shiner of the Mississippi River drainage.

Ecology.—The spottail shiner is a minnow of natural lakes and large rivers and is seldom found in other waters. In Lake Michigan large schools occur near the shoreline. According to Forbes & Richardson (1908:143), it feeds on a variety of items, including algae, higher plants, and both terrestrial and aquatic invertebrates. No information is available on its reproductive habits.

Distribution.—The spottail shiner is abundant in shallow waters of Lake Michigan and in the Rock, Illinois, and Mississippi rivers, but it is sporadic in the Mississippi below the mouth of the Missouri River. Formerly, when water levels were more stable, the species ascended tributary streams for greater distances than it does at present. Most tributaries now become too low during late summer and fall to provide suitable habitat for a large-river species.

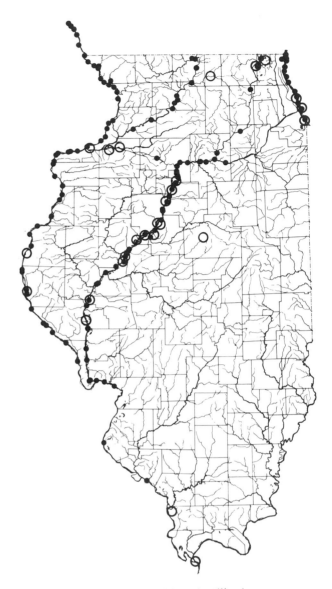

Distribution of the spottail shiner in Illinois.

Red shiner
Notropis lutrensis (Baird & Girard)

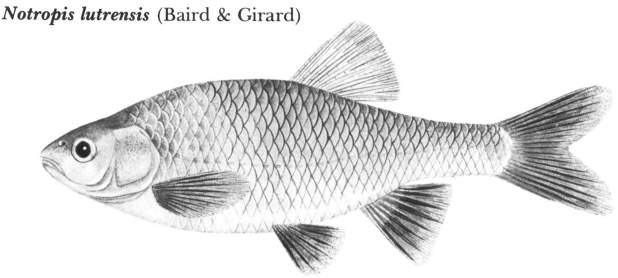

Leuciscus lutrensis Baird & Girard 1853*b*:391 (type-locality: Otter Creek [tributary of North Fork of Red River], Arkansas).
Cyprinella forbesi Jordan 1878:57 (type-locality: southern Illinois).
Notropis lutrensis: Forbes 1884:77; Large 1903: 17; Forbes & Richardson 1908:143–145; Smith 1965:7.
Cyprinella lutrensis: O'Donnell 1935:482.

Diagnosis.—The red shiner is an extremely deep-bodied and compressed shiner, tan or bluish silvery on the back and sides (males have bright blue bodies and brilliant red fins), with the interradial membranes of the dorsal fin uniformly pigmented with melanophores, a prominent dark scapular bar, usually nine anal rays, 32–36 lateral-line scales, diamond-shaped scales on its upper sides, 4—4 pharyngeal teeth, a bluntly rounded snout, a small eye situated equidistant between the top and bottom of the head, the dorsal fin convex and located slightly behind the pelvic fin insertions, and a terminal oblique mouth. In coloration the red shiner resembles the redfin shiner, but they are separable by the red shiner's much larger scales, well-developed scapular bar, and fewer anal rays. It resembles the related steelcolor shiner but has a much deeper body than that species (depth contained 3–3.5 times in standard length), a blunter snout, and no dark blotch on the posterior rays of the dorsal fin. The young resembles those of these same species and of the spotfin shiner, but it can be distinguished from them by its blunter head and its eye position. The species attains a length of almost 75 mm (3 inches).

Variation.—Considerable geographic variation is evident in this wide-ranging species, particularly in eye size, body color, and body depth, and both subspecies and synonyms have been described. Because of the overlap of many characteristics and the likelihood that some of them are environmentally produced, most present authors do not recognize subspecies.

Ecology.—The adaptable and aggressive red shiner prefers creeks with moderate flow and bottom materials of sand or mixed sand-silt-gravel, but it is extremely tolerant of turbidity, siltation, and fluctuating water levels. It is abundant in the relatively unstable streams of prairie and heavily farmed regions. Its food presumably consists of both terrestrial and aquatic invertebrates. Spawning occurs from late May into August. The brightly colored and densely tuberculate males and whitish distended females congregate in pools below riffles or in other rather quiet waters, such as those near submerged logs or brush. Eggs, which average more than 1,000 per female, are fertilized and settle to the bottom, where they adhere to various objects. Spawning over sunfish nests was reported by Minckley (1959:421–422). Young fish are more than 25 mm (1 inch) long at the end of their first season. Lewis & Gunning (1959), who misidentified the species as the steelcolor shiner, reported that it has a life span of no more than 2 years and that 2-year-old fish spawn in July and 1-year-old fish in late August and early September.

Distribution.—The red shiner is abundant in creeks and small rivers throughout Illinois except in the Wabash drainage and the northern and northeastern counties. An adult specimen from Channel Lake in Lake County is regarded as a bait-minnow introduction and is not plotted on the accompanying map. The species has gradually spread eastward across Illinois (Larimore & Smith 1963:332–333) and recently entered Indiana; still more recently it has penetrated the Wabash drainage in the upper reaches of the Middle Fork. It has hybridized with and ultimately supplanted the spotfin shiner in much of central Illinois and has displaced the steelcolor shiner to a lesser extent (Page & R. L. Smith 1970:271–272). In Clear Creek in southwestern Illinois, the red shiner and blacktail shiner have hybridized occasionally for many years. The red shiner is rare in ponds and artificial lakes and rather uncommon in large rivers although it does occur in the Mississippi River. Because of its wide ecological tolerances, the species is more generally distributed and more abundant than formerly. It has filled niches vacated by less tolerant minnows and through competition and hybridization has displaced populations of some of its relatives.

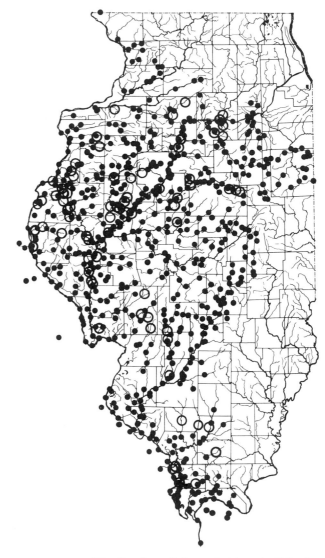

Distribution of the red shiner in Illinois.

Rosyface shiner
Notropis rubellus (Agassiz)

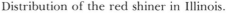

Alburnus rubellus Agassiz 1850:364 (type-locality: Sault Ste. Marie and the Pic [Ontario], Lake Superior).

Minnilus rubrifrons: Nelson 1876:47 (recorded from Illinois).

Notropis rubrifrons: Jordan 1878:60; Large 1903:18; Forbes & Richardson 1908:153–154; O'Donnell 1935:482.

Notropis dinemus: Forbes 1884:76 (part.).

Notropis rubellus: Smith 1965:7.

Diagnosis.—The rosyface shiner is an extremely slender and somewhat compressed shiner with a long and sharply pointed snout (longer than eye diameter), a bluish or greenish dorsum, an intense dusky lateral band, a silvery or white venter, 10–13 anal rays, 2, 4—4, 2 pharyngeal teeth, 36–40 lateral-line scales, a rounded dorsal fin situated well behind the pelvic fin insertions, fewer than 25 rows of predorsal scales, a large terminal and oblique mouth, and in the breeding male bright orange on the head, gill cleft margin, and pectoral fin bases. The species most closely resembles the emerald shiner, differing from it by the longer and sharply pointed snout and by the rounded rather than pointed dorsal fin. The young superficially resembles that of the redfin and ribbon shiners but can be distinguished from them by the snout shape, the larger predorsal scales (fewer than 25 rows), and by the gently decurved lateral line. The species attains a length of about 75 mm (3 inches).

Variation.—No studies of geographic variation have been published, and the rosyface shiner is currently regarded as a monotypic species. A closely related species (*N. micropteryx*) of Tennessee may be conspecific.

Ecology.—The rosyface shiner occurs in clear, fast large creeks and small rivers with bottoms of clean gravel. It schools in riffles and clear pools with silt-free substrates. Spawning occurs in May and probably early June. The finely tuberculate males have bright orange heads. The species aggregates in clear, clean-bottomed pools, and the males vigorously pursue and collide with the plain females. During these contacts, eggs are released and fertilized. Pfeiffer (1955) reported spawning in New York when water temperatures were between 21° and 25° C and described the spawning behavior in detail. The egg averages 1.5 mm in diameter. The rosyface shiner has been reported spawning over nests of common shiners, hornyhead chubs, and sunfishes by various authors. The food of the species, according to Starrett (1950), consists of aquatic and terrestrial invertebrates, bottom ooze, and some plant material.

Distribution.—The rosyface shiner occurs in large gravelly and clear streams throughout the northeastern counties of the state. It is intolerant of turbidity and silt and probably cannot stand high water temperatures during the summer months. Its range in Illinois is much the same as it has always been, but it is disappearing from streams that have been modified by impoundments and excessive siltation in recent years.

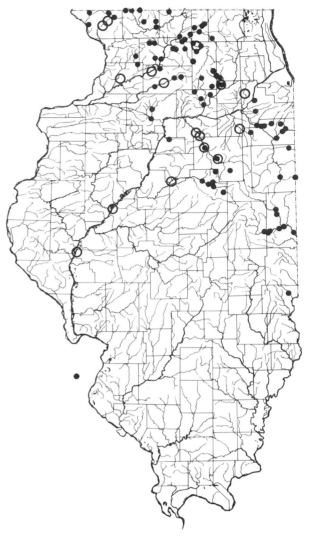

Distribution of the rosyface shiner in Illinois.

Silverband shiner
Notropis shumardi (Girard)

Alburnops shumardi Girard 1856:194 (type-locality: Arkansas River near Fort Smith, Arkansas).
Notropis illecebrosa: Hubbs & Bonham 1951:97 (recorded from Illinois).
Notropis shumardi: Smith 1965:7.

Diagnosis.—The silverband shiner is a nondescript pale olive minnow with a vague dusky lateral band over which is laid a silvery band; a rather slab-sided body; eight or nine anal rays; a large sharply pointed dorsal fin situated distinctly in advance of the pelvic fin insertions; 34–37 lateral-line scales; 2, 4—4, 2 pharyngeal teeth; a terminal and sharply oblique mouth; immaculate fins; and a thin

Silverband shiner

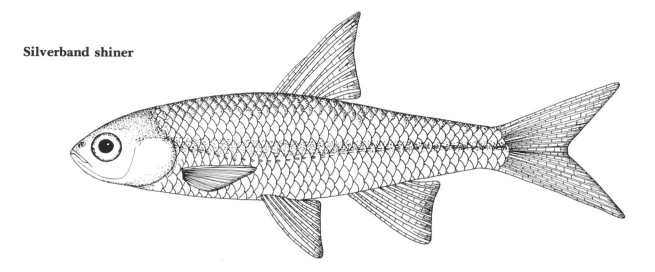

predorsal stripe. The species resembles a chubby emerald shiner but can be distinguished by the anteriorly placed dorsal fin and fewer anal rays. It bears an amazing resemblance to the cypress minnow (*Hybognathus hayi*) but lacks the long, much coiled gut of that species. The young resembles the ghost shiner but lacks the elevated lateral-line scales. The species attains a length of 65 mm (2½ inches).

Variation.—Gilbert & Bailey (1962) summarized all of the information known at the time about this rare fish, resurrected the name *shumardi* to replace *illecebrosus*, and synonymized *brazosensis* of Texas under *shumardi*. No subspecies are recognizable.

Ecology.—The silverband shiner is restricted to large-river habitats and ascends only slight distances up major tributaries of the great rivers. It occurs in flowing water over bottoms of sand and fine gravel. Its tolerance for extremely turbid conditions was cited by Gilbert & Bailey (1962:817), but its greater abundance in the Mississippi River below the mouth of the Ohio suggests that the diluting effect of the Ohio River favors the species. The species is not abundant but rather general in occurrence in the large rivers. Its feeding and reproductive habits are unknown.

Distribution.—Since this minnow was not known until recently, there is no evidence of changes in its range and abundance in the state. It presently occurs in the lower reaches of the Illinois and Mississippi rivers but is more common in the Ohio River.

Distribution of the silverband shiner in Illinois.

Spotfin shiner
Notropis spilopterus (Cope)

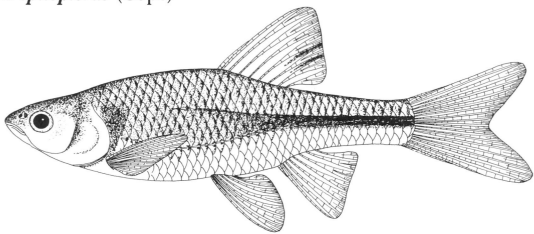

Photogenis spilopterus Cope 1866:378 (type-locality:
St. Joseph River, southwestern Michigan).
Cyprinella galacturus: Nelson 1876:47 (part., re-
corded from Illinois).
Photogenis analostanus: Jordan 1878:57 (part.).
Notropis whipplei: Forbes 1884:77 (part.).
Notropis whipplii: Large 1903:17 (part.); Forbes &
Richardson 1908:145–147 (part.).
Cyprinella whipplii: O'Donnell 1935:482 (part.).
Notropis spilopterus hypsisomatus Gibbs 1957*b*:195
(type-locality: Wonder Lake—bay in north end,
McHenry County, Illinois).
Notropis spilopterus (Cope) subspecies: Smith 1965:
7.

Diagnosis.—The spotfin shiner is a compressed
and bluish-silvery shiner with a dusky lateral band;
a pointed snout; a small eye; a black blotch in the
posterior rays of the dorsal fin; a dorsal fin situated
slightly behind the pelvic fin insertions; scales on
the sides of the body diamond shaped and sharply
outlined with melanophores; modally eight anal
rays; 35–40 lateral-line scales; usually 1, 4—4, 1
pharyngeal teeth; the membranes of the dorsal fin
clear with melanophores restricted to the margins
of the fin rays and to the posterior blotch (except
in the breeding male, which has entire dorsal fin
blackened); other fins of the breeding male yellow; and nuptial tubercles of breeding males only
slightly smaller on the nape than on the top of the
head. The spotfin is exceedingly similar to the
steelcolor shiner, differing from that species in
having eight rather than nine anal rays, the melanophores in the anterior dorsal fin restricted to
the ray margins, a more pronounced dusky lateral
band, and 14 or fewer pectoral rays, and in lacking

the extremely convex margin (flag) of the dorsal
fin in the breeding male. The spotfin differs from
the red shiner in having a more attenuate body, a
blotch in the posterior rays of the dorsal fin, a more
pointed snout, and yellow rather than red fins in
the male. The young resembles young of these
species and can best be distinguished from them by
the anal ray count, body shape, and presence of
melanophores only along the margins of the dorsal
fin rays. The species attains a length of 100 mm (4
inches).

Variation.—An excellent account of variation in
the species was published by Gibbs (1957*b*), who
described a western subspecies (*hypsisomatus*) having a relatively deeper body and 36 or 37 lateral-
line scales rather than 38–40. The resemblance of
this subspecies to the red shiner led Forbes & Richardson (1908:146) and Thompson (1935:493) to
regard Illinois specimens as hybrids between these
species. Proof that hybrid swarms of *spilopterus* X
lutrensis do occur in Illinois has been provided by
Page & R. L. Smith (1970).

Ecology.—The spotfin shiner occurs chiefly in
large creeks and small rivers but sometimes is
found in smaller populations in large rivers and
even lakes and reservoirs. The preferred habitat is
clear raceways over gravel pools with some current
and with a firm substrate of mixed gravel, sand,
and silt. Where it occurs, it is usually an abundant minnow. Forbes & Richardson (1908:146)
described the food of *"Notropis whipplii,"* which
included the spotfin shiner, as consisting of terrestrial and aquatic insects, aquatic and terrestrial vegetable materials, and small fishes. Starrett (1950)

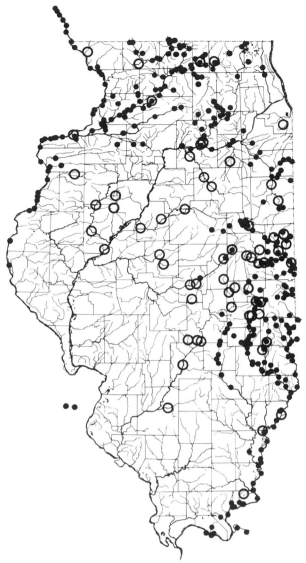

Distribution of the spotfin shiner in Illinois.

found the same items in the stomachs of Iowa specimens. White & Wallace (1973) found that the peak of feeding in the Huron River occurred just before dusk and that ants were important food items in the evening. In Ohio streams Pflieger (1965) observed spawning from early June until mid-August with a peak in June and early July. Submerged logs with loosely adhering bark and exposed tree roots near riffles were chosen for spawning, and eggs were secreted under the bark of newly inundated logs and in crevices. The same author compared the spawning development and behavior of the spotfin and steelcolor shiners, and he surmised that turbidity was a factor contributing to occasional hybridization with other species, since visual species recognition is essential to intraspecific spawning.

Distribution.—The spotfin shiner was once virtually statewide in Illinois although sporadic in occurrence in the western and southern parts of the state. It is now restricted to northern and eastern Illinois, but it follows the Mississippi and Wabash rivers southward for somewhat greater distances. The reasons for its decimation over most of Illinois are habitat alteration and the inability to compete with the allied red shiner. Page & R. L. Smith (1970) have shown that the red shiner hybridizes with the spotfin shiner and ultimately supplants it in areas highly modified by agricultural practices.

Sand shiner
Notropis stramineus (Cope)

Hybopsis stramineus Cope 1864:283 (type-locality: Detroit River, Grosse Isle, Michigan); Nelson 1876:46 (recorded from Illinois).
Alburnops stramineus: Jordan 1878:57.

Notropis stramineus: Forbes 1884:58.
Notropis blennius: Large 1903:17 (part.); Forbes & Richardson 1908:137–138 (part.).
Notropis phenacobius Forbes 1884:78 (*nomen nudum*); Forbes 1885:137 (type-locality: Peoria, Illinois); Forbes & Richardson 1908:138–139.
Hybopsis volucellus: O'Donnell 1935:481.
Hybopsis deliciosus: O'Donnell 1935:481.
Notropis stramineus stramineus: Smith 1965:7.

Diagnosis.—The sand shiner is a terete straw-colored shiner with silvery sides and venter, a distinctly punctate and complete lateral line, usually seven anal rays, 34–38 lateral-line scales, 4—4 pharyngeal teeth, a rather small mouth, a relatively large eye, and a middorsal dark stripe that is expanded into a wedge-shaped blotch in front of the dorsal fin origin and that does not encircle the dorsal fin base, and without elevated lateral-line scales, bright colors on the body and fins, and dark crescent-shaped markings between the nostrils. The sand shiner closely resembles the mimic and bigmouth shiners. The sand shiner differs from both of these fishes in having only seven anal rays rather than eight, a discrete middorsal dark stripe that terminates in a wedge-shaped blotch in front of the dorsal fin, and a pointed snout (when viewed from above) rather than a rounded snout. It further differs from the mimic shiner in lacking elevated lateral-line scales and widened middorsal scales and from the bigmouth shiner in having a rounded head in cross section rather than one that is flattened ventrally and eyes directed laterally rather than dorsolaterally, and in lacking dark crescents between the nostrils. The sand shiner differs from the river shiner in having a much smaller mouth, more pronounced lateral-line pore punctations, and a dark middorsal stripe interrupted at the dorsal fin rather than surrounding it. It differs from the bigeye shiner in having a smaller eye and a rounded dorsal fin, and in lacking the discrete black marking on the side of the snout. The young differs from young of these species by the same characters that distinguish the adult. The species attains a length of about 75 mm (3 inches).

Variation.—For many years this shiner was called *Notropis blennius,* a name applied to several similar, nondescript, and poorly known minnows. Hubbs (1926) resurrected Girard's name *deliciosa* for the sand shiner, and this name was widely used in the fishery literature until Suttkus (1958) pointed out that *deliciosa* was a junior synonym of *N. texanus* and that *stramineus* was the next oldest name for the species. Since that time authors have used *N.*

stramineus almost exclusively and have recognized two subspecies: *N. s. stramineus* in the eastern part of the range and *N. s. missuriensis* in the Great Plains.

Ecology.—The sand shiner occurs in permanent streams ranging in size from creeks to the Mississippi River and in clear natural and artificial lakes if they have bottoms of sand or gravel. However, it reaches its greatest abundance in large, fast-flowing creeks with bottoms of mixed gravel and sand and is seldom, if ever, found in turbid streams flowing over clay or silt. Despite its wide occurrence and abundance, little information is available on its reproductive habits. Spawning is presumed to occur from late spring until early fall although Starrett (1951) found that the greatest spawning

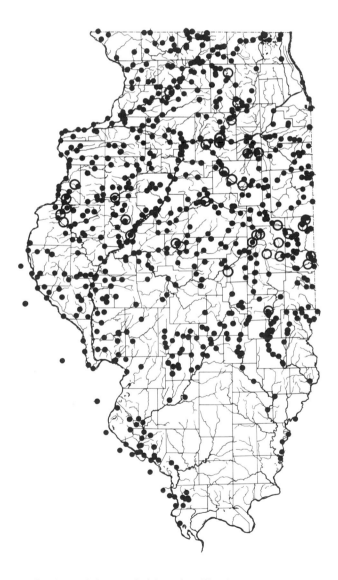

Distribution of the sand shiner in Illinois.

activity in the Des Moines River of Iowa occurred in August and early September. According to Starrett (1950), the sand shiner feeds on a variety of plant and animal items, but the fry and adults in the summer months feed heavily on microflora (bottom ooze); the adult at other seasons feeds primarily on aquatic insects.

Distribution.—The sand shiner is abundant throughout the northern four-fifths of Illinois but is absent in the low-gradient streams of the south-central counties and in the streams of the Shawnee Hills and Coastal Plain Province. In extreme southern Illinois it occurs only in the tributaries of the Mississippi River on the western side of the state. Its overall range in Illinois is probably unchanged since it was first recorded here, but it is likely that the species was even more abundant in northern and central Illinois before pollution and siltation deteriorated the quality of many streams in those parts of the state.

Weed shiner
Notropis texanus (Girard)

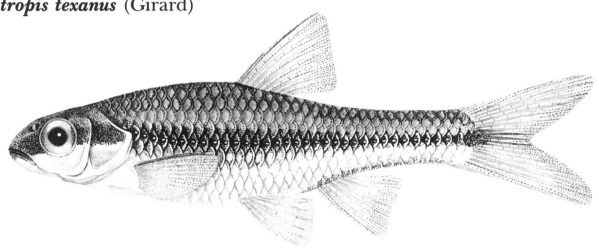

Cyprinella texana Girard 1856:198 (type-locality: Rio Salado and Turkey Creek, Texas).
Hemitremia heterodon: Jordan 1878:62 (?part.).
Notropis heterodon: Forbes 1884:78 (part.); Forbes & Richardson 1908:134–136 (part.; specimen figured is *N. texanus*, presumably from Illinois).
Hybopsis nux richardsoni: O'Donnell 1935:482.
Notropis texanus: Smith 1965:7.

Diagnosis.—The weed shiner is a terete straw-colored shiner with an intense black lateral stripe extending onto the snout and the tip of the chin; a diffuse light-colored stripe just above the black lateral band; several scales below the black lateral stripe outlined with melanophores; the posterior rays of the anal fin often margined with melanophores; usually seven anal rays; the dorsal fin origin in advance of the pelvic fin insertions; pharyngeal teeth usually 2, 4—4, 2; 34–37 lateral-line scales; the mouth moderate in size and somewhat oblique; and a broad black predorsal stripe. This species is the only black-striped shiner with seven anal rays except for the pugnose shiner, which differs in having a small and nearly vertical mouth and a black peritoneum. The weed shiner closely resembles the ironcolor shiner and often occurs with it but can be distinguished from that species by the lower anal ray count and the presence of melanophores around some of the scales below the black lateral stripe. The young differs from the young of similar species by the same characters that distinguish adults. The species attains a length of slightly more than 65 mm (2½ inches).

Variation.—Within the last 25 years this species has been referred to as *xaenocephalus*, *nux*, *roseus*, *aletes*, and *richardsoni*. Its status and correct name now seem to be settled, and a thorough study of geographic variation, as yet unpublished, has been done by Dr. Camm C. Swift, then at Florida State University. Populations in Illinois are more variable than those on the Gulf Coast, and one of the species' key characters (posterior rays of the anal fin margined with melanophores, anterior rays plain) is not always reliable in Illinois specimens.

Distribution of the weed shiner in Illinois.

Redfin shiner
Notropis umbratilis (Girard)

Alburnops umbratilis Girard 1856:193 (type-locality: Sugar Loaf Creek, tributary of Poteau River, near Fort Smith, Arkansas).

Lythrurus diplaemius: Nelson 1876:47 (recorded from Illinois).

Lythrurus cyanocephalus: Nelson 1876:47 (*nomen nudum*).

Lythrurus cyanocephalus Copeland *in* Jordan 1877c: 70 (type-locality: Root River, tributary of Rock River, Racine County [Wisconsin]); Jordan 1878:59.

Lythrurus diplaemius: Jordan 1878:59.

Lythrurus diplaemius var. *gracilis:* Forbes *in* Jordan 1878:59.

Lythrurus atripes Jordan 1878:59 (type-locality: streams in Union and Johnson counties [Illinois]).

Notropis atripes: Forbes 1884:76.

?*Notropis macrolepidotus:* Forbes 1884:76 (part., *nomen nudum*).

?*Notropis macrolepidotus* Forbes 1885:12 (part., type-locality not stated but somewhere in Illinois; type lost and description equally applicable to the ribbon shiner).

Notropis umbratilis: Large 1903:18.

Notropis umbratilis atripes: Forbes & Richardson 1908:154–156.

Lythrurus umbratilis cyanocephalus: O'Donnell 1935: 482.

Notropis umbratilis (Girard) subspecies: Smith 1965: 7.

Ecology.—The weed shiner is most common in sand-bottomed creeks with some submerged aquatic vegetation. Outside Illinois it is also known to occupy sloughs and large rivers (the Mississippi). Its feeding and reproductive habits are virtually unknown. Collections taken in Kankakee County in late August contained males with dense but minute tubercles and females distended with eggs.

Distribution.—The weed shiner is extremely rare everywhere in Illinois except in some tributaries of the Kankakee River in Kankakee and Iroquois counties. It was evidently more widespread in northern and central Illinois in the last century but probably never was an abundant minnow in Illinois. The principal likely reasons for its decline are siltation and the general deterioration of water quality.

Diagnosis.—The redfin shiner is a deep-bodied, slab-sided, whitish shiner with small and closely crowded predorsal scales in 25 or more rows; a strongly decurved lateral line; lateral-line scales in 38 or more rows; the dorsal ray origin distinctly behind the pelvic fin insertions; 10 or more anal rays; pharyngeal teeth 2, 4—4, 2; an intense black spot at the origin of the dorsal fin; scales on the upper sides and in the predorsal region uniformly pigmented and not outlined by peripheral melanophores; and the greatest body depth of the adult going less than four times into the standard length. The breeding male has a bright blue body, red fins, and white or pale gray on the top of the head and is suggestive of the unrelated red shiner, which has much larger scales. The species most closely resembles the ribbon shiner, with which it occurs, and is distinguishable (as an adult) from that species by its deeper body, smaller eye, black spot at the dorsal fin origin, and uniform pigmentation on

Redfin shiner

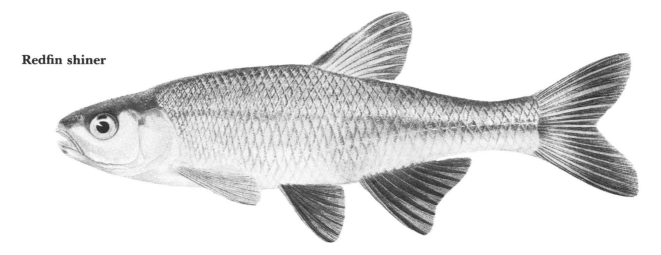

the upper sides. The young is whitish with round melanophores in the middle predorsal region that tend to be in regular rows. It can usually be distinguished from the young of the ribbon shiner by the predorsal spot and predorsal pigmentation. The young also resembles that of the more slender and larger-scaled emerald shiner. The species attains a length of about 75 mm (3 inches).

Variation.—Snelson and Pflieger (1975) analyzed geographic variation in the Mississippi Valley and found two distinctive subspecies. That in Illinois is *N. u. cyanocephalus.*

Ecology.—The redfin shiner inhabits clear, low-gradient creeks, but it is tolerant of a considerable amount of turbidity and silt. In streams it is most abundant in pool habitats where there is little or no current. It is a schooling species that often is the most abundant fish in silt-bottomed pools. Nothing is known of its feeding habits. Hunter & Wisby (1961) gave a detailed description of redfin shiners using green sunfish nests for spawning. They noted large schools of shiners appearing over the nests, especially those guarded by the male sunfish. Several spawning males pursued a female until she was in or above a sunfish nest, and the fertilized eggs dropped into the gravel of the nest alongside the sunfish eggs. In most cases, the guarding male sunfish permitted the intrusion of redfin shiners but drove off other fishes. In eastern Illinois, redfin shiners spawn over nests of longear sunfish.

Distribution.—The redfin shiner is statewide in distribution and extremely abundant in eastern and southern Illinois. It is somewhat sporadic in western and extreme northeastern Illinois. In both areas it was once more generally distributed. Its disappearance from some stream systems may be due to a combination of siltation and pollution.

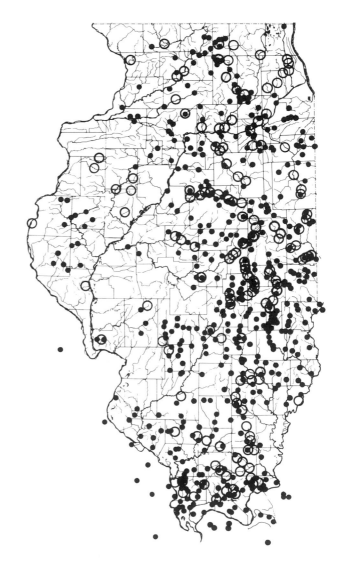

Distribution of the redfin shiner in Illinois.

Blacktail shiner
Notropis venustus (Girard)

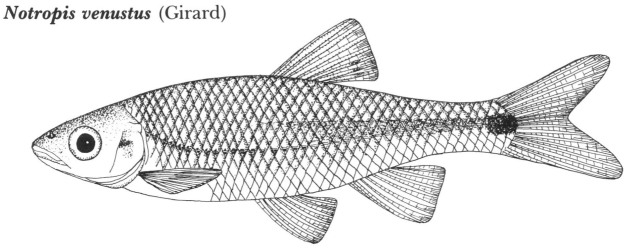

Cyprinella venusta Girard 1856:198 (type-locality: Rio Sabinal, Texas).
Notropis venustus: Bailey, Winn, & Smith 1954:28 (recorded from Illinois).
Notropis venustus venustus: Smith 1965:7.

Diagnosis.—The blacktail shiner is a slab-sided and bluish-silvery shiner with a large black squarish blotch on the caudal peduncle; a dusky lateral band on the posterior part of the body; the dorsal fin well pigmented and becoming darker posteriorly but without an evident spot; the preopercle and subopercle lightly pigmented; a pointed snout; the dorsal fin origin slightly behind the pelvic fin insertions; diamond-shaped scales outlined with melanophores on the anterior portion of the body; the mouth relatively large and oblique; 36–39 lateral-line scales; anal rays modally 8; pharyngeal teeth usually 1, 4—4, 1; and a moderate-sized eye (about equal to snout length). The blacktail shiner bears a superficial resemblance to the spottail shiner of northern Illinois but is more slab-sided, has diamond-shaped scales and a pointed snout, and occurs only in extreme southern Illinois. Among cohabiting species the blacktail shiner is most like the spotfin and steelcolor shiners but differs from both in usually having a conspicuous black caudal spot and in lacking a discrete spot in the dorsal fin. The blacktail and red shiners hybridize in the Clear Creek drainage of Union County, and intermediates between these species are sometimes found. The young is as distinctive as the adult and can be distinguished from other minnows with a caudal spot by its slab-sided body and pointed snout. The species attains a length of over 100 mm (4 inches).

Distribution of the blacktail shiner in Illinois.

Variation.—A thorough account of variation in the species has been published by Gibbs (1957*a*), who recognized three subspecies: *venustus, cercostigma,* and *stigmaturus.* The wide-ranging *venustus* is the subspecies occurring from southern Illinois to Texas.

Ecology.—The blacktail shiner occurs in clear, rather fast-flowing streams with sand as the predominant bottom type. Its food is unknown, and the meager information available on its reproduction consists of an account of repeated hybridizing of the species with the red shiner in Texas (Hubbs & Strawn 1956). These species hybridize in the only stream within Illinois in which the blacktail shiner is known to occur, and, although hybridization has been occurring for many years, hybridization and the increased rate of modification of the stream in recent years may result in the extirpation of the blacktail shiner before long.

Distribution.—Within Illinois the species is known only from Clear Creek in Union and Alexander counties, but it also occurs in the Ohio River and is extremely abundant in the drainage canals in the Missouri bootheel.

Mimic shiner
Notropis volucellus (Cope)

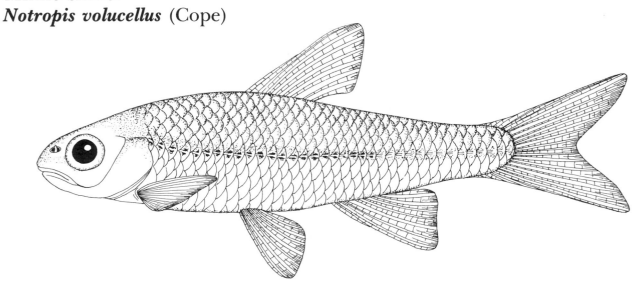

Hybognathus volucella Cope 1864:283 (type-locality: Detroit River, Grosse Isle, Michigan).
?*Hybopsis volucellus:* Nelson 1876:46 (possible misapplication of name to another species).
?*Alburnops volucellus:* Jordan 1878:57 (possible misapplication of name to another species).
Notropis volucellus: Large 1903:15 (not certainly known in Illinois).
Notropis deliciosus: Hubbs 1926:43 (recorded from Illinois; believed to be a senior synonym of *volucellus*).
?*Hybopsis deliciosus:* O'Donnell 1935:481 (misapplication of name).
Notropis volucellus (Cope) subspecies: Smith 1965:8.

Diagnosis.—The mimic shiner is a terete shiner, straw-colored above and white below, with punctate lateral-line pores, a diffuse lateral band that does not extend onto the head, lateral-line scales somewhat elevated (about two times higher than long), the median row of predorsal scales wider than the paravertebrals, anal rays modally 8, 35–37 lateral-line scales, pharyngeal teeth 4—4, the snout broadly rounded in dorsal profile, the dorsal fin rounded and situated over the pelvic fin insertions, the mouth subterminal and horizontal, and a rather large protruding eye that is directed laterally. The species resembles the sand shiner but differs from it in having eight rather than seven anal rays, a broadly rounded rather than a pointed snout, and elevated lateral-line scales. It differs from the bigmouth shiner in having the eyes directed laterally rather than dorsolaterally and in lacking dark crescents between the nostrils. It differs from the ghost shiner in having the lateral-line scales only moderately elevated, more pigment on the body, and a rounded dorsal fin. The young is superficially similar to the young silverband shiner but differs in having elevated lateral-line scales, a subterminal and horizontal mouth, and a punctate lateral line. The mimic shiner attains a length of about 65 mm (2½ inches).

Variation.—Hubbs & Greene (1928) showed that *"Notropis blennius"* of preceding authors was a composite of the sand shiner, mimic shiner, and ghost shiner. They resurrected *volucellus* from the synonymy for the mimic shiner and *buchanani* for the ghost shiner, which they believed to be a subspecies of the mimic shiner. Trautman (1931) described *Notropis volucellus wickliffi* as a subspecies within the range of the nominate subspecies but one that presumably was restricted to the channels of large rivers. The last named is currently recognized, but its status is uncertain. It may be specifically distinct from *volucellus* or may not be valid at all. Too few specimens of the nominate subspecies are known from Illinois to shed any light on the problem.

Ecology.—If *volucellus* and *wickliffi* are different taxa, the form *volucellus* occurs in a few glacial lakes in extreme northeastern Illinois and a few tributaries of the Wabash River. It is sporadic and rare. The form presumably referable to *wickliffi* is abundant in the Wabash, Ohio, and Mississippi (below the mouth of the Ohio) rivers and ascends short distances up a very few tributaries. Thus, a variety of aquatic habitats is encompassed. The key factor for *volucellus* seems to be clear water of high quality; that for *wickliffi,* channels of large rivers. Neither form is known from the Illinois River or the Mississippi River above the mouth of the Missouri. Speaking of *wickliffi* in southern Ohio, Trautman (1931) noted that schools ascended tributaries of the Ohio River in the spring to spawn. Cross (1967:138) found tuberculate males and females distended with eggs spawning over broad rocky riffles in July and August in Kansas. Presumably the Kansas form is also *wickliffi.* Although data on reproduction were not reported, Black (1945) described other aspects of the ecology of the form *volucellus* in a northern Indiana lake. Moyle (1973) noted that in a Minnesota lake *N. volucellus* fed in the mid-water and at the surface in large schools and did not compete appreciably with other common minnows in the lake. Its food consisted primarily of dipteran larvae and pupae, cladocerans, small terrestrial insects, and amphipods, the main type depending on the time of day that the fish were feeding. He believed that *volucellus* lives no longer than 3 years.

Distribution.—See ecology section. Since the mimic shiner was not recognized until 1928, no data are available on its former range and abundance. It is certain that the *volucellus* form is much decimated in the Midwest because of siltation and the deterioration of water quality. However, the *wickliffi* form is so abundant in the Wabash and Ohio rivers, that it is difficult to conceive of its ever being any more common in those rivers than it is now.

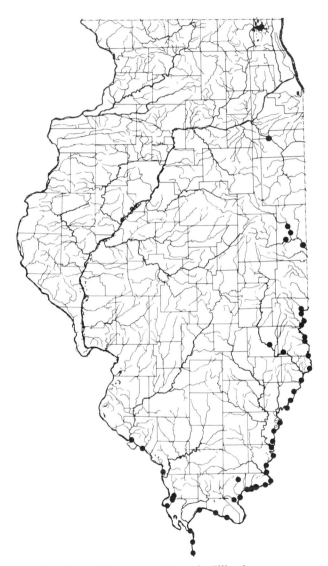

Distribution of the mimic shiner in Illinois.

Steelcolor shiner
Notropis whipplei (Girard)

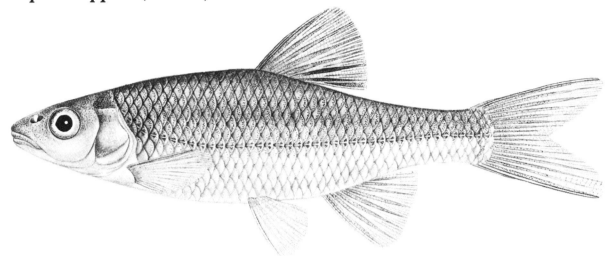

Cyprinella whipplii Girard 1856:198 (type-locality: Sugar Loaf Creek, tributary of Poteau River, near Fort Smith, Arkansas [Oklahoma]); O'Donnell 1935:482 (part.).

?*Cyprinella galacturus:* Nelson 1876:47 (part.).

Cyprinella analostanus: Jordan 1878:57 (part., recorded from Illinois but wrong name applied).

Notropis whipplei: Forbes 1884:77 (part.); Smith 1965:8.

Notropis whipplii: Large 1903:17 (part.); Forbes & Richardson 1908:145 (part.).

Diagnosis.—The steelcolor shiner is a compressed and bluish-silvery shiner with a faint lateral band on the caudal peduncle; usually a well-developed scapular bar; a pointed snout; a small eye; a black blotch in the posterior rays of the dorsal fin; the dorsal fin situated slightly behind the pelvic fin insertions; scales on the sides of the body diamond shaped and sharply outlined with melanophores; modally nine anal rays; 36–38 lateral-line scales; usually 1, 4—4, 1 pharyngeal teeth; the membranes of the dorsal fin well speckled with melanophores that do not outline the margins of the rays; usually 15 pectoral rays; the nape tubercles of the breeding male appreciably smaller than those on the head; the dorsal fin of the breeding male extremely convex and flaglike; bright yellow fins except for the blackened dorsal in the breeding male. The steelcolor shiner is most like the spotfin shiner, differing from it by possessing usually nine anal rays rather than eight, having the dorsal membranes well speckled with melanophores between rays, and having 15 rather than 14 or fewer pectoral rays. It differs from the red shiner in having a more attenuate body, a blotch in the posterior rays of the dorsal fin, and a more pointed snout, and in never having red fins. The young most closely resembles that of the same two species and can be distinguished from them by the same characters that separate adults. The steelcolor shiner attains a length of 130 mm (5 inches).

Variation.—Gibbs (1963) studied geographic variation throughout the range of the species and found no major genetic differentiation.

Ecology.—The steelcolor shiner occurs in clear, gravelly, large creeks and small rivers in central and southern Illinois. It prefers large riffles and pools just below them or eddies beside raceways, especially in relatively unmodified, tree-margined streams. Forbes & Richardson (1908:146) described the food of *"Notropis whipplii"* (also includes the spotfin shiner) as consisting of terrestrial and aquatic invertebrates and some vegetable matter. Pflieger (1965) described spawning similarities of the steelcolor and spotfin shiners in Ohio. Both selected submerged logs, especially those with loose bark or numerous crevices, and tree roots in portions of streams near riffles. Spawning occurred from early June until mid-August. Spawning adults were usually in their third year, sometimes in their second. Pflieger described the behavior in detail and suggested that sexual dimorphism and behavior kept the species from hybridizing except when the water was too turbid for the fish to see each other clearly. The spawning male of the steelcolor shiner has a bright blue body, yellow fins, and a rose-colored snout tip.

Distribution.—The steelcolor shiner once occurred throughout central Illinois but has now retreated to streams toward the eastern side of the state. It is still common in some of the large tributaries of the Wabash River but is sporadic and uncommon in streams of the Mississippi River drainage. Its retreat is probably due to a combination of siltation, the removal of trees margining streams, the deterioration of water quality, and the inability to compete with the related and more ecologically tolerant red shiner and spotfin shiner.

Ericymba Cope

This genus is restricted to the eastern United States. Except for the unique pearl organs on the head, the single species in the genus, which occurs in Illinois, would be included in the shiner genus *Notropis*.

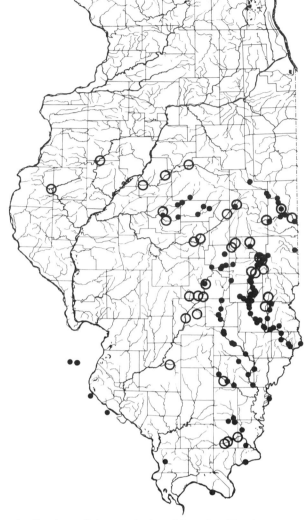

Distribution of the steelcolor shiner in Illinois.

Silverjaw minnow
Ericymba buccata Cope

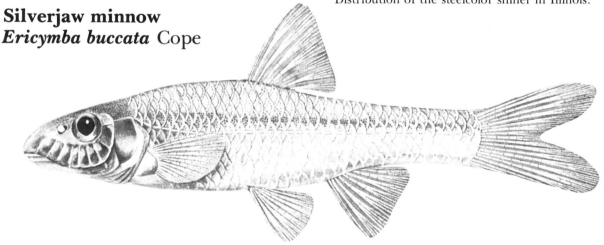

Ericymba buccata Cope 1865:88 (type-locality: Kiskiminitas River, a tributary of the Monongahela, western Pennsylvania); Nelson 1876:45 (recorded from Illinois); Jordan 1878:61; Forbes 1884:76; Large 1903:18; Forbes & Richardson 1908:156–158; O'Donnell 1935:483; Smith 1965:7.

Diagnosis.—The silverjaw minnow is a terete and plain shiner-like minnow, pale tan above and silvery below, with highly distinctive pearl organs (cavernous chambers separated by thin septa) occurring on the lower cheeks and ventral surface of the head and having the appearance of mother-of-pearl, the ventral surface of head greatly flattened, the eyes directed upward, and a small and horizontal subterminal mouth. No other Illinois fish should be confused with this species, but the bigmouth shiner has a similar form and color. The bigmouth shiner lacks the pearl organs and has a larger mouth. The young of the silverjaw minnow is as distinctive as the adult. The species attains a length of about 90 mm (3½ inches).

Variation.—Wallace (1973*a*) discussed distribution and dispersal but did not comment on any differences between the northern (Ohio River valley) and the southern (Gulf Coast) populations. Specimens from the Gulf Coast have a somewhat different appearance, and Wallace may discuss geographic variation in a future paper.

Ecology.—The silverjaw minnow lives on the shifting sand bottom in riffles and raceways with moderate flow. It is common in many clear headwaters. It can tolerate some pollution and even mine wastes but not fine silt. Hoyt (1970) found its food in Kentucky to consist primarily of immature chironomids but also to include substantial amounts of detritus, mayfly nymphs, and cladocerans and to be more varied in the winter than in the summer. Hoyt (1971) noted that adults school over fine gravel while spawning, the female produces an average of 748 eggs, .75 mm in diameter, spawning occurs from late March through June, sexual maturity is attained in 1 year, and the species lives for 4 years. Wallace (1973*b*) published similar results for a central Indiana population but noted two spawning peaks: one in early May and another in late June and early July. Wallace believed that most adults die after spawning in their 3rd year.

Distribution.—The silverjaw minnow is an abundant species in much of eastern Illinois. It occurs in the tributaries of the upper Illinois, those of the Wabash, and in many of those of the Kaskaskia River. It is difficult to conceive of the species ever being more abundant and widespread than it is at present, and it may have expanded its range somewhat in Illinois. It is a pioneering species that quickly occupies the newly dredged ditches if they have sand bottoms and clear water. In many shallow sand-bottomed creeks in eastern Illinois, the silverjaw minnow is the predominant fish.

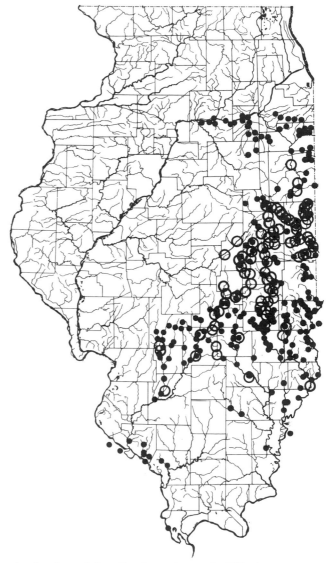

Distribution of the silverjaw minnow in Illinois.

Phoxinus Agassiz

Four eastern North American species and a number of Eurasian species are currently assigned to this Holarctic genus, which must replace the generally used name, *Chrosomus,* if the two groups are congeneric and if the first-revisor rule is applied. Some current authors are resisting the name change because *Chrosomus* has been in use for such a long time and because they feel the American and Eurasian species are not intimately related. The American species lack the three spinous rays in the dorsal fin characteristic of the Eurasian species. One species occurs in Illinois.

Southern redbelly dace
Phoxinus erythrogaster (Rafinesque)

Luxilus erythrogaster Rafinesque 1820*a*:47 (type-locality: Ohio River).
Leuciscus erythrogaster: Kennicott 1855:594 (recorded from Illinois).
Chrosomus erythrogaster: Nelson 1876:47; Jordan 1878:61; Forbes 1884:79; Large 1903:14; Forbes & Richardson 1908:112–114; O'Donnell 1935:480; Smith 1965:6.
Oxygeneum pulverulentum Forbes 1885:136 (type-locality: Illinois River at Peoria); Forbes 1884:79; Large 1903:14; Hubbs & Bailey 1952:143 (type: a stoneroller X redbelly dace hybrid).

Diagnosis.—The southern redbelly dace is a minnow with small scales, olive above and white (or red) below, with two dusky stripes on each side separated by a silvery yellowish band and with scattered dusky spots, some of which are arranged in rows down the back. The tiny scales and two lateral stripes distinguish this species from all other Illinois fishes. The breeding male has bright yellow fins, a crimson belly, and a red spot in the base of the dorsal fin. The young slightly resembles that of the stoneroller but can be distinguished by its smaller scales and two lateral stripes although the uppermost may be poorly developed. The species attains a length of 75 mm (3 inches).

Variation.—Apparently no studies of variation throughout the range of the species have been published. Phillips (1969) analyzed Minnesota samples of the northern (*P. eos*) and southern redbelly daces and found no evidence of interbreeding.

Ecology.—The southern redbelly dace occurs in spring-fed brooks and other clear cool streams in wooded ravines. It is a species found in headwaters, and it occurs in permanent seeps that have very little water in them. Schools of dace are often found under bank overhangs among tree roots, especially in clear pools with a muck bottom. Forbes & Richardson (1908:113–114) noted that the species nibbles on surface slime on objects in the water and that stomachs of dace contained mud, algae, and entomostraca. Spawning occurs in May and

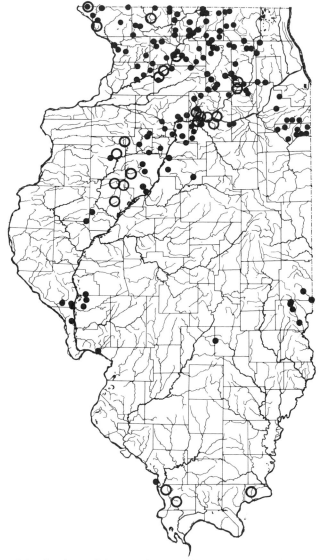

Distribution of the southern redbelly dace in Illinois.

June in swift shallow water over gravel. According to Smith (1908), the males are highly competitive when a female appears. The successful male wraps his body around that of the female during oviposition and holds her against the gravel of the bottom. The minute body tubercles help hold the female. Often the gravel nests constructed by other fishes are used. Like other minnows, the young dace grows rapidly and is sexually mature in 1 year.

Distribution.—The southern redbelly dace is general in occurrence in wooded areas throughout the northern third of Illinois but is sporadic elsewhere in the state. In east-central and west-central

Illinois, relict colonies occur in some wooded areas that have permanent springs. It once occurred in spring-fed streams in Union County in extreme southern Illinois, but it has evidently disappeared from this area in recent years, possibly because of the great fluctuations in the water table and instability of the springs in recent decades.

Dionda Girard

This North American genus contains three currently recognized U.S. species, one of which was described from northern Illinois. Other species are known from Mexico. Dr. Camm C. Swift of the Los Angeles County Museum of Natural History believes that the Illinois species belongs in the shiner genus *Notropis,* but pending publication of Dr. Swift's thesis, current authors retain for the Illinois species the genus *Dionda,* which shares with *Hybognathus* a long and much-coiled gut. The species are mostly southwestern in distribution in the United States.

Ozark minnow
Dionda nubila (Forbes)

Alburnops nubilus Forbes *in* Jordan 1878:56 (type-locality: Rock River, Ogle County, Illinois).
Hybognathus nubilus: Forbes 1884:79.
Hybognathus nubila: Large 1903:14; Forbes & Richardson 1908:116–117.
Dionda nubila: O'Donnell 1935:483; Smith 1965:7.

Diagnosis.—The Ozark minnow is shinerlike but has a long and coiled gut (at least twice the fish's standard length). It is a dirty straw color above and whitish beneath with a prominent black lateral stripe that extends to the snout tip but not onto the chin, dorsal scales broadly outlined with melanophores, a black peritoneum, the dorsal fin situated over the pelvic fin insertions, a large and protuberant eye (the diameter is greater than snout length), an inferior and almost horizontal mouth, 36–38 lateral-line scales, 4—4 pharyngeal teeth, and a modal anal ray count of eight. It is superficially similar to the bluntnose minnow but lacks the small and crowded predorsal scales and the intense caudal spot. It differs from species of *Hybognathus* in having a large eye and a well-defined lateral stripe. It differs from all Illinois species of

Ozark minnow

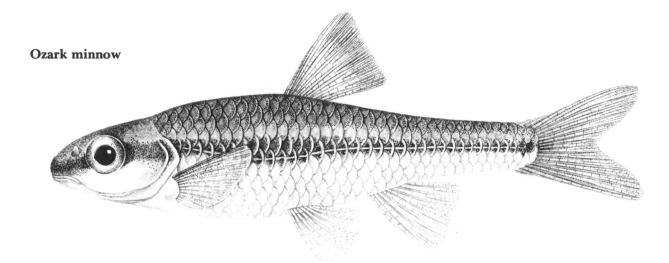

Notropis in having the very long gut. The species attains a length of about 65 mm (2½ inches).

Variation.—The species has been studied by Dr. Camm C. Swift, who presumably will discuss variation when he transfers the species to the genus *Notropis*.

Ecology.—The Ozark minnow lives in clear fast creeks with gravel bottoms. Its food probably consists of algae, ooze, and surface slime on pebbles in the stream bed. The spawning adult is a dirty yellow and the fins of the male are orange. Spawning occurs in May and June, but no other details are available.

Distribution.—This species occurs sporadically in clear gravelly streams of northwestern Illinois, where it was first found. It is also known from the Mississippi River of southwestern Illinois at three localities, where single specimens, believed to be stragglers from Missouri streams, have been taken. The Ozark minnow is abundant in Missouri streams but absent from small streams in southern Illinois. The evidence available suggests that the species is decimated in all of Illinois. Forbes & Richardson (1908) found the species in the Illinois River farther south than it now occurs.

Distribution of the Ozark minnow in Illinois.

Hybognathus Agassiz

This genus of minnows occurs primarily in middle North America and consists of five or six species, depending upon the final decision about the status of an Atlantic Coast population. Five species (one discovered recently and found in the Mississippi River) have been recorded from Illinois, one of which is now extirpated in the state. Three of the four still present are difficult to distinguish. Minnows of this genus are stout and rather shinerlike. They all possess a long and much-coiled gut and a small, hard knob at the tip of the lower jaw.

KEY TO SPECIES

1. Dorsal fin rounded, its first ray conspicuously shorter than second and third rays; anal fin rounded or straight edged; top of head and dorsum dusky, sides yellowish; greatest body depth in advance of dorsal fin . . . . *hankinsoni*
   Dorsal fin sharply pointed anteriorly, its first ray equal to or longer than second and third rays; anal fin somewhat falcate; top of head and dorsum pale straw color, sides silvery, dusky, or yellowish; greatest body depth at origin of dorsal fin 2
2. Eye diameter equal to or greater than snout length; scales on back and sides sharply outlined with melanophores; head pointed in lateral view; caudal peduncle slender, its depth going about 2.5 times into head length; dorsal fin origin distinctly closer to tip of snout than caudal origin; pectoral and pelvic fins long and pointed . . . . *hayi**
   Eye diameter less than snout length; scales on back and sides not sharply outlined with melanophores; head bluntly rounded in lateral view; caudal peduncle thick, its depth going into head length less than 2.5 times; dorsal fin origin about equidistant between snout tip and caudal origin; pectoral and pelvic fins shorter and less pointed 3
3. Eye small, its diameter going 4.5–5 times into head length and no more than twice diameter of nostril (eye pupil and nostril subequal); scale rows across belly (in front of pelvic insertions), usually more than 15; posterior process of basioccipital (cut isthmus and bend head sharply backward) uniformly narrow and peglike (Fig. 12a) . . . . *placitus*

Eye moderate, its diameter going 4–4.5 times into head length and more than twice diameter of nostril (pupil usually larger than nostril); scale rows across belly usually fewer than 15; posterior process of basioccipital gradually widening posteriorly, not peglike with parallel sides 4
4. Posterior process of basioccipital longer than wide and shallowly concave or truncate posteriorly (Fig. 12b) . . . . *argyritis*
   Posterior process of basioccipital wider at tip than its greatest length and deeply concave posteriorly (Fig. 12c) . . . . *nuchalis*

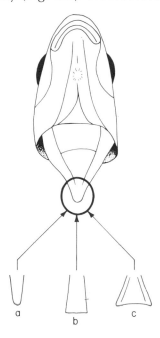

Fig. 12. Basioccipital processes of: a) *Hybognathus placitus;* b) *H. argyritis;* c) *H. nuchalis.*

Western silvery minnow
Hybognathus argyritis Girard

Hybognathus argyritis Girard 1856: 182 (type-locality: Milk River [Montana]); Pflieger 1971:366–368 (resurrection of name, recorded from Mississippi River).

Diagnosis.—The western silvery minnow, like other members of the genus, differs most markedly from shiners by the nature of the gut. It is a terete and robust minnow, pale olivaceous above and yellowish or whitish beneath with a vague dusky band along each side, a small eye (pupil a little larger than nostril), a sharply pointed dorsal fin whose origin is situated in front of the pelvic fin insertions, a very small subterminal and horizontal mouth, 37–39 lateral-line scales, and a basioccipital process that is longer than wide and truncate or shallowly concave posteriorly. It can be distinguished with certainty from the silvery and plains minnows only by examining the basioccipital process. Its eye size is intermediate between those of the same two species. The young superficially resembles that of the river shiner, from which it

differs by the long and coiled gut (and soft black belly), a smaller mouth, and eight rather than seven anal rays. The species attains a length of 100 mm (4 inches).

Variation.—Pflieger (1971:365–369) compared the species with related forms. No other information on variation is available.

Ecology.—This newly rediscovered species is poorly known, and information on its ecology must be inferred from its morphology, which is similar to that of an East Coast form (*regius*) studied by Raney (1939). The western silvery minnow occurs in large silty rivers over a substrate of sand or sandy silt. Like other members of the genus, it probably has strong schooling tendencies. Its mouth and intestine suggest that it is an ooze and mud feeder. Raney (1939) observed that males of *Hybognathus regius* become yellow on the sides and fins and dusky on the upper surfaces, while the females remain silvery. Breeding adults migrate to coves. Each female is accompanied by several males and commonly deposits her eggs over muck on the bottom with males on each side of her. Spawning occurs when water temperatures are between 13° and 20.5° C. Males wait in shallow water around the grassy borders of the pool until the females come into the pool. A female may contain 6,600 developed eggs. After a female is spent, the males seek other females and spawn with them.

Distribution.—The western silvery minnow is a characteristic fish of the Missouri River and in Illinois is restricted to the Mississippi River below the mouth of the Missouri. It probably does not extend much south of Illinois, but in the Missouri it ranges west to Montana.

Distribution of the western silvery minnow in Illinois.

Brassy minnow
Hybognathus hankinsoni
C. L. Hubbs

Hybognathus hankinsoni C. L. Hubbs *in* Jordan 1929:88 (type-locality: Dead River, Section 1, T 48 N, R 26 W, Marquette County, Michigan, subsequently designated by Bailey 1954); Bailey 1954:290 (recorded from Illinois); Smith 1965: 7.

Diagnosis.—The brassy minnow is a rather compressed minnow, blackish above and yellowish on the sides, with a broad dusky predorsal stripe, a rounded dorsal fin situated in advance of the pelvic fin insertions, a rounded or straight-edged anal fin, usually eight anal rays, 36–38 lateral-line scales, and a bluntly rounded head in lateral profile. It is the deepest-bodied species in the genus and the only one with a rounded dorsal fin and nonfalcate anal fin. Except for its long gut, it might be confused with the common shiner, with which it occurs, but it differs in lacking elevated lateral-line scales and in having fewer anal rays and a smaller mouth. The species attains a length of about 65 mm (2½ inches).

Variation.—Bailey (1954) provided the first adequate description of the species, based on the lectotype, and he discussed dispersal and distribution. Presumably no geographic variation was evident.

Ecology.—The brassy minnow occurs in quiet mud-bottomed pools of creeks. Starrett (1950) found that the species fed exclusively on bottom ooze (mud and diatoms) in the Des Moines River. In addition to mud and diatoms Copes (1975) found mosquito larvae in stomachs of brassy minnows. He described afternoon feeding in summer by large schools of the species. He found that spawning occurs over vegetation in quiet pools of

Distribution of the brassy minnow in Illinois.

creeks in late May in Wisconsin. One to several distinctly brassy colored males attend one female. Eggs settle to the bottom and hatch in a week to 10 days. His population consisted of four age classes.

Distribution.—The species occurs sporadically in the northern third of Illinois and is rather rare. Since it was unknown prior to 1929, no data are available on its former distribution and abundance. Its scarcity is surprising because apparently suitable habitat is widespread and actually increasing as a result of siltation.

Cypress minnow*
Hybognathus hayi Jordan

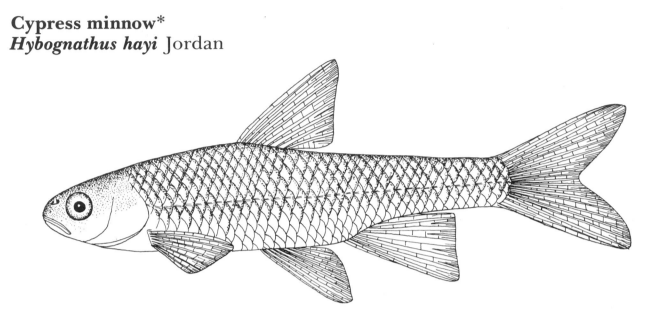

Hybognathus hayi Jordan 1885a:548 (type-locality: Pearl River, Jackson County, Mississippi).

Diagnosis.—The cypress minnow is a relatively slender and somewhat compressed minnow, dark olive above and silvery or whitish below, with the scales on the back and sides narrowly but sharply outlined with melanophores, a large eye (its diameter equal to or exceeding snout length), a relatively long and slender caudal peduncle (its least depth going 2½ times into the head length), falcate median fins, sharply pointed and long pectoral and pelvic fins, a narrow and diffuse predorsal stripe, and an angular head in the side view. This minnow is the most slender species in the genus and has the largest eye, sharpest snout, most anteriorly placed dorsal fin, and the most distinctly margined diamond-shaped scales. Except for its long (shorter than in other members of the genus) and coiled gut, this species might be confused with the silverband shiner, which has, however, a larger and more oblique mouth and a more attenuate and compressed body. The cypress minnow attains a length of 90 mm (3½ inches).

Variation.—Fingerman & Suttkus (1961) compared this species and the silvery minnow and described the differences in morphology and habitat. The cypress minnow is still too poorly known for studies of geographic variation to have been undertaken.

Ecology.—Fingerman & Suttkus (1961) reported that this species occupies mud-bottomed backwaters of streams and lagoons in Louisiana. Along the Ohio River in Kentucky it inhabits cypress-lined oxbow lakes over a bottom of muck and detritus. Presumably it feeds on ooze and algae. Its life history is completely unknown but is probably similar in many respects to that described for the brassy minnow, except that the cypress minnow lives in floodplain lakes.

Distribution.—Extirpated in Illinois. Specimens of this species were found in a Forbes & Richardson collection of *"Hybognathus nuchalis"* from a floodplain lake across the Ohio River from Cairo but not in any Illinois collections. However, Dr. M. B. Trautman found the species in the Little Muddy drainage of southwestern Illinois in the mid-1930's, but these specimens, deposited in the University of Michigan Museum of Zoology, have not been formally reported. The specimens reported from the Mississippi River (Smith 1965:7) were misidentified juveniles of another species. The searching of suitable habitat in the most likely areas of Illinois has not yielded additional specimens, and the Little Muddy, where the cypress minnow once occurred, has suffered extensive oil field pollution in recent decades. Thus, it appears that the cypress minnow was extirpated from Illinois before it was ever reported in the literature.

Silvery minnow
Hybognathus nuchalis Agassiz

Distribution of the cypress minnow in Illinois.

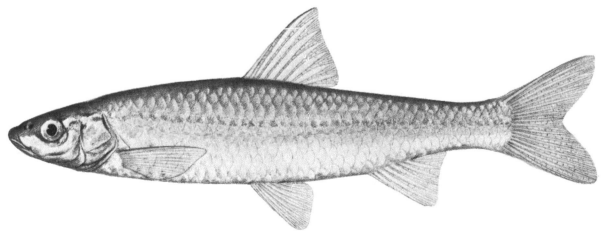

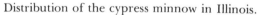

Hybognathus nuchalis Agassiz 1855:224 (type-locality: Quincy, Illinois); Nelson 1876:45; Jordan 1878:56; Forbes 1884:79; Large 1903:14; Forbes & Richardson 1908:114–116; O'Donnell 1935:483.

Hybognathus argyritis: Nelson 1876:45; Jordan 1878:56.
Hybognathus nuchalis nuchalis: Smith 1965:7.

Diagnosis.—The silvery minnow is a terete and robust minnow, pale olivaceous above and silvery below, with a vague dusky band along each side, a small eye (its diameter less than snout length), a sharply pointed dorsal fin whose origin is in front of the pelvic fin insertions, a small subterminal and horizontal mouth, 37–39 lateral-line scales, and a basioccipital process wider than long and distinctly concave posteriorly. It can be distinguished with certainty from the western silvery minnow and plains minnow only by examining the basioccipital process, which is the widest and flares out more than that of any other species in the genus. The eye of this species is slightly larger than that of the closely related species but smaller than that of the cypress minnow. The young superficially resembles the young river shiner but differs in having a smaller mouth, eight rather than seven anal rays, and a long and coiled gut (belly soft and black). The species attains a length of 100 mm (4 inches).

Variation.—Currently, authors recognize two subspecies: *H. n. regius* on the Atlantic Coast and *H. n. nuchalis* in the trans-Appalachian region. However, Al-Rawi & Cross (1964:161) noted that the basioccipital process of *regius* is more like that of *H. placitus* than of *H. nuchalis*, which suggests that the disjunct *regius* may be specifically distinct. No one has yet carefully compared populations throughout the range of the species.

Ecology.—The silvery minnow is a characteristic species of clear rivers and large creeks that have sandy bottoms. Where it occurs, the species is usually abundant and obvious because of the large schools that flash silver when individuals turn on their sides. Forbes & Richardson (1908:115) found mud, diatoms, filamentous algae, and other vegetable matter in the gut and commented on the role of the hard knob at the tip of the lower jaw in scraping algae and ooze from objects on the bottom. Spawning occurs in June. No other details are available, but the ecology is presumably very similar to that described for the western silvery minnow.

Distribution.—The silvery minnow is abundant in the Illinois, Kaskaskia, and Wabash and their larger tributaries. It is almost statewide in distribution, avoiding the northeastern corner of Illinois, but it is far less generally distributed than formerly. Its decimation in central and southern Illinois is probably due to a combination of siltation, pollution, and widely fluctuating water levels, particularly reductions in stream sizes during droughts.

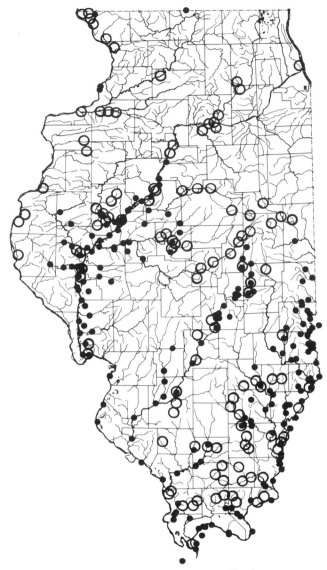

Distribution of the silvery minnow in Illinois.

Plains minnow
Hybognathus placitus Girard

Hybognathus placitus Girard 1856:182 (type-locality: sluices of the Arkansas River near Fort Makee [Kansas *fide* Al-Rawi & Cross 1964:162]); Smith 1965:7 (recorded from Illinois).

Diagnosis.—The plains minnow is very similar to the silvery minnow and to the western silvery minnow, differing from them in having a simple peg-like basioccipital process, a smaller eye (the diameter goes 4.5–5.5 times into the head length; the pupil is subequal to the nostril), and slightly smaller scales (usually more than 15 rows across the belly in front of the pelvic fin insertions). Like other species in the genus, it differs from the sympatric river shiner in having a long coiled gut. In life the plains minnow is more yellow than specimens of the silvery minnow in the same sample. Certain identification requires an examination of the basioccipital process because of overlap in other characters. The species attains a length of 100 mm (4 inches) or more.

Variation. — Al-Rawi & Cross (1964) concluded that subspecies were not recognizable but that populations at the northern and southern ends of the Great Plains had higher circumferential counts than those in the intermediate area. They con-

cluded that the higher counts were either environmentally induced or the result of gene introgression from sympatric *H. nuchalis*.

Ecology. — Al-Rawi & Cross (1964) noted that the species occurs in shallow and silty headwaters of streams in the Great Plains. In Illinois the species occurs only in the silt-laden Mississippi River. The feeding and reproductive habits of this species are probably similar to those described for the western silvery minnow.

Distribution. — The plains minnow occurs in Illinois only in the Mississippi River below the mouth of the Missouri and in the mouths of tributary streams.

Distribution of the plains minnow in Illinois.

Pimephales Rafinesque

This North American genus contains four species, three of which are common in most parts of Illinois. All are rather terete and stout bodied with a thickened splint in front of, but separate from, the first dorsal ray and a flattened predorsal region covered with small, irregular, crowded scales. The gut is long in most species but relatively short in one. Most authors regard the genus as distinctive enough to warrant recognition as a subfamily, the Pimephalinae.

KEY TO SPECIES

1. Body rather deep, greatest depth going fewer than four times into standard length; upper sides with herringbone lines; mouth sharply upturned; predorsal dark stripe present; lateral line not punctate .... *promelas*
   Body almost terete, greatest depth going more than four times into standard length; sides usually without herringbone pattern; mouth almost horizontal; predorsal stripe absent; lateral line partly punctate 2
2. Mouth terminal, slightly upturned; intestine short; peritoneum silvery; body without a dark lateral stripe; blotches in anterior rays of dorsal fin and at caudal base intense ......
   .... *vigilax*
   Mouth subterminal, almost horizontal; intestine long and much coiled; peritoneum black; body with distinct lateral stripe and discrete caudal spot; blotches in anterior rays of dorsal fin small and diffuse .... *notatus*

Bluntnose minnow
Pimephales notatus (Rafinesque)

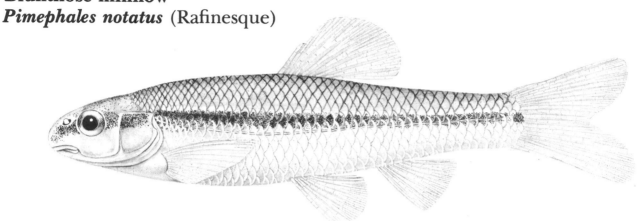

Minnilus notatus Rafinesque 1820a:47 (type-locality: Ohio River).

Hyborhynchus notatus: Nelson 1876:45 (recorded from Illinois); Jordan 1878:55; O'Donnell 1935:483.

Hyborhynchus superciliosus: Jordan 1878:56.

Pimephales notatus: Forbes 1884:78: Large 1903:14; Forbes & Richardson 1908:119–121; Smith 1965:8.

Diagnosis.—The bluntnose minnow is a terete minnow, olivaceous above and whitish below (belly of preserved specimen turns black), with a distinct black lateral band ending in a prominent caudal spot, a small black blotch in the anterior rays of the dorsal fin, the predorsal region flattened and containing many small crowded scales, a bluntly rounded snout, a subterminal and nearly horizontal mouth, and no predorsal stripe. This distinctive minnow is easily recognized by the combination of an intense black stripe along each side ending in a discrete caudal spot, a blackened (and soft) belly, and the tiny crowded predorsal scales. The young is as easily distinguished as the adult. It differs from the bullhead minnow in having a black peritoneum, a longer gut, a subterminal mouth, and a black lateral stripe. It differs from those shiners that have a caudal spot in having a soft black belly and crowded predorsal scales. The species attains a length of 90 mm (3½ inches).

Variation.—This abundant and widespread minnow is evolutionarily conservative. There are few synonyms and no described subspecies.

Ecology.—The bluntnose minnow is the most abundant and widespread fish in Illinois. It prefers hard-bottomed pools in creeks and small rivers but occurs almost everywhere except in swamps and

Distribution of the bluntnose minnow in Illinois.

heavily silted ditches and ponds. Several authors have described its feeding habits and agree that, while it is primarily a mud eater, vegetable matter and small aquatic invertebrates are also taken occasionally. The breeding male blackens and develops a barbel-like protuberance at the angle of the jaws and three rows of large tubercles on the snout. Breeding occurs in May and June. Several authors have described the reproductive behavior of the species, the most complete and detailed accounts being those of Van Cleave & Markus (1929) and Hubbs & Cooper (1936) for an Illinois and a Michigan population, respectively. According to these authors, spawning occurs in gravelly or sandy shoals. The male excavates a shallow depression beneath some object on the bottom and carefully cleans its undersurface with its tail and horny snout. When the nest is completed, a female moves in and deposits the adherent eggs on the underside of the object. The male guards the nest and will permit additional females to deposit eggs but will drive away other intruders. The male may guard the nest for as much as a day after all eggs have hatched.

Distribution.—The bluntnose minnow is abundant in all parts of the state except those regions that are principally swampy or have been so badly polluted that few fishes can survive in them.

Fathead minnow
Pimephales promelas Rafinesque

Pimephales promelas Rafinesque 1820*a*:53 (type-locality: pond near Lexington, Kentucky); Nelson 1876:45 (recorded from Illinois); Jordan 1878: 55; Forbes 1884:79; Large 1903:14; Forbes & Richardson 1908:117–119; O'Donnell 1935:45.
Pimephales milesii: Nelson 1876:45.
Pimephales promelas promelas: Smith 1965:8.

Diagnosis.—The fathead minnow is a stout and somewhat compressed (body depth goes fewer than four times into standard length) minnow, dark olive above and yellowish olive below, with a long and coiled gut, a terminal and sharply oblique mouth, herringbone lines on the upper sides, a brownish black peritoneum, predorsal scales small and closely crowded, an incomplete lateral line that is not punctate, and a dusky predorsal stripe. This species differs from other members of the genus in being darker in color and deeper bodied and having an oblique mouth and a predorsal stripe. It is superficially similar to the stoneroller but differs in having an upturned mouth and lacking patches of darker pigment on the sides. The young is similar to the young of the creek chub but has a much smaller mouth, a soft and darkened belly, and a more compressed body form. The species attains a length of about 75 mm (3 inches).

Variation.—For many years a northern and a southern subspecies of the fathead minnow were recognized. After comparing adults from the extreme ends of the range, Taylor (1954) concluded that the variation in several characters was clinal and that subspecies should not be recognized.

Ecology.—The fathead minnow occurs most commonly in sluggish creeks, ditches, and ponds with a mud bottom. In larger streams it occupies backwaters and muck-bottomed pools. It usually is abundant where the bluntnose minnow is absent, suggesting that it cannot compete successfully with species of similar habits. Starrett (1950) found in the Des Moines River that this species fed exclusively on detritus. Forbes & Richardson (1908:119) noted, in addition to mud and algae, fragments of both terrestrial and aquatic insects in the guts of specimens they examined. The fathead minnow is extremely prolific and has an extended breeding season from May well into the summer. The male develops broad, black vertical bands; three rows of tubercles on the snout; and a thick dorsal pad in front of the dorsal fin. Several authors have described the reproductive biology, which is similar to that of the bluntnose minnow. A good summary has been presented by Hubbs & Cooper (1936:

74–77), but a wealth of more recent papers has been published. The fathead is more defensive of its nest and more attentive to the eggs than are the bluntnose and most other minnows. It keeps the eggs clean and aerated by nibbling at them and rubbing the dorsal pad against them. Because of its fecundity, the species is widely propagated as a bait minnow.

Distribution.—The fathead minnow is abundant and widespread in suitable habitat throughout northern and western Illinois. While it has entered the Wabash drainage, it is strangely absent, or extremely sporadic, in eastern and southern Illinois. Human modification of the landscape has increased the amount of suitable habitat, and the species is undoubtedly more common and more widespread now than in former times.

Bullhead minnow
Pimephales vigilax (Baird & Girard)

Ceratichthys vigilax Baird & Girard 1853*b*:391 (type-locality: Otter Creek [fork of Red River], Arkansas); O'Donnell 1935:483.
Hybopsis tuditanus: Nelson 1876:46 (recorded from Illinois).
Alburnops tuditanus: Jordan 1878:56.
Cliola vigilax: Forbes 1884:78; Large 1903:15; Forbes & Richardson 1908:129–130.
Pimephales vigilax perspicuus: Smith 1965:8.

Diagnosis.—The bullhead minnow is a terete and rather stout-bodied minnow, greenish- to yellowish-olive above and silvery below, with conspicuous, small black blotches in the anterior rays of the dorsal fin and at the caudal base; a short intestine; a silvery peritoneum; a terminal and slightly upturned mouth; and a nearly complete and punctate lateral line. It is most like the bluntnose minnow but differs in having a silvery peritoneum, a short gut, more intense spots in the dorsal fin, and a terminal mouth. It differs from all shiners and other minnow genera in the nature of the dorsal fin rays and predorsal squamation. The young differs from similar and related species by the same characters as those found in the adult. The species attains a length of about 90 mm (3½ inches).

Variation.—Variation in this species and its relatives was thoroughly reviewed by Hubbs & Black (1947). A nominal species (*perspicuus*) was formally reduced to subspecies status by Cross (1953), and it

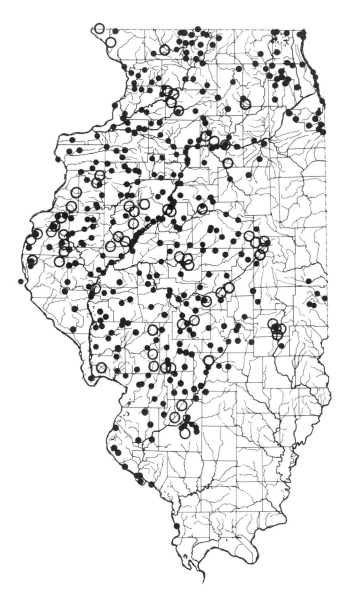

Distribution of the fathead minnow in Illinois.

Bullhead minnow

is this subspecies that occurs in Illinois. The nominate form, *P. v. vigilax,* occurs in Texas and parts of adjacent Oklahoma.

Ecology.—The bullhead minnow is a characteristic species of large rivers although it is found in some lakes and certain smaller rivers. It is most abundant in clear water over a bottom of mixed sand, mud, and fine gravel and, in Illinois, occurs both in the strong current of channels and in quiet backwaters. Its food has been described by several authors as quite varied, and Starrett (1950) regarded the species as a semispecialized feeder. The reproductive habits are in general similar to those of the bluntnose minnow. Parker (1964) reported on some aspects of its ecology. Spawning occurs from late May well into July.

Distribution.—The species is statewide and abundant in all of the large rivers, in some glacial lakes, and in two small rivers (the Embarras River in eastern Illinois and Clear Creek of Union and Alexander counties). It is much decimated in tributaries of the large rivers in the interior of Illinois, presumably because these streams now fluctuate in water depth and flow and no longer contain large-stream habitat throughout the year.

Campostoma Agassiz

This Nearctic genus contains two species in eastern North America (both occurring in Illinois) and a third in the Southwest and in central Mexico. The genus is curious because all species have a hard cartilaginous ridge on the lower jaw, used to scrape algae from stones on the bottom, and two of the

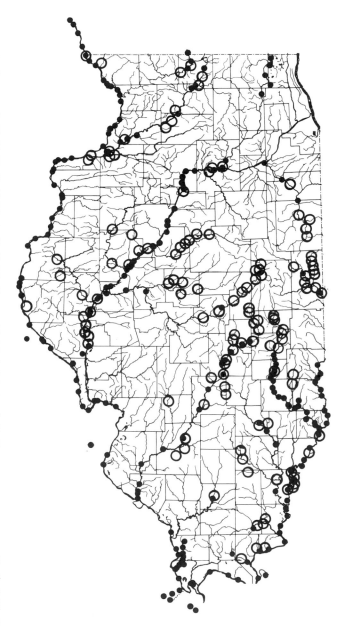

Distribution of the bullhead minnow in Illinois.

three species have long, much-coiled intestines that ordinarily encircle the air bladder. Members of the genus are sometimes called rot-gut minnows because of the black peritoneum and soft viscera.

KEY TO SPECIES

1. Body scales larger (sum of lateral-line and body-circumferential rows usually fewer than 85); breeding male without intense black band traversing anal fin and without row of one to three tubercles along inner margin of nostril .... *oligolepis*
   Body scales smaller (sum of lateral-line and body-circumferential rows usually more than 85); breeding male with intense black band traversing anal fin and with row of one to three tubercles along inner margin of nostril .... *anomalum*

Common stoneroller
Campostoma anomalum (Rafinesque)

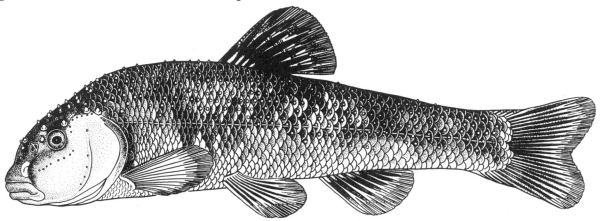

Rutilus anomalus Rafinesque 1820a:52 (type-locality: Licking River, Kentucky).

Campostoma anomalum: Nelson 1876:44–45 (recorded from Illinois); Jordan 1878:55; Forbes 1884:79; Large 1903:14; Forbes & Richardson 1908:110–112 (part.); O'Donnell 1935:483.

Oxygeneum pulverulentum Forbes 1885:136 (type-locality: Illinois River at Peoria); Hubbs & Bailey 1952:143 (shown to be a stoneroller X redbelly dace hybrid).

Campostoma anomalum (Rafinesque) subspecies: Smith 1965:6.

Diagnosis.—The common stoneroller is a dusky minnow with irregular patches of black or brown pigment scattered over the body. It is highly distinctive in its generic characters (long and coiled gut, black peritoneum, cartilaginous scraping edge on mandible) but closely resembles the allied large-scale stoneroller. It differs in having smaller scales, a flatter and less projecting snout, and a more highly arched nape, and in the nuptial characters of the breeding male as cited in the key. Scale counts will enable one to identify virtually every specimen in northern and central Illinois (where the two are sympatric), but they are less reliable in extreme southern Illinois (where only the common stoneroller occurs). The small young can be distinguished only by scale count differences. Superficially the common stoneroller resembles the white sucker, from which it can be distinguished by the lack of a fleshy lower lip, and the blacknose dace, which has much smaller scales and a white rather than black peritoneum. The species attains a length of about 180 mm (7 inches).

Variation.—Two subspecies are generally recognized, and both occur in Illinois. *C. a. anomalum* is restricted to direct tributaries of the Ohio River in southeastern Illinois, and it intergrades with *C. a. pullum* in extreme southwestern Illinois. *C. a. pullum* occupies the rest of the state and shows no clinal variation. A careful study of variation in Illinois was published by Burr (1976), from which these statements were extracted. One or two other nominal subspecies in the east are of uncertain status and have limited ranges.

Ecology.—The common stoneroller occurs in creeks with substrates of gravel, bedrock, or mixed sand and gravel and occurs in riffles and raceways. In summer it may occur in pools when water levels become low in raceways. It is primarily a creek species, and it is intolerant of silt. An excellent account of reproduction in the species, published by Miller (1962), was based on studies in western New York. The strongly tuberculate males begin nest construction when the water temperature reaches 15.5° C. Pits are excavated by digging, pushing stones with the snout, and picking up pebbles by mouth. The nest, in a riffle or gravel-bottomed pool, is often used by several males. Spawning is communal, but some territoriality exists. Females move in from a nearby school and deposit eggs while accompanied by several males. The spawning period is from late March into May. Sexual maturity is reached at 1 year of age and at a length of 50 mm (2 inches).

Distribution.—The common stoneroller is abundant in creeks throughout Illinois, except for an area in the south-central part of the state where suitable habitat is lacking. In this area the low-gradient turbid streams flow over clay or mud. The Illinois range of this species has not changed appreciably, and the species is probably as common as it has ever been. While many of the streams it inhabits have deteriorated, the species is rather tolerant, and its preferred habitat has increased because many streams once large and stable now have characteristics of headwaters in late summer.

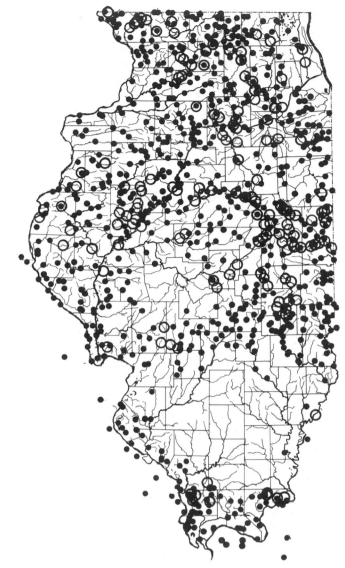

Distribution of the common stoneroller in Illinois.

Largescale stoneroller
Campostoma oligolepis Hubbs & Greene

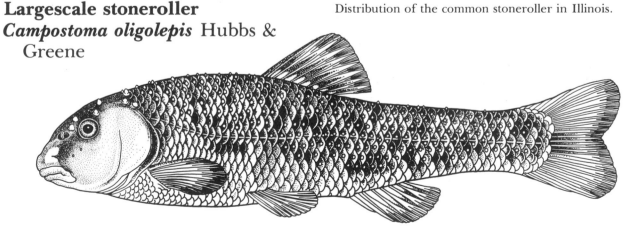

Campostoma anomalum oligolepis Hubbs & Greene 1935:89 (type-locality: Little Rib River, 5 km E of Hamburg, Marathon County, Wisconsin).
Campostoma anomalum: Forbes & Richardson 1908:

110–112 (part.).
Campostoma oligolepis: Burr & Smith 1976:521 (recorded from Illinois).

Diagnosis.—The largescale stoneroller is, as noted in the diagnosis of the preceding species, exceedingly similar to the common stoneroller, differing from that species primarily in having larger (and fewer) scales and in lacking a black band across the anal fin and a row of tubercles along the inner margin of the nostrils. It also tends to have a more globose and projecting snout and a less arched dorsal profile. Its lateral-line scales are usually 43–47; body circumferential scales, usually 31–36; and the sum of these counts, usually 74–83. The scale counts permit virtually 100 percent separation from *Campostoma anomalum pullum,* which occurs with the largescale stoneroller in northern and central Illinois, but *C. a. anomalum,* which occurs only in extreme southern Illinois, has counts that approach those of the largescale stoneroller. The species attains a length of about 180 mm (7 inches).

Variation.—Pflieger (1971) and Burr & Smith (1976) intensively studied geographic variation in the species and concluded that local variation was discernible in some Ozarkian streams but no subspecies were recognizable.

Ecology.—The habitat of the largescale stoneroller is generally similar to that of the common stoneroller, except that it is less tolerant of turbidity, reduced flow, and silt than is the common stoneroller. Its feeding and reproductive habits are also presumed to be much the same. The differences in snout tuberculation and breeding pattern suggest that these features may be important in species recognition during spawning, since both species occur together in many areas.

Distribution.—The largescale stoneroller is restricted to streams in the northern third of Illinois, except for two populations in tributaries of the Sangamon River in McLean County. Its range is much reduced, and it is far less common than formerly, if one judges by the numerous collections of large series taken in central Illinois by Forbes and Richardson before 1908 (Burr & Smith 1976). It is similarly decimated in such agriculturized states as Iowa, Minnesota, and southern Wisconsin but is still common in Missouri and Arkansas.

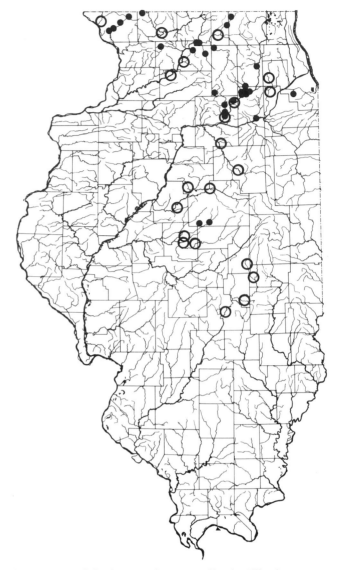

Distribution of the largescale stoneroller in Illinois.

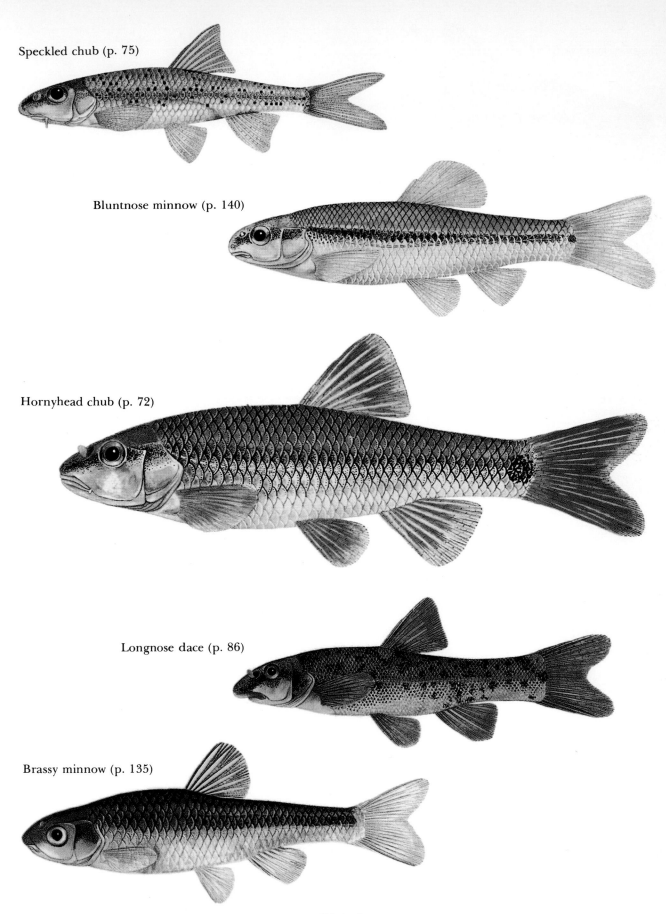

Speckled chub (p. 75)

Bluntnose minnow (p. 140)

Hornyhead chub (p. 72)

Longnose dace (p. 86)

Brassy minnow (p. 135)

Plate 1

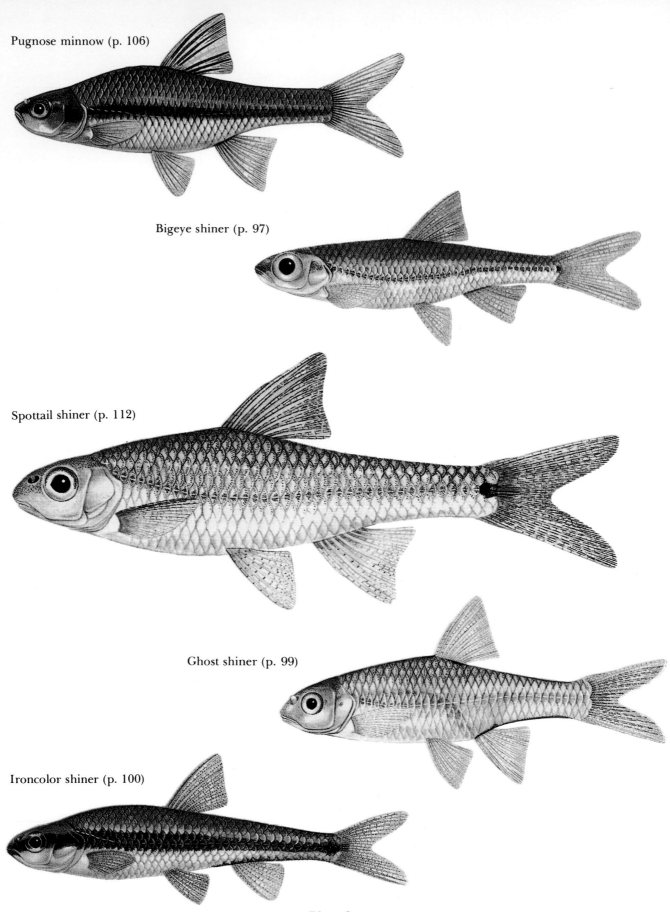

Pugnose minnow (p. 106)

Bigeye shiner (p. 97)

Spottail shiner (p. 112)

Ghost shiner (p. 99)

Ironcolor shiner (p. 100)

Plate 2

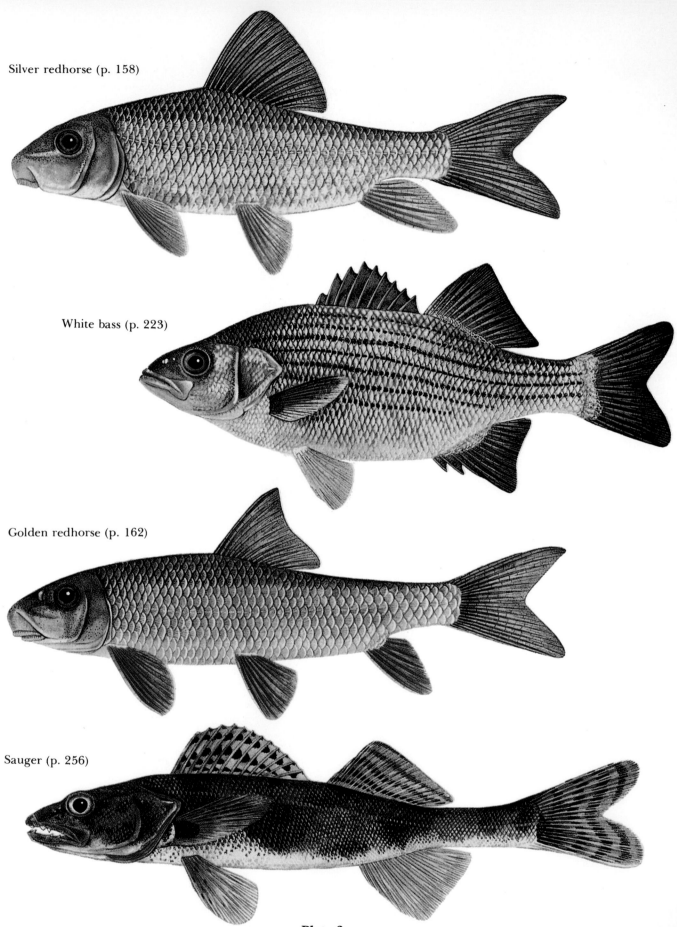

Silver redhorse (p. 158)

White bass (p. 223)

Golden redhorse (p. 162)

Sauger (p. 256)

Plate 3

Flier (p. 251)

Bantam sunfish (p. 245)

Redear sunfish (p. 242)

Plate 4

Longear sunfish (p. 241)

Pumpkinseed (p. 235)

Warmouth (p. 237)

Plate 5

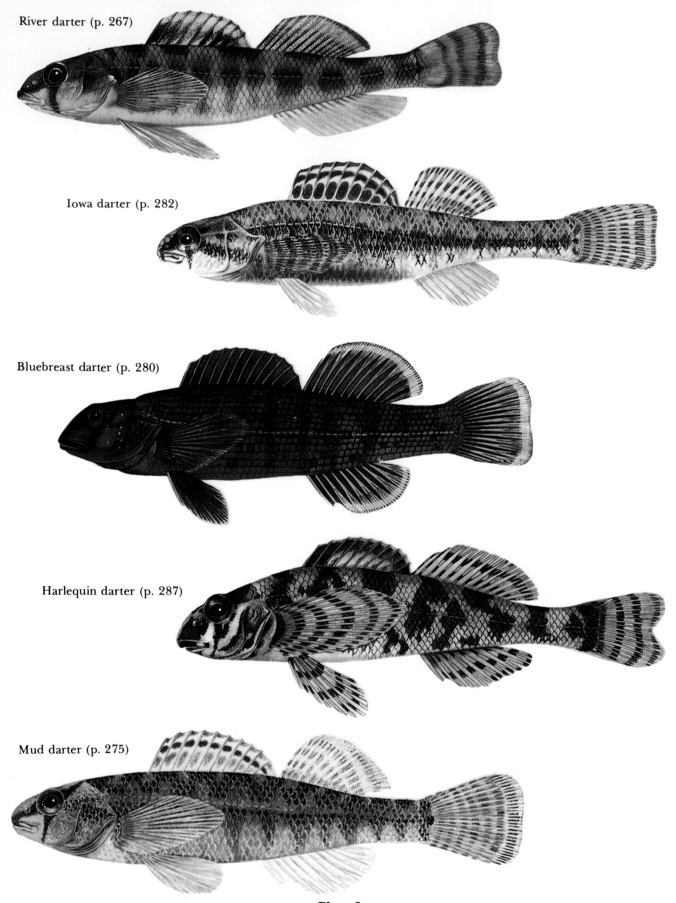

River darter (p. 267)

Iowa darter (p. 282)

Bluebreast darter (p. 280)

Harlequin darter (p. 287)

Mud darter (p. 275)

Plate 6

Slough darter (p. 285)

Eastern sand darter (p. 272)

Banded darter (p. 296)

Cypress darter (p. 292)

Least darter (p. 289)

Plate 7

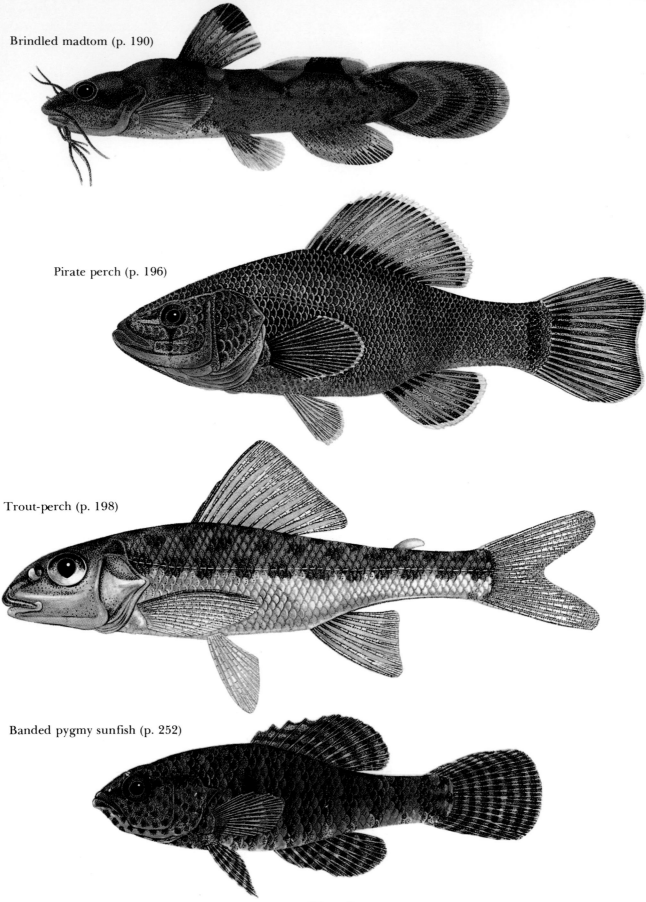

Brindled madtom (p. 190)

Pirate perch (p. 196)

Trout-perch (p. 198)

Banded pygmy sunfish (p. 252)

Plate 8

Suckers—Catostomidae

This Nearctic family of cypriniform fishes contains 10 genera of living fishes (the genus *Lagochila* became extinct in the last century), eight of which are known in Illinois. This family of bottom-dwelling fishes is most obviously distinguished from the minnow family Cyprinidae by the usually specialized lips and premaxillaries (adapted for sucking), the posteriorly placed anal fin, the high dorsal ray count, and the distinctive pharyngeal arch. Suckers generally are clean-water fishes that cannot tolerate extensive modification of their habitats. The buffalos and larger redhorse species are important commercial fishes of the large rivers, and the redhorses are also popular sport fishes, particularly in early spring. The flesh of most species is firm and said to be delicious, but suckers are excessively bony.

KEY TO GENERA

1. Dorsal fin long, containing more than 20 principal rays 2
    Dorsal fin short, containing 18 or fewer rays 4
2. Head small, its length contained five or more times in standard length; lateral-line scales more than 50; caudal peduncle long, considerably exceeding length of depressed anal fin; head and body terete .... *Cycleptus*
    Head large, its length contained fewer than five times in standard length; lateral-line scales fewer than 50; caudal peduncle short, its length less than that of depressed anal fin; head and body compressed 3
3. Sides of body brownish, bronzy olive, or dusky blue; subopercle broadest at its middle, its free edge forming an even curve (Fig. 13a); caudal peduncle deep and thick; anal and pelvic fins well pigmented with melanophores .... *Ictiobus*
    Sides of body whitish or silvery; subopercle broadest below its middle, its free edge somewhat angular (Fig. 13b); caudal peduncle not excessively deep and thick; anal and pelvic fins usually lacking melanophores .... *Carpiodes*
4. Lateral line complete and well developed 5
    Lateral line incomplete or wholly lacking 7
5. Head strongly depressed between eyes, forming a concavity (Fig. 13c); head decidedly squarish in cross section; mouth large; lips extremely protractile, strongly papillose; body traversed with four prominent black oblique bars .... *Hypentelium*
    Head rounded between eyes, forming a convex curve (Fig. 13d); head round in cross section; mouth small to moderate; lips somewhat protractile, plicate or papillose; body pattern variable but without four strong black oblique bars 6

Fig. 13. Key characters: a) head of *Ictiobus*, showing hemispherical subopercle; b) head of *Carpiodes*, showing triangular subopercle; c) head of *Hypentelium*, showing concavity; d) head of *Catostomus*, showing rounded head.

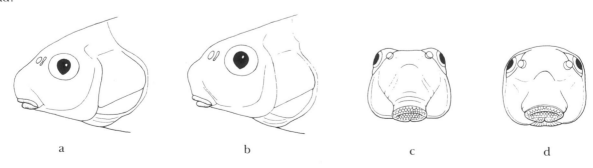

a   b   c   d

6. Scales small and closely crowded, more than 55 in lateral line; ground color dusky; lips entirely papillose .... *Catostomus*
   Scales large, not closely crowded, fewer than 50 in lateral line; ground color silvery or bronzy; lips plicate or both plicate and papillose .... *Moxostoma*
7. Body terete; dorsal fin slightly falcate; body with many distinct longitudinal rows of small brown dots, each dot being a spot at the scale base; lateral-line scales, 43 or more .... *Minytrema*
   Body slab-sided; dorsal fin convex; body pattern not consisting of longitudinal rows of small brown dots; lateral-line scales, fewer than 43 .... *Erimyzon*

Cycleptus Rafinesque

This bizarre genus contains only one species, which is restricted to rivers of the central and southern United States.

Blue sucker
Cycleptus elongatus (Lesueur)

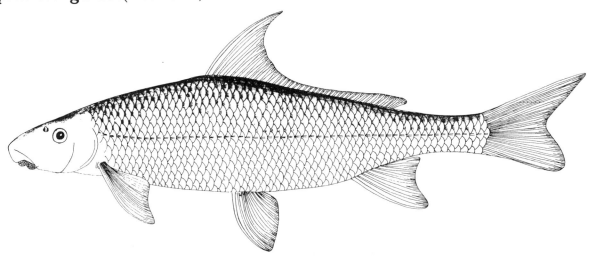

Catostomus elongatus Lesueur 1817*b*:103 (type-locality: Ohio River).

Cycleptus elongatus: Nelson 1876:50 (recorded from Illinois); Jordan 1878:64; Forbes 1884:81; Large 1903:12; Forbes & Richardson 1908:65–66; O'Donnell 1935:478; Smith 1965:8.

Diagnosis.—The blue sucker is an elongate and terete fish unique in the Catostomidae because of its small head (the length contained five or more times in the standard length) and long caudal peduncle (greatly exceeding length of adpressed anal fin). It has a blue-black or dark gray dorsum, darkly pigmented fins, a somewhat paler venter, 50 or more lateral-line scales, and a long and ex-

tremely falcate dorsal fin; the lower lobe of its caudal fin is black. So bizarre are the proportions that neither adult nor young can be confused with any other sucker. The species attains a length of about 890 mm (35 inches).

Variation.—No studies of geographic variation have been published and no subspecies have been described. The scientific name of this fish has been remarkably stable.

Ecology.—The blue sucker is a large-river species most often found in deep riffles and fast chutes over rocky or gravelly bottom in March and April, when the species is probably spawning. It is a strongly migratory fish that occasionally ascends

Distribution of the blue sucker in Illinois.

tributary streams for considerable distances and then is not recognized by the small-river fishermen who catch them. Many such discoveries are reported to authorities, but the specimens rarely reach a museum collection. Almost nothing is known about the feeding and reproductive habits of the species, and no one publication summarizing the available information can be cited.

Distribution. — The blue sucker has been declining in abundance for many years; its decimation has been attributed to the construction of dams on navigable rivers, the deterioration of water quality, excessive catches of adults in spawning runs, and the gradually decreasing depths of river channels through sand and silt choking. The blue sucker still

occurs in the Mississippi River at least as far north as Rock Island County but is generally uncommon. It is probably more common in the less turbid Wabash and Ohio rivers than available records indicate but, according to long-time commercial fishermen, much less common now than formerly. How generally it occurs is difficult to assess because of its habit of occasionally ascending great distances into medium-sized rivers.

Ictiobus Rafinesque

This genus, restricted to Mexico, Central America, and the Mississippi River valley of the central United States, contains five currently recognized species, three of which occur in Illinois. Juveniles are similar to each other and to the young of the quillback and are difficult to distinguish.

KEY TO SPECIES

1. Mouth large, terminal, and extremely oblique; tip of upper lip about on level with lower margin of eye; lips faintly striate . . . . *cyprinellus*
   Mouth small, somewhat subterminal, and not extremely oblique; tip of upper lip well below level of lower margin of eye; lips thicker and more striate 2
2. Mouth small, almost horizontal, decidedly inferior; body deep and slab-sided in the adult, its greatest depth contained less than three times in standard length; back in front of dorsal fin highly arched, thin, and keeled; eye large, its diameter contained fewer than two times in snout length; parietal and occipital region not appreciably swollen . . . . *bubalus*
   Mouth large, slightly oblique, almost terminal; body thick, not deep and not slab-sided in the adult; back in front of dorsal fin not highly arched, thin, and keeled; eye small, its diameter contained two or more times in snout length; parietal-occipital region swollen . . . . *niger*

Smallmouth buffalo
Ictiobus bubalus (Rafinesque)

?*Amblodon bubalus* Rafinesque 1818*b*:421 (type-locality: Ohio River).

Ichthyobus cyanellus Nelson 1876:49 (type-locality: Illinois River and Mississippi River at St. Louis).

Bubalichthys cyanellus: Jordan 1878:66.

Ictiobus bubalus: Forbes 1884:82; Large 1903:11; Forbes & Richardson 1908:72–73; O'Donnell 1935:478–479; Smith 1965:8.

Diagnosis.—The smallmouth buffalo is a deep-bodied sucker, bronzy to dark slate above and somewhat paler below, usually with well-pigmented lower fins, a long and falcate dorsal fin, a deep and thick caudal peduncle, the free edge of the subopercle forming a symmetrically even curve, a small and horizontal mouth that is decidedly inferior, the greatest body depth of the adult contained less than three times in the standard length, the back highly arched and keeled in front of dorsal fin, and the eye diameter contained less than twice in the snout length of the adult, and without a swollen parietal-occipital region. The smallmouth buffalo most closely resembles the black buffalo, differing from it in having a smaller and horizontal mouth and, in the adult, a much deeper and more slab-sided body. The young of the two species are especially difficult to separate, since the size and position of the mouth are the only characters that can be used. Very small specimens are similar to young quillbacks but are usually more heavily pigmented, have a thicker caudal peduncle and more pointed snout, and have a rounded and symmetrical subopercle. The species attains a length of more than 760 mm (30 inches), but most adults range from 250 to 410 mm (10 to 16 inches).

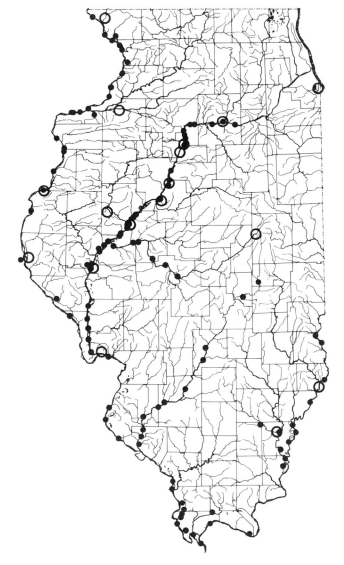

Distribution of the smallmouth buffalo in Illinois·

Variation.—The smallmouth buffalo is variable, but its diagnostic characters are rather conservative. No subspecies, but a number of synonyms, have been described.

Ecology.—The smallmouth buffalo is typically a species of large rivers, but it is taken occasionally in lakes and medium-sized rivers although less frequently than the other two species of buffalos. It prefers firm-bottomed channels but is sometimes taken in backwaters and in mouths of tributaries. Like most suckers, it feeds on benthic organisms and spawns in the spring. It feeds in schools at mid-water or near the bottom. Except for some data on growth rates (Minckley 1959:416), little is known of its reproductive biology. It spawns in late spring in quiet pools or backwaters, and the eggs are merely dropped over the bottom. Hatching takes about 10 days at 15° C. The species lives at least 8 years and possibly much longer.

Distribution.—Probably the most abundant buffalo in the state, this species is not the most widely distributed, because it is less often found in smaller streams and swamps. A change in its distribution and abundance in the state cannot be documented, but numerous authors have surmised that it declined with the advent of the carp in American waters.

Bigmouth buffalo
Ictiobus cyprinellus (Valenciennes)

Sclerognathus cyprinella Valenciennes *in* Cuvier & Valenciennes 1844:477 (type-locality: Lake Pon- chartrain, Louisiana).

Ichthyobus bubalus: Nelson 1876:49 (recorded from Illinois, misapplication of name); Jordan 1878: 65.

Ictiobus cyprinellus: Forbes 1884:82; Smith 1965:8.

Ictiobus cyprinella: Large 1903:11; Forbes & Rich- ardson 1908:68–70.

Megastomatobus cyprinella: O'Donnell 1935:478.

Fig. 14. Buffalo heads: a) *Ictiobus cyprinellus*, b) *I. niger*, c) *I. bubalis*.

a   b   c

Diagnosis.—The bigmouth buffalo is a stout bronzy or slate-colored sucker with the long and falcate dorsal fin characteristic of the genus. It differs from all other Illinois suckers in having a large, sharply oblique, and terminal mouth. Nevertheless, experience is required to separate this species from the black buffalo, which has a sub- terminal mouth that is quite similar to that of the bigmouth. The adult bigmouth buffalo is deeper bodied than the black buffalo but much less com- pressed than the smallmouth buffalo. The small young can usually be separated from young of other buffalos and carpsuckers by the terminal mouth. Larger young and adults are more difficult to identify unless comparative material is avail- able. Occasionally reaching weights of 36 kg (80

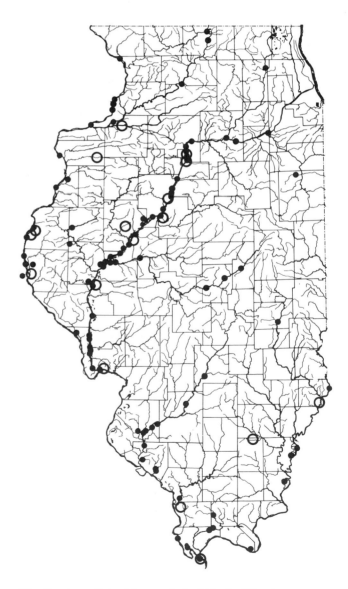

Distribution of the bigmouth buffalo in Illinois.

pounds), the majority of adults are under 4.5 kg (10 pounds) and less than 510 mm (20 inches) in length.

Variation.—No subspecies are recognized, but sufficient ontogenetic and individual variation occurs that some commercial fishermen believe there are several "kinds" of buffalos.

Ecology.—The bigmouth buffalo is most common in large and medium-sized rivers, oxbows, and bottomland lakes marginal to large rivers. It is less of a bottom-dwelling fish than most other suckers. It feeds primarily on plankton and small immatures of aquatic insects. Like most suckers, it spawns in the spring and scatters its thousands of eggs over debris on the bottom. Its reproductive habits, which are not elaborate, have been described by Johnson (1963).

Distribution.—The bigmouth buffalo occurs in all parts of the state but is extremely sporadic in small rivers and present in creeks only at their confluences with large rivers. There is no evidence that the species is any more or any less common than formerly. It is more abundant in the low-gradient Illinois River and its associated floodplain lakes than elsewhere in the state.

Black buffalo
Ictiobus niger (Rafinesque)

Bubalichthys niger Rafinesque 1820a:56 (type-locality: Ohio River); Nelson 1876:50 (recorded from Illinois).
Bubalichthys urus: Jordan 1878:65.
Ictiobus urus: Forbes 1884:82; Forbes & Richardson 1908:70–72; O'Donnell 1935:478.
Ictiobus niger: Large 1903:11; Smith 1965:8.

Diagnosis.—The black buffalo is a slate-colored or bronzy sucker similar to the preceding two species and intermediate between them in virtually all characters. However, large adults are more slender bodied and thicker headed than either the smallmouth or the bigmouth buffalo, and they frequently have a swollen parietal-occipital region. Young and subadults are sometimes very difficult to separate from similar-sized specimens of the smallmouth buffalo. The black buffalo attains a length of about 640 mm (25 inches).

Variation.—No subspecies have been described. For many years fishermen and some fishery biologists have believed that this species is a hybrid

between the other two species in the genus and have referred to it as the mongrel buffalo.

Ecology.—The black buffalo occurs in large and medium-sized rivers and their marginal lakes. In Illinois it is often found with the bigmouth buffalo. Its feeding and reproductive habits are similar to those of other buffalos. Greer & Cross (1956: 359–360) reported growth rates of the species in a Kansas reservoir.

Distribution.—This species occurs sporadically in most parts of the state. Hubbs & Lagler (1941: 41) reported it common in marginal lakes at the southern part of Lake Michigan, but it is presumably now extirpated in northeastern Illinois. No other data are available on the status of this comparatively rare buffalo.

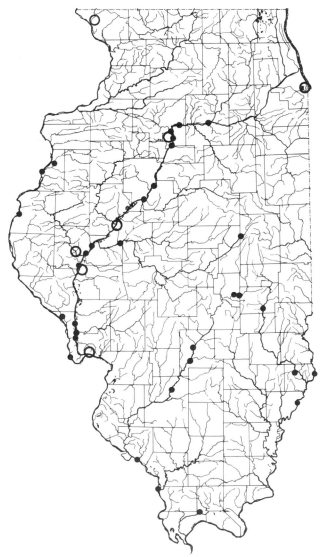

Distribution of the black buffalo in Illinois.

Carpiodes Rafinesque

This North American genus contains three currently recognized species, all of which occur in Illinois. The genus is related to *Ictiobus,* differing from it in being silvery or whitish with little or no dark pigment on the fins and in having a more slender caudal peduncle, a more angular and lopsided subopercle, and a well-developed anterior fontanelle as well as a posterior one. The two genera constitute the subfamily Ictiobinae. Juveniles are difficult to distinguish at the species level.

KEY TO SPECIES

1. Snout produced, anterior tip well in advance of anterior nostril; no dentary "nipple" at tip of lower jaw; scales, 37–41 in lateral line . . . . *cyprinus*
   Snout bluntly rounded, not produced; nipple-like protuberance at tip of lower jaw; scales, 33–37 in lateral line 2
2. Anterior dorsal fin rays of adult longer than fin base (if unbroken); snout bluntly rounded; body very deep and much compressed in adult . . . . *velifer*
   Anterior dorsal fin rays of adult shorter than fin base; snout tip rounded and bullet shaped; body elongate, not deep and much compressed . . . . *carpio*

River carpsucker
Carpiodes carpio (Rafinesque)

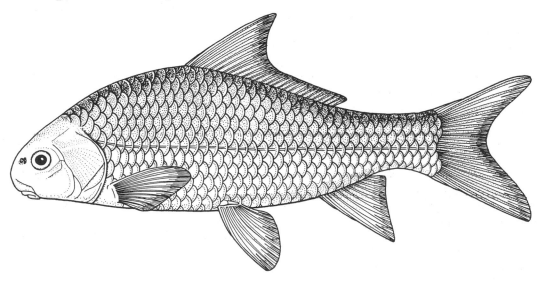

Catostomus carpio Rafinesque 1820*a*:56 (type-locality: falls of the Ohio River).
Ichthyobus carpio: Nelson 1876:49 (recorded from Illinois).
?Ichthyobus bison: Nelson 1876:49.
?Carpiodes bison: Jordan 1878:65.
Carpiodes carpio: Jordan 1878:65; Large 1903:11; Forbes & Richardson 1908:76–77; O'Donnell 1935:479.
Carpiodes carpio carpio: Smith 1965:8.
Ictiobus cyprinus: Forbes 1884:81 (part., only one species of carpsucker recognized).

Diagnosis.—The river carpsucker is a somewhat compressed but not excessively deep-bodied sucker, pale olive or bronze above but whitish or silvery on the sides, with a long dorsal fin (more than 20 rays), a nipple-like knob at the tip of the lower jaw, and a bullet-shaped snout, and without extremely elongated anterior rays in the dorsal fin. It is most like the highfin carpsucker, differing from it (in the adult stage) by lacking the long rays in the dorsal fin, having a more pointed snout, and being much less deep bodied (its greatest body depth contained three times or more in the standard length). It differs from the quillback in having the "nipple" at the tip of the lower jaw, usually less than 38 lateral-line scales, a rounded rather than a squarish snout, and a more elongate body. It differs from all the buffalos in having the sides and fins whitish, a more slender caudal peduncle, and an asymmetrical subopercle. The young less than 100 mm (4 inches) in total length are indistinguishable from the young of the highfin carpsucker. The species attains a length of about 610 mm (2 feet), but most adults are less than 410 mm (16 inches).

Variation.—A northern (*C. c. carpio*) and a southern subspecies (*C. c. tumidus*) are currently recognized. The nominate subspecies occurs in Illinois. No detailed study of variation in this species has been undertaken, probably because of the more urgent need for investigations in other species of carpsuckers.

Ecology.—The river carpsucker is abundant in very large rivers, less common in middle-sized rivers. It prefers quiet pools over a substrate of silt or mixed sand, silt, and fine gravel. Large individuals are often associated with carp around brush piles and log jams. Buchholz (1957) described the food as bottom ooze, consisting primarily of diatoms, green algae, blue-green algae, desmids, immature stages of Diptera, and other small invertebrate animals. He believed that spawning in the Des Moines River occurs intermittently from May through July. An adult female produces over 100,000 eggs, which are merely broadcast over the bottom. Although the female may be sexually mature at 2 years, most of the breeding adults are older. Buchholz found nine year classes and calculated the growth per year of the species.

Distribution.—The species occurs in all of the major rivers, ascending the Illinois River to the point where it cannot tolerate the polluted waters. It is sporadic in middle-sized rivers and only accidental in smaller streams. There is no evidence of either an increase or decrease in its distribution and abundance. It does not occur in northeastern Illinois.

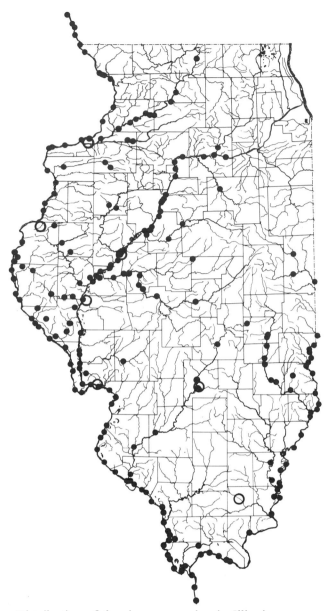

Distribution of the river carpsucker in Illinois.

Quillback
Carpiodes cyprinus (Lesueur)

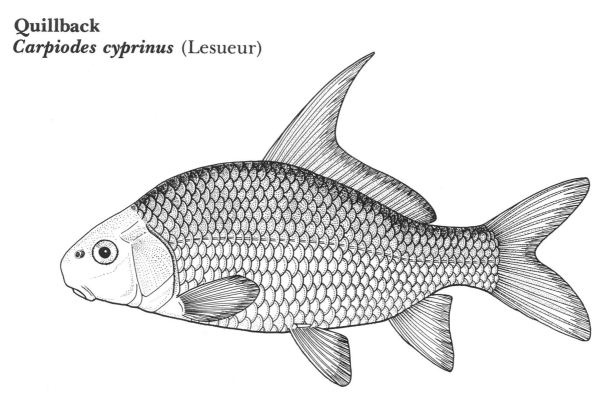

Catostomus cyprinus Lesueur 1817b:91 (type-locality: Elk River and other tributaries of Chesapeake Bay).

Ichthyobus velifer: Nelson 1876:49 (recorded from Illinois).

Ichthyobus thompsoni: Nelson 1876:49.

Carpiodes velifer: Jordan 1878:65; Large 1903:12; Forbes & Richardson 1908:78–79.

Carpiodes selene: Jordan 1878:65.

Ictiobus cyprinus: Forbes 1884:81 (part., only one carpsucker species recognized).

Carpiodes thompsoni: Jordan 1878:65; Forbes & Richardson 1908:79–80; O'Donnell 1935:479.

Carpiodes forbesi Hubbs 1930:13 (type-locality: Illinois River drainage of Illinois).

Carpiodes cyprinus: O'Donnell 1935:479.

Carpiodes cyprinus hinei Trautman 1956:35 (type-locality: Scioto River, northeastern Rush Township, Scioto County, Ohio—some Illinois specimens designated paratypes).

Carpiodes cyprinus (Lesueur) subspecies: Smith 1965: 8.

Diagnosis.—The quillback is a much compressed carpsucker, differing from the river carpsucker in having the anterior rays of the dorsal fin greatly elongate in the adult, a deeper body, a produced and squarish snout (the anterior tip of the snout well in advance of the anterior nostril), and usually more than 37 scales in the lateral line, and in lacking the nipplelike protuberance at the tip of the lower jaw. The adult can be distinguished from other carpsuckers by the combination of deep body form, produced snout, and lack of the jaw "nipple." The young is most easily separated from young of other carpsuckers by snout shape and absence of a jaw "nipple." The young differs from the young smallmouth buffalo in having a paler coloration, a more slender caudal peduncle, and an asymmetrical subopercle. The species attains a length of 560 mm (22 inches), but most adults are less than 380 mm (15 inches) in total length.

Variation.—The great range of ontogenetic and individual variation is reflected by the complex synonymy of the quillback. In addition to the several synonyms, early authors frequently misapplied names to the entities that they recognized. Hubbs (1930:13–16) straightened out the confusion in the early literature and reluctantly proposed *Carpiodes forbesi* as a substitute name for the Illinois River form that Forbes & Richardson had called *C. thompsoni,* a preoccupied name in the genus. Trautman (1956) described a western subspecies (*hinei*) on the basis of its more elongate body form and relatively larger eye. Bailey & Allum (1962:81) synonymized both *forbesi* and *hinei* under *C. cyprinus,* thus reducing the number of carpsucker taxa to three.

Ecology.—The quillback is common in creeks, rivers, and some lakes. In streams it feeds on bottom ooze in pools and eddies of backwaters. It has a wider range of ecological tolerance than other carpsuckers, occurring in clear and silty habitats and in streams of various sizes. Forbes & Richardson (1908:79) reported spawning in mid-April, but the season likely extends into June. Vanicek (1961) found 10 different year classes in a population he studied in the Des Moines River. Spawning, as in other carpsuckers, consists of broadcasting the eggs over the bottom.

Distribution.—The quillback is statewide in occurrence in Illinois but rather sporadic and uncommon in the southern half of the state. In northern and much of central Illinois it is widely distributed and abundant in streams of all sizes and in some lakes. It is seemingly more widespread and common now than during the censusing by Forbes & Richardson prior to 1908.

Highfin carpsucker
Carpiodes velifer (Rafinesque)

Catostomus velifer Rafinesque 1820a:56 (type-locality: Ohio River).
Ichthyobus difformis: Nelson 1876:49 (recorded from Illinois).
Carpiodes difformis: Jordan 1878:65; Large 1903: 12; Forbes & Richardson 1908:77–78; O'Donnell 1935:479.
Carpiodes cutisanserinus: Jordan 1878:65.
Ictiobus cyprinus: Forbes 1884:81 (part., only one carpsucker species recognized).
Carpiodes velifer: Smith 1965:8.

Diagnosis.—The highfin carpsucker is extremely deep bodied as an adult, differing from the quillback in having a nipplelike protuberance at the tip of the lower jaw, usually less than 37 lateral-line scales, and a very short and bluntly rounded snout. It differs from the river carpsucker in having the anterior rays of the dorsal fin greatly elongated, a very deep body, and a shorter and much deeper snout. Specimens less than 130 mm (5 inches) in total length usually cannot be distinguished from young river carpsuckers but can be separated from young quillbacks and smallmouth buffalos by the dentary "nipple" and shorter and rounded snout. The species attains a length of about 310 mm (12 inches).

Variation.—No studies of geographic variation have been published, in part due to the difficulty of distinguishing the young of this species from other carpsuckers and buffalos.

Ecology.—The highfin carpsucker inhabits clear water in small and large rivers that flow over gravel or mixed gravel-sand-silt. Presumably its feeding and reproductive habits are similar to those of related species, except that the highfin carpsucker is more of a riffle-inhabiting species. Vanicek (1961) found eight age classes in a population he studied in the Des Moines River.

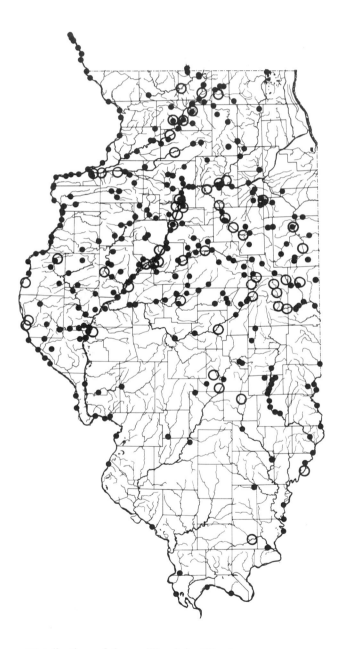

Distribution of the quillback in Illinois.

Highfin carpsucker

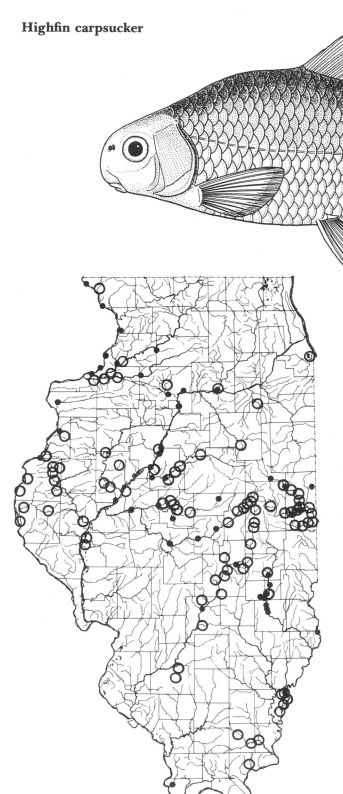

Distribution of the highfin carpsucker in Illinois.

Distribution.—The highfin carpsucker occurs in almost all parts of the state but is most common across central Illinois. It is decimated over the entire state, probably because of excessive siltation and the deterioration of water quality. Forbes and Richardson found that this species was the most generally distributed and most abundant carpsucker in the state; it is now the least.

Moxostoma Rafinesque

This North American genus contains 20 recognized species; six of them have been reported in Illinois, but one has long been extirpated. Young specimens of some species of redhorses are difficult to distinguish.

KEY TO SPECIES

1. Caudal fin red or pink in life; scales on upper sides with small dark spots (on scale bases), forming rows of faint dark spots above lateral line 2

   Caudal fin slate colored in life; scales on upper sides without dark spots on scale bases that form rows of dots above lateral line 4

2. Head small, its length usually going 4.2 or more times into standard length; mouth small, lower lip thicker than upper, its posterior border forming a nearly straight line; free edge of dorsal fin concave .. *macrolepidotum*

Head large, its length usually going four or fewer times into standard length; mouth large, upper lip thick and lower lip very thick, its posterior border forming a U-shaped curve; free edge of dorsal fin convex or straight edged 3

3. Pharyngeal teeth heavy and molarlike; occipital region flattened and snout squarish; eye large, diameter contained four or fewer times in head length of young specimens; caudal peduncle scales, usually 12 or 13 ....
.... *carinatum*
Pharyngeal teeth thin and comblike; occipital region and snout bluntly rounded; eye small, diameter contained more than four times in head length of young specimens; caudal peduncle scales, usually 15 or 16 ....
.... *valenciennesi**

4. Dorsal fin rays, 15 or 16; free edge of dorsal fin straight or convex; body relatively deep, its greatest depth usually exceeding head length;

lower lip distinctly bilobed, the cleft between the lobes forming an acute angle; lips somewhat papillose .... *anisurum*
Dorsal fin rays, 13 or 14; free edge of dorsal fin concave; body nearly terete; lower lip not distinctly bilobed and its posterior border usually forming a U-shaped curve; lips plicate
.... 5

5. Scales in lateral line, 39–43; pelvic fin rays, usually nine; caudal peduncle stout, its depth usually contained 1.8 or fewer times in distance from caudal fin to front of anal fin; rear edge of lower lip distinctly U-shaped ......
.... *erythrurum*
Scales in lateral line, 44–48; pelvic fin rays, usually 10 on one or both sides; caudal peduncle slender, its depth usually contained more than 1.8 times in distance from caudal fin to front of anal fin; rear edge of lower lip shallowly U-shaped .... *duquesnei*

Silver redhorse
Moxostoma anisurum (Rafinesque)

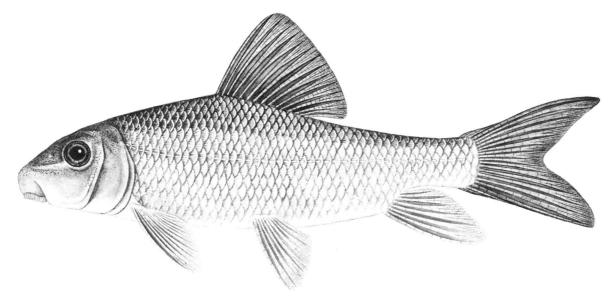

Catostomus anisurus Rafinesque 1820*a*:54 (type-locality: Ohio River); ?Kennicott 1855:594 (recorded from Illinois).
Teretulus carpio: Nelson 1876:49.
?*Teretulus velatus:* Nelson 1876:49.
?*Teretulus anisurus:* Nelson 1876:49.
Myxostoma carpio: Jordan 1878:63.
?*Myxostoma velatum:* Jordan 1878:64.
Moxostoma carpio: Forbes 1884:80.
Moxostoma anisurum: Large 1903:11; Forbes & Richardson 1908:89–90; O'Donnell 1935:479; Smith 1965:8.

Diagnosis.—The silver redhorse is a relatively deep-bodied (body depth going about three times into standard length and greater than greatest head length) redhorse with a slate-colored tail, whitish ventral fins, a convex or straight-edged dorsal fin usually containing 15 or 16 rays, and a full lower lip that is distinctly bilobed and somewhat papillose as well as plicate. The adult is readily distinguished from other species in the genus by the deep body shape (at the origin of the dorsal) and the convex dorsal fin. The young is most readily recognized by the distinctive lower lip, which has two strong lobes separated by a deep and acutely angled cleft. It differs from the river redhorse in lacking a red tail and spots on the scale bases of the back and sides, and in having a smaller

and strongly bilobed lower lip. The species attains a length of slightly over 510 mm (20 inches).

Variation.—A thorough analysis of variation in the species has been undertaken by Dr. Robert E. Jenkins of Roanoke College but is not yet published.

Ecology.—The silver redhorse is most common in long deep pools of medium-sized rivers. It is most often taken in deep, rather firm-bottomed pools that have undercut banks and tree roots protruding into the water. The most complete account of feeding and reproductive behavior in the species is that of Meyer (1962). In the Des Moines River he found the food to be almost entirely immatures of aquatic insects. Spawning occurred in early May in rather deep, clear riffles in the main channels. Many thousand eggs were produced by each female. Growth was rapid during the 1st year. Sexual maturity was reached at age five, and nine year classes were present in the population.

Distribution.—The silver redhorse is occasional in small and medium-sized rivers in northern and central Illinois but extremely rare in the southern half of the state. There is no real evidence of decimation because the species was seldom taken before the advent of electrofishing gear. It is likely that it was more abundant before siltation became so extensive and fluctuations in water level so drastic.

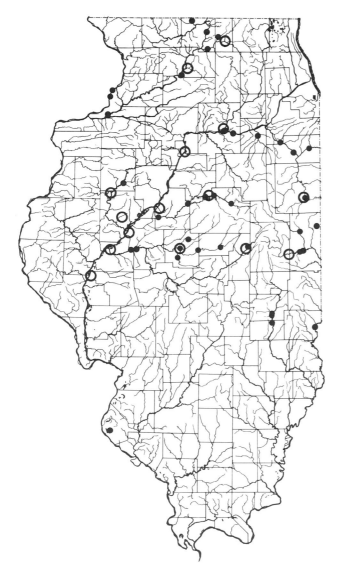

Distribution of the silver redhorse in Illinois.

River redhorse
Moxostoma carinatum (Cope)

Placopharynx carinatus Cope 1870b:467 (type-locality: Wabash River, Lafayette, Indiana); Nelson 1876:49 (recorded from Illinois); Forbes 1884: 80; O'Donnell 1935:480.

Placopharynx carinatns: Jordan 1878:63 (misspelling).

Placopharynx duquesnei: Large 1903:13; Forbes & Richardson 1908:93–94.

Moxostoma carinatum: Smith 1965:8.

Moxostoma valenciennesi: Smith 1965:8 (misidentification).

Diagnosis.—The river redhorse is a slightly compressed and red-tailed redhorse (the illustration in Forbes & Richardson—1908:93—was inadvertently colored gray) with dark spots on the scale bases of the back and sides, a large head (length contained fewer than four times in standard

River redhorse

length), a large mouth and heavy plicate lips, posterior border of lower lip broadly U-shaped, the distal edge of the dorsal fin convex or with a straight edge, and pharyngeal teeth heavy and molarlike. The large head, squarish snout, large eye, and molariform teeth distinguish this species from the related but extirpated (in Illinois) greater redhorse. The juvenile most closely resembles that of the golden redhorse but can be separated from that species by the red tail, heavier lips, straight-edged dorsal fin, and molarlike pharyngeal teeth. A specimen 690 mm (27 inches) in total length was taken from the Fox River in 1958.

Variation.—As in other species of the genus, a study not yet published on variation has been done by Robert E. Jenkins of Roanoke College.

Ecology.—In Illinois this poorly known sucker occurs in deep, swift, gravelly riffles of small and medium-sized rivers and is seemingly intolerant of silty bottoms, turbid waters, and pollution. The specialized pharyngeal teeth of this species enable it to feed heavily on molluscs as well as benthic insects. Although a common species in some Ozark streams, little information is available on its reproduction. Carlander (1969:508–509) summarized unpublished data and noted that 12 age classes were present in Missouri populations.

Distribution.—No inferences can be drawn about the changes in status of the river redhorse, since it was known to Forbes & Richardson (1908) from only one locality and is known at present from only a few localities. The species is common in the Kankakee River but extremely uncommon elsewhere in the state.

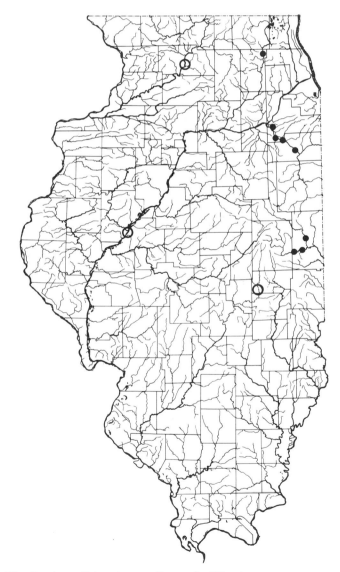

Distribution of the river redhorse in Illinois.

Black redhorse
Moxostoma duquesnei (Lesueur)

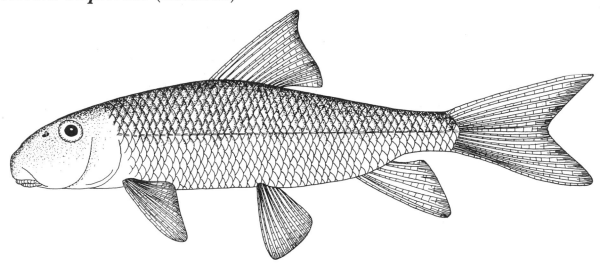

Catostomus duquesnii Lesueur 1817*b*:105 (type-locality: Ohio River at Pittsburgh, Pennsylvania); ?Kennicott 1855:594 (recorded from Illinois).

Moxostoma aureolum: Forbes & Richardson 1908: 90–91 (part.).

Moxostoma duquesnii: Hubbs 1930:23 (name resurrected, recorded from Illinois).

Moxostoma duquesnei: Smith 1965:8.

Diagnosis.—The black redhorse is a terete and gray-tailed redhorse with 44–48 lateral-line scales, a slender caudal peduncle (its least depth contained 1.8 times or more in the distance from the caudal base to the front of the anal fin), a rather small mouth, lips relatively thin and plicate, the rear edge of lower lip shallowly U-shaped to straight edged, and the snout rounded rather than squarish. The snout of the breeding male lacks tubercles. This species most closely resembles the golden redhorse, especially when young, but it has head-body proportions and a mouth structure suggesting the northern redhorse. The best character for distinguishing it from the golden redhorse is its higher lateral-line scale count and from the northern redhorse, the slate-colored tail and relatively longer head. The species is usually less than 380 mm (15 inches) in length.

Variation.—This species was not recognized until Hubbs (1930) resurrected the name *duquesnei* from the synonymy of *M. erythrurum.* It is said to have 10 pelvic fin rays in one or both fins, but most Illinois specimens have only 9. A study of variation in the species by Dr. Robert E. Jenkins is as yet unpublished.

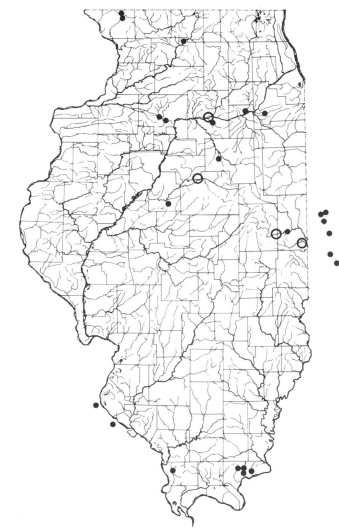

Distribution of the black redhorse in Illinois.

Ecology.—The black redhorse occurs in clean, high-gradient creeks and rivers and probably has always been uncommon in Illinois. It is less tolerant of pollution, siltation, and turbidity than are most other suckers and thus differs from them somewhat in feeding and reproductive habits. An excellent account of its life history in Missouri streams was published by Bowman (1970). Like other redhorses, it feeds in schools near the bottom. Spawning, which is similar to that of related species, occurs in rather deep, clear riffles over gravel or rubble. The species lives 8–10 years.

Distribution.—The black redhorse occurs sporadically in the northern half of the state and in some of the high-gradient and little modified streams in the Shawnee Hills of southern Illinois. It is uncommon everywhere except in Lusk Creek in Pope County and Big Creek in Hardin County. No inferences can be drawn about changes in its distribution, since it has evidently always been rare in this state, but several specimens have been found mixed with Forbes and Richardson's "*Moxostoma aureolum*" taken between 1883 and 1901.

Golden redhorse
Moxostoma erythrurum (Rafinesque)

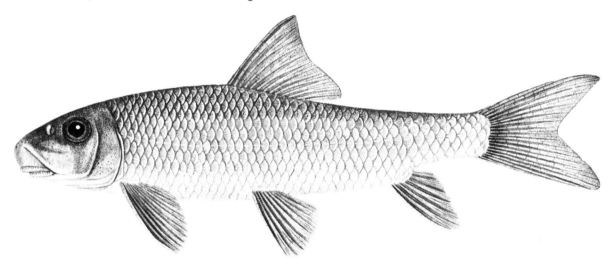

Catostomus erythrurus Rafinesque 1818d:355 (type-locality: Ohio River).

?*Teretulus duquesnii:* Nelson 1876:49 (recorded from Illinois).

Teretulus macrolepidotum: Nelson 1876:49.

?*Myxostoma macrolepidotum* var. *duquesnii:* Jordan 1878:63.

Moxostoma macrolepidotum: Forbes 1884:80.

Moxostoma aureolum: Large 1903:12; Forbes & Richardson 1908:90–91; O'Donnell 1935:479.

Moxostoma erythrurum: Smith 1965:8.

Diagnosis.—The golden redhorse is a terete and gray-tailed redhorse with a relatively large head and mouth, plicate lips that form a V- or U-shaped curve posteriorly, a rather thin lower lip, a squarish snout, usually 39–43 lateral-line scales, a concave dorsal fin, and a rather thick caudal peduncle (its least depth contained fewer than 1.8 times in the distance from the caudal base to the front of the anal fin). It is most like the black redhorse, differing primarily in the lower lateral-line scale count, stouter caudal peduncle, larger mouth, squarish snout, and tuberculate snout (in the breeding male). It differs from the river redhorse in having a slate-colored tail, a smaller head and mouth, a concave dorsal fin, and thin comblike pharyngeal teeth. Very small young are sometimes difficult to distinguish from those of other redhorse species and young spotted suckers. The species is said to attain a length of more than 610 mm (2 feet), but most adults are under 380 mm (15 inches).

Variation.—Considerable individual variation is found in young specimens. Dr. R. E. Jenkins of Roanoke College studied variation in the species and will presumably soon publish his results.

Ecology.—The golden redhorse is the most wide-spread and common species in the genus but is seldom found in large rivers, where the shorthead redhorse is relatively common. The preferred habitat is raceways and firm-bottomed pools of creeks and small rivers. Like other species, the golden redhorse feeds on bottom ooze, molluscs, and benthic insects. Spawning occurs in April and May in riffles. The reproductive behavior is similar to that of other redhorses. A life-history study was published by Meyer (1962); other details have been summarized by Carlander (1969:511–514).

Distribution.—The species occurs in all parts of the state except those south-central Illinois counties having predominantly clay soils and low-gradient creeks. It is abundant in most of northern and central Illinois but somewhat decimated in the streams west of the Illinois River. The species is probably as widely distributed as formerly but less abundant because of the deterioration of water quality and the siltation of many streams.

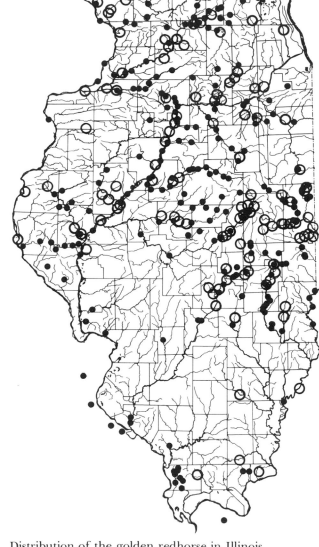

Distribution of the golden redhorse in Illinois.

Shorthead redhorse
Moxostoma macrolepidotum
(Lesueur)

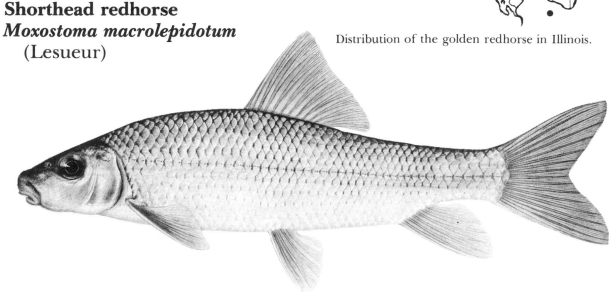

Catostomus macrolepidotus Lesueur 1817*b*:94 (type-locality: Delaware River).

?*Catostomus aureolus:* Kennicott 1855:594 (recorded from Illinois).

Teretulus aureolum: Nelson 1876:49.
Myxostoma aureoleum: Jordan 1878:63.
Moxostoma aureolum: Forbes 1884:80.
Moxostoma macrolepidotum: Large 1903:12; Smith 1965:8.
Moxostoma breviceps: Forbes & Richardson 1908: 91–92.
Moxostoma lesueurii: O'Donnell 1935:480.

Diagnosis.—The shorthead redhorse is a somewhat compressed and red-tailed redhorse with rows of dark spots (on the scale bases) on the back and sides, a small head (its length usually going into the standard length well over four times), a small mouth with thinly plicate lips and some cross striae, and a lower lip that is straight edged posteriorly. The combination of red tail, short head, and small mouth serves to distinguish the adult from all other Illinois suckers. The small young may resemble young black and golden redhorses, but tail fin color and mouth shape permit identification of most juveniles. The species attains a length of 610 mm (2 feet), but most adults are much smaller.

Variation.—Several nominal species close to the shorthead redhorse have been shown to be conspecific by Dr. R. E. Jenkins of Roanoke College. Presumably they will be regarded as southeastern subspecies, but the study has not yet been published. The nominate subspecies (*M. m. macrolepidotum*) occupies all of this state except southwestern and southeastern Illinois. Material from the Mississippi River below the mouth of the Missouri is referable to the Ozark subspecies, *M. m. pisolabrum,* but when more specimens are available, the southwestern Illinois population may be found to consist of *macrolepidotum* X *pisolabrum* intergrades. Specimens from the Wabash and Embarras rivers are intergrades between *M. m. macrolepidotum* and *M. m. breviceps.*

Ecology.—The shorthead redhorse occurs in rivers, including the Mississippi, but is rarely found in creeks. The preferred habitat is deep raceways and firm-bottomed pools with some flow. While clear, fast water over a gravel bottom is the optimal habitat, the species is sometimes taken in turbid waters and in bays of large rivers where there is little current. Its feeding and reproductive habits are similar to those of other redhorses. Its life history in the Des Moines River has been described by Meyer (1962). Burr & Morris (1977) reported over a hundred shorthead redhorse spawning off a sandbar in a high-gradient northeastern Illinois

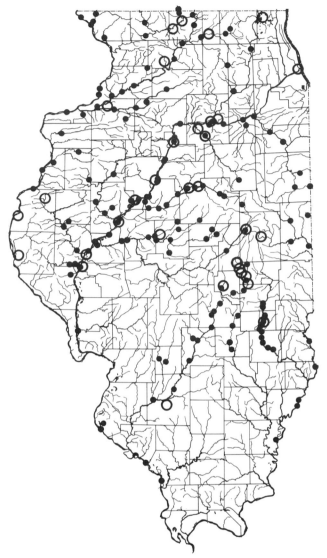

Distribution of the shorthead redhorse in Illinois.

stream in mid-May. They observed no territoriality or aggressive displays. Groups of three to seven with the female in the middle or below the males, violently rolled and undulated until troughlike nests were formed in the sand and gravel. The spawning site was shared by white suckers and northern hog suckers in similar-sized groups. The tuberculate shorthead redhorse captured were all 5 years old.

Distribution.—The species occurs in all parts of the state except extreme southern Illinois. It is widely distributed and, although less common than the golden redhorse, apparently more general in occurrence now than formerly, probably because it has greater ecological tolerance than other species in the genus.

Greater redhorse*
Moxostoma valenciennesi Jordan

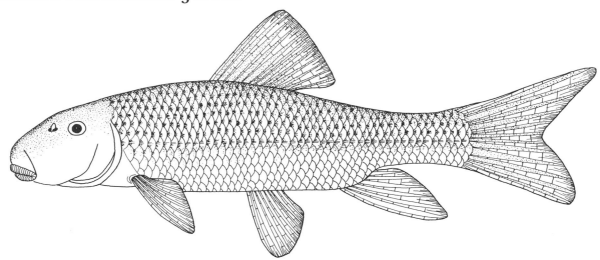

Moxostoma valenciennesi Jordan 1886:73 (type-locality: Lake Ontario).

Moxostoma aureolum: Forbes & Richardson 1908: 90–91 (part.).

Moxostoma rubreques Hubbs 1930:24–25 (type-locality: Au Sable River, just below Foote Dam, Michigan; also recorded from Illinois).

Diagnosis.—The greater redhorse is a somewhat compressed and red-tailed redhorse with rows of dark spots (one per scale base) on the back and sides, a large mouth, full and plicate lips, usually 15 or 16 caudal peduncle scales, a convex or straight-edged dorsal fin, a bluntly rounded snout and occiput, a small eye (its diameter usually contained four or more times in the head length even in young), and thin and comblike pharyngeal teeth. Superficially, the species resembles the river redhorse, differing from it in lacking the molarlike pharyngeal teeth and the squared snout, and in having a higher caudal peduncle scale count. If the red tail fin has not faded, the species can easily be distinguished from the golden redhorse. If it has, dorsal fin shape and caudal peduncle scale counts will separate the species. The large head and U-shaped lips preclude confusion with the shorthead redhorse. The species attains a length of about 610 mm (2 feet).

Variation.—Dr. R. E. Jenkins will presumably publish the results of his study of variation in the species.

Ecology.—Almost nothing is known about the habits of this sucker. Scott & Crossman (1973: 585–586) have summarized the small amount of

Distribution of the greater redhorse in Illinois.

data available, and the life history of the species is apparently quite similar to that of other redhorse species.

Distribution.—Extirpated in Illinois. The species has long been gone from Illinois. Dr. R. E. Jenkins found a specimen among the Forbes and Richardson holdings of *M. erythrurum*. It was col-lected in Salt Creek, Du Page County, in 1901. No other specimens have been found, and Salt Creek is now highly modified by industrial and suburban development. The species is known to occur at present in adjacent Wisconsin (George C. Becker, personal communication) and adjacent Indiana (Whitaker & Wallace 1973:458).

Hypentelium Rafinesque

This bizarre, eastern North American genus contains three recognized species, one of which occurs in Illinois.

Northern hog sucker
Hypentelium nigricans (Lesueur)

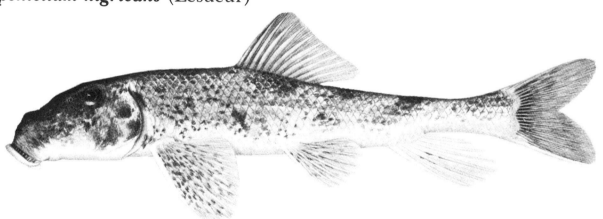

Catostomus nigricans Lesueur 1817*b*:102 (type-locality: Lake Erie); Kennicott 1855:594 (recorded from Illinois); Jordan 1878:64; Forbes 1884:64; Large 1903:12; Forbes & Richardson 1908:86–88.
Hypentelium nigricans: Nelson 1876:48; O'Donnell 1935:479; Smith 1965:8.

Diagnosis.—The northern hog sucker is a terete and large-headed sucker easily distinguished from other Illinois species by its squarish head (in cross section), depressed area between the eyes, large and protractile mouth, strongly papillose lips, flattened breast, large and expansive pectoral fins, and three to five prominent black bars traversing the back. Sometimes young redhorses have four black bands crossing the back, but the distinctive head and mouth of the hog sucker make it recognizable at a glance. The species attains a length of about 460 mm (18 inches).

Variation.—Hubbs (1930:41–43) noted little geographic variation throughout the range of the species. Raney & Lachner (1947) discussed its taxonomic relationships with other species in the genus.

Ecology.—The northern hog sucker inhabits clear, fast riffles and raceways with pebbly or gravel-sand bottoms that are free of silt and vegetation. It feeds primarily on benthic insects, molluscs, and other invertebrates that it sucks up while overturning pebbles on the bottom. It is highly migratory and ascends clean gravelly streams in April and May to spawn. Raney & Lachner (1946) gave a detailed account of the ecology and life history of the species in New York. The species is intolerant of pollution, silt, and the modification of stream channels. It overwinters in quiet water of large streams. It occurs in impoundments only as a straggler and has not been found at all in natural lakes

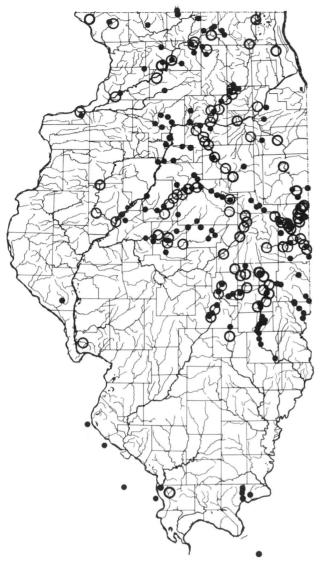

Distribution of the northern hog sucker in Illinois.

or sloughs. It is less of a schooling fish than are redhorses, but groups of two and three are commonly seen. Spawning is communal in early spring. The species lives 5 or more years.

Distribution.—The northern hog sucker occurs in the high-quality streams of northern and central Illinois and in a few clean streams of the Shawnee Hills in extreme southern Illinois. It is absent in much of south-central and western Illinois. Although still common in parts of northern and east-central Illinois, the species is decimated even here, probably because of a combination of silt and pollution.

Catostomus Lesueur

This genus of small-scaled suckers is confined to North America except for one species that also extends across the Bering Strait into Siberia. It includes 25 recognized species, 2 of which occur in Illinois, one of these being restricted to Lake Michigan.

KEY TO SPECIES

1. Lateral-line scales, more than 85; prominent bulbous snout extending far beyond tip of lower lip; lower lip flaring widely posteriorly; posterior end of mouth extending backward behind nostrils .... *catostomus*
   Lateral-line scales, 55–85; snout rounded and projecting only slightly beyond tip of lower lip; lower lip not flaring appreciably posteriorly; posterior end of mouth extending backward only as far as nostrils .... *commersoni*

Longnose sucker
Catostomus catostomus (Forster)

Cyprinus catostomus Forster 1773:158 (type-locality: streams about Hudson Bay).

Catostomus longirostris: Jordan 1878:64 (abundant in Lake Michigan).

Catostomus catostomus: Large 1903:11 (uncertain occurrence in Illinois); Forbes & Richardson 1908: 84 (doubtlessly occurring in Lake Michigan off Illinois shore); O'Donnell 1935:479 (presumably in lower Lake Michigan).

Catostomus catostomus catostomus: Smith 1965:11 (presumably in Illinois waters of Lake Michigan).

Diagnosis.—The longnose sucker is a terete and small-scaled sucker, dark olive above and white below (rather sharply bicolored), with more than 85 lateral-line scales, a bulbous snout that extends well beyond the tip of the lower jaw, the rear edge of the mouth extending back to the anterior nostril, the lower lip flaring widely posteriorly, and large papillose lips. The high scale count and bulbous snout readily separate this species from the white sucker, which it most resembles. The breeding male has a rosy lateral band. The longnose sucker attains a length of about 510 mm (20 inches).

Longnose sucker

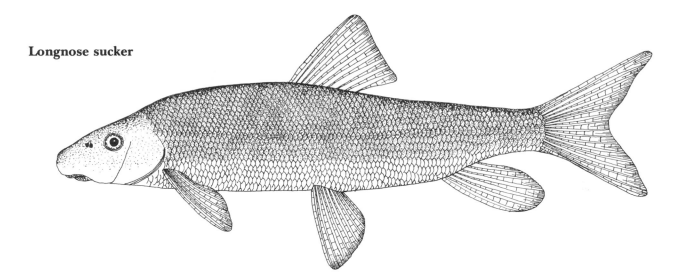

Variation.—Several populations with restricted ranges have been described as subspecies, but most current workers do not recognize them because of the great amount of individual variation throughout the range of the species.

Ecology.—Spawning presumably occurs in the spring in shallow waters of Lake Michigan. The species feeds almost entirely on benthic invertebrates. Good summaries of the ecology, which is not well known, of the longnose sucker in Canadian waters are provided by McPhail & Lindsey (1970:287) and Scott & Crossman (1973:532–535). The longnose sucker spawns earlier in the spring in Canada than do most suckers, and spawning is a communal affair, each female broadcasting many thousands of adhesive eggs over the bottom. Hatching in nature is believed to require about 2 weeks. In Canada this slow-growing fish may live almost 20 years.

Distribution.—As indicated in the synonymy, the longnose sucker has long been expected in the Illinois waters of Lake Michigan. An old record of *Catostomus hudsonius* (a synonym of *C. catostomus*) from the Rock River (Nelson 1876:48) is almost certainly based on a misidentified white sucker. In May 1969 Bruce Muench, then with the Illinois Department of Conservation, collected an adult specimen just off Montrose Beach, Chicago. Since then Harry L. Wight (personal communication) advises that he has seen specimens at four other sites in the lake.

Distribution of the longnose sucker in Illinois.

White sucker
Catostomus commersoni (Lacépède)

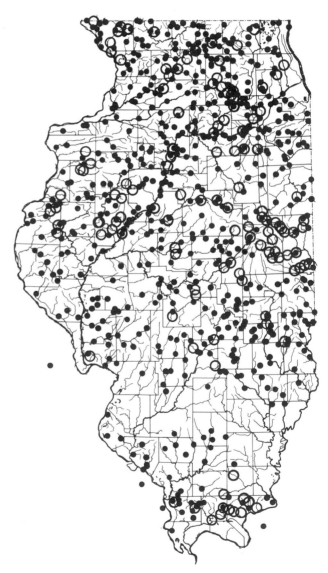

Cyprinus commersonii Lacépède 1803:503 (type-locality: unknown).

?*Catostomus hudsonius:* Nelson 1876:48.

Catostomus teres: Nelson 1876:48 (recorded from Illinois).

Catostomos teres: Forbes 1884:81 (misspelling).

Catostomus commersonii: Jordan 1878:64; Large 1903:12; Forbes & Richardson 1908:85–86; O'Donnell 1935:479.

Catostomus commersoni: Smith 1965:8.

Diagnosis.—The white sucker is a terete and small-scaled sucker, bronzy slate or olive above and whitish below, with 55–85 lateral-line scales, a large and papillose mouth, a distinctly bilobed lower lip, a rounded snout that projects only slightly beyond the tip of the lower lip, and the posterior end of the mouth extending backwards only as far as the nostrils, and without a widely flaring lower lip posteriorly. The young has a distinctive pattern of small, blackish, tesselated blotches on the predorsum and upper sides, giving the fish a mosaic appearance, and three vague dark blotches along the side. The species can be distinguished from all other suckers except the longnose sucker by the very small scales and is separable from the longnose by its much shorter snout and lower lateral-line scale count. It attains a length of slightly more than 510 mm (20 inches).

Variation.—Several subspecies have been described and soon after have been synonymized in this wide-ranging species. A Great Plains subspecies (*C. c. suckleyi*) was recognized for many years, but Bailey & Allum (1962:85–86) synonymized it also.

Distribution of the white sucker in Illinois.

Ecology.—The white sucker is typically a species of clear, sandy or gravelly creeks and small rivers, but it has extremely wide ecological tolerances and occasionally can be found in almost any kind of stream or lake, even in badly silted streams. Spawning occurs in gravelly riffles and pools in late March to May. The tuberculate males sometimes are reddish or purplish and have a well-defined lateral band. Eggs are broadcast over the pebbly bottoms of riffles and in nature hatch in about 3 weeks. The young grow rapidly. The food consists primarily of benthic invertebrates. Good summaries of the ecology are presented by Cross (1967: 195–196) and Scott & Crossman (1973:540–543).

The species is known to attain an age of 15 years.

Distribution.—The white sucker is statewide in distribution, including Lake Michigan, and it is abundant everywhere except in the block of south-central counties between the limits of the Wisconsinan and Illinoian glacial advances, where most streams have clay or mud bottoms. Despite the wholesale deterioration of its preferred habitat in Illinois, there is no evidence of the decimation of the species, except in localized areas that are chronically polluted. It is very common except in the largest rivers.

Minytrema Jordan

This genus contains only one species, which occurs in eastern North America barely extending into Canada.

Spotted sucker
Minytrema melanops (Rafinesque)

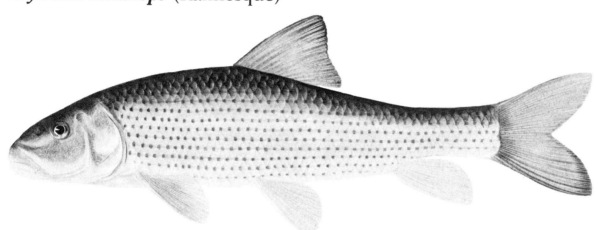

Catostomus melanops Rafinesque 1820*a*:57 (type-locality: Ohio River).

Erimyzon melanops: Nelson 1876:48 (recorded from Illinois).

Minytrema melanops: Jordan 1878:64; Forbes 1884: 80; Large 1903:12; Forbes & Richardson 1908: 83; O'Donnell 1935:479; Smith 1965:8.

Diagnosis.—The spotted sucker is a terete sucker, pale olive above and white below, with many longitudinal rows of squarish brown spots (located on scale bases), a slate-colored tail, a short and slightly concave dorsal fin with 11 or 12 rays, usu-ally 43–45 lateral-line scales but few or no lateral-line pores, and rather thin and striate lips. Specimens more than 75 mm (3 inches) long are readily distinguished by the rows of prominent brown spots, but the small young resembles the young of redhorses and also of the white sucker. The young of the spotted sucker, if it has not yet developed the characteristic pattern, can be distinguished from young redhorses and white suckers by its mouth shape and reddish dorsal fin, which is blackish distally. The species attains a length of 460 mm (18 inches).

Variation.—No studies of geographic variation in the species have been published and no subspecies are recognized.

Ecology.—The spotted sucker is usually found in clear firm-bottomed creeks and small rivers but in Illinois occurs occasionally in a wide variety of habitats, ranging from small turbid creeks to the Mississippi River and even in overflow lakes and impoundments. Spawning males develop two blackish lateral bands on each side and often have a lavender coloration. McSwain & Gennings (1972) gave a detailed account of spawning behavior during April in a Georgia river. Spawning behavior is similar to that of other suckers. Feeding habits of the species have not been well studied. The species lives no longer than 6 years.

Distribution.—The spotted sucker still occurs in all parts of the state, except perhaps in extreme northeastern Illinois, where it was never known. However, it is sporadic and uncommon, except in east-central Illinois, and even in that part of the state it is decidedly less widespread and common than formerly. The Forbes and Richardson records indicate a rather general distribution in Illinois in the last century. Siltation is probably the factor most responsible for decimation of the species, and it is possible that it is disappearing from many areas of the state.

Distribution of the spotted sucker in Illinois.

Erimyzon Jordan

This eastern North American genus of cyprinid-like suckers includes three recognized species, two of which occur in Illinois.

KEY TO SPECIES

1. Lateral-line scales, usually 39–43; dorsal rays, 9 or 10; body depth contained more than 3.3 times in standard length; head bluntly rounded; immature pattern consisting of 5–8 confluent lateral blotches .... *oblongus*
   Lateral-line scales, usually 35–37; dorsal rays, 11 or 12; body depth contained 3.3 or fewer times in standard length; head pointed; immature pattern consisting of an intense black lateral band .... *sucetta*

Creek chubsucker
Erimyzon oblongus (Mitchill)

Cyprinus oblongus Mitchill 1815:459 (type-locality: New York).
?*Catostomus tuberculatus:* Kennicott 1855:594 (part., recorded from Illinois).
?*Erimyzon oblongus:* Nelson 1876:48 (part.).
Erimyzon sucetta: Jordan 1878:64 (part.); Forbes 1884:80 (part.).
Erimyzon sucetta oblongus: Large 1903:12 (part.); Forbes & Richardson 1908:81–82 (part.); O'Donnell 1935:479 (part.).
Erimyzon oblongus claviformis: Smith 1965:8.

Creek chubsucker

Diagnosis.—The creek chubsucker is a slab-sided (body depth going 3.3 times or more into standard length) and olive-colored sucker, lacking a lateral line but possessing a short and convex dorsal fin located on the anterior part of the body, 9 or 10 dorsal rays, 5–8 confluent dark blotches along the side that extend over the back as weak saddles or (in young) a black stripe along the side, usually 39–41 lateral scales, rather thin lips, the two halves of the lower lip meeting at about a right angle, and a distinctly bilobed anal fin in the breeding male. The young superficially resembles small minnows but has the anal fin located more posteriorly and has the sucker mouth. The species most closely resembles the related lake chubsucker, differing from it in having fewer dorsal rays, larger scales, a blunter snout, and a more definite pattern in the adult. The species attains a length of slightly more than 150 mm (6 inches).

Variation.—Hubbs (1930:37–41) presented the most thorough analysis of geographic variation in the species, recognizing three subspecies. Two of these (*E. o. oblongus* of the Atlantic drainage and *E. o. claviformis* of the Mississippi valley) are still recognized.

Ecology.—The creek chubsucker occurs in low-gradient creeks and is most abundant in quiet pools with muck, debris, vegetation, and overhanging roots. The young are pioneering fish, among the first to ascend headwaters and previously dry stream courses. Very little is known of the feeding and reproductive habits. The food presumably consists of plankton and small benthic invertebrates. Specimens in breeding condition have been

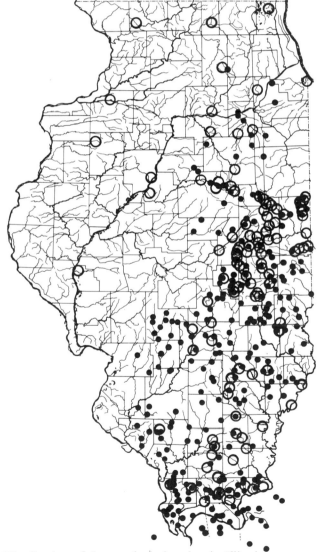

Distribution of the creek chubsucker in Illinois.

collected in April and May, and spawning is probably similar to that in other suckers. Lewis & Elder (1953:199–200) presented limited data on the growth rate in southern Illinois. The species lives no longer than 5 years.

Distribution.—The creek chubsucker is a common fish in the low-gradient creeks of southern and eastern Illinois. It once occurred sparingly in all parts of the state but has been decimated in northern and western Illinois.

Lake chubsucker
Erimyzon sucetta (Lacépède)

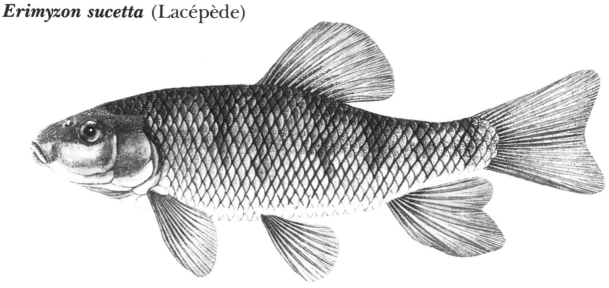

Cyprinus sucetta Lacépède 1803:606 (type-locality: South Carolina).
Erimyzon oblongus: Nelson 1876:48 (part., recorded from Illinois).
Erimyzon sucetta: Jordan 1878:64 (part.); Forbes 1884:80 (part.); Smith 1965:8.
Erimyzon sucetta oblongus: Large 1903:12 (part.); Forbes & Richardson 1908:81–82 (part.); O'Donnell 1935:479 (part.).

Diagnosis.—The lake chubsucker is a slab-sided (body depth going fewer than 3.3 times into standard length of adult) and olivaceous sucker, lacking a lateral line and possessing a short and rounded dorsal fin on the anterior part of the body, 11 or 12 dorsal fin rays, 35–38 lateral scales, thin lips, the two halves of the lower lip meeting at a right angle, a distinctly bilobed anal fin in the breeding male, and a jet black lateral band in the young but usually no definite markings in the adult. The species is more deep bodied and has a sharper snout than the creek chubsucker, from which it also differs in numbers of dorsal fin rays and lateral scales. The young superficially resembles certain minnows but is most like the young creek chubsucker, differing from it in having a more intense black lateral stripe and the blackened anterior border of the anal fin as well as in meristic characters. The species attains a length of over 250 mm (10 inches).

Variation.—Hubbs (1930:35–37) studied variation in the species and recognized two weakly differentiated subspecies. Current authors do not recognize any subspecies.

Ecology.—The lake chubsucker occurs primarily in clear, well-vegetated natural lakes and in some quarries but may also be present in drainage ditches where extensive marshes once occurred. It has been transplanted in some reservoirs as a forage fish for largemouth bass and does well if the water is clear and vegetation is luxuriant. An excellent summary of the small amount of information available on the reproductive biology of the lake chubsucker is given in Scott & Crossman (1973: 552–553). Eggs are broadcast over beds of vegetation and require about a week to hatch in nature.

Distribution.—The present natural distribution of the species consists of "islands" of localities. It is

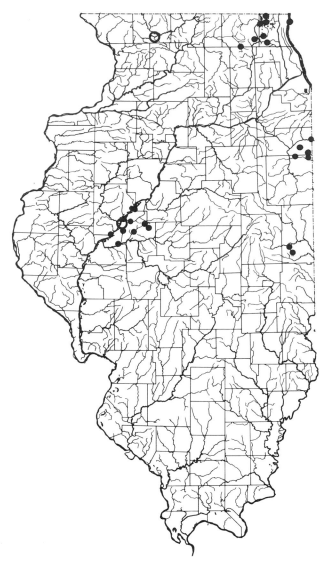

Distribution of the lake chubsucker in Illinois.

present in several of the glacial lakes in northeastern Illinois, in the Kankakee-Iroquois County sand area, the Mason-Tazewell County sand area, and in some very old limestone quarry lakes in southern Vermilion County. Gunning & Lewis (1956a:23–24) reported it from a strip-mine pond in Perry County, where it may still occur. The University of Michigan Museum of Zoology has collections from various localities in extreme southern Illinois made in the 1930's and 1940's, but the species evidently no longer occurs at these localities.

Freshwater catfishes—Ictaluridae

In the United States this family of strictly North American catfishes includes five genera, three of which are found in Illinois. It includes the bullheads and madtoms; the remaining species are simply called catfishes, some of which are similar to the bullheads. The family consists of summer breeders that locate or construct a nest. One or both parents care for the eggs until hatching. In some species the young form tight schools, which are guarded by a parent for some time. Small species feed mostly on benthic organisms. Larger species also scavenge and feed on fish. Bullheads mature in 3 or 4 years and live 7 or 8. Large catfish species may require a longer period to attain sexual maturity and live much longer. Most madtoms probably are sexually mature in their 2nd year and likely live only 3 or 4 years. The large species of catfishes are important commercial and sport fishes, the channel catfish being especially popular. The small species (madtoms) are often good indicators of water quality and habitat modification.

KEY TO GENERA

1. Adipose fin short, its posterior margin free and well separated from caudal fin 2
   Adipose fin a long, keel-like fleshy ridge without a free posterior margin and separated from caudal fin by only a notch .... *Noturus*
2. Lower jaw strongly projecting beyond upper; snout greatly flattened; premaxillary band of teeth with a backward extension on each side of jaw; upper margin of caudal fin white .... *Pylodictis*
   Lower jaw not strongly projecting beyond upper; snout not greatly flattened; premaxillary band of teeth without a backward extension on each side of jaw; upper margin of caudal fin not white .... *Ictalurus*

Ictalurus Rafinesque

In the United States this widespread genus contains 11 recognized species, of which 5 are native to Illinois and a 6th has been introduced. Other species occur in Mexico.

KEY TO SPECIES

1. Caudal fin distinctly forked; upper jaw usually projecting beyond lower 2
   Caudal fin not distinctly forked; upper and lower jaws about equal 4
2. Anal rays, 19–23; greatest head width exceeding length of anal fin base; body squat and greatly widened .... *catus*
   Anal rays, 24 or more; greatest head width less than length of anal fin base; head and body narrow, not greatly widened 3
3. Anal fin with 30–36 rays, its distal margin forming a nearly straight line; eye situated equidistant between top and bottom of head ... . *furcatus*
   Anal fin with 24–30 rays, its distal margin convex; eye situated on dorsal half of head ... . *punctatus*
4. Chin barbels white or yellow; anal fin long, with 24–27 rays .... *natalis*
   Chin barbels gray, black, or dusky; anal fin short, with 16–24 rays 5
5. Anal rays, 16–20; pectoral spine without strong "teeth" along back side; sides of body not mottled .... *melas*
   Anal rays, 21–24; pectoral spine with prominent "teeth" along back side; sides mottled or marbled .... *nebulosus*

White catfish
Ictalurus catus (Linnaeus)

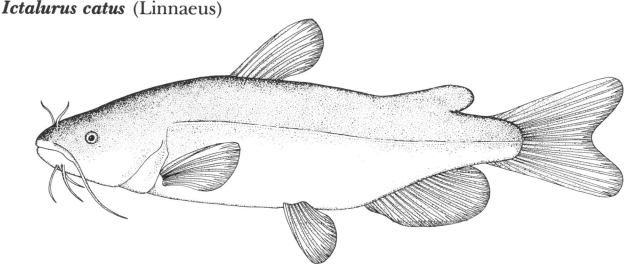

Silurus catus Linnaeus 1758:305 (type-locality: northern part of America).
Ictalurus catus: Smith et al. 1971:8 (recorded from Illinois).

Diagnosis.—The white catfish is a blue-black and frequently mottled bullhead with a moderately forked tail fin, the upper jaw projecting beyond the lower, a short and rounded anal fin usually containing 19–23 rays, and a very wide head (width exceeding the length of the anal fin base). The combination of forked tail fin and short anal fin distinguishes this species from all other Illinois catfishes. The young most closely resembles the young channel catfish, but it is much stouter bodied than that species. None of the Illinois specimens has exceeded 250 mm (10 inches) in length.

Variation.—No subspecies are recognized. Occurring naturally in the Atlantic Coast drainage, the species has been so widely introduced there as well as elsewhere that a study of geographic variation would be meaningless.

Ecology.—In Illinois the white catfish occurs in fee-fishing lakes and large rivers, presumably having escaped from those lakes. Elsewhere in its range the species occupies rivers of various sizes and ponds. It is said to be intermediate ecologically between the bullheads and the channel catfish. No actual evidence of reproduction in Illinois is available, except that several specimens have been taken over a several-year period. Breder (*in* Breder & Rosen 1966:257–258) described the spawning of captive individuals. Miller (*in* Calhoun 1966: 430–434) summarized the literature on the ecol-

Distribution of the white catfish in Illinois.

ogy of the species. In nature both parents participate in excavating a saucer-shaped nest that may be more than 300 mm (12 inches) deep. The mass of rather large and adhesive eggs is covered with sand and silt and with gravel if it is available. At an average water temperature of 26° C hatching requires 6 or 7 days. The rate of growth of the young varies widely.

Distribution.—The first white catfish to be taken in the Illinois River was collected in late 1965, and several specimens have been taken in the middle section of the river by commercial fishermen since. It is also known from widely separated localities in the Mississippi and Kaskaskia rivers and is no doubt present at least temporarily in many of the fee-fishing lakes. When the first Illinois specimens were found, I checked the possibility that they might represent the nominal *Ictalurus anguilla* Evermann & Kendall, long believed to be a synonym of *I. punctatus*. However, the anal ray count of Illinois specimens makes them definitely referable to *I. catus*.

Blue catfish
Ictalurus furcatus (Lesueur)

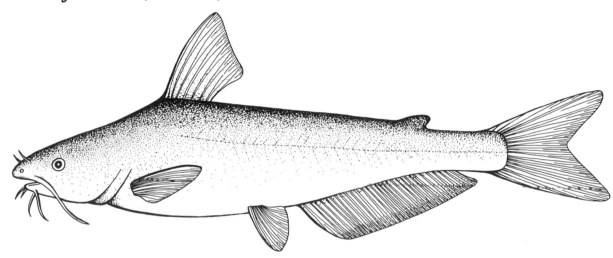

Pimelodus furcatus Lesueur *in* Cuvier & Valenciennes 1840:136 (type-locality: New Orleans).
Ictalurus furcatus: Nelson 1876:50 (recorded from Illinois); Forbes 1884:82; Large 1903:9; Forbes & Richardson 1908:178–179; O'Donnell 1935: 483; Smith 1965:8.
Ichthaelurus furcatus: Jordan 1878:66 (no Illinois specimens known).
Amiurus nigricans: Jordan 1878:66 (part.).
Ictalurus nigricans: Forbes 1884:83.
Ictalurus ponderosus: Forbes 1884:83 (part.).

Diagnosis.—The blue catfish is a pale blue and unspotted catfish with a distinctly forked tail, the upper jaw projecting well beyond the lower, 30–36 anal rays, the distal edge of the anal fin nearly straight, and a small eye situated equidistant between the top and bottom of the head. The species most closely resembles the channel and white cat-fishes but can be easily distinguished from both by the much longer and straight-edged anal fin. Small young are equally distinctive in the same characters. Formerly, giants of more than 45 kg (100 pounds) were taken occasionally; even in recent years specimens in excess of 22.5 kg (50 pounds) and 1 meter in length have been caught.

Variation.—Early workers were confused by the very large catfishes and described the same species several times. Currently, two subspecies are recognized: *I. f. furcatus* in the central U.S. and northern Mexico and *I. f. meridionalis* in eastern Mexico and Guatemala.

Ecology.—The blue catfish occurs in channels of large rivers and lower reaches of their major tributaries. Because of its rather inaccessible habitat, little is known of the species. Spawning occurs in June, and the nest, constructed by the parents, is cared for until the young hatch. Brown & Dendy (1962) reported a varied diet for the species in Alabama, but the food is primarily animal matter and includes fish. Conder & Hoffarth (1965) studied age and growth of individuals up to 10 years old in Kentucky Lake, but much older individuals are known.

Distribution.—The blue catfish occurs in the Mississippi River virtually up to the Wisconsin state line, but it is infrequent except in that portion of the river below the mouth of the Missouri, where commercial fishermen take individuals with regularity. It is not common in other streams but is taken occasionally in the lower Illinois River. There is little evidence that its status is any different than it was formerly. Coker (1930:175) noted that all records in the Keokuk region were for summer months, that navigation dams block the upstream migration of this migratory species, and that its abundance varies from year to year.

Distribution of the blue catfish in Illinois.

Black bullhead
Ictalurus melas (Rafinesque)

Silurus melas Rafinesque 1820*b*:51 (type-locality: Ohio River).
Amiurus confinis: Nelson 1876:50 (recorded from Illinois).
Amiurus pullus: Nelson 1876:50.

Amiurus melas: Jordan 1878:67.
Ictalurus nebulosus: Forbes 1884:83 (part.).
Ameiurus melas: Large 1903:10; Forbes & Richardson 1908:190–192; O'Donnell 1935:484.
Ictalurus melas: Smith 1965:8.

Diagnosis.—The black bullhead is a robust bullhead, uniformly black or olive above and whitish or pale yellow below, with a squared caudal fin, dusky chin barbels, 16–20 anal rays, a light vertical bar on the caudal peduncle, black interradial membranes on most fins, and a roughened (but not serrate) rear edge of the pectoral spine. The species most closely resembles the brown bullhead, differing from it in lacking the conspicuous "teeth" on the back edge of the pectoral spine and the mottling on the sides of the body. The young is distinctive because of the very black chin barbels, the short anal fin, and blackened interradial membranes in the fins. The species attains a length of more than 380 mm (15 inches), but most adults are smaller.

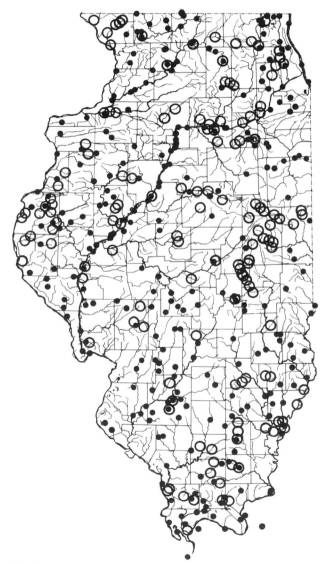

Distribution of the black bullhead in Illinois.

Variation.—Some authors recognize a southern population on the Gulf Coast and in northern Mexico as the subspecies *I. m. catulus;* other authors do not believe that subspecies are recognizable.

Ecology.—The black bullhead inhabits lakes, ponds, swamps, and pool habitats of streams of all sizes, particularly those in low-gradient creeks. Its feeding and breeding habits are similar to those of other species of *Ictalurus.* The compact schools of very small young are well known. An extensive literature exists on the fishery biology of the species. References are cited and information is summarized in Breder & Rosen (1966) and Carlander (1969). Spawning occurs in May and June over excavated nests in mud.

Distribution.—The black bullhead is common in all parts of the state. Yet there is evidence from an examination of the distribution map of the species in Forbes & Richardson (1908) that it was formerly even more ubiquitous than it is now. In view of its wide ecological tolerance, the apparent decimation cannot be easily explained.

Yellow bullhead
Ictalurus natalis (Lesueur)

Pimelodus natalis Lesueur 1819:154 (type-locality: northern Canada).
Amiurus cupreus: Nelson 1876:50 (recorded from Illinois).
Amiurus natalis: Jordan 1878:66.
Ictalurus natalis: Forbes 1884:83; Smith 1965:8.
Ameiurus natalis: Large 1903:9; Forbes & Richardson 1908:185–186; O'Donnell 1935:484.

Diagnosis.—The yellow bullhead is a robust bullhead, olive or brownish above and yellowish below, with a paddle-shaped caudal fin, immaculate white or yellow chin barbels, 24–27 anal rays, a vague dark stripe running through the middle of the anal fin, and a finely serrate rear edge on the pectoral spine. The species most closely resembles the brown bullhead but is easily distinguished from that species by the unpigmented chin barbels. The young is distinctive because of the long anal fin and immaculate chin barbels. The species attains a length of more than 380 mm (15 inches) but is usually much smaller.

Variation.—Currently no subspecies are recognized. For a time the Atlantic Coast form was believed to be a different race, but its name (*ereben-*

Yellow bullhead

nus) was synonymized by Bailey, Winn, & Smith (1954:154).

Ecology.—The yellow bullhead is said by most authors to be a stream species, whereas the black bullhead is more typically a pond species. This idea is somewhat borne out in Illinois, but the two are frequently taken together. The yellow bullhead is the most abundant and most widespread catfish in the state, possibly because it is primarily a creek species and has abundant habitat. Its ecology is relatively well known because of its extensive fishery literature. For references and summaries, see Breder & Rosen (1966) and Carlander (1969). It is an omnivorous feeder. Its life history is similar to that of the black bullhead.

Distribution.—The yellow bullhead is statewide and common, evidently more so than formerly, since Forbes & Richardson (1908:185) noted that it was then much less common than the black bullhead.

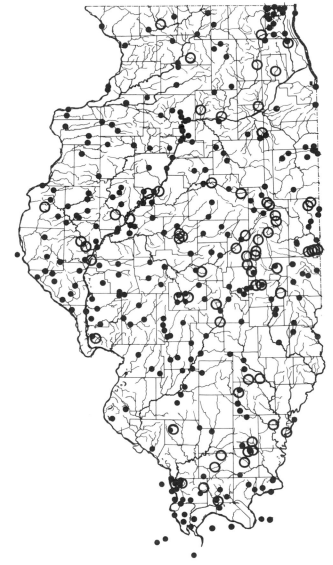

Distribution of the yellow bullhead in Illinois.

Brown bullhead
Ictalurus nebulosus (Lesueur)

Pimelodus nebulosus Lesueur 1819:149 (type-locality: Delaware River at Philadelphia, Pennsylvania).

?*Pimelodus catus:* Kennicott 1855:594 (recorded from Illinois).

Amiurus atrarius: Nelson 1876:50.

Amiurus albidus: Nelson 1876:50.

Amiurus vulgaris: Nelson 1876:50; Jordan 1878:66.

?*Amiurus xanthocephalus:* Jordan 1878:67.

Amiurus marmoratus: Jordan 1878:67.

Amiurus catus: Jordan 1878:67.

Ictalurus nebulosus: Forbes 1884:83 (part.); Smith 1965:8.

Ameiurus nebulosus: Large 1903:10; Forbes & Richardson 1908:187–190; O'Donnell 1935:484.

Diagnosis.—The brown bullhead is a stout-bodied bullhead, olive, yellowish brown, or blue-black above and heavily mottled or marbled along the sides, with dusky chin barbels, a squarish caudal fin, 21–24 anal rays, and large "teeth" on the rear edge of the pectoral spine. The species most closely resembles the yellow bullhead but differs in having pigmented chin barbels. It differs from the superficially similar black bullhead in having more anal rays, strong "teeth" on the back edge of the pectoral spine, and a mottled body. The small young is most easily distinguished by the "teeth" on the pectoral spine. The species attains a length of more than 380 mm (15 inches), but most adults are much smaller.

Variation.—Currently most authors do not recognize subspecies, but some recognize a northern (*I. n. nebulosus*) and a southern subspecies (*I. n. marmoratus*). The northern form occurs in Illinois. There is considerable geographic variation in me-

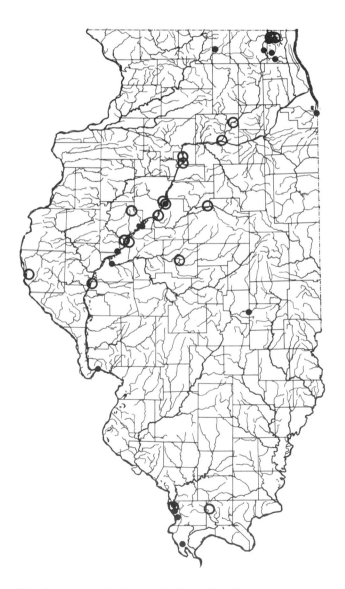

Distribution of the brown bullhead in Illinois.

ristic characters and patterns. In some parts of the range, the species is uniformly pigmented and not mottled. The complex synonymy reflects the confusion in the early literature due in part to the great amount of individual and geographic variation in the species.

Ecology.—In Illinois, the brown bullhead occurs in clear, well-vegetated lakes. Its habits are similar to those of other bullheads. While no detailed life-history study has been conducted, a great deal of information is available. Forbes & Richardson (1908:188–190) described some aspects of feeding and reproduction, and additional summaries and references are given in Breder & Rosen (1966:

251–257) and Carlander (1969:535–537). Spawning occurs in May and June over nests sometimes dug in roots and vegetation.

Distribution.—The brown bullhead is reputed to be an extremely hardy and ecologically tolerant species in many parts of its range, but such does not appear to be the case in Illinois. The species is nowhere abundant but is most often taken in the glacial lakes in the extreme northeastern part of the state, in floodplain lakes along the middle Illinois River, and in swamps of extreme southwestern Illinois. There is evidence of its decimation, as it once occurred more generally in the central part of the state.

Channel catfish
Ictalurus punctatus (Rafinesque)

Silurus punctatus Rafinesque 1818*d*:355 (type-locality: Ohio River).
Ictalurus punctatus: Nelson 1876:50 (recorded from Illinois); Forbes 1884:82; Large 1903:9; Forbes & Richardson 1908:180–183; Smith 1965:8.
Ichthaelurus punctatus: Jordan 1878:66.
Ichthaelurus robustus: Jordan 1878:66.
Ameiurus lacustris: Forbes & Richardson 1908:184–185.
Ictalurus anguilla: Forbes & Richardson 1908:179–180; O'Donnell 1935:483.
Villarius lacustris: O'Donnell 1935:483.

Diagnosis.—The channel catfish is a rather slender catfish, pale blue or greenish above and whitish or silvery below, usually with discrete black spots scattered over the sides, a distinctly forked tail, the upper jaw projecting well beyond the lower, 24–30 anal rays, the outer edge of the anal fin convex, and the eye situated on the dorsal portion of the

head. Individuals without black spots superficially resemble the blue catfish but can be distinguished from that species by the shape and length of the anal fin. The breeding male sometimes resembles the white catfish but has a longer anal fin, narrower head, more projecting upper jaw, and more forked caudal fin. The young is easily recognized by its slender body, deeply forked tail, and rounded anal fin. The species rarely may reach very large size—in excess of 1 meter (39 inches) and 13.6 kg (30 pounds)—but normally adults are less than 600 mm (24 inches) and 2.2 kg (5 pounds) in weight.

Variation.—Sexual and seasonal variation in the species confused early workers, who described the channel catfish as new several times. Geographic variation consists of weak clines, and Bailey, Winn, & Smith (1954:130) recommended that subspecies not be recognized. Prior to their work, the northern populations were referred to *I. p. lacustris*.

Ecology.—Although the channel catfish has been stocked in ponds and reservoirs, it is a stream fish that reaches its greatest abundance in clear, fast-flowing, and sand- or gravel-bottomed rivers of medium to large size. A tremendous literature exists on the fishery of this popular fish (Breder & Rosen 1966; E. E. Miller *in* Calhoun 1966; Carlander 1969). Its feeding and reproductive habits are similar to those of other species in the genus except that the female does not help in nest construction and guarding. This species may live longer than 6 years.

Distribution.—The channel catfish occurs throughout the state and is abundant in the larger streams—extremely so in the major rivers. It is somewhat decimated within the state, probably because streams once large throughout the year now become small during drought periods. Siltation is likely another adverse factor.

Pylodictis Rafinesque

This distinctive genus contains one species, found in the central United States and northern Mexico.

Flathead catfish
Pylodictis olivaris (Rafinesque)

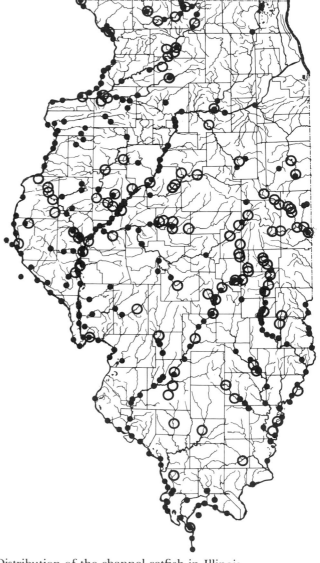

Distribution of the channel catfish in Illinois.

Silurus olivaris Rafinesque 1818*d*:355 (type-locality: Ohio River).
Hopladelus olivaris: Nelson 1876:50 (recorded from Illinois).
Pelodichthys olivaris: Jordan 1878:67.

Leptops olivaris: Forbes 1884:83; Large 1903:10; Forbes & Richardson 1908:193–194.
Opladelus olivaris: O'Donnell 1935:480.
Pylodictis olivaris: Smith 1965:9.

Diagnosis.—The flathead catfish is an often boldly mottled or marbled catfish with the head notably flattened between the eyes, the lower jaw protruding beyond the upper, a squarish caudal fin, a premaxillary band of teeth with a backward-projecting extension on each side, a rather large but free adipose fin, a short anal fin with 14–17 rays, and whitish dorsal and ventral edges on the caudal fin of small and medium-sized specimens. This combination of characters can apply to no other American catfish. The small young resembles some of the madtoms that occur in the same riffles but differs from them most markedly in having the posterior margin of the adipose fin free and separate from the caudal fin. The species attains a length of more than 1 meter (39 inches) and

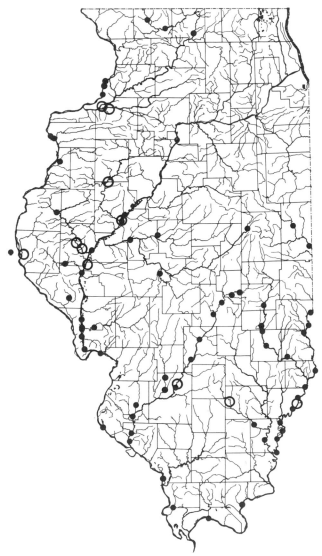

Distribution of the flathead catfish in Illinois.

a weight of over 22.5 kg (50 pounds). Adults weighing 4.5–6.7 kg (10–15 pounds) are rather common.

Variation.—There is great individual variation but little geographic variation in the species. No subspecies have been proposed.

Ecology.—The flathead catfish lives in the "deep holes" of large and medium-sized rivers. Often these habitats have submerged logs or undercut banks and bottoms of mud or detritus. The young lives in fast riffles of rivers, frequently under rocks. As for the preceding species of catfishes, there is a large fishery literature (Breder & Rosen 1966; Carlander 1969). The habits of the flathead catfish differ from those of other large catfishes chiefly in that sexual maturity is not reached until the fish is 3 or 4 years old and that individuals may live for 20 or more years. Its food is mostly fishes and crustaceans.

Distribution.—The flathead catfish occurs in all parts of Illinois except the northeastern part of the state and is more common than indicated by the records on the accompanying map. Adults are difficult to capture by conventional collecting techniques and are frequently of such a size that it is not feasible to preserve and store them. There is no evidence of a change in the status of the species, and it may be as common and widespread now as it has ever been.

Noturus Rafinesque

This eastern North American genus contains 24 described species, 7 of which occur in Illinois. Except for preferred habitats, the species of madtoms are similar ecologically and differ from the larger catfishes mostly in attaining sexual maturity much sooner, having shorter lives, and feeding almost exclusively on aquatic invertebrates. The life histories of most species have not been studied.

KEY TO SPECIES

1. Pectoral spines without prominent posterior "teeth"; dorsum uniformly colored or with only vague light and dark areas 2
   Pectoral spines with prominent posterior "teeth"; dorsum patterned with blotches or saddles 4

2. Premaxillary band of teeth with a backward extension on each side; body slender, uniformly colored or with vague areas of light and dark pigment .... *flavus*
   Premaxillary band of teeth without backward extensions 3
3. Upper and lower jaws subequal; ground color yellowish, reddish, or brown with one or two prominent axial stripes along sides; belly, sides, and head not profusely freckled with dark pigment .... *gyrinus*
   Upper jaw decidedly projecting beyond lower; ground color uniform or with faint axial stripes; belly, sides, and head profusely freckled with dark pigment .... *nocturnus*
4. Upper and lower jaws subequal; dorsal, anal, and caudal fins with black margins; body very slender; adipose fin without dark spot or saddle .... *exilis*
   Upper jaw projecting beyond lower; fins without black margins; body not very slender; dark spot or saddle on adipose fin 5
5. Dorsum with three bold, broad dark saddles, the last one completely traversing the adipose fin; distal tip of dorsal fin with a large black spot; eye relatively large .... *miurus*
   Dorsum with three irregular, narrow, dark saddles, the last one not completely traversing the adipose fin; dorsal fin without a discrete, distal black spot; eye small 6
6. Caudal fin with three vertical dark bands; pectoral fin sharply pointed; upper half of caudal fin usually with 25–28 rays; sides and belly prominently mottled with dark pigment .... *stigmosus*
   Caudal fin with one or two dark vertical bands; pectoral fin rounded; upper half of caudal fin usually with 22–25 rays; sides and belly dimly mottled .... *eleutherus*

Mountain madtom
Noturus eleutherus Jordan

Noturus eleutherus Jordan 1877a:371 (type-locality: Big Pigeon River near Newport, Cocke County, Tennessee); Smith 1965:8 (recorded from Illinois).
Schilbeodes miurus: Forbes & Richardson 1908:200–201 (part., a Wabash River series found in their collection labeled as brindled madtom).

Diagnosis.—The mountain madtom is a small, tan-colored catfish with a long, keel-like adipose fin separated from the caudal fin only by a shallow notch; prominent "teeth" on the rear edge of the pectoral spine; the upper jaw projecting beyond the lower; the dorsal fin flecked but without a discrete, distal black spot; three narrow and irregular dark saddles over the back, the last of which is interrupted on the upper edge of the adipose fin; a dimly mottled belly and lower sides; the upper half of the caudal fin usually with 22–25 rays; 10 preoperculomandibular pores; rounded pectoral fins; and one or two prominent, dark vertical bars in the caudal fin. The species closely resembles the northern madtom, differing from it most obviously in having one or two rather than three dark vertical bands in the tail and a rounded rather than pointed pectoral fin. The mountain madtom differs from the brindled madtom in having the last dorsal saddle interrupted on the adipose fin and in lacking the black spot on the dorsal fin. The young is separable from those of other madtoms by the same characters. The species attains a length of about 100 mm (4 inches).

Variation.—Taylor (1969:164) noted that the species was relatively uniform throughout its range.

Ecology.—The mountain madtom lives in large and medium-sized rivers in fast and sandy-gravelly riffles, especially those with some algae or other aquatic vegetation. It often lives within the valves of long-dead mussels. Like other madtoms, it is nocturnal and hides under rocks during the day. Almost nothing else is known of the species. Presumably its feeding and reproductive habits are similar to those of other small catfishes.

Distribution.—The species is widely distributed and abundant in riffles of the lower Wabash River and occasional in the lower reaches of major tributaries. It is the most common madtom in the Wabash. No information is available on its former abundance, as there is only one old record for Illinois.

Distribution of the mountain madtom in Illinois.

Slender madtom
Noturus exilis Nelson

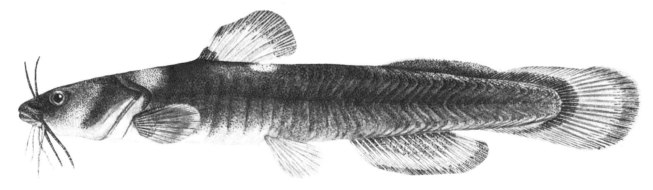

Noturus exilis Nelson 1876:51 (type-locality: McLean County, Illinois); Jordan 1878:69; Forbes 1884:84; Smith 1965:8.

Noturus elassochir Swain & Kalb 1883:638 (type-locality: Naperville, Illinois; presumably West Branch, Du Page River).

Schilbeodes exilis: Large 1903:10; Forbes & Richardson 1908:199–200.

Rabida exilis: O'Donnell 1935:484.

Diagnosis.—The slender madtom is an attenuate, dark gray or blackish madtom with vague yellowish blotches on the back; a long, keel-like adipose fin separated from the caudal fin only by a shallow notch; the upper and lower jaws equal in length; the dorsal, anal, and caudal fins margined with black; prominent "teeth" on the rear edge of the pectoral spine; and without a dark saddle or blotch on the adipose fin. The combination of slender body, subequal jaws, and black margins on the fins separates this species from all other Illinois catfishes. The species attains a length of about 100 mm (4 inches).

Variation.—Taylor (1969:63–64) noted considerable geographic variation in pigmentation of fins

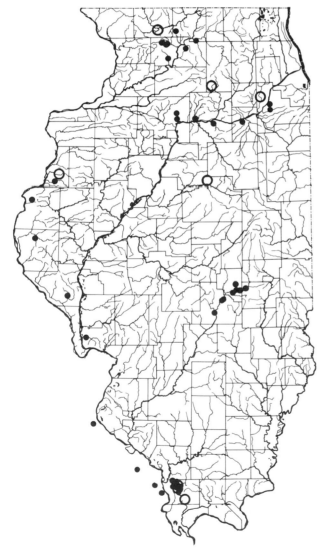

Distribution of the slender madtom in Illinois.

and in body shape but concluded that subspecific separation was not warranted.

Ecology.—The slender madtom occurs in clear fast creeks over gravelly riffles. Stegman & Minckley (1959:341) found large numbers in the gravel interstices of Hutchins Creek in Union County. Except for its preference for fast riffles, it is probably similar in habits to other stream-inhabiting madtoms.

Distribution.—The species is extremely sporadic and usually uncommon in Illinois although it is known from widely scattered parts of the state. Too few old records are available to draw any inferences regarding its former distribution. Its erratic distribution in Illinois is surprising in view of its abundance in the Ozark streams of Missouri.

Stonecat
Noturus flavus Rafinesque

Noturus flavus Rafinesque 1818*a*:41 (type-locality: falls of the Ohio River; restricted to Eagle Creek, 3.5 miles E of Jonesville, Grant County, Kentucky, by Taylor 1969:118); Nelson 1876:50 (recorded from Illinois); Jordan 1878:67; Forbes 1884:84; Large 1903:10; Forbes & Richardson 1908:194–196; O'Donnell 1935:484; Smith 1965:8.

Diagnosis.—The stonecat is a rather slender, slate-colored madtom with a long, keel-like adipose fin separated from the caudal fin by only a notch; the upper jaw projecting beyond the lower; uniform color above or vague blotches of yellowish white; a discrete, small white spot immediately behind the dorsal fin; a long backward extension on each side of the band of premaxillary teeth; and a squarish caudal fin with a whitish margin. The species most closely resembles the slender madtom but differs in the shape of the patch of premaxillary teeth, the projecting upper jaw, and white-margined fins. The species attains a length of about 250 mm (10 inches).

Variation.—Taylor (1969:122) noted relatively little geographic variation in this wide-ranging species but commented on the small-eyed form that occurs occasionally in very large and turbid rivers. Such a specimen is available in the Illinois Natural History Survey collection from the Kaskaskia River near its mouth. Others are known from the Mississippi below the mouth of the Missouri River.

Stonecat

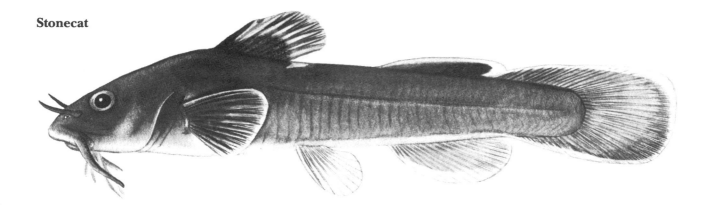

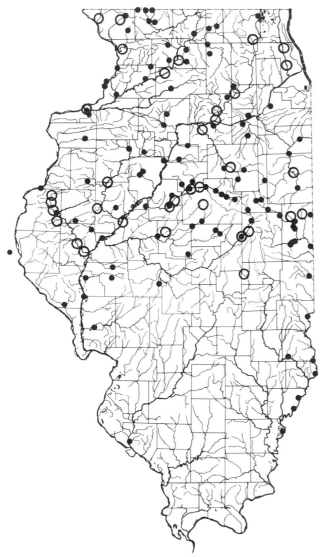

Distribution of the stonecat in Illinois.

Ecology.—The stonecat is most abundant in strong riffles of large creeks and rivers, especially in areas having boulders or large flat rocks. It also occurs in strong riffles over gravel but seems to prefer large rocks. Being a larger species, the stonecat lives 2 or 3 years longer than most madtoms. The small amount of information available is summarized in Carlander (1969:555).

Distribution.—Except for the Wabash River and one record near the confluence of the Kaskaskia and Mississippi rivers, the stonecat is confined to the northern half of Illinois, where it is common and generally distributed in suitable habitat. There is no evidence that it is any more or less common than formerly. It has always been restricted to high-gradient rocky streams, most of which have remained relatively unmodified unless dammed or channelized.

Tadpole madtom
Noturus gyrinus (Mitchill)

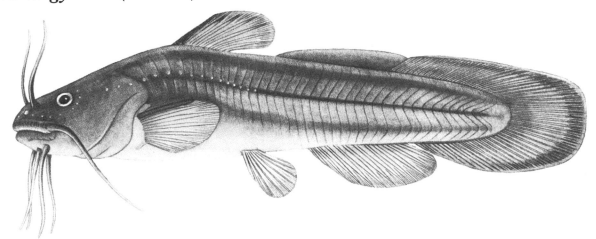

Silurus gyrinus Mitchill 1817:289 (type-locality: Wallkill River, New York).

Noturus sialis: Jordan 1878:68 (recorded from Illinois).

Noturus gyrinus: Forbes 1884:84; Smith 1965:9.

Schilbeodes gyrinus: Large 1903:10; Forbes & Richardson 1908:197–198; O'Donnell 1935:484.

Diagnosis.—The tadpole madtom is a robust little catfish, reddish, tan, or dark brown above, with one or two dark axial stripes along each side; a long, keel-like adipose fin separated from the caudal fin by only a notch; upper and lower jaws equal in length; a rounded and uniformly dusky caudal fin; the dorsum unmarked; and the rear edge of the pectoral spine smooth. The species resembles the freckled madtom but is easily distinguished by its subequal jaws and unfreckled belly and sides. It attains a length of about 100 mm (4 inches).

Variation.—Taylor (1969:48–49) described clinal and individual variation but concluded that recognition of an eastern and western subspecies (*sialis*) was not warranted. In Illinois individual variation in color and body shape is extreme. Taylor (1969:50) believed the variation in form is a function of nutrition during growth. The wide use of the name *Schilbeodes mollis* for the tadpole madtom during the 1940's and 1950's was the result of a nomenclatural misunderstanding and had nothing to do with geographic variation.

Ecology.—The tadpole madtom is typically a species of lakes, swamps, and sluggish muck-bottomed pools of creeks. When found in high-gradient streams, it is usually over vegetated sand bottom. Such individuals tend to be reddish or yellow and

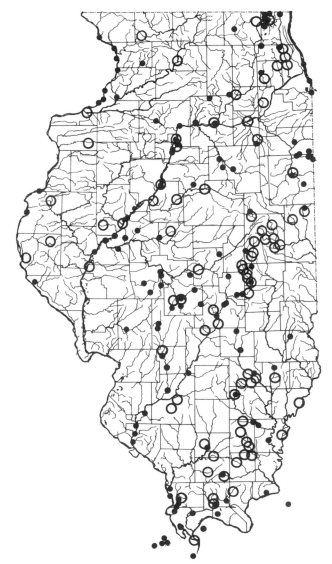

Distribution of the tadpole madtom in Illinois.

noticeably more slender bodied than other individuals. Information on the ecology of this madtom is meager, but it appears to be more diurnal than other Illinois species. Scott & Crossman (1973: 617–618) summarized the data available; Forbes & Richardson (1908:108) described feeding habits.

Distribution.—The tadpole madtom is statewide in distribution and locally common, but it is considerably less general in occurrence than formerly, especially in eastern Illinois. Its decimation is likely the result of increased water turbidity in recent decades.

Brindled madtom
Noturus miurus Jordan

Noturus marginatus: Nelson 1876:50 (recorded from Illinois).

Noturus miurus Jordan 1877c:370 (type-locality: White River, Indianapolis, Indiana); Jordan 1878:68; Forbes 1884:84; Smith 1965:9.

Schilbeodes eleutherus: Large 1903:10 (misidentification).

Schilbeodes miurus: Large 1903:10; Forbes & Richardson 1908:200–201.

Rabida miurus: O'Donnell 1935:484.

Diagnosis.—The brindled madtom is a tan or gray catfish with three bold, broad black saddles, the last one completely traversing the adipose fin, and numerous flecks and mottlings of black or brown on the back and sides; a discrete black spot near the apex of the dorsal fin; a subdistal black vertical band in the caudal fin; a long, keel-like adipose fin separated from the caudal fin by only a notch; the upper jaw projecting beyond the lower; strong "teeth" on the rear edge of the pectoral spine; a paddlelike caudal fin; and a relatively large

eye. It resembles the mountain madtom and northern madtom somewhat but differs from both most obviously in that the third black saddle is broad and extends completely over the adipose fin. It differs from the slender madtom in its squat rather than slender shape and in having a projecting upper jaw. The species attains a length of over 100 mm (4 inches).

Variation.—Taylor (1969:198) found a remarkable uniformity in appearance throughout the range of the species.

Ecology.—The brindled madtom occupies clear shallow pools of creeks and small rivers over mixed bottoms of sand, fine gravel, silt, and detritus. The only information available on reproduction is the summary in Scott & Crossman (1973:620), which is credited to Taylor (1969) but does not appear in that publication. If, indeed, the statements apply to the brindled madtom, its reproductive behavior parallels that of other catfishes.

Distribution.—The brindled madtom is now restricted to the Wabash-Ohio watershed and, although still general in occurrence, it is not abundant. It has disappeared from the headwaters of the Kaskaskia River (Mississippi drainage) and evidently has been extirpated in the Skillet Fork, Saline system, and in some branches of the Vermilion River system (Wabash-Ohio drainage). Its decimation is due in large part to the deterioration of water quality (coal mine wastes, sewage, and excessive siltation above impoundments of streams).

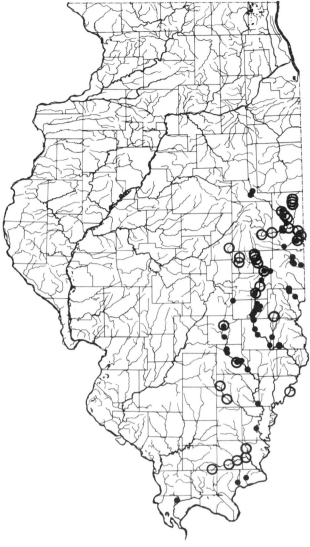

Distribution of the brindled madtom in Illinois.

Freckled madtom
Noturus nocturnus Jordan & Gilbert

Noturus nocturnus Jordan & Gilbert 1886:6 (type-locality: Saline River at Benton, Arkansas); Smith 1965:9.

Schilbeodes nocturnus: Large 1903:10 (recorded from Illinois); Forbes & Richardson 1908:198–199; O'Donnell 1935:484.

Diagnosis.—The freckled madtom is a moderately robust catfish, dark slate or brownish above and densely freckled with black or brown on the lower sides, with one or two dim axial stripes in many specimens; a long, keel-like adipose fin separated from the caudal fin by only a notch; the upper jaw projecting beyond the lower; a rounded caudal fin; a uniformly dark caudal fin; the dorsum unmarked; and the rear edge of the pectoral spine nearly smooth. Among Illinois species the freckled madtom looks most like the tadpole madtom but is more slender, more freckled, and easily distinguished by the protruding upper jaw. The species attains a length of about 150 mm (6 inches), but most individuals are much smaller.

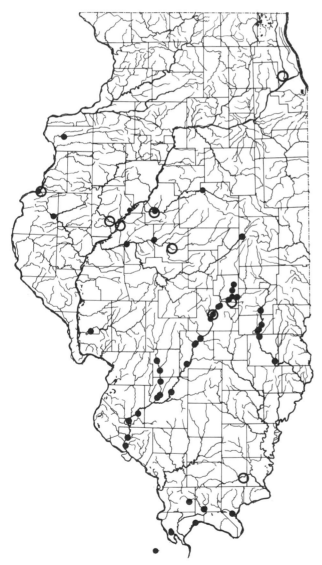

Distribution of the freckled madtom in Illinois.

Variation.—Taylor (1969:79–81) noted that the species is variable and tends to form distinctive localized populations, but no subspecies have been proposed.

Ecology.—The freckled madtom occurs in deep slow-moving riffles and shallow pools with some current of medium-sized and large rivers. It is most common over bottoms of mixed fine gravel, sand, and silt, often with some detritus and brush, and it is fairly tolerant of turbid water. Its ecology is presumably similar to that of other madtoms, but no details are available.

Distribution.—Occurring sporadically throughout most of the southern three-fourths of Illinois, this species is abundant only in the Kaskaskia River system. Too few old records are available to draw any inferences regarding its former distribution in the state, but it is certain that the recent creation of Lake Shelbyville and Carlyle Lake and the channelizing of the lower river eliminated the species for long stretches in the Kaskaskia River proper.

Northern madtom
Noturus stigmosus Taylor

Noturus species: Smith 1965:9 (recorded from Illinois).

Noturus stigmosus Taylor 1969:173 (type-locality: Huron River north of Dexter [Section 13, T1S, R4E], Washtenaw County, Michigan).

Diagnosis.—The northern madtom is a relatively slender madtom, tan to brownish, with narrow dark brown or black saddles across the back, the last of which is interrupted on the distal edge of the adipose fin; the sides and part of the venter prominently mottled with clumps of dark pigment; the caudal fin with three vertical dark bars, the midcaudal one as well developed as the other two; a long, keel-like adipose fin distinctly separated (almost free) from the adjacent caudal fin; the pectoral fin sharply pointed; 25–28 rays in the upper half of the caudal fin; the upper jaw projecting beyond the lower; the rear edge of the pectoral spine with large "teeth"; and a rather squarish caudal fin. The northern madtom most closely resembles the mountain madtom, the resemblance being especially noticeable in the young, and is most easily distinguished from that species by the midcaudal dark crescent. The northern madtom is most readily distinguished from the brindled madtom

Northern madtom

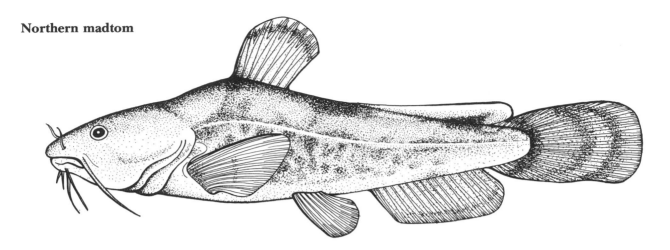

by its interrupted dark saddle across the adipose fin. The species attains a length of about 100 mm (4 inches).

Variation.—Taylor (1969:178–179) found no geographic variation trends. No subspecies have been proposed for this recently described species. The northern madtom was once thought to represent sexual dimorphism in the related mountain madtom.

Ecology.—The species evidently occurs in different-sized streams in different geographic areas, but in Illinois it has been taken from one large river and one of medium size. At all localities the habitat was rather strong current over a bottom of sand and gravel with some detritus. Virtually nothing has been published on its ecology.

Distribution.—The species is thus far known only from the Vermilion River, 6.4 km E of Westville, Vermilion County, Illinois; the Wabash River opposite Rochester (Illinois), Gibson County, Indiana; and from the Wabash in adjacent Indiana 1.6 km NE of Summit Grove, Vermillion County. It is extremely rare in Illinois, which is on the western periphery of its range.

Distribution of the northern madtom in Illinois.

Cavefishes—Amblyopsidae

This family of eastern U.S. fishes contains four genera, of which one occurs in Illinois, represented by a partially pigmented but largely subterranean species. The other three genera include eyeless and unpigmented fishes confined to caves. Some of the species are known to carry eggs in their mouths, and it may be a universal habit within the family. Cavefishes are small fishes generally unknown except as novelties. They are incredibly well adapted to precarious environments and specialized for life in subterranean waters. Until recently their relationships to other fishes have defied understanding but now seem to be clearly established. They pose several important problems yet to be solved such as their manner of dispersal, distribution, and details of reproduction. The local species is of interest because it is transitional between an epigean and hypogean (subterranean) way of life. It is sometimes dipnetted from springs or seined in spring runs.

Chologaster Agassiz

This genus contains two species of quite different habits. One of them has degenerate eyes, is subterranean, and occurs in southern Illinois, southeastern Missouri, Kentucky, and Tennessee. The other has well-developed eyes and occurs in bogs and marshes on the Coastal Plain of the southeastern United States.

Spring cavefish
Chologaster agassizi Putnam

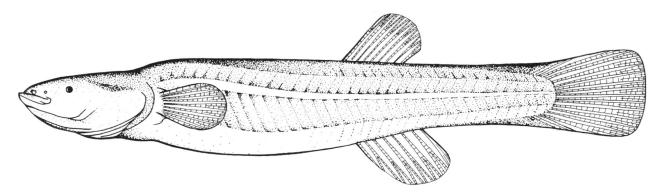

Chologaster agassizii Putnam 1872:30 (type-locality: a well at Lebanon, Tennessee).
Chologaster: Forbes 1881:232–233 (species uncertain; recorded from Illinois).
Chologaster papilliferus Forbes 1882:1 (type-locality: spring, Union County, Illinois); Large 1903:22; Forbes & Richardson 1908:218–219.
Chologaster papiliferus: Forbes 1884:72 (misspelling).
Forbesella papillifera: O'Donnell 1935:485.
Chologaster agassizi: Smith 1965:9.

Diagnosis.—The spring cavefish is a small, terete, and salamanderlike fish that is brown or flesh colored and rather translucent with a thin light-colored stripe along each side in most specimens. It lacks pelvic fins and has degenerate eyes covered over with skin and numerous short and broken rows of sensory papillae that are most conspicuous in the head region. In life this species resembles a larval salamander, but closer examination reveals a short anal fin and a paddle-shaped caudal fin. It is

194

so distinctive that no other Illinois species can be confused with it. It attains a length of 75 mm (3 inches), but most adults are much smaller.

Variation.—Woods & Inger (1957:239–240), who synonymized *papilliferus* under the older name *agassizi*, noted that populations from southern Illinois, central Kentucky, and central Tennessee all differed slightly, but these authors felt that subspecies were not warranted.

Ecology.—The spring cavefish is subterranean but is found in mouths of springs and cave streams and occasionally is washed out into streams or pools when the water table is high. At night it may be seen swimming in tiles or springs; during the day it hides beneath stones in spring runs. A year-long study conducted by Norbert M. Welch for the U.S. Forest Service, which permitted me to abstract his findings, revealed that abundance above ground depends upon the amount of flow of ground water, darkness, and season (spawning occurs underground from January through March). Using the Petersen Index, Welch calculated the total population of seven springs to be less than 1,000 individuals. Four age classes were represented. Growth averaged 10–20 mm per year but was slight during summer and fall. Some individuals spawned in their 2nd year. Poulson (1963:267) found three age classes. Weise (1957) described behavior (well-developed positive thigmotaxis and negative phototaxis), the wide temperature tolerance, feeding habits (*Gammarus* was the principal food), and other aspects of its ecology. He noted that the cavefish has vision but seems not to rely on it appreciably. Hill (1969) noted that in Kentucky caves the species is strongly cannibalistic.

Distribution.—The spring cavefish occurs in several springs issuing from the Mississippi River bluffs from southern Jackson County to northern Alexander County and in springs in Hardin and Johnson counties. It was known to occur in a spring near Golconda in Pope County (Forbes & Richardson 1908:219), but this colony has never been rediscovered. The species presumably occurs in springs and spring runs throughout the Shawnee Hills.

Distribution of the spring cavefish in Illinois.

Pirate perches—Aphredoderidae

This family consists of one genus confined to the eastern United States. Although small, pirate perch are sometimes taken on baited hook and are frequently encountered in minnow-seine catches. The fish is usually regarded more as a curiosity than anything else, and is kept merely to find out what kind of fish it is. Detailed morphological studies indicate that the relationship of this strange fish is with the trout-perches and cavefishes. The most pressing needs are for studies of its reproductive biology. The anterior position of the genital pore suggests that it may be a mouthbreeder, but as yet no observations are available.

Aphredoderus Lesueur

This genus contains one species, common in many parts of Illinois.

Pirate perch
Aphredoderus sayanus (Gilliams)

Scolopsis sayanus Gilliams 1824:81 (type-locality: near Philadelphia, Pennsylvania).

Aphredoderus sayanus: Kennicott 1855:593 (recorded from Illinois); Nelson 1876:39–40; Forbes 1884: 70; Large 1903:22; Forbes & Richardson 1908: 229–231; O'Donnell 1935:485–486; Smith 1965: 9.

Sternotremia isolepis Nelson 1876:39–40 (type-locality: Calumet River near Chicago and small stream in southern Illinois).

Aphredoderus isolepis: Jordan 1878:48–49.

Diagnosis.—The pirate perch is a robust and large-mouthed fish, blackish or iridescent purple on the sides with a dark vertical bar on the caudal peduncle and a pronounced tear drop; ctenoid scales on the body and cheeks; usually three dorsal, two anal, and one pelvic spine; and, in all but the very small young, an anal opening far in advance of the anal fin. In the adult the anus is just behind the isthmus. Superficially resembling a small bass or sunfish, the pirate perch has so many distinctive characters that it cannot be confused with any other Illinois fish. The species attains a length of more than 100 mm (4 inches).

Variation.—For many years the Mississippi River valley pirate perch was assigned to the subspecies *A. s. gibbosus*. Bailey, Winn, & Smith (1954:135) noted that the western populations differed from those in the Middle Atlantic States in several characters but suggested that subspecies not be recognized until a thorough study of geographic variation in the species had been published. Since that time most authors have not used subspecific names.

Ecology.—The pirate perch occurs in swamps, ponds, ditches, and muck-bottomed pools of low-gradient creeks and small rivers. It is most common over soft silt bottoms with organic debris and occurs in both turbid and clear water with vegetation. Forbes & Richardson (1908:230–231) reported that the species feeds on a variety of animal foods, predominantly insects. They reported spawning throughout May and that a nest is constructed and guarded for some time after the eggs hatch. Hall & Jenkins (1954:49) studied age and growth in an Oklahoma impoundment and reported four age classes.

Distribution.—The pirate perch is generally distributed and common in suitable habitat throughout the southern half of Illinois. In the northern half of the state it is localized in a few scattered populations, the largest being in the Kankakee County and Mason County sand areas. In this state the pirate perch evidently does not occur west of the Illinois River. Despite its abundance in southern Illinois, it shows some evidence of decimation, possibly because of the general deterioration of water quality.

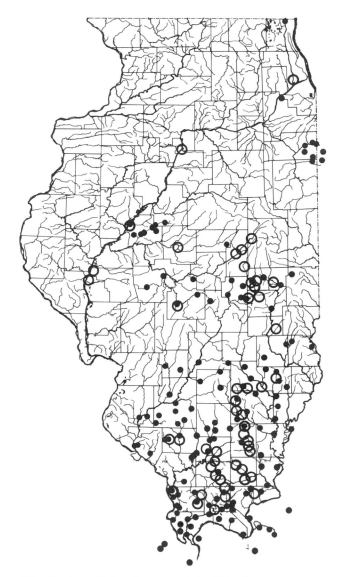

Distribution of the pirate perch in Illinois.

Trout-perches — Percopsidae

This boreal North American family contains one genus. The family, distantly related to cavefishes and the pirate perch, is of evolutionary interest because it is a relict of a once important group and because many of its characters are transitional between the primitive salmoniforms and the more advanced perciforms. Trout-perch are small fishes unknown to almost everyone except ichthyologists. They are most often encountered in minnow-seine and otter trawl samples. In Illinois, they are too uncommon to be of importance to fishermen as a bait minnow. They undoubtedly serve as forage fish in Lake Michigan, and they help characterize certain distinctive aquatic habitats.

Percopsis Agassiz

This genus contains two species; one occurs only in the Pacific Northwest and the other ranges widely across Canada and occurs as far south as Illinois.

Trout-perch
Percopsis omiscomaycus (Walbaum)

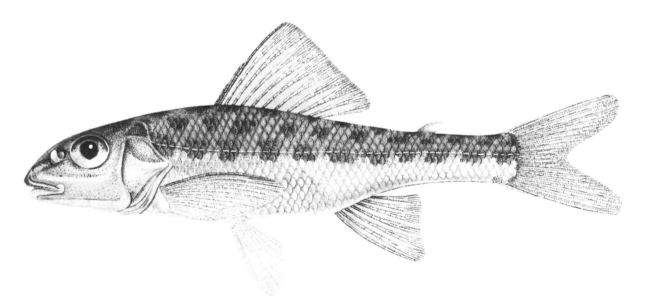

Salmo omiscomaycus Walbaum 1792:65 (type-locality: Hudson Bay).
Percopsis guttatus: Nelson 1876:43 (recorded from Illinois); Jordan 1878:53; Forbes 1884:72; Large 1903:22; Forbes & Richardson 1908:225–226.
Percopsis omiscomaycus: O'Donnell 1935:485; Smith 1965:9.

Diagnosis. — The trout-perch is a large-headed and rather translucent little fish, pale straw color above and silvery below, with a series of linear dark spots along the middorsum, another along the lateral line, and one or two less well-developed rows in between; strongly ctenoid scales; a free adipose fin; a forked tail; a subterminal and horizontal mouth; and one to three weak spines in the dorsal, anal, and pelvic fins. The combination of ctenoid scales and an adipose fin distinguishes this species from all other Illinois fishes, and it bears no real resemblance to any other species. The trout-perch attains a length of about 130 mm (5 inches).

Variation.—McPhail & Lindsey (1970:292) and Scott & Crossman (1973:679) commented that little geographic variation is shown by the species.

Ecology.—In Illinois the trout-perch occurs only in large rivers and their associated floodplain lakes and in Lake Michigan. It is most abundant over bottoms of such organic debris as sticks, leaves, and other detritus. Age, growth, fecundity, and spawning season for the species in Lake Michigan were described by House & Wells (1973). The species feeds on benthic organisms, primarily insects, and spawns from May to August over gravel. No information is available for Illinois, but it is likely that spawning may begin earlier, and the adhesive eggs are probably deposited over bottoms of muck in the floodplain lakes.

Distribution.—The trout-perch occurs in the Illinois River and associated floodplain lakes and in Lake Michigan. The only other record for the species in the state is for the Mississippi River in Henderson County. It is more common in the Mississippi farther north. There is no evidence of any change in its distribution or abundance in Illinois.

Distribution of the trout-perch in Illinois.

Codfishes—Gadidae

This large and important family of marine fishes contains many genera, only one of which enters any appreciable distance into fresh water in the United States. Many of the codfishes are tremendously important commercial fishes of the oceans, particularly the North Atlantic, and the food is highly esteemed both fresh and frozen. They are of interest to ichthyologists because of their species diversity and morphological adaptations to different environments. The Illinois species, which is seldom recognized by most fishermen, is not often taken on hook and line but sometimes caught in trawls or other nets in Lake Michigan and more rarely in the large rivers of the state. It is not a highly regarded food species.

Lota Linnaeus

This genus contains one Holarctic and essentially boreal species that extends southward into Illinois waters.

Burbot
Lota lota (Linnaeus)

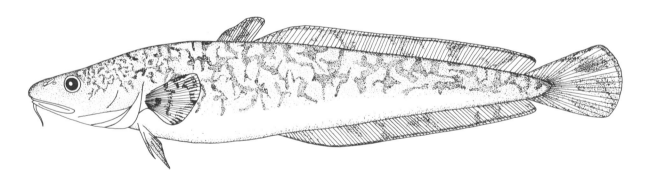

Gadus lota Linnaeus 1758:1172 (type-locality: Europe).

Lota lacustris: Nelson 1876:42 (recorded from Illinois); Jordan 1878:51.

Lota maculosa: Forbes 1884:62; Large 1903:30; Forbes & Richardson 1908:331–332; O'Donnell 1935:490–491.

Lota lota: Smith 1965:9.

Diagnosis.—The burbot is an elongate and terete fish, usually mottled and marbled with dark brown, with one median barbel at the chin tip, a short first dorsal fin followed by a long second dorsal containing more than 60 rays, a rounded and separate caudal fin, a long anal fin containing more than 60 rays, and scales so small that the body appears smooth skinned. It is superficially somewhat intermediate between the eel and catfishes but is easily distinguished from all other Illinois fishes. The species attains a length of more than 760 mm (30 inches).

Variation.—Three subspecies have been described: one in Eurasia, one in Alaska, and a third for the remainder of North America. The North American subspecies has been assigned the subspecific names of *lacustris* and *maculosa*, but present authors do not recognize subspecies. A good summary of the systematic history of the species appears in McPhail & Lindsey (1970:298).

Ecology.—The burbot is a deep-water species occurring in Illinois only in large rivers and the lower reaches of their major tributaries and in Lake Michigan. It feeds on a great variety of animal foods, depending upon its size. It spawns over gravel in deep water during the winter months. Although not regarded as a desirable commercial species, it has a rather large fishery literature. An excellent summary of the ecology of the species is presented in Scott & Crossman (1973:642–644).

Distribution.—In view of the discovery of a specimen of burbot in the lower Big Muddy River (Lewis 1955:24), the species must be regarded as sporadic in large rivers throughout Illinois. Evidently it has never been common in our rivers. Coker (1930:214) reported it as so rare in the Keokuk area on the Mississippi River that it was unknown to most commercial fishermen. However, in Lake Michigan it was abundant enough to be regarded as a nuisance until the arrival of the sea lamprey. The species is clearly decimated in Lake Michigan and probably less frequently encountered in the Illinois River now than formerly.

Distribution of the burbot in Illinois.

Killifishes—Cyprinodontidae

This large family of surface-dwelling fishes is virtually worldwide in tropical and temperate areas and contains many genera of marine, brackish-water, and freshwater species. One genus is represented in Illinois. Killifishes or topminnows are small fishes popular in the aquarium fish trade and in behavioral studies. They are also used in genetics research. Many are undoubtedly of value in the control of mosquitoes and other aquatic insect nuisances. They make hardy bait minnows and serve to some extent as forage fish. Because they swim at the water's surface, they are frequently observed in nature but usually caught only in dipnets or minnow seines.

Fundulus Lacépède

This North American genus contains 27 described species in the United States; five occur in Illinois. Topminnows, or killifishes, are easily recognized by the superior mouth, short and posteriorly placed dorsal fin, and rounded caudal fin, and by the absence of an intromittent organ in the male.

KEY TO SPECIES

1. Dorsal fin originating approximately over or in advance of anal fin; lateral-line scales, 38 or more; dorsum tesselated with brown 2
   Dorsal fin originating behind anal fin; lateral-line scales, fewer than 38; dorsum not distinctly tesselated with brown 3
2. Dorsal fin approximately over anal fin insertion; dorsal fin with 13 or more rays; anal fin with 15 or more rays; sides plain or with many thin longitudinal stripes ... *catenatus*
   Dorsal fin in advance of anal fin insertion; dorsal fin with 12 or fewer rays; anal fin with 11 or fewer rays; sides with thin vertical bars .... *diaphanus*
3. A prominent blue-black blotch below eye; males with thin and well-separated, dark vertical bars; females with several thin horizontal dark lines; greatest body depth contained in standard length less than four times .... *dispar*
   No blue-black blotch below eye; both sexes with a prominent, black lateral band that extends from tip of snout to caudal base; body rather terete, its greatest depth contained about four times or more in standard length .. 4
4. Back and upper sides plain or with relatively large, diffuse dusky spots; lateral stripe distinct but not intensely black .... *notatus*
   Back and upper sides with few to many discrete, intense black dots; lateral stripe intensely black and in sharp contrast to ground color .... *olivaceus*

Northern studfish
Fundulus catenatus (Storer)

Poecilia catenata Storer 1846:430 (type-locality: Tennessee River, Florence, Alabama).
Fundulus catenatus: Heidinger 1974:364 (recorded from Illinois).

Diagnosis.—The northern studfish is a terete and stout-bodied topminnow, olivaceous in color, with thin brown stripes along the sides or mottling so vague as to give the fish a plain appearance, 13–16 dorsal rays, the dorsal fin origin approximately over the anal fin insertion; 15–18 anal rays; and 40–45 scales in the lateral series. The species has more dorsal rays, anal rays, and lateral scales than any other Illinois topminnow and is distinctive in form and pattern. The breeding male develops a blue-green iridescence and orange lon-

Northern studfish

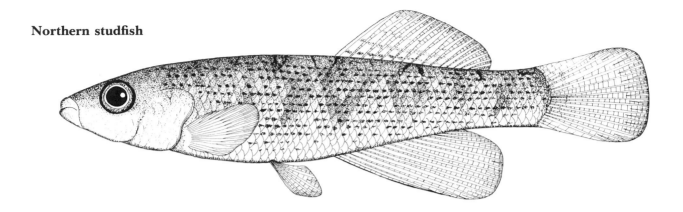

gitudinal stripes, and some individuals have a subterminal black band on the caudal fin. The species attains a length of 130 mm (5 inches).

Variation.—Thomerson (1969) analyzed variation in this species and the related southern studfish. He noted too little geographic variation to justify recognition of subspecies.

Ecology.—In Missouri this species is abundant in backwaters adjacent to clear gravelly creeks and in high-water pools near creeks. Surprisingly little else is known about its habits. It probably feeds on terrestrial invertebrates that alight on, or fall into, the water as well as on aquatic forms. Presumably spawning occurs over gravel in the summer months. Adults are vividly colored in May. The northern studfish cruises about the surface of pools in small schools.

Distribution.—This topminnow is known in Illinois from one young-of-the-year female taken in the Mississippi River at River Mile 48 in Alexander County (Heidinger 1974). The specimen is probably a straggler from a Missouri tributary, and there is no evidence of a population in Illinois. The species is nevertheless included here, since other such stragglers are likely to appear in the Mississippi River (Smith et al. 1971:11).

Distribution of the northern studfish in Illinois.

Banded killifish
Fundulus diaphanus (Lesueur)

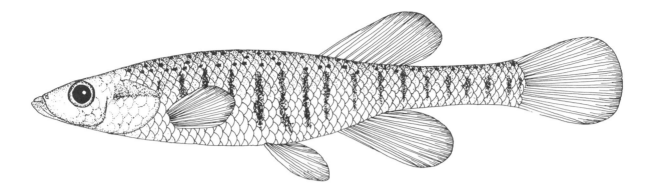

Hydrargira diaphana Lesueur 1817c:130 (type-locality: Saratoga Lake, New York).

Fundulus diaphanus: Nelson 1876:42 (recorded from Illinois); Jordan 1878:51; Forbes 1884:72.

Fundulus menona: Jordan 1878:52.

Fundulus diaphanus menona: Large 1903:21; Forbes & Richardson 1908:211–212; O'Donnell 1935: 485; Smith 1965:9.

Diagnosis.—The banded killifish is a slender and terete topminnow, light olivaceous above and silvery white below with the dorsum tesselated with brown, and with many thin, well-separated, dark vertical bars along the sides in both sexes; the dorsal fin originating in advance of the anal fin; 38 or more lateral-line scales; and a rather attenuate snout. The species attains a length of a little more than 75 mm (3 inches).

Variation.—The species consists of two rather well-marked subspecies: *F. d. diaphanus* along the Atlantic Coast and *F. d. menona* in the Great Lakes basin, the latter being the Illinois subspecies.

Ecology.—The banded killifish occurs in clear glacial lakes with much aquatic vegetation. It is usually in schools of a few to many individuals that cruise about the surface of weedy lakes. Keast & Webb (1966:1860–1861) confirmed the findings of Forbes & Richardson (1908:212) that this killifish feeds on a great variety of organisms and that it feeds as much in mid-water and on the bottom as at the surface. Spawning occurs in late spring and early summer. The small clusters of eggs adhere to aquatic vegetation. The best account of reproductive behavior in nature is that of Richardson (1939).

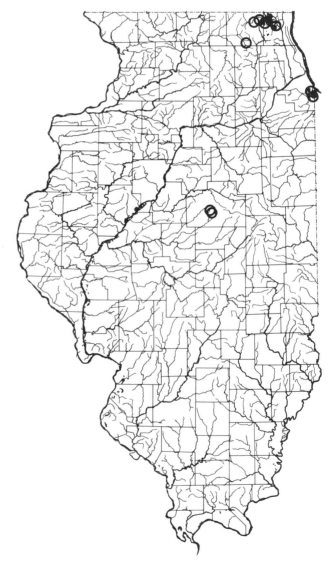

Distribution of the banded killifish in Illinois.

Distribution.—The banded killifish still occurs in a few glacial lakes (Greys, Cedar, Turner, Wolf, and Loon) in Lake and Cook counties and is common in some of them. It once occurred in McHenry County and, as isolated populations, in McLean County. The destruction and general deterioration of natural lakes must account for the decimation of the species in Illinois.

Starhead topminnow
Fundulus dispar (Agassiz)

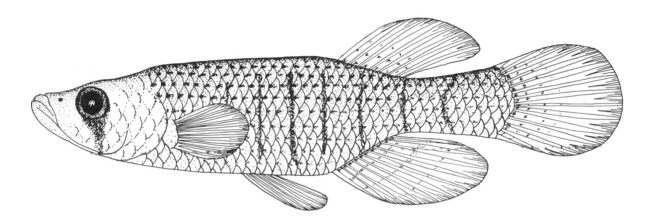

Zygonectes dispar Agasssiz 1854:353 (type-locality: creeks opposite St. Louis, Missouri, and Beardstown, Illinois); Nelson 1876:42; Forbes 1884:72; O'Donnell 1935:485.

Zygonectus dispar: Jordan 1878:52 (misspelling).

Fundulus dispar: Large 1903:21; Forbes & Richardson 1908:212–213.

Fundulus dispar dispar: Smith 1965:9.

Diagnosis.—The starhead topminnow is a rather deep-bodied killifish, olive above and yellow on the sides with minute flecks of red, blue, or green, with a prominent blue-black blotch or tear drop beneath the eye; 10–14 thin, well-separated, dark vertical bars along the side of the male; numerous thin, longitudinal, dark stripes along the side of the female; a dorsal fin origin distinctly behind the anal fin insertion; and, in life, a metallic silver spot on top of the head and another in front of the dorsal fin. The dark tear drop distinguishes this species from all other Illinois topminnows but not from the mosquitofish. However, the mosquitofish lacks the vertical bars and longitudinal stripes and has instead the scales boldly outlined with dark pigment and, frequently, a large blue-black blotch above the pelvic fin insertion. The starhead topminnow attains a length of 65 mm (2½ inches).

Variation.—Griffith (1974) and Wiley & Hall (1975) have given *dispar* full specific rank rather than that of a subspecies of *F. notti*. No subspecies of *F. dispar* are recognized.

Ecology.—The starhead topminnow occurs in some glacial lakes and in clear, well-vegetated floodplain lakes, swamps, and marshes. Gunning & Lewis (1955:555) found snails, crustaceans, aquatic insects, and algae to be the major food items of the species. Spawning occurs in late spring and early summer among dense beds of aquatic vegetation. No details are available.

Distribution.—The starhead topminnow is extremely sporadic in Illinois but often common in those few lakes and swamps where it occurs. The reason for its erratic occurrence is unknown. Its range is much the same as formerly except for its disappearance in the Wabash River valley, where oil pollution and drainage have eliminated the ideal floodplain swamp habitats.

Distribution of the starhead topminnow in Illinois.

Blackstripe topminnow
Fundulus notatus (Rafinesque)

Semotilus notatus Rafinesque 1820a:86 (type-locality: tributary of the Ohio River in Kentucky).
?*Zygonectes tenellus:* Kennicott 1855:594 (recorded from Illinois).
Zygonectes notatus: Nelson 1876:42 (part.); Jordan 1878:52 (part.); Forbes 1884:72 (part.); O'Donnell 1935:485 (part.).
Fundulus notatus: Large 1903:22 (part.); Forbes & Richardson 1908:213–215 (part.); Smith 1965:9.

Diagnosis.—The blackstripe topminnow is a terete killifish, pale olive above and white below, with a broad, purplish black, lateral band extending along each side from the snout tip to the caudal fin and with the back and upper sides uniform in color or with rather diffuse dusky spots on many of the scales. It can be confused only with the blackspotted topminnow, which has discrete and intense black dots on some of the scales above the lateral band. The blackstripe topminnow attains a length of almost 75 mm (3 inches).

Variation.—The blackstripe and blackspotted topminnows were badly confused in the upper Mississippi River valley until Braasch & Smith (1965) clarified their relationships. Thomerson (1966) thoroughly analyzed geographic variation throughout the range of the species and found some differences but not sufficient to justify recognition of subspecies.

Ecology.—The blackstripe topminnow occupies quiet waters of creeks, rivers, lakes, swamps, and ponds. It has wide ecological tolerances but reaches its greatest numbers in low-gradient creeks and small rivers. It feeds on a variety of arthropods (primarily dipteran larvae) and algae. A detailed study of food habits was made by Thomerson (1970). Spawning occurs from late spring into the summer, and details are similar to those for other topminnows except that in Illinois eggs are probably attached to detritus and leaf litter in the absence of aquatic vegetation. The male has a strongly serrate black lateral band; the female a straight-edged band. Carranza & Winn (1954) studied reproductive behavior of the species in Michigan.

Distribution.—The blackstripe topminnow is generally distributed and abundant throughout most of eastern and southern Illinois except in the Shawnee Hills, where it is replaced in upland

Blackstripe topminnow

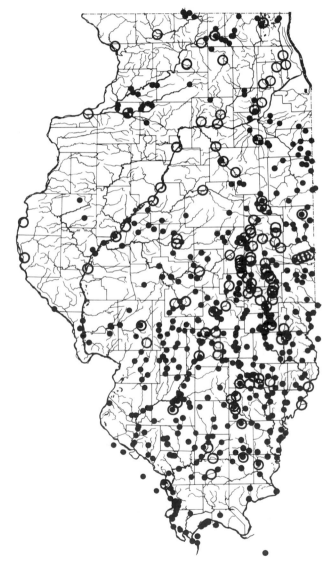

Distribution of the blackstripe topminnow in Illinois.

streams by the blackspotted topminnow. In northern and western Illinois it is present only in widely scattered colonies, but it may be locally common. The reasons for the gaps in its range in these parts of the state are not known. Throughout the rest of the state, it is difficult to imagine that the species was ever more common than now. It is extremely hardy and often present in habitats that harbor few other fishes.

Blackspotted topminnow
Fundulus olivaceus (Storer)

Paecilia olivicea Storer 1845b:51 (type-locality: Florence, Alabama).
Zygonectes notatus: Nelson 1876:42 (part.); Jordan 1878:52 (part.); Forbes 1884:72 (part.); O'Donnell 1935:485 (part.).
Fundulus notatus: Large 1903:22 (part.); Forbes & Richardson 1908:213–215 (part.).
Fundulus olivaceus: Miller 1955:10 (recorded from Illinois); Smith 1965:9.

Diagnosis.—The blackspotted topminnow is a terete killifish, pale olive or yellowish above and white below, with a broad, purplish-black, lateral band extending from the snout tip to the caudal fin and a few to many discrete and intense black dots on some of the scales above the lateral band. It looks most like the blackstripe topminnow but differs in having intense black dots scattered over the upper sides. The black lateral band and spots are more intense than those of the blackstripe, resulting in greater contrast. The species attains a length of almost 100 mm (4 inches).

Variation.—Braasch & Smith (1965) clarified the relationships between this species and the blackstripe topminnow in the upper Mississippi River

Blackspotted topminnow

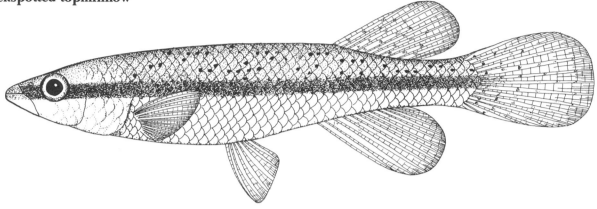

valley, and Thomerson (1966) presented a detailed account of variation in the species. No subspecies have been described, but for many years this species was believed to be merely a southern subspecies of the blackstripe topminnow.

Ecology.—The habitat relationships of the blackspotted and blackstripe topminnows differ markedly in different parts of their ranges. In Illinois and adjacent states, the blackspotted topminnow is almost entirely restricted to clear, gravelly, upland streams of high gradient, whereas the blackstripe topminnow is found in lowland areas with low-gradient streams. The food of the two species is similar except that the blackspotted topminnow, being larger, can ingest larger prey items (Thomerson 1970). Presumably its reproductive behavior is similar to that of related species, but details are lacking. The lateral band of the male is serrate, as in the blackstripe topminnow.

Distribution.—The blackspotted topminnow is extremely abundant in the clear fast streams of the Shawnee Hills. It occurs with the blackstripe topminnow in some of the slower, more turbid streams along the northern border of the Shawnee Hills but is restricted to the southern fifth of Illinois. A hardy and pioneering species, this topminnow could hardly be more common and widespread within its range than it presently is.

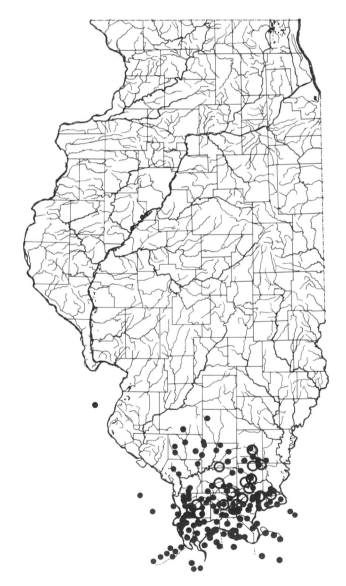

Distribution of the blackspotted topminnow in Illinois.

Livebearers—Poeciliidae

This strictly New World family is represented in this country by six genera, one of which is known from Illinois. Although primarily freshwater fishes, many livebearers are tolerant of rather high salinities. They are the predominant fishes of brackish water in the Caribbean region. The male has a distinctive intromittent organ (gonopodium) consisting of modified anal rays. Virtually all species bear living young. Most livebearers are very small fishes and of great value in the aquarium fish trade, behavioral studies, cancer research experiments, and control of mosquitoes. The Illinois species has been used extensively in studies of pesticide cross resistance. Although they bear a strong resemblance to killifishes, their reproductive biology is greatly different.

Gambusia Poey

This genus contains eight United States species and numerous Neotropical species. Only one, which is wide ranging in the southeastern states, reaches Illinois.

Mosquitofish
Gambusia affinis (Baird & Girard)

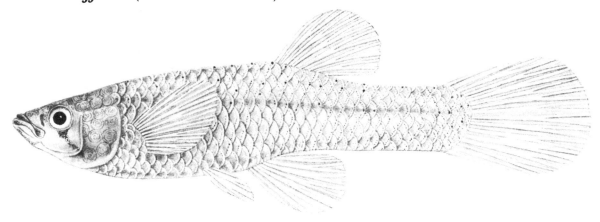

Heterandria affinis Baird & Girard 1853a:390 (type-locality: Rio Medina and Rio Salado, Texas).

Zygonectes melanops: Jordan 1878:52 (recorded from Illinois).

Gambusia patruelis: Forbes 1884:71–72; O'Donnell 1935:485.

Gambusia nobilis: Large 1903:22.

Gambusia affinis: Large 1903:22; Forbes & Richardson 1908:215–217.

Gambusia affinis affinis: Smith 1965:9.

Diagnosis.—The mosquitofish is a diminutive, dusky, surface-dwelling fish that resembles a top-minnow but differs in having a prominent intromittent organ on the anal fin of the adult male; viviparous habits; the dorsal fin far behind the anal fin insertion; the third anal ray unbranched; scales boldly outlined with dark pigment; a blue-black blotch below the eye but no definite body pattern other than a few scattered black dots; and, in some specimens, a large black spot above the pelvic fin.

Among Illinois fishes the mosquitofish resembles only the starhead topminnow and is easily distinguished by the modified anal fin of the male, bulging abdomen of the gravid female, and absence of both vertical bars and horizontal stripes. It attains a length of about 50 mm (2 inches).

Variation.—Two subspecies are recognized: an Atlantic Coast form (*holbrooki*) and an inland form (*affinis*).

Ecology.—The mosquitofish abounds in swamps, ditches, and ponds within its range and occupies practically all types of water that is shallow and has little current. It has been widely introduced to control mosquitoes although it feeds on whatever insects and crustaceans are most abundant. It breeds throughout the summer, each female producing several broods of live young. The most thorough study of its ecology is that of Krumholz (1948).

Distribution.—The mosquitofish is widely distributed and abundant throughout the southern third of Illinois and ascends a considerable distance upstream in the floodplains of large rivers. Outside its natural range, it may persist for several years where it has been introduced or permitted to escape. It is thus likely to be found almost anywhere in the state, but a severe winter may eliminate populations north of the natural range of the species.

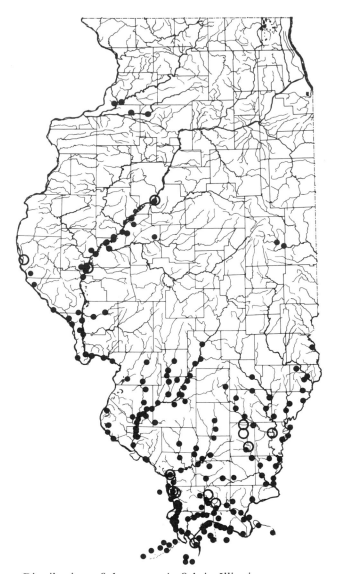

Distribution of the mosquitofish in Illinois.

Silversides—Atherinidae

This enormous family of marine fishes has only two genera that occur with regularity in fresh waters of this country. One of them contains a species widely distributed in Illinois; the other (*Menidia*) has a species that extends northward in the Mississippi River of Missouri to a point opposite Cairo, Illinois, but had not been taken in this state until recently.[1] This family of small fishes is of great value as food for larger species and is of interest because of the extraordinary diversity of marine species. The common Illinois species is too slender and delicate to be a good bait minnow. It is most often seen in minnow-seine catches or leaping above the surface of the water when pursued by another fish.

Labidesthes Cope

This eastern North American genus contains only one species, which occurs throughout Illinois.

Brook silverside
Labidesthes sicculus (Cope)

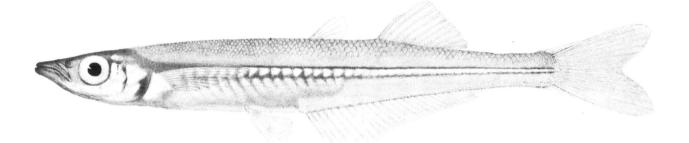

Chirostoma sicculum Cope 1865:81 (type-locality: Grosse Isle, Detroit River, Michigan).
Labidesthes sicculus: Nelson 1876:42 (recorded from Illinois); Jordan 1878:51; Forbes 1884:70; Large 1903:22; Forbes & Richardson 1908:227–228; O'Donnell 1935:486; Smith 1965:9.

Diagnosis.—The brook silverside is an extremely slender and frail little fish, pale straw color above and silvery below, with a somewhat pellucid body; a distinct beak; two separate dorsal fins, the first short with four to six weak spines; and a long anal fin, its origin far in advance of the insertion of the first dorsal fin. It is superficially minnowlike but differs sharply by such characters as two dorsal

[1]After this book was completed, a Mississippi silverside was found in the Mississippi River of southern Illinois by Dr. B. M. Burr.

fins, the long anal fin, and the beaked snout. It differs from the Mississippi silverside, which occurs in adjacent Missouri, in having the mouth produced into a beak. The species attains a length of about 100 mm (4 inches).

Variation.—For several years a peninsular Florida subspecies (*vanhyningi*) was recognized, but Bailey, Winn, & Smith (1954:150) recommended that subspecies should not be recognized.

Ecology.—The brook silverside is a surface-dwelling fish with a strong schooling tendency. It occurs in lakes, ponds, small rivers, and sometimes in brooks that are clear and have quiet water. In new impoundments, it quickly becomes abundant, particularly in those with clear water and sandy gravel bottoms. It is a schooling species that preys on small insects and zooplankton near the surface; feeding individuals in a school often leap clear of the surface of the water. Forbes & Richardson (1908:230–231) and Cahn (1927:83) described types of food taken. Nelson (1968) studied this species' reproductive behavior and growth in Indiana and found extremely rapid growth in this short-lived fish. Spawning occurs throughout the summer in quiet pools over aquatic vegetation or gravel beds. Each egg has an adhesive filament that attaches to some object as it sinks to the bottom of the pool; it hatches in approximately a week in nature.

Distribution.—The brook silverside is statewide in occurrence, but in Illinois is usually associated with large rivers and their marginal waters. Where it occurs it is abundant, but it is not ubiquitous by any means. While not strikingly evident on the distribution map, there can be no doubt that this silverside is somewhat decimated in Illinois because of the present turbidity and excessive siltation in so many streams.

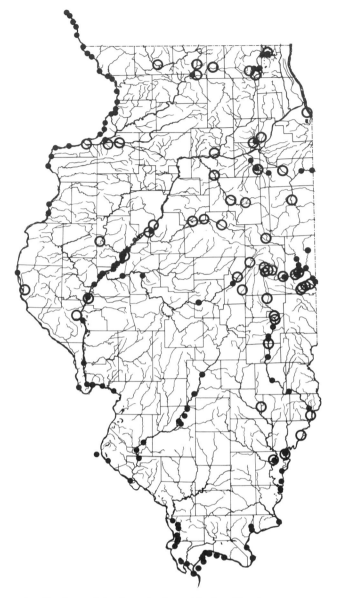

Distribution of the brook silverside in Illinois.

Sticklebacks—Gasterosteidae

This Holarctic family of small, nest-building fishes contains five United States genera, of which some are marine, some freshwater, and some both. Two are represented in Illinois. Sticklebacks are strange little fishes that have been popular as aquarium fishes and as subjects of behavioral studies. They are sometimes used as bait minnows and serve to some extent as forage fishes if other fishes are not abundant even though they are so spiny as to appear unfit for food. In some hatcheries they are accused of preying heavily on the fry of sport fishes. They are extremely pugnacious toward other small fishes.

KEY TO GENERA

1. Dorsal spines, usually 5; caudal peduncle without bony lateral keels; body black, greenish, or
     olive with yellowish markings .... *Culaea*
   Dorsal spines, usually 9 or 10; caudal peduncle with flattened bony plates forming a keel on
     each side; body silvery with brown markings .... *Pungitius*

Culaea Whitley

This boreal North American genus contains only one species, which extends southward into Illinois. *Culaea* is a substitute name for the long-used *Eucalia,* preoccupied by a butterfly genus.

Brook stickleback
Culaea inconstans (Kirtland)

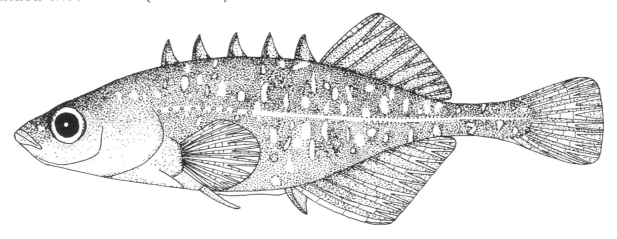

Gasterosteus inconstans Kirtland 1841*a*:273 (type-locality: brooks of Trumbull County, Ohio; revised to vicinity of Poland, Mahoning County, by Trautman 1957:617); Kennicott 1855:594 (recorded from Illinois); Forbes 1884:70.

Eucalia pygmaea: Nelson 1876:42.
Eucalia inconstans: Nelson 1876:42; Jordan 1878:51; Large 1903:22; Forbes & Richardson 1908:222–223; O'Donnell 1935:468.
Culaea inconstans: Smith 1965:9.

Diagnosis.—The brook stickleback is a compressed and scaleless small fish, olive, greenish, or entirely black usually with dark vermiculations and small yellowish spots scattered over its sides; two to seven (usually five) unconnected dorsal spines; a slender and compressed caudal peduncle without a lateral keel; and a stout spine in the anal and in each pelvic fin. It is distinctive enough to be easily recognized. The species attains a length of 65 mm (2½ inches).

Variation.—Nelson (1969) studied clinal variation in spine length and in development of the supportive skeleton of this species throughout its range. Hansen (1939) analyzed spine and ray count variation among Illinois populations.

Ecology.—The brook stickleback occurs in almost any kind of water that remains cool all year long, but it is most abundant in small, shallow brooks with much aquatic vegetation. It spawns in late spring and early summer in nests that are constructed just above the bottom on vegetation. A number of papers have been published on the reproductive biology of the species. Excellent summaries of them are given in Winn (1960) and Scott & Crossman (1973:662–663). Highly predaceous, the brook stickleback feeds on a variety of aquatic invertebrates and on algae.

Distribution.—The brook stickleback is restricted to the northern three tiers of counties in Illinois and is common in most small, grassy-bottomed brooks. It also occurs in Lake Michigan. There is no evidence that its range and abundance have changed in Illinois although it may presently be threatened by pollution from the runoff of cattle feedlots.

Pungitius Costa

This Holarctic genus contains one boreal species that occurs in marine and fresh waters of North America and Eurasia.

Ninespine stickleback
Pungitius pungitius (Linnaeus)

Gasterosteus pungitius Linnaeus 1758:296 (type-locality: Europe).

Pygosteus pungitius: Nelson 1876:42 (recorded from Illinois); Forbes & Richardson 1908:224.

Pygosteus occidentalis var. *nebulosus:* Jordan 1878:51.

Pungitius pungitius: O'Donnell 1935:486; Smith 1965:9.

Diagnosis.—The ninespine stickleback is a slender little fish, pale greenish-gray above and silvery white below with bold brown reticulations on the upper sides. It is easily distinguished from other sticklebacks by its large number (9 or 10) of dorsal spines that alternately project to the right and to the left (instead of vertically), by its much depressed caudal peduncle that has a bony keel along each side, and by its distinctive color pattern. The species attains a length of 65 mm (2½ inches).

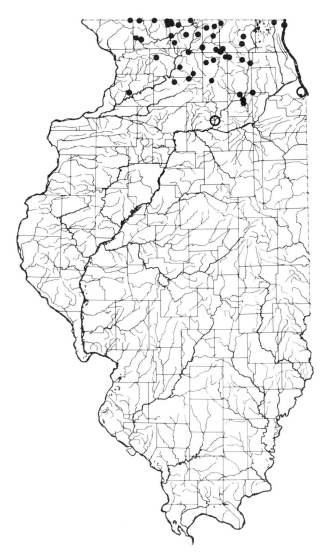

Distribution of the brook stickleback in Illinois.

Ninespine stickleback

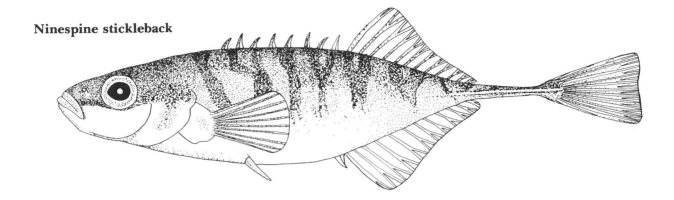

Variation.—McPhail (1963) found that in North America the species consists of a Bering Strait coastal form and an inland freshwater form but that differences were not great enough to warrant subspecific recognition of either. Nelson (1971) studied variation in the pelvic skeleton.

Ecology.—The ninespine stickleback is restricted to waters that remain cold all year. The food of the species is principally aquatic insects and crustaceans. Scott & Crossman (1973:672–673) have summarized the published information on reproductive habits. In Canada spawning occurs in the summer months. The all-black male constructs a nest among the weeds, using plant fragments glued together by a threadlike kidney secretion. The nest is tunnel shaped with an opening at either end. Courtship is rather elaborate, culminating in the female's depositing 10–30 eggs in the nest. Several females may use the same nest, and each one may spawn twice each season. As in the brook stickleback, the male guards the nest. Most ninespine sticklebacks survive only 1 year, but occasional ones may live more than 3 years.

Distribution.—In Illinois the ninespine stickleback is restricted to the shore waters of Lake Michigan. It occurs generally, but not in large numbers, in the bays and harbors and along the shallow shoreline. Occasionally during winter floods individuals enter the Des Plaines and upper Illinois rivers, but there is presently no evidence of reproduction outside of Lake Michigan.

Distribution of the ninespine stickleback in Illinois.

Sculpins—Cottidae

This large Nearctic family contains many marine genera but only four that have species occurring in fresh water. Two genera are represented in Illinois. The distribution of the family is mainly circumpolar, but several species reach the southern United States. All sculpins are bottom dwellers in cold and highly oxygenated water. As such they are of some value as indicators of the proximity of springs, waters suitable for stocking trout, and high water quality. They are too delicate to be suitable for bait minnows. They have been accused of preying heavily on eggs of other fishes and competing for the limited food supply of trout streams, but there is little evidence to support either accusation. Sculpins are distinctive and recognized by many people, who may have their own names for them. In the deeper parts of Lake Michigan, they are among the few forage fishes.

KEY TO GENERA

1. Gill membranes free from isthmus; dorsal fins separated by a distance at least equal to the eye diameter . . . . *Myoxocephalus*
   Gill membranes broadly attached to isthmus; dorsal fins not separated by a distinct gap . . . . *Cottus*

Myoxocephalus Tilesius

This genus contains seven Nearctic marine species, one of which also occurs in fresh water in North America and Eurasia. The genus reaches its southernmost limit in the deep water of southern Lake Michigan.

Fourhorn sculpin
Myoxocephalus quadricornis
   (Linnaeus)

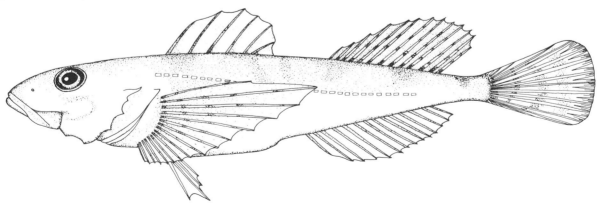

Cottus quadricornis Linnaeus 1758:264 (type-locality: Baltic Sea).
Triglopsis thompsoni: Nelson 1876:41 (recorded from Illinois).
Triglopsis stimpsoni: Jordan 1878:50.
Myoxocephalus quadricornis: Smith 1965:11.

216

Diagnosis.—The fourhorn sculpin is a grayish-brown sculpin with four to seven rows of thin dark saddles, well-separated dorsal fins, a prominent second preopercular spine directed backward rather than downward, the gill membranes completely free from the isthmus, and with one pelvic spine and three rays. It is easily recognized as a sculpin by its head and body shape, expansive pectoral fins, naked body, and double dorsal fin, and it is sharply set off from other Illinois sculpins by the key characters. The species usually attains a length of about 130 mm (5 inches).

Variation.—Despite considerable study, the number of subspecies to be recognized is still uncertain. Most authors recognize the marine form as *M. q. quadricornis* and the freshwater form as *M. q. thomp-soni.* An excellent summary of the taxonomic history of the species is given in McPhail & Lindsey (1970:320–322).

Ecology.—Because the fourhorn sculpin is restricted to the bottom in deep water, little is known of its ecology. Many of the early records were from the stomachs of lake trout. Wells (1968:12) reported a specimen from 4 fathoms (about 7.4 m or 24 feet) but noted that the species was uncommon in water less than 40 fathoms and that it occurred in the deepest basin of Lake Michigan. The most complete summary of the feeding and reproductive behavior is that of McPhail & Lindsey (1970: 322–323), who cited the food of the species as crustaceans and chironomids. It appears that in southern Lake Michigan breeding probably occurs in June and, although no details are available, it is presumed that eggs are deposited on the undersides of rocks (as in most other sculpins) and are guarded by the male.

Distribution.—The species probably occurs throughout the Illinois portion of Lake Michigan except for the shallow water near shore. A series of specimens is available in the Illinois Natural History Survey collection from 48 km (30 miles) ENE of the mouth of the Chicago River. Moffett (1957: 394) believed that the fourhorn sculpin increased in abundance after its principal predators (lake trout and burbot) had been decimated by the sea lamprey.

Distribution of the fourhorn sculpin in Illinois.

Cottus Linnaeus

This Holarctic genus contains 22 North American species, 4 of which occur in Illinois. Most of them inhabit fast-flowing streams along the Pacific Coast, but two of the four Illinois species occur in Lake Michigan. Insofar as is known, spawning takes place in the late winter and early spring while the water is still cold. Typically the male selects a nest site, usually under a flat rock, and several females deposit adhesive eggs on the nest ceiling. The male guards the nest until the young are able to feed.

KEY TO SPECIES

1. Pelvic fin with one spine and three rays (spine and first ray bound together); body plain or mottled and rather smooth .... *cognatus*

Pelvic fin with one spine and four rays; body with three or four saddles or, if mottled, extremely prickly 2
2. Head spatulate, triangular, and greatly flattened; preopercular spine enlarged and strongly curved upward; body vaguely blotched or mottled and extremely prickly; body slender .... *ricei*
Head rounded and not greatly flattened; preopercular spine small and almost straight; body with four transverse saddles; body robust 3

3. Lateral line complete; pectoral fin with 16 rays; spinous dorsal without black blotch posteriorly; body bands sharply contrasting with ground color; dorsal fins separate ....
.... *carolinae*
Lateral line ending before caudal peduncle; pectoral fin with 14 or 15 rays; spinous dorsal fin with a posterior black blotch; body bands somewhat subdued; dorsal fins slightly connected .... *bairdi*

Mottled sculpin
Cottus bairdi Girard

Cottus bairdii Girard 1850:410 (type-locality: Mahoning River, Poland, Ohio); O'Donnell 1935: 490 (part.).
Pegedichthys alvordi: Nelson 1876:41 (recorded from Illinois).
Potamocottus alvordi: Jordan 1878:50.
Potamocottus wilsoni: Jordan 1878:50 (not in Illinois).
Uranidea richardsoni: Forbes 1884:62 (part.).
Cottus ictalops: Forbes & Richardson 1908:326–327 (part.).
Cottus bairdi: Smith 1965:10.

Diagnosis.—The mottled sculpin is a brownish or blackish sculpin with three or four black saddles, numerous small whitish spots scattered over the back and sides, one or two black spots in the first dorsal fin, the lateral line ending before the caudal peduncle, dorsal fins somewhat connected, a smooth skin, the pelvic fin with one spine and four

rays, and 14 or 15 pectoral fin rays. The species is similar to the slimy sculpin, but Illinois specimens can be reliably separated by the number of pelvic fin rays. It is also similar to the banded sculpin but has more subdued dorsal saddles and scattered small light spots. The two can also be distinguished by characters listed in the key. The mottled sculpin attains a length of about 100 mm (4 inches).

Variation.—A thorough, but as yet unpublished, study of the mottled sculpin and its relatives was done in the early 1950s by Dr. C. Richard Robins, then at Cornell University. Several subspecies have been recognized for many years. In Illinois the Lake Michigan form was called *C. b. kumlieni* and the stream form, *C. b. bairdi*. Currently most authors regard the species as highly variable without recognizable subspecies.

Ecology.—In Illinois the mottled sculpin occurs in springs, spring-fed seeps, and clear fast creeks, often called runs. It also occurs in the shallow water along the pebbly shoreline of Lake Michigan. In streams it is most abundant in gravelly or rocky riffles. It feeds on benthic organisms (largely aquatic insects and crustaceans) and sometimes other fishes. Spawning occurs in April and perhaps much earlier. The spawning behavior is elaborate but typical of that of other sculpins. The male cleans and guards the approximately 200 eggs attached to the underside of a flat rock. Details were presented by Savage (1963).

Distribution.—The mottled sculpin is relatively common in tributaries of the Fox River in northeastern Illinois but extremely sporadic elsewhere in the northern part of the state. There is no evidence that it has become decimated, but its habitats are rapidly being destroyed by stream alteration.

Distribution of the mottled sculpin in Illinois.

Banded sculpin
Cottus carolinae (Gill)

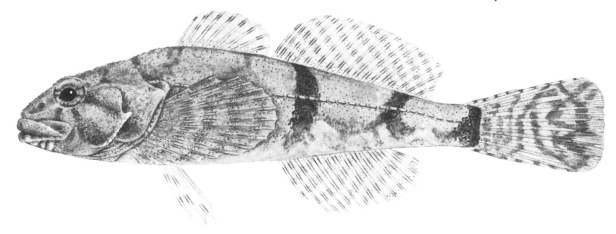

Potamocottus carolinae Gill 1861:41 (type-locality: Maysville, Kentucky).
Potamocottus meridionalis: Jordan 1878:50 (not in Illinois).
Uranidea richardsoni: Forbes 1884:62 (part.).

Cottus ictalops: Large 1903:30 (recorded from Illinois); Forbes & Richardson 1908:326–327 (part.).
Cottus bairdii: O'Donnell 1935:490 (part.).
Cottus carolinae: Smith 1965:10.

Diagnosis.—The banded sculpin is a grayish or brownish sculpin with three or four intense black or brown saddles and small flecks of dark pigment, a complete lateral line, the dorsal fins contiguous but separate, a smooth skin, pelvic fins with one spine and four rays, and 16 pectoral fin rays. It most closely resembles the mottled sculpin but can be distinguished by the characters given in the key. It has the most pronounced dorsal saddles of all Illinois sculpins. The species attains a length of about 150 mm (6 inches).

Variation.—Until Bailey and Dimick (1949) elevated *carolinae* to specific rank, this sculpin was regarded as a southern subspecies of *C. bairdi*. A study of variation in the species in the 1950's by Dr. C. Richard Robins has not been published, but

Distribution of the banded sculpin in Illinois.

Williams & Robins (1970) recognized three subspecies and compared their new subspecies, *C. c. infernatis,* with *C. c. zopherus.* The Illinois subspecies is *C. c. carolinae.*

Ecology.—The banded sculpin occupies springs, spring-fed streams, and cave streams. In Illinois it probably occurs only in streams that are spring-fed. Its feeding habits, like those of other sculpins, include preying on benthic insects, crustaceans, and small fishes. Since it is a large sculpin, fishes probably are more important prey items to the banded sculpin than to other Illinois species. Robins (*in* Williams & Robins 1970:376) expressed the opinion that the banded sculpin probably does not build a nest but lays its eggs singly or broadcasts them over gravel. Spawning probably occurs in March and April in Illinois.

Distribution.—The banded sculpin is limited to clear cold streams that are spring fed in extreme southern Illinois and streams issuing from the bluffs along the lower Illinois River and Mississippi River in western Illinois. It still occurs at some of the sites where Forbes and Richardson collected it prior to 1908, and evidently these springs and caves have not been greatly altered over the years. While there is no evidence of decimation of the species, its habitat is being reduced by stream alteration.

Slimy sculpin
Cottus cognatus Richardson

Cottus cognatus Richardson 1836:40 (type-locality: Great Bear Lake [Canada]); O'Donnell 1935:490 (not in Illinois); Smith 1965:11.

Uranidea hoyi: Nelson 1876:41 (recorded from Illinois); Jordan 1878:50; Large 1903:30.

Uranidea kumlieni: Nelson 1876:41; Jordan 1878:50.

Uranidea kumlienii: Large 1903:30; Forbes & Richardson 1908:328–329.

Diagnosis.—The slimy sculpin is a smooth-skinned, coarsely mottled sculpin with the first dorsal fin darkly pigmented basally and clear distally, the dorsal fins separate, an incomplete lateral line, and the pelvic fins with one spine but only three rays. Superficially it resembles the mottled sculpin, but in Illinois the pelvic ray count suffices to separate the species. The slimy sculpin is more mottled and less spotted, and it has a smoother skin. The

Slimy sculpin

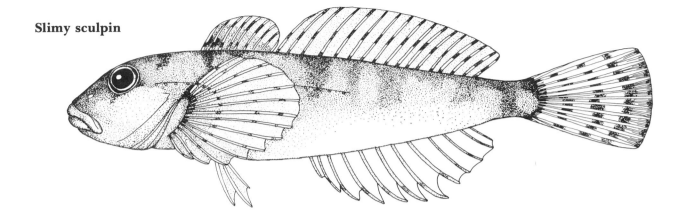

species attains a length of a little more than 100 mm (4 inches).

Variation.—Several nominal species have been described, and many authors have recognized a far northern race as *C. c. cognatus* and a southern and eastern form as *C. c. gracilis*. Currently Canadian workers point out that subspecies recognition is not warranted and that in some areas the traditional pelvic ray count does not even serve to separate the slimy sculpin from the mottled sculpin (McPhail & Lindsey 1970:334; Scott & Crossman 1973:831–832). The name *kumlieni* that Hubbs (1926:75) has shown to apply to the *bairdi* complex was unfortunately misapplied to *cognatus* by early workers, as can be seen in the synonymy.

Ecology.—In Illinois the slimy sculpin is known only in Lake Michigan and occurs along the shoreline as well as in deep water, but probably much more commonly in the latter. Like its relatives in the lake, it probably subsists mostly on crustaceans and chironomid larvae. Its spawning behavior is similar to that of the mottled sculpin in that it deposits adhesive eggs on the ceiling of the nest, which the male guards.

Distribution.—Collections are available at the Illinois Natural History Survey from a few sites along the Lake Michigan shoreline near Zion and from deep water 48 km (30 miles) ENE of the mouth of the Chicago River.

Distribution of the slimy sculpin in Illinois.

Spoonhead sculpin
Cottus ricei (Nelson)

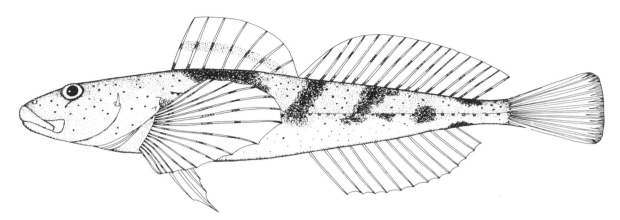

Cottopsis ricei Nelson 1876:40 (type-locality: shore of Lake Michigan near Evanston, Illinois).

Tauridea spilota: Jordan 1878:50.

Cottus ricei: Large 1903:30; Forbes & Richardson 1908:327–328; O'Donnell 1935:490; Smith 1965:11.

Diagnosis.—The spoonhead sculpin is a slender-bodied and prickly sculpin, mottled with brown but usually with about four vague saddles across the back, with the pelvic fin with one spine and four rays, a much depressed and spatulate head, preopercular spines much enlarged and strongly curved upward, the dorsal fins close together, and a complete lateral line. The flattened triangular-shaped head, slender caudal peduncle, and well-developed preopercular spines are said to distinguish this species from all other American sculpins. The species attains a length of more than 100 mm (4 inches).

Variation.—The spoonhead sculpin is geographically rather stable in meristic and proportional characters (Scott & Crossman 1973:839).

Ecology.—In Illinois this species probably occupies the deep water of Lake Michigan. It is so rare everywhere that little is known of its ecology. Scott & Crossman (1973:841) noted that it probably spawns in the fall.

Distribution.—To my knowledge, the only Illinois records for the species are the type and four Lake Michigan specimens in the Field Museum.

Distribution of the spoonhead sculpin in Illinois.

Temperate basses—Percichthyidae

This widely distributed family of primarily marine genera is represented in the fresh waters of North America by only one genus. They are extremely popular sport fishes since they strike artificial lures, some attain large size, and they are valued as food. In some parts of the country the striped bass is sometimes sought as a trophy fish. Temperate basses tend to do well in reservoirs and are among the most prized of impoundment species. Some are of commercial importance. They were formerly placed in the large marine family Serranidae.

Morone Mitchill

This Nearctic genus includes four species, two of which are native to Illinois and one of which has recently found its way into this state as a result of stockings in nearby Kentucky. The introduced species appeared in Illinois waters for the first time in 1974. Whether it will persist or disappear is at present unknown. These fishes were formerly placed in the genus *Roccus*.

KEY TO SPECIES

1. First anal spine about one-third length of second and third, which are about equal in length; dorsal fins partly joined; jaws about equal in length; bold dark stripes on a yellow or white ground color interrupted on sides above anal fin insertion ..... *mississippiensis*
   Second anal spine intermediate in length between first and third; dorsal fins separate; lower jaw protruding beyond upper; longitudinal lines along sides usually not interrupted 2
2. Longitudinal dark lines rather dim; longest anal spine equal to or longer than half of greatest height of anal fin; soft anal rays, 12 or 13; back highly arched and body rather deep .. .. *chrysops*
   Longitudinal dark lines rather prominent; longest anal spine less than half as long as the greatest height of anal fin; soft anal rays, 9–11; back little arched and body rather slender .... *saxatilis*

White bass
Morone chrysops (Rafinesque)

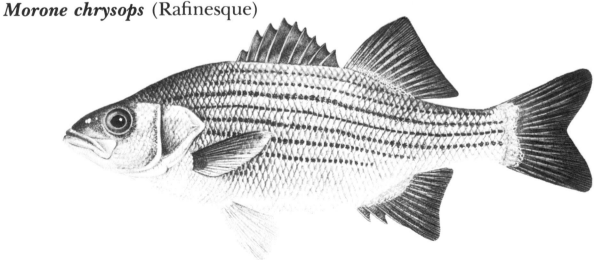

Perca chrysops Rafinesque 1820*a*:22 (type-locality: falls of the Ohio River).
Labrax multilineatus: Kennicott 1855:593 (recorded from Illinois).

Roccus chrysops: Nelson 1876:36; Jordan 1878:44; Forbes 1884:63; Large 1903:29; Forbes & Richardson 1908:319–320; Smith 1965:9.
Lepibema chrysops: O'Donnell 1935:490.

Diagnosis.—The white bass is a moderately compressed bass, bluish-white on the sides, with several thin and rather faded longitudinal brownish lines not conspicuously interrupted above the anal fin, a spinous dorsal fin separated from the soft dorsal fin, a protruding lower jaw, the second anal spine intermediate in length between the first and third, the length of the longest anal spine more than half the greatest height of the anal fin, and 9–11 soft anal rays. The white bass differs from the introduced striped bass in having a less prominent pattern of longitudinal stripes, a proportionately deeper body, longer anal spines, and more anal rays. It differs from the yellow bass in color and pattern as well as in the several morphological characters cited in the key. The small young may lack longitudinal stripes but is easily recognized by the shape of the body and head. The species attains a length of over 410 mm (16 inches).

Variation.—No subspecies are recognized and relatively few synonyms exist. Evidently little geographic variation occurs in this species.

Ecology.—The white bass occurs in schools in large and medium-sized rivers, floodplain lakes, and large reservoirs. It prefers clear water over a firm bottom. Adults are primarily fish eaters; the young feed on a variety of invertebrates (Voightlander & Wissing 1974). In reservoirs it preys heavily on shad. A large literature on age and growth exists (Sigler 1949; Lewis 1950), but details of spawning are not as well known. For a good summary of the knowledge available on the ecology of the species, see Chadwick et al. (*in* Calhoun 1966:412–422). Spawning occurs over about 1 week, usually in April or May, depending on water temperature, and is gregarious with males outnumbering females. Males arrive first. Each female lays several hundred thousand eggs near the surface over shoals. The adhesive eggs sink, attaching to rocks, sticks, or vegetation near the bottom. Hatching requires about 2 days, and the growth of the young is rapid. The species lives 5 or 6 years and is usually sexually mature at the beginning of its 3rd year.

Distribution.—The white bass is common in large rivers and in some large lakes but not present in most of the small streams and ponds within the interior of the state. No data are available to indicate changes in its overall distribution pattern and abundance in Illinois, except that it no longer occurs in southern Lake Michigan.

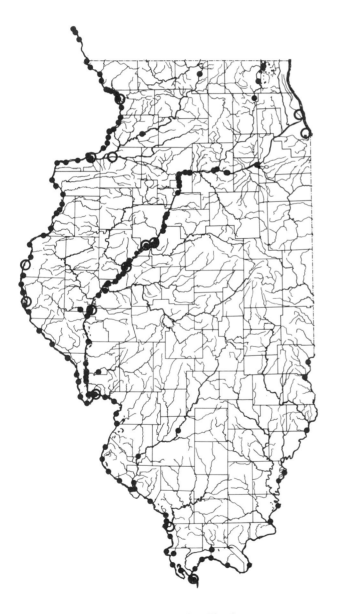

Distribution of the white bass in Illinois.

Yellow bass
Morone mississippiensis Jordan & Eigenmann

Morone mississippiensis Jordan & Eigenmann *in* Eigenmann 1887:295 (substitute name for preoccupied *Morone interrupta* Gill; type-locality: St. Louis—thus assumed to occur in Illinois waters—and New Orleans).

Morone interrupta: Nelson 1876:36; Jordan 1878: 44; Large 1903:29; Forbes & Richardson 1908: 321–322.

Roccus interruptus: Forbes 1884:63.

Chrysoperca interrupta: O'Donnell 1935:490.

Roccus mississippiensis: Smith 1965:9.

Diagnosis.—The yellow bass is a moderately compressed bass, yellow or greenish white on the sides, with several bold, brown or black longitudinal lines, those just above the anal fin being conspicuously interrupted and offset; the median fins and throat region bluish; the spinous and soft dorsal fins slightly conjoined; the spinous dorsal as large as or larger than the soft dorsal fin; the lower jaw contained within the upper; the second anal spine about the size of the third; and the first anal spine about a third as long as either the second or third. The species most closely resembles the white and striped basses but is easily distinguished by the characters in the key. Most Illinois specimens are less than 260 mm (10 inches) in length although Forbes & Richardson (1908:321) reported a size range of 310–460 mm (12–18 inches).

Variation.—No subspecies have been described for this distinctive species, which seemingly varies little in different parts of its range.

Ecology.—The yellow bass is primarily a fish of reservoirs and bottomland lakes, and its presence

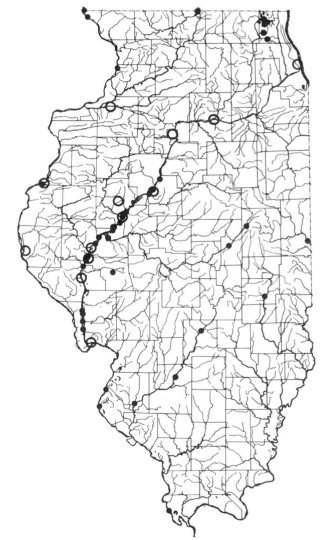

Distribution of the yellow bass in Illinois.

in streams is usually the result of individuals dispersing from nearby lakes. It does occur naturally in large rivers although the source may also be marginal lakes. Except for its preference for lakes, its ecology is presumably similar to that of the white bass. The yellow bass is a smaller species with a shorter life, but like the white bass, it grows fast (Lewis & Carlander 1948) and can quickly become abundant in newly stocked lakes. Detailed life-history information is extremely scanty, but spawning time and behavior are similar to those described for the white bass.

Distribution.—The yellow bass is general in occurrence in the lower Illinois River, upper Mississippi, and in the glacial lakes of northeastern Illinois. It also occurs in reservoirs—and is sometimes extremely abundant—throughout the state, but its distribution is sporadic. Contrary to the statement of Forbes & Richardson (1908:321) that it is nearly twice as abundant as the white bass, it is now much less generally distributed and less common than that species even though it is widely introduced. It is relatively rare in most of the Mississippi, Ohio, and Wabash rivers. Reasons for its decline are unknown although currently high turbidities of most Illinois lakes may be an important factor.

Striped bass
Morone saxatilis (Walbaum)

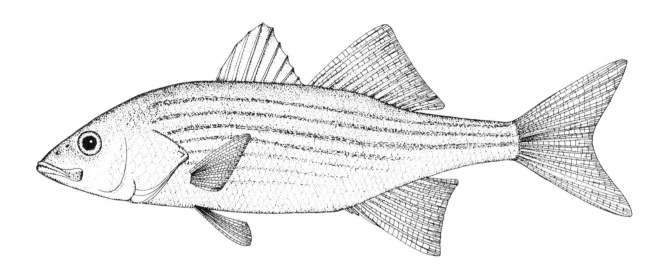

Perca saxatilis Walbaum 1792:330 (type-locality: New York).

Diagnosis.—The striped bass is a rather elongate temperate bass, silvery white on the sides, with bold longitudinal lines, the spinous and soft dorsal fins separate, a projecting lower jaw, and rather small anal spines (the longest being less than half the greatest height of the anal fin), and without dim secondary stripes between the primary stripes and without the highly arched back of the other Illinois temperate basses. It differs from them in being much larger and more slender and in having bold dark stripes neither interrupted in the anal fin region nor alternating with dim secondary stripes. The species attains a length of more than 610 mm (2 feet).

Variation.—Several authors have studied geographic variation. For a summary, see Lewis (1957). No subspecies are recognized despite the presence of several recognizable intraspecies-level populations.

Ecology.—The striped bass is an anadromous species that is landlocked in some geographic areas. Because of its popularity as a sport species, it has been widely introduced, and a massive literature on its ecology is available. For a summary, see Goodson (*in* Calhoun 1966). Raney (1952) described its life history. It feeds in schools, primarily on crustaceans and fishes. Spawning occurs in large rivers, probably in May in southern Illinois, in a fashion similar to that described for the white bass. The semibuoyant eggs, which may number

Distribution of the striped bass in Illinois.

several million from a large female, are cleaned by the current's sweeping them along the bottom. The species is known to live 14 years.

Distribution.—The striped bass first appeared in Illinois waters in 1974, presumably having escaped from impoundments in western Kentucky. Within a few months it had spread from the Ohio River to as far north as the lower Kaskaskia River. Its future status is unknown in the state; it is presently known from a few very large specimens caught in the Ohio River and Crab Orchard Lake by anglers.

Sunfishes—Centrarchidae

This Nearctic freshwater family includes nine genera, six of which occur in Illinois. Originally restricted to North America, the family is now virtually worldwide through deliberate introduction of several popular sport species. Members of this family typically construct saucer-shaped nests in gravel, and the male guards the nest until after the eggs have hatched into fry. Longevity and the attainment of sexual maturity vary with the sizes reached by the species, the larger ones living to a greater age and requiring more time to become sexually mature. The black basses, crappies, and larger sunfishes are among the most popular sport fishes known and can be caught on artificial lures and baited hooks. Breeding males of some of the sunfishes are among the most colorful and attractive of American freshwater fishes.

KEY TO GENERA

1. Lateral line absent; caudal fin rounded; dorsal fin with four or five spines; adults less than 40 mm (1½ inches) in length .... *Elassoma*
   Lateral line present; caudal fin forked; dorsal fin with six or more spines; adults longer than 40 mm (1½ inches) 2
2. Anal fin spines, five to eight; anterior dorsal fin with 6–8 or 11–13 spines (rarely 10) 3
   Anal fin spines, usually three; anterior dorsal fin usually with 10 spines 5
3. First dorsal fin with 11–13 spines; dorsal fin origin well in advance of anal fin origin; dorsal spines not stepped, the middle ones as long as or longer than posterior ones; adult body pattern consisting of dark longitudinal streaks 4
   First dorsal fin with six to eight spines; dorsal fin origin slightly in advance of anal fin origin; dorsal spines distinctly stepped, the first being shortest and the last longest; adult body pattern not consisting of dark longitudinal streaks .... *Pomoxis*
4. Mouth large, posterior end of upper jaw extending almost to below middle of eye; length of anal fin base a little more than half length of dorsal fin base; body robust, not strongly compressed; dark bar below eye extending obliquely backward .... *Ambloplites*
   Mouth small, posterior end of upper jaw extending to below front of eye; length of anal fin base more than two-thirds length of dorsal fin base; body thin, strongly compressed; dark bar below eye vertically aligned .... *Centrarchus*
5. Body elongate, its depth usually going three or more times into standard length; scales in lateral line, 55 or more; mouth large, the length of the maxilla more than 1.5 times distance from rear edge of maxilla to tip of opercle .... *Micropterus*
   Body deep and compressed, its depth usually going 2.5 times or fewer into standard length; scales in lateral line, fewer than 55; mouth small, the length of the maxilla less than 1.5 times distance from rear edge of maxilla to end of opercle .... *Lepomis*

Micropterus Lacépède

This genus, native to east-central North America, includes six species, three of which occur in Illinois. Two of them have been widely introduced around the world and are among the most popular of sport fishes.

KEY TO SPECIES

1. Deep notch between spinous and soft dorsal fins, free edge of first dorsal fin hemispherical or sickle shaped, spines 8 and 9 less than

half height of longest spines; mouth large, the maxilla extending behind eye in adult; caudal fin not tricolored in juvenile ......
.... *salmoides*
Shallow notch between spinous and soft dorsal fins, free edge of first dorsal fin curved but not hemispherical, spines 8 and 9 more than half height of longest spines; mouth small, the maxilla not extending behind eye; caudal fin tricolored in juvenile, with a band of orange-yellow and a white margin distally ..
.... 2

2. Ground color olive-green or brown with a series of brown vertical bars along sides or without markings; sides below lateral line without thin, dark horizontal stripes; scales, usually more than 67 in lateral line ...... *dolomieui*
Ground color whitish, yellowish, or pale olive with a series of dark, nearly confluent blotches that forms a distinct lateral band; sides below lateral line with several thin, dark horizontal stripes; scales larger, usually fewer than 66 in lateral line .... *punctulatus*

Smallmouth bass
Micropterus dolomieui Lacépède

Micropterus dolomieu Lacépède 1802:324 (type-locality: not given); Large 1903:25; Forbes & Richardson 1908:263–266; O'Donnell 1935:486.
Centrarchus fasciatus: Kennicott 1855:594 (recorded from Illinois).
Micropterus salmoides: Nelson 1876:37; Jordan 1878:44.
Micropterus dolomiei: Forbes 1884:67 (misspelling).
Micropterus dolomieui: Smith 1965:10.

Diagnosis. — The smallmouth bass is a somewhat compressed bass, dark olive or yellowish brown, without prominent markings on the sides or with vague dark vertical bars, dark stripes across the cheeks, a gently curved spinous dorsal fin broadly joined to the soft dorsal, usually more than 67 scales in the lateral line, and a moderate-sized mouth (the end of the upper jaw usually not ex-

tending behind the eye), and without a lateral band or rows of longitudinal stripes on the lower sides. The absence of a lateral band or row of nearly confluent blotches and the dark pigmentation distinguish the species from the largemouth and spotted basses. The darkly pigmented young has a tricolored caudal fin like that of the spotted bass except that it lacks the black caudal spot. The species attains a length of more than 510 mm (20 inches), but in Illinois adults over 300 mm (12 inches) are unusual.

Variation. — For several years the population at the southwestern edge of the species' range was recognized as a separate subspecies (*M. d. velox*), but Bailey (*in* Harlan & Speaker 1956:336) recommended that it not be given nomenclatorial status.

Ecology.—The smallmouth bass occurs in clear, gravelly or rocky rivers that have moderate to fast current and remain relatively cool during the summer months. Although a lake species farther north, in Illinois it is predominantly a stream fish that lurks near cover in large clear pools. A large fishery literature exists for the species, and a great deal of experimental work on the species has been done by Dr. R. W. Larimore and other members of the Section of Aquatic Biology, Illinois Natural History Survey. For an excellent summary of the ecology of the smallmouth bass, see Emig (*in* Calhoun 1966:354–366). The species feeds on crustaceans, insects, and other fishes and has a voracious appetite. Spawning occurs in May or June over saucer-shaped nests excavated in gravel.

From 2,000 to several thousand eggs are guarded by the male, who continues to guard the school of black, tadpole-like fry for a day or so. Hatching times depend on water temperature, and hatching may require as little as 2 or 3 days. The adults have rather circumscribed home ranges. They may live more than 10 years and are usually sexually mature in 3 or 4 years.

Distribution.—The smallmouth bass is widely distributed and common in suitable habitats throughout the northern two-thirds of Illinois but extremely sporadic in the southern third and absent from many areas. Despite its present general distribution in northern and central Illinois, it was more generally distributed formerly. Siltation, fluctuating water levels, and a general deterioration of water quality have contributed to its decline in the state.

Spotted bass
Micropterus punctulatus
(Rafinesque)

Calliurus punctulatus Rafinesque 1819:420 (type-locality: Ohio River).
Micropterus salmoides: Forbes & Richardson 1908: 267–269 (part.).
Micropterus pseudaplites: O'Donnell 1935:486 (recorded from Illinois).
Micropterus punctulatus punctulatus: Smith 1965:10.

Diagnosis.—The spotted bass is a rather compressed bass, pale olive, with a black or brown lateral band or row of nearly confluent blotches, dark stripes across the cheeks, several longitudinal rows of dark dots on the lower sides, a gently curved spinous dorsal fin broadly joined by the soft dorsal, usually less than 67 scales in the lateral line, and a moderate-sized mouth (the end of the upper jaw usually does not extend behind the eye). The adult resembles the largemouth bass in color and pattern but differs in lacking the sickle-shaped spinous dorsal fin and in having longitudinal rows of dark dots on the lower sides and a smaller mouth. The young differs from the young largemouth in having a black caudal spot, a tricolored tail, and more prominent cheek stripes. It differs from the young smallmouth bass in having a black caudal spot, a black or brown lateral band rather than vertical bars, and a pale ground color. The species attains a length of more than 500 mm (20 inches), but in Illinois adults more than 310 mm (12 inches) are rare.

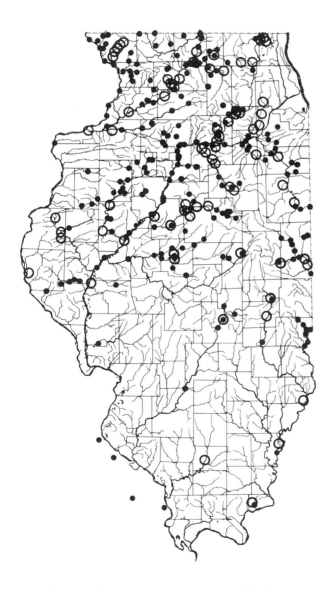

Distribution of the smallmouth bass in Illinois.

Spotted bass

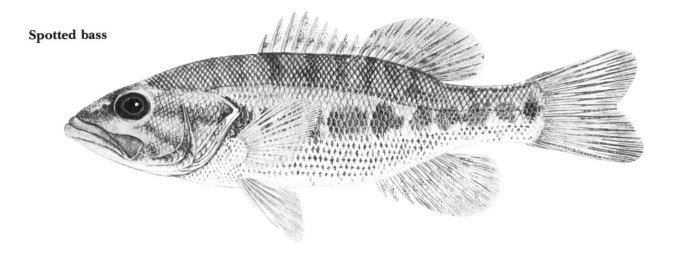

Variation.—Hubbs & Bailey (1940) studied geographic variation and recognized three subspecies, two of which have rather restricted ranges. The wide-ranging subspecies, and the one occurring in Illinois, is *M. p. punctulatus.*

Ecology.—The spotted bass occurs in small and large rivers that are clear, gravelly, and have moderate current. It is most common in firm-bottomed pools. Although occupying reservoirs in other states, in Illinois it is primarily a stream species. Its feeding habits are similar to those of other species in the genus, although Smith & Page (1969) found that in Illinois streams aquatic insects were the principal food items. McKechnie (*in* Calhoun 1966:366–370) summarized other aspects of the ecology of the species. Spawning occurs in May and June and is similar to that described for the smallmouth bass.

Distribution.—The spotted bass is a widely distributed and common species in suitable habitats in the Wabash-Ohio drainage in Illinois, and it occurs commonly in Clear Creek, a direct tributary of the Mississippi River, in southwestern Illinois. No evidence of decimation or range expansion is available, since the species was not recognized by early authors.

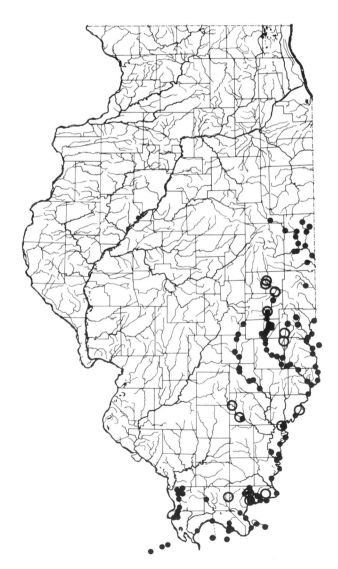

Distribution of the spotted bass in Illinois.

Largemouth bass
Micropterus salmoides (Lacépède)

Labrus salmoides Lacépède 1802:716 (type-locality: [South] Carolina).

Micropterus nigricans: Nelson 1876:36 (recorded from Illinois).

Micropterus pallidus: Jordan 1878:44.

Micropterus salmoides: Forbes 1884:67; Large 1903: 25; Forbes & Richardson 1908:267–269.

Huro salmoides: O'Donnell 1935:486.

Micropterus salmoides salmoides: Smith 1965:10.

Diagnosis.—The largemouth bass is a rather compressed bass, pale olive, with a black or brown lateral band or row of nearly confluent blotches, vague stripes across the cheeks, a hemispherical or sickle-shaped spinous dorsal fin separated from the soft dorsal by a notch, spines 8 and 9 less than half the height of longest spines, usually less than 67 scales in the lateral line, and a large mouth (the end of the upper jaw extending behind the eye in the adult), and without longitudinal rows of dark dots on the lower sides. The species most closely resembles the spotted bass but can be distinguished by the shape of the spinous dorsal fin, the large mouth, and details of pattern (largemouth adults tend to have fewer spots on the body and no markings at all or a continuous but vague lateral band). The young differs from the young of other members of the genus in lacking the tricolored tail and striped cheeks. The species attains a length of 610 mm (24 inches) or more, but most adults are under 460 mm (18 inches).

Variation.—Bailey & Hubbs (1949) described the peninsular Florida population as a new subspecies, resurrecting for it the name *floridanus* from the

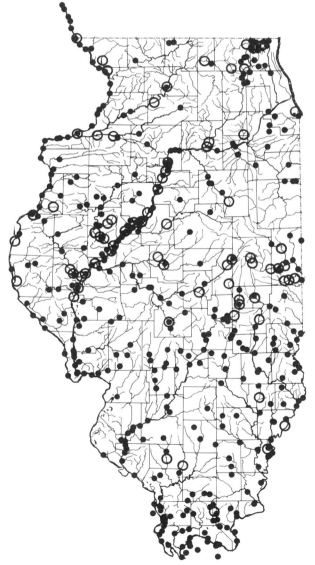

Distribution of the largemouth bass in Illinois.

synonymy. The wide-ranging subspecies, the one occurring in Illinois, is the nominate form, *M. s. salmoides*.

Ecology.—The largemouth bass is an ecologically tolerant species that occurs in virtually all types of water, including swamps, ponds, lakes, reservoirs, creeks, and large rivers. The preferred habitat is weedy oxbows and clear floodplain lakes. There are few other fishes in the world that have been so intensely studied, and an enormous fishery literature exists. Many studies have been performed at the Illinois Natural History Survey by Dr. George W. Bennett and his associates. For an excellent summary, see Emig (*in* Calhoun 1966:332–353). The tiny young feed on plankton; larger individuals, on insects and crustaceans; adults take a variety of foods, consisting mostly of crustaceans and fishes. Spawning occurs over nests constructed in gravel or vegetation in the quiet water of bays and inlets in May or June. The spawning behavior parallels that reported for the smallmouth bass. In cold lakes the species may live 16 years, but in Illinois it probably does not survive more than 8 or 10. It is usually sexually mature at 2 years of age.

Distribution.—The largemouth bass is statewide and abundant. It doubtlessly occurs in every township in Illinois. However, there was no point in collecting voucher specimens from every locality to document the distribution of a species that has been so widely introduced.

Lepomis Rafinesque

This genus, native to eastern North America, contains 11 species, 9 of which occur in Illinois. Some species in the genus have been widely introduced outside their natural ranges as sport fishes.

KEY TO SPECIES

1. Several distinct dark lines radiating out from eye; mouth large, the maxilla extending below middle of eye; fins boldly marbled and mottled; body robust, little compressed .... *gulosus*
   No dark lines radiating out from eye; mouth small (except in *cyanellus*), not extending to below middle of eye; fins plain or mottled; body usually thin and rather compressed (except in *cyanellus*) 2

2. Pectoral fin long and sharply pointed, when bent forward its tip reaching at least to front of eye; rear edge of maxilla not extending to front of eye; body rather thin and compressed 3
   Pectoral fin short and rounded, when bent forward its tip usually not reaching front of eye; rear edge of maxilla usually extending to beyond front of eye; body not conspicuously thin and compressed 5

3. Opercular flap flexible, dark to its posterior margin, without red spot; rear edge of second dorsal fin with distinct black spot; gill rakers long and slender; sides usually with prominent chainlike vertical bands, separated by immaculate interspaces ..... *macrochirus*
   Opercular flap stiff or moderately flexible, its posterior tip with a red spot or red margin (in life); rear edge of second dorsal fin without distinct black spot; gill rakers short and thick; body plain, mottled, or with dim vertical bands, separated by interspaces containing numerous dusky flecks 4

4. Dorsal and anal fins mottled and spotted; opercular flap in adult with a round red or orange spot; opercular flap stiff to its margin; cheeks of adult with wavy blue lines (in life) .... *gibbosus*
   Dorsal and anal fins plain; opercular flap of adult with a red or orange semilunar margin; opercular flap moderately flexible; cheeks of adult without wavy blue lines (in life) .... *microlophus*

5. Greatest body depth equal to or less than head length; mouth large; usually 41 or more scales in lateral line; posterior rays of soft dorsal fin with black spot; adult with thin green lines on face and yellowish white distal margin on anal fin .... *cyanellus*
   Greatest body depth exceeding head length; mouth small or medium; usually fewer than 41 scales in lateral line; posterior rays of soft dorsal fin with or without black spot; adult without green lines on face and yellowish white distal margin on anal fin 6

6. Adult male with a prolonged, flexible opercular flap extending posterior to opercle; opercular flap of both sexes margined with white; head and body of adult male brilliantly colored 7
   Adult male without a prolonged, flexible opercular flap; opercular flap of both sexes without white margin; head and body of adult male usually not brilliantly colored 8

7. Opercular flap broadly margined with white; a distinctly protruding snout; body of male with numerous scattered red or orange spots, that of female with scattered irregular brown spots; adult without alternating lines of blue and orange across face; gill rakers rather thin and long .... *humilis*

   Opercular flap thinly margined with white; snout not protruding; body of male without red or orange spots, that of female without irregular brown spots; adult with alternating lines of blue and orange across face; gill rakers short and thick .... *megalotis*

8. Lateral line usually incomplete; body chubby; head relatively wide, its width greater than distance from tip of snout to rear edge of eye; second dorsal fin with light spots and a dark posterior blotch in all except large adults; scales in lateral line, usually fewer than 35; adult without red markings; juvenile with dark vertical bands and distinct black spot on posterior portion of dorsal fin .... *symmetricus*

   Lateral line complete; body and head compressed, head width less than distance from tip of snout to rear edge of eye; fins without spots; scales in lateral line, usually more than 35; sides of adult with parallel rows of red or orange spots on dusky background and a wash of reddish color above opercular flap; juvenile without blotch on soft dorsal fin but with small dusky flecks over sides of body .... *punctatus*

Green sunfish
Lepomis cyanellus Rafinesque

Lepomis cyanellus Rafinesque 1819:420 (type-locality: Ohio River); Forbes 1884:69; Forbes & Richardson 1908:248–250; Smith 1965:9.

Telipomis cyanellus: Nelson 1876:37 (recorded from Illinois).

Telipomis microps: Nelson 1876:37.

Telipomis nephelus: Nelson 1876:37.

Ichthelis aquiliensis: Nelson 1876:37.

Lepiopomis ischyrus Jordan & Nelson *in* Jordan 1877*b*:25 (part., type-locality: Illinois River); Jordan 1878:45 (part.); Hubbs & Hubbs 1932:436 (= green sunfish X bluegill hybrid).

Apomotis cyanellus: Jordan 1878:45; Large 1903:24; O'Donnell 1935:486.

Lepomis ischyrus: Forbes 1884:68; Forbes & Richardson 1908:250–251.

Apomotis ischyrus: Large 1903:24; O'Donnell 1935:486.

Lepomis euryorus: Forbes & Richardson 1908:252–253; Hubbs 1920:103 (= green sunfish X pumpkinseed hybrid).

Apomotis euryorus: O'Donnell 1935:486.

Diagnosis.— The green sunfish is a rather shallow-bodied and robust sunfish, dark olive on the sides, with indistinct rows of greenish or coppery spots in the adult, a black spot on the posterior rays of the soft dorsal fin, thin blue-green lines on the

Distribution of the green sunfish in Illinois.

for this wide-ranging and widely introduced species. Much of the confusion in its synonymy is due to its frequent hybridization with other sunfishes to produce highly variable F_1 and backcross generations that appear to be different species.

Ecology.—The green sunfish abounds in small ponds and sluggish creeks but is seldom found in rivers and large lakes. It is a pioneering species that soon finds its way into newly created farm ponds and borrow pits. Although not prized as a sport fish, it has a large fishery literature because it is so frequently associated with the popular largemouth bass in ponds. It feeds on a variety of organisms and can ingest surprisingly large prey. The reproductive biology is similar to that of other centrarchids, and a detailed account was reported by Hunter (1963). Spawning occurs in May and continues into the summer over excavated nests in gravel or whatever coarse bottom material is available. Sometimes in the shallow water of coves or pools nests are close together, each one guarded by the male for the approximately 1 week required for the hatching and emergence of the fry. The species is usually sexually mature in 2 years and lives for 4 or 5 years.

Distribution.—The green sunfish is statewide in occurrence and abundant everywhere that suitable habitat exists. It has wide ecological tolerances and may be more abundant and ubiquitous now than in former times.

face, a yellowish-white distal margin on the anal fin, a large mouth (the rear edge of the maxilla extending at least to the front of the eye in the adult), 41 or more lateral-line scales, and a short and rounded pectoral fin. The adult resembles the warmouth but differs in lacking the pattern of dark lines radiating out from the eye and in usually lacking teeth on the tongue. The young is superficially similar to the young longear sunfish but has a much larger mouth and more robust body. It differs from the young warmouth in lacking any definite pattern on the body and head. The species attains a length of more than 200 mm (8 inches), but most individuals are much smaller.

Variation.—No subspecies have been described

Pumpkinseed
Lepomis gibbosus (Linnaeus)

Perca gibbosa Linnaeus 1758:292 (type-locality: Carolina).
?*Pomotis vulgaris:* Kennicott 1855:594 (recorded from Illinois).
Pomotis auritus: Nelson 1876:38.
Eupomotis aureus: Jordan 1878:46.
Lepomis gibbosus: Forbes 1884:67; Smith 1965:9.
Eupomotis gibbosus: Large 1903:25; Forbes & Richardson 1908:260–262; O'Donnell 1935:487.
Lepomis euryorus: Forbes & Richardson 1908:252–253; Hubbs 1920:103 (= green sunfish X pumpkinseed hybrid).
Apomotis euryorus: O'Donnell 1935:486.

Diagnosis.—The pumpkinseed is a deep-bodied and thin sunfish, olive to grassy green on the sides with many irregular spots of bright copper or gold,

Pumpkinseed

a round red or orange spot at the tip of the opercular flap, wavy blue lines across the cheeks, the dorsal and anal fins mottled and spotted, the opercular flap stiff to its margin, the gill rakers short and blunt, the pectoral fin long and sharply pointed (the tip reaching to at least the front of the eye when bent forward), and a rather small mouth (the rear edge of the maxilla not reaching to the front of the eye). The adult most closely resembles the redear sunfish but differs in having a round red spot on the opercular flap, which is stiff to its margin rather than moderately flexible, and in possessing mottled dorsal and anal fins and wavy blue lines across the cheeks. The young has vertical chainlike bands down the sides, as have several other juvenile sunfishes, but differs from other juveniles in having some dark vertical bars in the interspaces between the primary bands. The species attains a length of 250 mm (10 inches) but is usually much smaller.

Variation.—No subspecies have been described for this wide-ranging northern species. It has been widely introduced in this country and Europe, and studies of geographic variation would now be meaningless.

Ecology.—The pumpkinseed is typically a species of well-vegetated natural lakes but also occurs in quiet pools of rivers. A rather large fishery literature exists for the species in Canada and the northern states, where it is commonly associated with the more popular sport fishes. Its food consists mostly of invertebrate animals, and its reproductive biology is similar to that of the green sunfish and other sunfishes. The information avail-

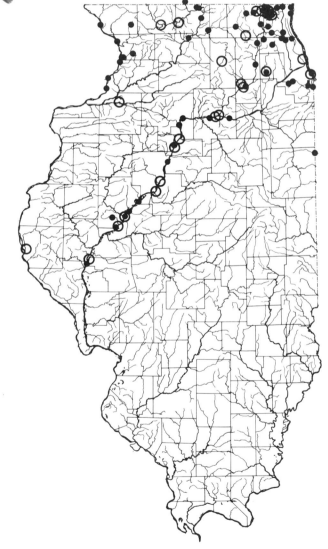

Distribution of the pumpkinseed in Illinois.

able on reproduction in the pumpkinseed has been summarized by Breder & Rosen (1966:415–418) and Scott & Crossman (1973:715–717).

Distribution.—The pumpkinseed is generally distributed across the northern fourth of Illinois and is common in the glacial lakes of the northeastern part of the state. It descends the low-gradient Illinois River at least to Morgan County but is common only in marginal bottomland lakes and backwaters. While difficult to document, the species is probably decimated in northern Illinois because of the elimination of natural lakes and the general deterioration of water quality in the Illinois River and its associated bays and lakes. The two records for southern Illinois plotted in Forbes & Richardson's atlas of maps undoubtedly were based on misidentified specimens of the redear sunfish.

Warmouth
Lepomis gulosus (Cuvier)

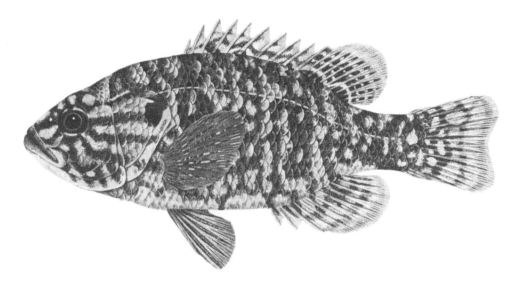

Pomotis gulosus Cuvier *in* Cuvier & Valenciennes 1829:367 (type-locality: Lake Ponchartrain and lagoons about New Orleans).
Chaenobryttus gulosus: Nelson 1876:37 (recorded from Illinois); Jordan 1878:45; Forbes 1884:69; Forbes & Richardson 1908:245–247; O'Donnell 1935:487; Smith 1965:9.
Choenobryttus gulosus: Large 1903:23.

Diagnosis.—The warmouth is a shallow-bodied and robust sunfish, greenish-yellow to olive and heavily mottled with brown, with prominent dark lines radiating out from the eye, a large mouth (the rear edge of the maxilla extending at least to the front of the eye in the adult), a patch of teeth on the tongue, a short and rounded pectoral fin, a small red spot at the base of the soft dorsal in the male, highly vermiculate dorsal and anal fins, and a reddish eye. The species somewhat resembles the rock bass, differing in having only three anal spines, and the green sunfish, differing in having strong dark lines radiating out from the eye. The young lacks the distinctive pattern of dark lines radiating out from the eye but can be distinguished from other baby sunfishes by the heavily stippled face and head and the six or seven broad dark bands that extend from the middorsum to the venter. The species attains a length of more than 310 mm (12 inches), but most adults are less than 155 mm (6 inches).

Variation.—Considerable ontogenetic and individual variation occurs, but there is little, if any, geographic variation. Prior to 1970 the warmouth was placed in the monotypic genus *Chaenobryttus.* During the early 1950's the species was called *C. coronarius,* a name now considered invalid because its author was not consistent in using binomial nomenclature.

Ecology.—The warmouth occurs in swamps, ponds, lakes, and streams of various sizes that are low gradient and have mud or debris over the bottom. In streams it is a pool species and is often abundant around beds of vegetation or roots of trees or stumps. Larimore (1957) published a thorough study of the life history of the species. The warmouth is somewhat more piscivorous than other sunfishes, but in general its feeding and reproductive habits are like those of the green sunfish. It lives 6 or 7 years.

Distribution.—The warmouth is statewide in Illinois but much more generally distributed in the southern third of the state than elsewhere. It is doubtlessly more widely distributed than available records indicate because it tends to frequent waters difficult to sample by conventional collecting techniques, but there is clear evidence that the species

was formerly more general in occurrence. The decimation is probably due to the drainage of natural marshes, lakes, and ponds and the siltation that has destroyed aquatic vegetation in most parts of Illinois.

Orangespotted sunfish
Lepomis humilis (Girard)

Bryttus humilis Girard 1857:201 (type-locality: Sugar Loaf Creek, Arkansas).
Ichthelis anagallinus: Nelson 1876:38 (recorded from Illinois).
Lepiopomus anagallinus: Jordan 1878:45.
Lepomis humilis: Forbes 1884:68; Large 1903:24–25; Forbes & Richardson 1908:255–257; Smith 1965:9.
Allotis humilis: O'Donnell 1935:487.

Diagnosis.—The orangespotted sunfish is a somewhat compressed sunfish, light olive in ground color, with many scattered spots of dark brown in the female and red or orange in the male, a red eye and breast (in the male), a broad white margin around the flexible black opercular flap, usually fewer than 40 lateral-line scales, a somewhat protruding snout, a rather large mouth (the rear edge of the maxilla extending behind the front of the eye), a short and rounded pectoral fin, and elongated sensory pores along the free edge of the preopercle. This distinctive and beautiful species differs from other Illinois sunfishes in details of pattern and in having the broad white margin around the opercular flap. The young closely resembles the young bluegill but has fewer and larger dark vertical bands on the sides. The species attains a length of about 100 mm (4 inches).

Variation.—There is considerable sexual and ontogenetic variation but evidently little geographic variation. No subspecies have been proposed.

Ecology.—The orangespotted sunfish has wide ecological tolerances, occurring in almost all types of waters except swiftly flowing streams. In streams it occupies pools with silt or debris on the bottom. It occurs in small ponds, large lakes, creeks, and large rivers. Its feeding and reproductive habits are similar to those of other sunfishes, but it probably does not live as long as others. Barney & Anson (1923) described its life history.

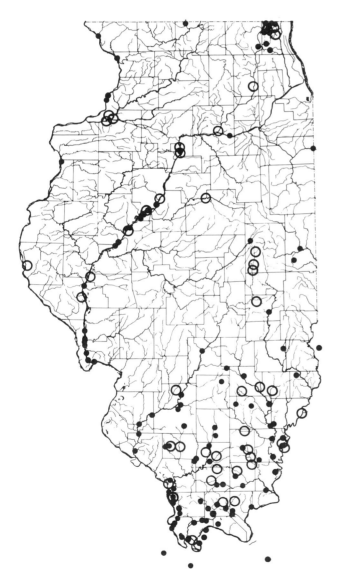

Distribution of the warmouth in Illinois.

Orangespotted sunfish

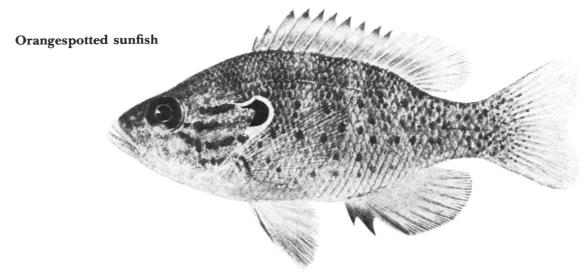

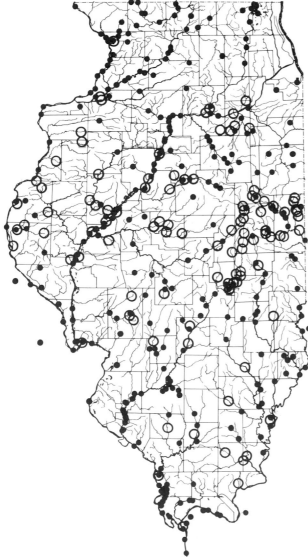

Distribution of the orangespotted sunfish in Illinois.

Distribution.—The orangespotted sunfish is statewide and common in suitable habitats. It has been expanding its range within historic times and, although it is now more generally distributed in Illinois than formerly, it is less common in central Illinois than it once was. It must have abounded in the sloughs and meandering streams before the wet prairie was drained.

Bluegill
Lepomis macrochirus Rafinesque

Lepomis macrochira Rafinesque 1819:420 (type-locality: Ohio River, Licking River).

Ichthelis speciosus: Nelson 1876:37 (recorded from Illinois).

Ichthelis incisor: Nelson 1876:37.

Lepiopomus ischyrus Jordan & Nelson *in* Jordan 1877b:25 (type-locality: Illinois River); Jordan 1878:45; Hubbs & Hubbs 1932:436 (= green sunfish X bluegill hybrid).

Lepiopomus macrochirus: Jordan 1878:45.

Lepomis macrochirus: Forbes 1884:68.

Lepomis pallidus: Forbes 1884:67; Large 1903:25; Forbes & Richardson 1908:257–259.

Lepomis ischyrus: Forbes 1884:68; Forbes & Richardson 1908:250–251.

Apomotis ischyrus: Large 1903:24; O'Donnell 1935: 486.

Helioperca incisor: O'Donnell 1935:487.

Lepomis macrochirus macrochirus: Smith 1965:9.

Bluegill

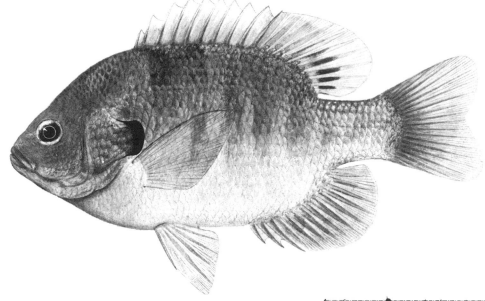

Diagnosis.—The bluegill is a thin and much compressed sunfish, bluish or yellow-green, with six to eight olive, chainlike, vertical bands down the sides (the sides are unicolorous in large adults and fish from turbid water); a black blotch in the posterior rays of the soft dorsal fin (in the adult); an orange belly and bluish cheeks (in the adult male); a long and pointed pectoral fin; a flexible and uniformly dark opercular flap; a small mouth (the rear of the maxilla not reaching the front of the eye); and long, thin gill rakers. The adult most closely resembles the redear sunfish but differs in lacking red or orange on the opercular flap and in having a black spot on the soft dorsal fin and long and thin gill rakers. The young resembles the young orangespotted sunfish but has more numerous, more regular, and narrower vertical bands. The baby bantam sunfish differs from the baby bluegill in having an intense black spot on the soft dorsal fin (not yet developed in baby bluegill) and in having a blackish head and a more chubby body. The baby pumpkinseed has scattered dark spots and flecks in the interspaces between the vertical bands. The baby warmouth has a blackish head and face. Other Illinois sunfishes lack vertical bands as juveniles. The species attains a length of about 310 mm (12 inches) but is usually much smaller.

Variation.—For many years, three subspecies have been recognized: *L. m. speciosus* in the Southwest, *L. m. purpurescens* in the Southeast, and *L. m. macrochirus* from Lake Superior to the Gulf Coast. Bailey, Winn, & Smith (1954:139) acknowledged that subspecies may be recognizable but recom-

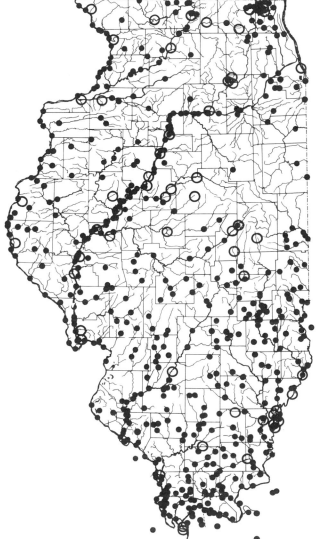

Distribution of the bluegill in Illinois.

mended that names be withheld until a thorough study of geographic variation in the species had been made. In recent years much genetic mixing of local stocks has occurred with the wholesale stocking of bluegills in reservoirs.

Ecology.—The bluegill reaches its greatest abundance in clear well-vegetated lakes but also occurs in swamps, ponds, and in pools of streams of various sizes, especially large rivers. Its feeding and reproductive behavior are similar to those of other centrarchids. An enormous fishery literature exists, which is well summarized by Emig (*in* Calhoun 1966:375–392). It lives at least 5 years.

Distribution.—The bluegill is statewide and common, and there is no evidence that it was ever any more so than at present.

Longear sunfish
Lepomis megalotis (Rafinesque)

Ichthelis megalotis Rafinesque 1820a:29 (type-locality: Licking and Sandy rivers, Kentucky); Nelson 1876:38 (recorded from Illinois).
Ichthelis sanguinolentis: Nelson 1876:38.
Ichthelis macrochira: Nelson 1876:38.
Ichthelis inscriptus: Nelson 1876:38.
Xenotis lythrochloris: Jordan 1878:46.
Xenotis aureolus: Jordan 1878:46.
Xenotis inscriptus: Jordan 1878:46.
Xenotis peltastes: Jordan 1878:46 (recorded from Illinois).
Xenotis megalotis: Jordan 1878:46; O'Donnell 1935:487.
Lepomis megalotis: Forbes 1884:68; Large 1903:24; Forbes & Richardson 1908:254–255.
Xenotis megalotis peltastes: O'Donnell 1935:487.
Lepomis megalotis (Rafinesque) subspecies: Smith 1965:9.

Diagnosis.—The longear sunfish is a thin and deep-bodied sunfish, olive on the sides, with numerous spots of blue and orange, an orange breast, alternating stripes of bright blue and orange across the face (in the adult male), obscure vertical bands and subdued colors (in the female), a long and very flexible (in the male) opercular flap, the opercular flap black in both sexes except for a narrow whitish margin, a short and rounded pectoral fin, a rather large mouth (the rear edge of the maxilla extending beyond the front of the eye), and short and stumpy gill rakers. The adult male is highly distinctive, but the adult female superficially resembles the female redear sunfish, pumpkinseed, and bluegill, differing from all in having a short and rounded pectoral fin. The young is a unicolorous olive, lighter in color than the young green sunfish and with a more compressed and deeper body and a much smaller mouth. The species attains a length of more than 150 mm (6 inches).

Variation.—A northern subspecies (*L. m. peltastes*) is generally recognized and occurs in northeastern Illinois. It is an equally colorful but dwarfed race (usually less than 100 mm) with red or orange at the tip of the opercular flap, which is oblique rather than horizontal in the adult male. Although *L. m. peltastes* is regarded as a subspecies, there is no evidence of intergradation in Illinois. In the southern portion of the species' range considerable geographic variation exists. Several locally differentiated populations are known, some of which have subspecific names available for them.

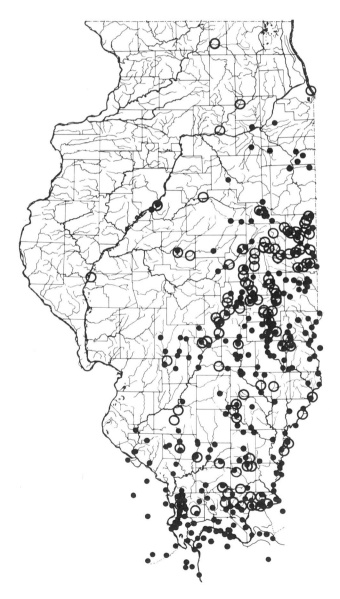

Distribution of the longear sunfish in Illinois.

Since their ranges and even the validity of some of them are as yet unknown, Bailey, Winn, & Smith (1954:138) preferred to withhold subspecific names until a thorough study of variation is undertaken. The population in the southern three-fourths of Illinois is the nominal *L. m. megalotis*.

Ecology.—The longear sunfish is characteristic of sand and gravel-bottomed pools of creeks and small rivers. It avoids strong current and turbid water over a silt bottom and is less tolerant of silt and pollution than other Illinois sunfishes. The communally spawning males are brilliant while guarding nests in clean gravel or sand. References to reproductive habits of the species are numerous but scattered. Breder & Rosen (1966:414–415) summarized many of them. It lives to be 6 years old.

Distribution.—The northern longear sunfish is known only from Kankakee, Will, Iroquois, and Grundy counties, where it is erratic and rare. The central longear sunfish is widely distributed and abundant in eastern and southern Illinois but strangely absent from the western part of the state. Although still common in central Illinois, it was evidently once far more widely distributed. It is probable that siltation and the general deterioration of water quality are responsible for its decimation.

Redear sunfish
Lepomis microlophus (Günther)

Pomotis microlophus Günther 1859:264 (substitute name for preoccupied *P. speciosus;* type-locality: St. Johns River, Florida).
Eupomotis notatus: Forbes 1884:67 (recorded from Illinois).
Eupomotis heros: Large 1903:25; Forbes & Richardson 1908:259–260; O'Donnell 1935:487.
Lepomis microlophus: Smith 1965:9.

Diagnosis.—The redear sunfish is a rather thin and deep-bodied sunfish, greenish-olive on the sides with or without dark vertical bands, with a yellowish belly, dark olive lines across the face, a light-bordered and semiflexible black opercular flap with a red or orange posterior margin, unspotted greenish yellow median fins, a long and sharply pointed pectoral fin, a rather small mouth (the rear of the maxilla barely extending to the front of the eye), and short and knobby gill rakers. The adult most closely resembles the pumpkinseed

Redear sunfish

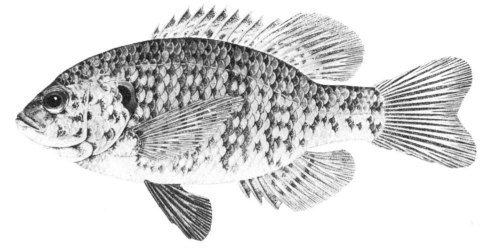

because of the reddish tip on the opercular flap but differs in that the spot is semilunar instead of round, the soft dorsal fin is plain rather than mottled, the opercular flap is somewhat flexible, and the face lacks bright colors. It differs from the longear sunfish in having a very long and pointed pectoral fin. The young is distinguished by the combination of a long, pointed pectoral fin and the weakly developed vertical bands down the sides. The species attains a length of about 250 mm (10 inches) but is usually much smaller.

Variation.—Hubbs & Lagler (1941:79) suggested that subspecies would eventually be recognized, but the redear has been so widely transplanted in artificial lakes and ponds in recent years that any geographic variation would now be obscured.

Ecology.—The redear sunfish originally occurred in swamps, bottomland lakes, and low-gradient streams but is most abundant in clear artificial lakes, where it has been introduced, usually along with the largemouth bass. Stocking by the Department of Conservation has been widespread, and the species frequently escapes into creeks and rivers, where it prefers pools with aquatic vegetation. Its fondness for molluscs has given it the common name of shellcracker in the southern states. Like other sunfishes, it is a communal breeder with reproductive habits similar to those of other species. It is less tolerant of low temperatures and more tolerant of silt than many other species. Emig (*in* Calhoun 1966:392–399) has summarized the pertinent literature on the species. It lives for 5 years.

Distribution.—The redear sunfish is native to the southern third of Illinois but now occurs, through stocking, in all parts of the state.

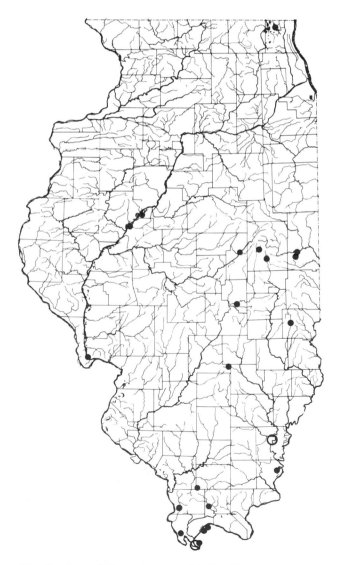

Distribution of the redear sunfish in Illinois.

Spotted sunfish
Lepomis punctatus (Valenciennes)

Bryttus punctatus Valenciennes *in* Cuvier & Valenciennes 1831:347 (type-locality: Charleston, South Carolina).

Lepomis garmani Forbes 1884:68 (*nomen nudum*); Forbes 1885:135 (type-locality: Little Fox River at Phillipstown, Wabash River, and Drew Pond at Carmi [Illinois]); Large 1903:24.

Lepomis miniatus: Forbes & Richardson 1908:253.

Sclerotis miniatus: O'Donnell 1935:486–487.

Lepomis punctatus miniatus: Smith 1965:9.

Diagnosis.—The spotted sunfish is a moderately thin and deep-bodied sunfish, dark olive, with longitudinal rows of paler spots (red-orange in the adult male), a blackish face and head, a small wash of pale red just above the opercular flap, three dark lines extending posteriorly behind the eye (in the female and juvenile), uniformly dusky median fins, rather evenly spaced dark spots on the side of the juvenile, a short and rounded pectoral fin, moderately short and stout gill rakers, a complete lateral line, and usually more than 35 lateral-line scales. The adult male is easily distinguished in life by its longitudinal rows of red-orange spots (scale centers) and wash of red above the opercular flap. The adult female resembles the bantam sunfish but differs in having the patch of pale red pigment above the opercular flap, three dark lines behind the eye, and a complete lateral line, and in being much less chubby. The young somewhat resembles the young longear sunfish but is much darker in color (dark olive instead of greenish) and has strongly mottled and spotted sides. The species attains a length of about 130 mm (5 inches).

Variation.—The species contains two well-marked subspecies: *L. p. punctatus* of the Atlantic Coast and peninsular Florida and *L. p. miniatus* of the Mississippi River valley (Bailey, Winn, & Smith 1954:137).

Ecology.—The spotted sunfish occupies well-vegetated swamps, sloughs, and bottomland lakes. Reproductive behavior in the eastern subspecies was studied by Carr (1946:101–106). Presumably her remarks apply also to the Illinois subspecies, inasmuch as she found the pattern similar to that of other centrarchids. Both sexes develop bright red above the opercular flap. It is not known where the spotted sunfish and other species occurring over a soft bottom find areas of gravel to construct nests, and they may use debris on the bottom or submerged logs and stumps if gravel or sand cannot be found. Presumably they live 4 or 5 years.

Distribution. — The spotted sunfish presently occurs in only a few bottomland lakes and swamps along the middle Illinois River valley and in the southern tip of the state. Formerly it occurred in several bottomland lakes in the lower Wabash River valley, where it has evidently become rare. Although never abundant in Illinois, it was once more widespread than at present, and its decimation is probably the result of the drainage of swamps and bottomland lakes and the general deterioration of water quality. In the lower Wabash Valley, oil pollution is likely an important factor.

Distribution of the spotted sunfish in Illinois.

Bantam sunfish
Lepomis symmetricus Forbes

Lepomis symmetricus Forbes *in* Jordan & Gilbert 1883:473 (type-locality: Illinois River, Illinois [at Pekin]); Forbes 1884:68; Forbes & Richardson 1908:251–252; Smith 1965:9.
Apomotis symmetricus: Large 1903:24.
Lethogrammus symmetricus: O'Donnell 1935:486.

Diagnosis. — The bantam sunfish is a very chubby and symmetrical sunfish, dusky olive, with many rows of paler spots (scale centers) in the adult, a blackened head and face, an unpatterned head and cheeks, several light spots in the soft dorsal fin, a prominent dusky blotch in the posterior rays of the soft dorsal fin and irregular vertical bands in the juvenile and subadult, a short and rounded pectoral fin, rather long and slender gill rakers, an incomplete lateral line, and usually fewer than 35 lateral-line scales, and without any bright colors. The adult most closely resembles the spotted sunfish, sharing with it rows of paler spots on a dusky ground color but differing in lacking a patch of pale pigment above the opercular flap, three dark lines behind the eye, and a complete lateral line, and in being much more robust and less compressed. The adult female somewhat resembles the warmouth but lacks dark lines radiating out from the eye and has a much smaller mouth. The young superficially resembles the young bluegill but is much chubbier; has less regular vertical bands, a blackened head and face, and an intense spot in the posterior rays of the soft dorsal fin (not yet developed in juvenile bluegill); and lacks the long and pointed pectoral fin. It attains a length of about 90 mm (3½ inches).

Variation. — The species is rather conservative throughout its range. Burr (1977) found only minor clinal variation in comparing central Illinois and Gulf Coast specimens. The only aberrant population was that which formerly occurred in the Wabash River valley of southeastern Illinois. It averaged more lateral-line and caudal peduncle scales and fewer dorsal soft rays, but that population is now extirpated.

Ecology. — The bantam sunfish occurs in swamps and bottomland lakes in association with dense beds of vegetation in the shallow water. Burr (1977) made a detailed study of the life history of the species and found that its food is varied but consists mostly of snails, crustaceans, and insects. He reported spawning typical of all other sunfishes

Bantam sunfish

Distribution of the bantam sunfish in Illinois.

in late May. The female produces from 200 to 1,600 eggs. Sexual maturity is attained at 1 year of age, and the species lives just over 3 years.

Distribution.—The species is known to occur at present only in two localities in northwestern Union County but was originally described from Pekin in the middle Illinois River valley and formerly occurred also in bottomland lakes in the lower Wabash River valley. The species is threatened because so few populations remain in the upper Mississippi valley, and little unaltered habitat for it is now extant.

Ambloplites Rafinesque

This eastern North American genus contains two species, one of which is wide ranging and common in many parts of Illinois.

Rock bass
Ambloplites rupestris (Rafinesque)

Bodianus rupestris Rafinesque 1817a:120 (type-locality: lakes of New York, Vermont, and Canada).
?*Centrarchus aeneus:* Kennicott 1855:594 (recorded from Illinois).
Ambloplites rupestris: Nelson 1876:37; Jordan 1878: 44; Forbes 1884:69; Large 1903:23; Forbes & Richardson 1908:243–244; O'Donnell 1935: 487.
Ambloplites rupestris rupestris: Smith 1965:9.

Rock bass

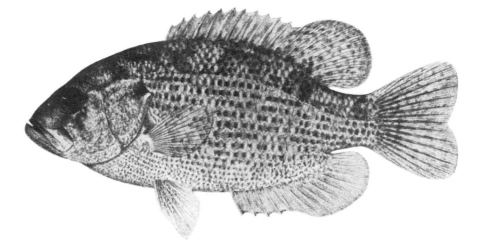

Diagnosis.—The rock bass is a robust sunfish, greenish or yellowish, with bronzy reflections and obscure brown saddles on the back and brown spots aligned in longitudinal rows along the sides, large red eyes, a large mouth (the end of the upper jaw extending backward to beneath the middle of the eye), dorsal spines 11–13 and not distinctly stepped in height, the dorsal fin origin well in advance of the anal fin origin, anal spines 5–7, the length of anal fin base a little more than half the length of the dorsal fin base, and a dark teardrop extending obliquely backward. The adult is somewhat similar to the warmouth but differs from that species and all *Lepomis* species in having more dorsal and anal spines. It has markings somewhat like those of the flier but is distinguishable by its robust body, large mouth, and shorter anal fin base. The young rock bass is attractive with large, vertically aligned chocolate blotches on the pale gray ground color of the sides. It superficially resembles a freshwater angel fish but not any native Illinois species. The species attains a length of more than 300 mm (12 inches), but most individuals are less than 150 mm (6 inches).

Variation.—Most authors recognize a wide-ranging northern subspecies (*A. r. rupestris*), that occurring in Illinois, and a southern subspecies (*A. r. ariommus*) in the lower Mississippi River valley. A study of geographic variation in the species is currently underway by Robert C. Cashner of Tulane University.

Ecology.—The rock bass occurs in clear gravelly rivers, often in pools with abundant vegetation or in eddies behind large boulders. It is intolerant of silt and turbid water and is most abundant in cold, well-oxygenated water. Its food is varied, insects,

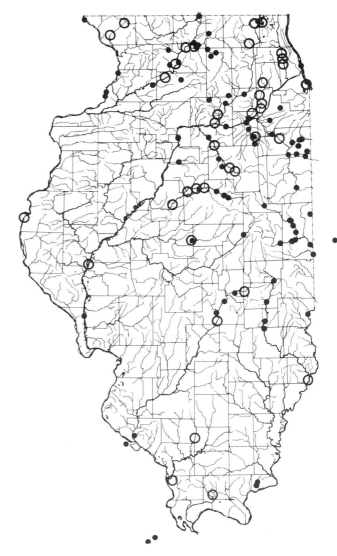

Distribution of the rock bass in Illinois.

crustaceans, and small fishes making up the bulk of the diet of the adult. Breder & Rosen (1966:421–422) described the details of spawning in aquarium-held fish. In nature the species is a solitary spawner, the male usually constructing its nest near a boulder. The reproductive behavior is quite similar to that of sunfishes, but spawning may begin a bit earlier. The species lives 5 or more years and occasionally produces very large, old individuals.

Distribution.—The rock bass is generally distributed in clear, gravel-bottomed and rocky streams in northern and central Illinois but is extremely sporadic in the western and southern parts of the state. It occurs along the pebbly beach of Lake Michigan and in some of the harbors. Although still common in many streams, it is less widely distributed than formerly because of siltation and the general deterioration of water quality.

Pomoxis Rafinesque

This eastern North American genus contains two species, both widespread in Illinois.

KEY TO SPECIES

1. Dorsal fin with six spines; length of dorsal fin base, when projected forward from dorsal fin origin, reaching a point on nape well behind eyes; pattern of broad, dark vertical bars on sides; fins partially vermiculate ... *annularis*
   Dorsal fin with seven or eight spines; length of dorsal fin base, projected from dorsal fin origin, reaching a point just behind eyes; pattern of dark blotches and irregular white spots on sides; fins strongly vermiculate ...
   .... *nigromaculatus*

White crappie
Pomoxis annularis Rafinesque

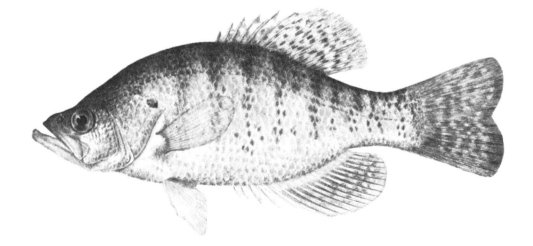

Pomoxis annularis Rafinesque 1818*a*:41 (type-locality: falls of Ohio River); Large 1903:23; Forbes & Richardson 1908:238–240; O'Donnell 1935: 487; Smith 1965:10.
Pomoxys annularis: Nelson 1876:37 (recorded from Illinois); Jordan 1878:47.
Pomoxys annuluris: Forbes 1884:69 (misspelling).

Diagnosis.—The white crappie is a thin and much compressed sunfish, white or silvery on the sides, with greenish reflections and six or seven dusky vertical bands; somewhat reticulate median fins; usually six dorsal spines; dorsal fin spines stepped in length; no notch between first and second dorsal fins; the dorsal fin origin in advance of the anal fin origin; five to seven anal spines; and the dorsal-fin base length, when projected forward from its origin, reaching only to the nape well behind the eyes. The only other Illinois species with which it can be confused is the black crappie, which is deeper bodied, is blotched on the sides, has more dorsal spines, and has a longer dorsal fin base. The young of the two are best separated by relative body depth and the length of the dorsal fin base. The species attains a length of more than 380 mm (15 inches).

Variation.—No trends in geographic variation have been noted in this species, and no subspecies have been recognized.

Ecology.—The white crappie has wide ecological tolerances, occurring in virtually all types of water except very small streams and ponds. It is most abundant in well-vegetated lakes and large rivers. Being larger than most sunfishes, it is more piscivorous as an adult but still relies heavily on insects and crustaceans. The biology of the species was thoroughly studied by Hansen (1951 and 1965). The white crappie is an important reservoir species and has a considerable fishery literature. Spawning occurs in April, May, and June in sites similar to those selected by the largemouth bass. The crudely constructed nest, fanned out of the bottom material, may not be evident except by the presence of the guarding male. The breeding male develops strong black blotching reminiscent of that of the related black crappie. The species is extremely prolific, a female depositing from 10,000 to 180,000 eggs that hatch in about 3 days, depending upon water temperature. Despite its comparatively large size, it appears to live no more than 7 years.

Distribution.—The white crappie is statewide and common in large rivers. It is more widespread than indicated on the distribution map, since it occurs also in virtually all reservoirs, most of which were not collected in because of their artificial nature. Its tolerance of turbid water and silt enables it to build up large populations in artificial lakes. Nevertheless, there is evidence that the species was even more generally distributed in Illinois in the past. It probably occupied the prairie marshes as well as the many connecting streams.

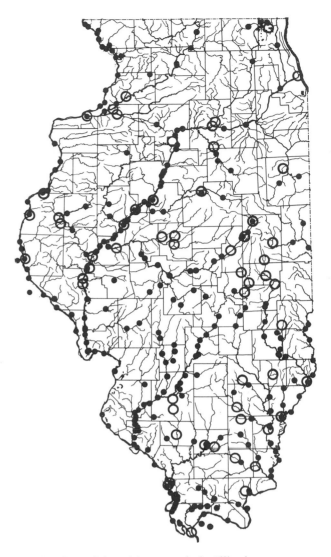

Distribution of the white crappie in Illinois.

Black crappie
Pomoxis nigromaculatus (Lesueur)

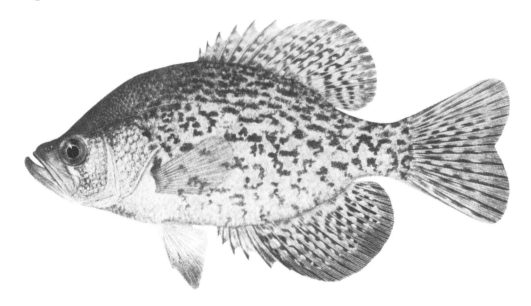

Cantharus nigro-maculatus Lesueur *in* Cuvier & Valenciennes 1829:65 (type-locality: Wabash River).

Pomoxys hexacanthus: Nelson 1876:37 (recorded from Illinois).

Pomoxys nigromaculatus: Jordan 1878:47.

Pomoxys sparoides: Forbes 1884:69.

Pomoxis sparoides: Large 1903:23; Forbes & Richardson 1908:240–241; O'Donnell 1935:487–488.

Pomoxis nigromaculatus: Smith 1965:10.

Diagnosis. — The black crappie is a much compressed sunfish, white or silvery on the sides, with greenish reflections and numerous irregular black vermiform blotches scattered over the sides as well as smaller patches of black pigment; highly reticulate median fins; usually seven or eight dorsal spines; dorsal fin spines stepped in length; no notch between the first and second dorsal fins; the dorsal fin in advance of the anal fin origin; five to seven anal spines; and the dorsal-fin base length, when projected from its origin, reaching to a point between the eyes. The black crappie is closest to the white crappie but differs in being deeper bodied and having black blotches instead of vertical bands, more dorsal spines, and a longer dorsal-fin base length. The young black crappie differs from the young white crappie in the same characters although it tends to have weakly developed vertical bands, as has the young white crappie. The species attains a length of 380 mm (15 inches) but is usually much smaller.

Variation. — No subspecies are recognized in the species, and the most obvious geographic variation is a trend toward heavier black pigmentation in northern populations. Dr. W. C. Childers (personal communication) believes that many Illinois populations of both black and white crappies are really hybrids through generations of gene introgression. Whether this is the situation, it is true that the species tend to look alike in the turbid waters of Illinois, where pattern features are subdued. The projection of dorsal-fin base length onto the predorsal length generally separates specimens of all ages without difficulty.

Ecology. — Like the white crappie, this species occupies almost all types of water except very small streams and ponds and streams with strong current. It is much less tolerant of turbidity and silt than the white crappie. The species is most abundant in well-vegetated lakes and clear backwaters of rivers. Aside from its preference for clear water and aquatic vegetation, it has an ecology similar to that of the white crappie and a rather large fishery literature. There are no breeding colors, and it may live a little longer than the white crappie.

Distribution.—The black crappie is statewide and moderately common but much less so than the white crappie. It is common in reservoirs that have suitable habitat as well as in natural lakes and backwaters. Despite its currently wide distribution, it is somewhat decimated because of the silt problem in so many Illinois lakes and rivers.

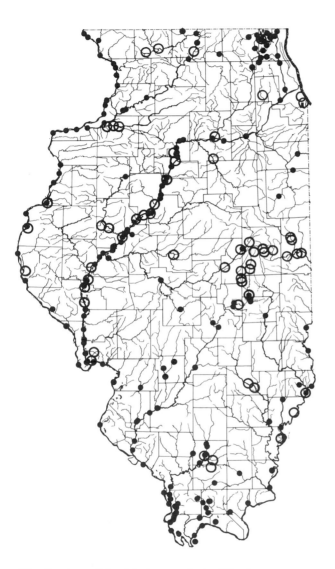

Distribution of the black crappie in Illinois.

Centrarchus
Cuvier & Valenciennes

This genus contains only one species, which is restricted to swamps and lowland lakes in the southeastern United States.

Flier
Centrarchus macropterus (Lacépède)

Labrus macropterus Lacépède 1802:447 (type-locality cited in error: presumably Charleston, South Carolina).
Centrarchus irideus: Nelson 1876:37 (recorded from Illinois); Jordan 1878:47.
Centrarchus macropterus: Forbes 1884:70; Large 1903:23; Forbes & Richardson 1908:241–242; O'Donnell 1935:488; Smith 1965:9.

Diagnosis.—The flier is a deeply compressed sunfish, greenish or yellowish on the sides, with many bronzy reflections and longitudinal rows of brown spots (in the adult), a vertically aligned teardrop, reticulated median fins, a small mouth (the posterior end of the jaw is below the front of the eye), the anal fin base more than two-thirds the length of the dorsal fin base, 11 or 12 dorsal spines, six to eight anal spines, and the dorsal fin origin well in advance of the anal fin origin. The species most closely resembles the rock bass but is easily distinguished by its more compressed body and small mouth. It is related to the crappies but differs markedly in pattern and in having more dorsal spines. The young is yellowish gray with four broad, brown, vertical bands and a prominent black and red ocellus in the posterior rays of the soft dorsal fin. The species attains a length of about 150 mm (6 inches).

Variation.—No subspecies are recognized in this distinctive species.

Ecology.—The flier occurs in swamps, lakes, sloughs, and low-gradient streams and is most abundant in well-vegetated waters. Gunning & Lewis (1955:557) reported that its major food consists of insects, crustaceans, and filamentous algae. Reproductive habits of the flier are presumably similar to those of other sunfishes, but no life-history information has been published. Conley & Witt (1966:433–434) described squamation development in the young. Burr (1974) reported a flier X white crappie hybrid from Clinton County, Illi-

Flier

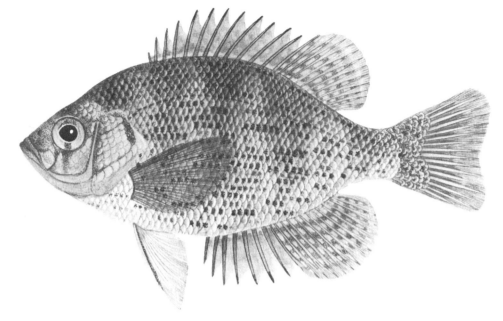

Distribution of the flier in Illinois.

nois. The flier probably lives about 5 years like most sunfishes.

Distribution.—The flier is generally distributed and common in suitable habitats in the southern third of Illinois. Too few old records are extant to draw inferences regarding decimation or range expansion of the species in the state.

Elassoma Jordan

This genus of diminutive fishes occurs only in southeastern United States and contains three described, and possibly one or two as yet undescribed, species. One species enters southern Illinois. Formerly the genus was placed in a separate family (Elassomidae), but it is now regarded by some specialists as a member of the Centrarchidae.

Banded pygmy sunfish
Elassoma zonatum Jordan

Elassoma zonata Jordan 1877*b*:50 (type-locality: Little Red River, Judsonia, White County, Arkansas).

Elassoma zonatum: Jordan 1878:47–48 (recorded from Illinois); Forbes 1884:70; Large 1903:23; Forbes & Richardson 1908:232; O'Donnell 1935: 488; Smith 1965:9.

Banded pygmy sunfish

Diagnosis.—The banded pygmy sunfish is a tiny slab-sided but robust sunfish, grayish (or greenish in the breeding male), with many pepperlike dark spots over the entire head and body, punctulate fins, 10–11 vertical bands (brown in the female, black in the breeding male) on the sides, a conspicuous dusky blotch on the side below the spinous dorsal fin, a dusky bar across the caudal peduncle, a rounded caudal fin, no notch between the first and second dorsal fins, four or five dorsal spines, no lateral line, and with cycloid scales covering the head and body. The species superficially resembles the young of the mudminnow and of the pirate perch but differs from both in many important details of structure and pattern. It differs from other Illinois sunfishes by the characters listed above, most obviously its rounded caudal fin and lack of a lateral line. The young resembles the adult female and is recognizable only with magnification. The species attains a length of about 40 mm (1½ inches).

Variation.—No subspecies are presently recognized, but there is reason to believe that this fish may be found to be a composite of two or more species when a detailed study of geographic variation is undertaken.

Ecology.—The banded pygmy sunfish is associated with dense beds of aquatic vegetation in swamps and sloughs. Gunning & Lewis (1955:556) found water fleas, rotifers, amphipods, and small Diptera in the stomachs of specimens from Union County. The life history of the species was thoroughly studied by Barney & Anson (1920) in southern Mississippi. In the pygmy sunfish, the

Distribution of the banded pygmy sunfish in Illinois.

nest-building habit is poorly developed. A few hundred eggs are merely dropped during spawning, and they adhere to vegetation or debris and hatch in about a week. The species probably never lives more than 3 years. The species was once popular as an aquarium fish.

Distribution.—The banded pygmy sunfish occurs only in extreme southern Illinois and is common at only a few sites. Formerly it also occurred in the lower Wabash River valley, where it has been extirpated probably as a result of extensive oil pollution and the drainage of natural swamps.

Darters and perches—Percidae

This large Holarctic family of mostly small fishes contains five North American genera, all of which are represented in Illinois. The majority of the species are too small to be well known to anglers and commercial fishermen, but the large ones (walleye, sauger, and yellow perch) are highly prized as sport and food fishes. Many people rank the walleye first as a desirable eating species. The vast array of small species (darters) are second only to the minnows in numbers of species and in abundance. While darters of one kind or another occupy almost every type of aquatic habitat, most of them live on the gravelly bottoms of riffles and raceways and must contribute heavily to the food of larger fish species. Most of the species are delicate indicators of water quality and other environmental modification of the watershed. Breeding males of several species are incredibly colorful.

KEY TO GENERA

1. Caudal fin deeply forked; preopercle strongly serrate behind and below; mouth large, the maxilla extending backward at least to middle of eye; genital papilla absent or much reduced 2
   Caudal fin usually not forked; preopercle smooth or weakly serrate behind and below; mouth small, the maxilla not extending backward to middle of eye; genital papilla prominent in the female 3
2. Canine teeth present; pelvic fins widely separated; body terete; anal rays, 11 or more; body pattern variable . . . . *Stizostedion*
   Canine teeth lacking; pelvic fins slightly separated; body deep and slab-sided; anal rays, eight or fewer; pattern of six to eight black vertical bars . . . . *Perca*
3. Body usually incompletely scaled, translucent in life, white in preservative; snout long and pointed; body elongate and cylindrical; dorsal fins well separated . . . . *Ammocrypta*
   Body fully or mostly scaled, opaque; snout variable; body shape variable; dorsal fins usually closely approximated 4
4. An enlarged and strongly toothed scale between pelvic fin bases; belly of male usually with a midventral row of enlarged scales; anal fin usually almost as large as second dorsal fin . . . . *Percina*
   No large specialized scale between pelvic fin bases; belly of male without a midventral row of enlarged scales; anal fin usually much smaller than second dorsal fin . . . . *Etheostoma*

Stizostedion Rafinesque

This Holarctic genus contains two North American species, both of which occur in Illinois. For percids they are rather large, and they are much prized as sport fishes because of their flavor.

KEY TO SPECIES

1. First dorsal fin with round, discrete black spots forming oblique rows; first dorsal fin without large black basal spot posteriorly; cheeks usually partly scaled; rays of second dorsal fin, 17–21; back with three or four dusky saddles; pyloric caeca five to eight . . . . *canadense*
   First dorsal fin with obscure mottling but without rows of discrete black spots; prominent black basal spot in posterior rays of first dorsal fin; cheeks with few or no scales; rays of second dorsal fin, 19–23; back and sides with 4–14 dark saddles, or unicolorous; pyloric caeca, three . . . . *vitreum*

Sauger
Stizostedion canadense (Smith)

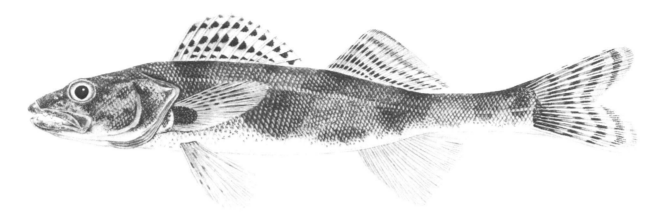

Lucioperca candensis Smith *in* Griffith's edition of
    Cuvier 1834:275 (type-locality: Canada).
Stizostedium griseum: Nelson 1876:36 (recorded
    from Illinois).
Stizostethium canadense: Jordan 1878:43.
Stizostedium canadense: Forbes 1884:63.
Stizostedion canadense: Large 1903:26; Smith 1965:
    10.
Stizostedion canadense griseum: Forbes & Richardson
    1908:274–275.
Cynoperca canadense grisea: O'Donnell 1935:490.

Diagnosis. — The sauger is an elongate and cylindrical perch, slaty or yellowish olive, with three or
four widely spaced dusky saddles that extend on
each side to form large oblique blotches, occasionally three or four additional brown spots on the
sides, several oblique rows of discrete black spots in
the first dorsal fin, a black spot at the pectoral fin
base, the tip of the anal fin white, a large mouth
(the rear of the maxilla extending to below the
back of the eye), enlarged canine teeth, partly
scaled cheeks, the preopercle strongly serrate below and behind, the caudal fin forked, the pelvic
fins widely separated, 12 or 13 anal rays, 17–21
rays in the second dorsal fin, five to eight pyloric
caeca, and the genital papilla absent or much reduced. The species most closely resembles the walleye but is easily distinguished by the many rows of
black spots in the first dorsal fin except in very
small young. The young has three or four widely
spaced dorsal saddles that extend obliquely onto
the sides, whereas the young walleye has 5–12
closely spaced saddles that extend vertically onto
the sides. Young that are bleached are difficult to
distinguish. The species attains a length of more

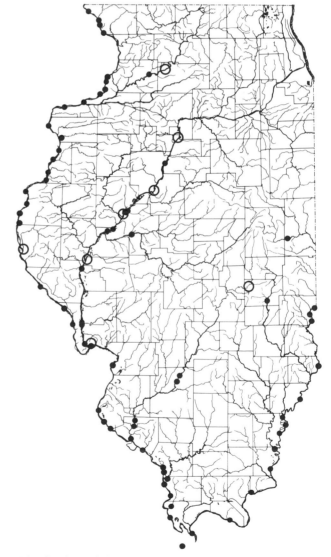

Distribution of the sauger in Illinois.

than 460 mm (18 inches), but most adults are less than 310 mm (12 inches).

Variation.—In the past three subspecies have been recognized, but nearly all current authors feel that subspecies are not justified in this wide-ranging but remarkably uniform species.

Ecology.—In other parts of its range, the sauger is a common lake species, but in Illinois it is virtually restricted to large rivers, occupying backwaters and the mouths of sluggish tributaries. It is tolerant of turbid water and a silty bottom and is often abundant in brushy high-water pools adjoining major rivers. As in other percids, the food depends upon the size of the fish, the young taking microcrustaceans and large individuals eating fishes. A substantial fishery literature exists and has recently been summarized in Scott & Crossman (1973:763–

766). The spawning season, in April in northern Illinois, is rather short and spawning occurs over gravel or rubble. The female is joined by one or more smaller males, which were already present on the spawning shoals. The 15,000–40,000 eggs are merely broadcast and adhere to rocks on the bottom. Hatching may require as much as 3 weeks when the water is cold. The species may live 7 years and is probably sexually mature in its 2nd year. The species is extremely prolific but not abundant.

Distribution.—The sauger is rather general in the Mississippi River and moderately common below the mouth of the Missouri. In other large rivers of the state, it is sporadic but probably more common than indicated by records on the distribution map. There are no recent records for northeastern Illinois.

Walleye
Stizostedion vitreum (Mitchill)

Perca vitrea Mitchill 1818:247 (type-locality: Cayuga Lake, New York).

Stizostedium salmoneum: Nelson 1876:36 (recorded from Illinois).

Stizostedium americanum: Nelson 1876:36.

Stizostethium vitreum: Jordan 1878:44.

Stizostethium vitreum var. *salmoneum:* Jordan 1878: 44.

Stizostedium vitreum: Forbes 1884:63.

Stizostedion vitreum: Large 1903:26; Forbes & Richardson 1908:272–274; O'Donnell 1935:490.

Stizostedion vitreum vitreum: Smith 1965:10.

Diagnosis.—The walleye is an elongate and cylindrical perch, olive brown to blackish, with

greenish yellow reflections, sides finely vermiculate in large adults, 5–12 vague and almost vertical bars on the sides of small young, a conspicuous black blotch in the posterior membranes of the first dorsal fin, a black spot at the pectoral fin base, the tip of the anal fin and the lower lobe of the caudal fin white, a large mouth (the rear of the maxilla extending to below the back of the eye), enlarged canine teeth, cheeks naked or with a very few scales, the preopercle strongly serrate below and behind, the caudal fin forked, the pelvic fins widely separated, 12 or 13 anal rays, 19–23 rays in second dorsal fin, three rather large pyloric caeca, and the genital papilla absent or much reduced. The species most closely resembles the sauger but is easily distinguished by the single posterior blotch in the first dorsal fin in all but very small specimens. The young has more vertical bands than has the young sauger, and they are vertically aligned and much less distinct. The species attains a length of 760 mm (30 inches), but most adults are much smaller.

Variation.—Two subspecies are recognized. The nominate form (*S. v. vitreum*), which occurs in Illinois, is wide ranging in eastern and central North America; another form (blue walleye, *S. v. glaucum*), which is presently endangered, occurs in Lake Erie.

Ecology.—The walleye occurs in large rivers and associated floodplain lakes. It is highly migratory, and stragglers may be found occasionally in small streams but never far from a major river. It is less tolerant of turbidity, silt, and high temperatures than is the sauger but has similar habitat preferences: beds of aquatic vegetation, holes among tree roots, and brushy areas. Its food consists of plankton at first, but after the 1st year of growth, it feeds mostly on fishes. Spawning in the Rock River occurs in early April in backwaters; flooded fields; and lakes over vegetation, debris, or gravel. In the Rock River it is common following a year of high spawning success but less common in other years. Feeding and breeding are similar to those described for the sauger, but the walleye, being larger, may live for 10 years. A tremendous fishery literature has been developed for this important sport fish. The most recent summary of its life history and other aspects of its ecology is Scott & Crossman (1973:770–773).

Distribution.—The walleye occurs in large rivers in all parts of the state but is sporadic and uncommon everywhere except in the Rock and upper Mississippi rivers. It is less general in occurrence in the Illinois River than formerly. The species does well for a short time in newly created large reservoirs and may temporarily be common enough to provide good fishing. Its present status in the Illinois waters of Lake Michigan is unknown.

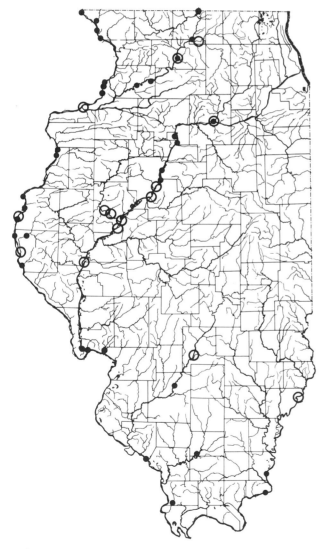

Distribution of the walleye in Illinois.

Perca Linnaeus

According to most current authors, this Holarctic genus contains one North American and one Eurasian species although a few workers regard them as conspecific. The North American species occurs southward into Illinois. The genus is centrarchid-like in many morphological and ecological ways and is an important sport fish.

Yellow perch
Perca flavescens (Mitchill)

Morone flavescens Mitchill 1814:18 (type-locality: near New York City).
Perca flavescens: Kennicott 1855:593 (recorded from Illinois); Nelson 1876:36; Large 1903:26; Forbes & Richardson 1908:276–278; O'Donnell 1935:490; Smith 1965:10.
Perca americana: Jordan 1878:43; Forbes 1884:63.

Yellow perch

Diagnosis.—The yellow perch is a deep-bodied and slab-sided perch, grayish-olive or greenish-yellow, with six to nine strong vertical bands of black or brown on the sides, usually a dusky blotch in the posterior rays of the first dorsal fin, two anal spines, six to eight anal rays, the caudal fin forked, the pelvic fins slightly separated, the preopercle strongly serrate behind and below, a large mouth (the rear of the maxilla extending backward to beneath the middle of the eye), no enlarged canine teeth, and a small and unspecialized genital papilla. The species is easily recognized by its deep body shape and distinctive pattern. The young somewhat resembles the logperch but is more slab-sided, has the serrate-edged preopercle, and has proportionately smaller anal and second dorsal fins. Young basses have at least three anal spines. The species attains a length of about 310 mm (12 inches).

Variation.—There is great individual variation in color and intensity of pattern but little geographic variation. No subspecies are recognized if the North American population is regarded as specifically distinct from the Eurasian perch.

Ecology.—The yellow perch occurs in clear, well-vegetated lakes and backwaters and clear pools of rivers. The species feeds on a variety of organisms. Spawning occurs in April and May over gravel, pebbles, brush, or submerged vegetation. The eggs are laid in long gelatinous masses. Because the perch is a popular sport fish during winter as well as summer, a considerable fishery literature exists. For an excellent summary of the life history of the species, see Scott & Crossman (1973:757–760).

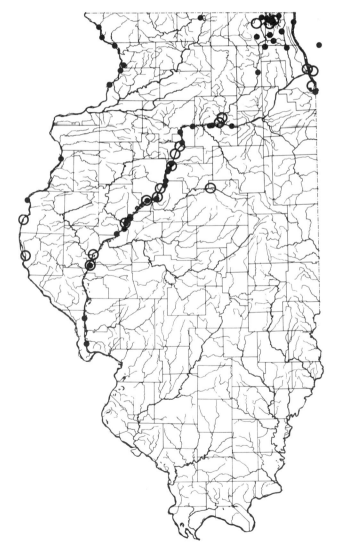

Distribution of the yellow perch in Illinois.

Distribution.—The yellow perch is common in Lake Michigan and the glacial lakes in northeastern Illinois, and rather common in the Illinois River and its associated bottomland lakes for its entire length. It is sporadic in other streams in the northern third of Illinois except in some parts of the upper Mississippi River, where it is fairly common. It has been widely transplanted in reservoirs and golf-course lakes outside its natural range, and these stocked populations may persist for several years if the lakes remain clear and have abundant submerged vegetation. The species is somewhat decimated in northern Illinois because of turbidity, the destruction of natural bodies of standing water, and the deterioration of water quality in the Illinois River.

Percina Haldeman

This eastern North American genus contains 27 described species, 7 of which have been reported for Illinois but 2 of which have long been extirpated in the state. Another species (*P. copelandi*) is known from adjacent Fountain, Posey, and Warren counties, Indiana, but not from Illinois. The genus contains relatively large and primitive darters generally characterized by an enlarged scale between the pelvic fin bases, a midventral row of specialized scales in the male, a large anal fin (almost as expansive as the second dorsal fin), and the absence of bright colors in most species. The species are diverse morphologically and ecologically but have similar feeding and reproductive habits.

KEY TO SPECIES

1. Mouth distinctly subterminal, a conical snout extending well beyond upper lip; scales in lateral line, more than 80; sides of body with more than 16 narrow, dark vertical bars ... . *caprodes*
   Mouth almost terminal, no conical snout; scales in lateral line, usually fewer than 80; sides of body without narrow dark vertical bars .. 2
2. Upper lip separated from snout by a groove, or if present, frenum weakly developed; anal fin of male, when depressed, extending far behind end of depressed second dorsal fin 3
   Upper lip bound to snout by a well-developed frenum; anal fin of male, when depressed, extending slightly behind tip of depressed second dorsal fin 4
3. First dorsal fin with an anterior and posterior inky black blotch; middorsum mottled or with five or more vague saddles; anterior lateral blotches deeper than long; teardrop directed slightly forward .... *shumardi*
   First dorsal fin without anterior and posterior black blotches; middorsum with four or five widely spaced saddles much narrower than interspaces; anterior lateral blotches rounded and more or less confluent; teardrop vertical or directed slightly backward .... *uranidea**
4. Snout sharply produced; body rather slender; first dorsal fin with a submarginal row of orange spots; middorsum with 11–13 vague greenish or brownish blotches; sides with 10–12 more or less confluent, vague blotches .. .. *phoxocephala*
   Snout not produced; body not slender; first dorsal fin without a submarginal row of orange dots; middorsum with 7–10 squarish black blotches; sides with 6–10 black blotches 5
5. Dorsal saddles directly over lateral blotches and usually confluent with them; body and fins with red, orange, yellow, blue, and green colors .... *evides**
   Dorsal saddles and lateral blotches alternating and separate from each other; body and fins without bright colors 6
6. An inky black, median caudal spot; last lateral blotch like preceding ones; teardrop strongly developed; gill covers not connected at isthmus; first dorsal fin with a black basal spot .... *maculata*
   No inky black, median caudal spot; last lateral blotch expanded downward and fused to lower caudal spot; teardrop weakly developed or missing; gill covers moderately joined at isthmus; first dorsal without a black basal spot .... *sciera*

Logperch
Percina caprodes (Rafinesque)

Sciaena caprodes Rafinesque 1818*d*:354 (type-locality: Ohio River).

Percina caprodes: Nelson 1876:36 (recorded from Illinois); Jordan 1878:39; Large 1903:26; Forbes & Richardson 1908:282–283; O'Donnell 1935: 488.

Percina manitou: Jordan 1878:39 (possible in Illinois).

Hadropterus evermanni: Forbes & Richardson 1908: 284–285; Hubbs 1926:60 (= logperch X blackside darter hybrid).

Alvordius evermanni: O'Donnell 1935:488.

Percina caprodes (Rafinesque) subspecies: Smith 1965:10.

Diagnosis.—The logperch is a cylindrical darter, pale straw color or olive, with 15–25 narrow vertical bands of black or brown (usually every other band extending below the lateral line), a conspicuous median caudal spot, a pointed and conical snout extending well beyond the mouth, and 80 or more lateral-line scales. The combination of the terete body, conical snout, and distinctively ringed pattern easily distinguishes this species from all other Illinois percids. The species attains a length of about 180 mm (7 inches).

Variation.—Three subspecies exert influences in Illinois, and much of the state is a broad area of intergradation among them. Logperch in the northern third of the state are *P. c. semifasciata;* those in southwestern Illinois show characteristics of *P. c. carbonaria*, which intergrades with *P. c. caprodes* in eastern and southern Illinois. No recent studies of geographic variation have been published, and the species needs a critical revision. Several species in the complex have been recog-

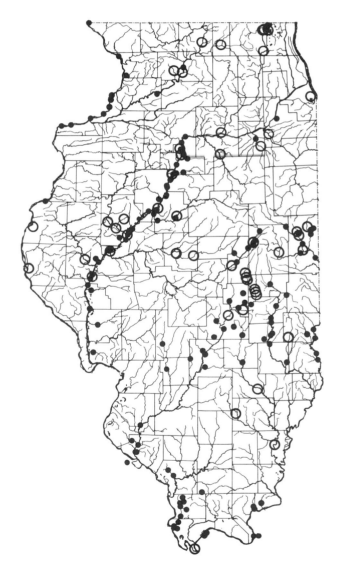

Distribution of the logperch in Illinois.

nized in recent years, and names in the synonymy have been resurrected for them or new names have been proposed.

Ecology.—The logperch prefers clear riffles over mixed sand and gravel in large creeks and rivers, but it also occurs in clear bottomland lakes, pools of streams, and low-gradient large rivers. In the riffle habitat it frequently hides in brush and log jams, and hence its common name. Where the bottom is sand, it may bury itself except for its eyes in the fashion of sand darters. The food consists primarily of immatures of aquatic insects (Thomas 1970:8–12), but, as in other darter species, the small young feeds on microcrustaceans. In searching for food, the logperch uses its conical snout to overturn rocks. Spawning occurs in April over

gravel in strong riffles. The mating pair partially buries the eggs by their vigorous spawning vibrations. Various aspects of the life history of the logperch have been described by several authors. The most detailed accounts are those of Winn (1958*a* and 1958*b*). The species lives for more than three years.

Distribution.—The logperch occurs in all parts of the state where streams are large and stable enough to provide habitat. It is particularly common in the sluggishly flowing and sand-bottomed Illinois River and its associated lakes. Although it is widely distributed and locally common, it has been somewhat decimated in the state because of the destruction of habitats and the deterioration of water quality in many streams and lakes.

Gilt darter*
Percina evides (Jordan & Copeland)

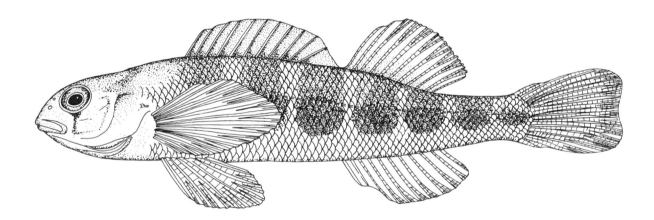

Alvordius evides Jordan & Copeland *in* Jordan 1877*c*:51 (type-locality: White River near Indianapolis, Indiana).

Etheostoma evides: Nelson 1876:36 (expected in southern Illinois).

Ericosoma evides: Jordan 1878:39 (known only from Indiana); O'Donnell 1935:489.

Hadropterus evides: Forbes 1884:65 (recorded from Illinois); Large 1903:27; Forbes & Richardson 1908:288–289.

Percina evides: Smith 1965:12 (extirpated, not collected since 1932).

Diagnosis.—The gilt darter is a stout-bodied darter nearly unique among species of *Percina* in

possessing bright reds and blues on the body and having dorsal saddles directly above the lateral blotches and often confluent with them. The species has 11–13 dorsal spines, two anal spines, usually 55–65 lateral-line scales, naked cheeks, a frenum, and the gill covers slightly connected at the isthmus. The breeding male has five to eight blue-green vertical bands, coppery red interspaces, an orange breast, orange dorsal fins, blue-black anal and pelvic fins, and a pair of orange spots at the caudal base. The species attains a length of about 75 mm (3 inches).

Variation.—Dr. Robert F. Denoncourt of York College analyzed geographic variation in the species in an as yet unpublished paper, concluding that three subspecies were recognizable. That which occurred in Illinois was *P. e. evides.*

Ecology.—The gilt darter lives in large, clear fast-flowing rivers and is frequently found over gravel or rubble riffles that have attached algae and beds of other aquatic vegetation. High-gradient large rivers are rare in Illinois, and the few present are highly modified by silt and other contaminants. Aside from habitat preference and associated species, almost nothing is known of the ecology of the gilt darter.

Distribution.—Extirpated in Illinois. The gilt darter was known to occur in the Rock River from Sterling to Rock Island between 1877 and 1932. It has not been taken in Illinois since. A published record for the mouth of the Kaskaskia River (Luce 1933:119) was based on a misidentified river darter.

Distribution of the gilt darter in Illinois.

Blackside darter
Percina maculata (Girard)

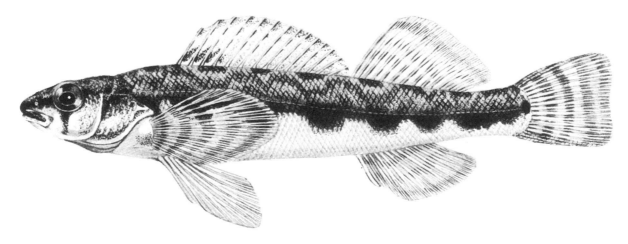

Alvordius maculatus Girard 1859a:68 (type-locality: Fort Gratiot [Michigan]); Jordan 1878:39; O'Donnell 1935:488–489.

Etheostoma blennioides: Nelson 1876:35 (misapplication of name, recorded from Illinois).

Hadropterus aspro: Forbes 1884:65; Large 1903:27; Forbes & Richardson 1908:286–288.

Hadropterus evermanni: Forbes & Richardson 1908: 284–285; Hubbs 1926:60 (= logperch X blackside darter hybrid).

Alvordius evermanni: O'Donnell 1935:488.

Percina maculata: Smith 1965:10.

Diagnosis. — The blackside darter is a moderately slender darter, pale olive green or grayish-yellow above and whitish below, with 8–10 squarish black saddles well separated from 6–10 rectangular lateral blotches; a well-developed teardrop; a small and inky black, median caudal spot; a small black spot in the anterior rays of the first dorsal fin; 13–15 dorsal spines; two anal spines; 65–75 lateral-line scales; the upper lip bound to the snout by a well-developed frenum; and gill covers not connected at the isthmus. The breeding male darkens, becomes more yellowish, and has a more intense pattern. The species most closely resembles the dusky darter but differs in having the median black dot on the caudal peduncle, gill covers free at the isthmus, and a strong teardrop, and in lacking a downward expansion of the terminal lateral blotch. The small young lacks the teardrop but otherwise can be distinguished by the characters just listed. The species attains a length of about 100 mm (4 inches).

Variation. — No subspecies have been described for this rather wide-ranging species, and no trends in geographic variation are known.

Ecology. — The blackside darter is most abundant in firm-bottomed pools of creeks and small rivers, but it sometimes ascends into headwaters. According to Thomas (1970:8–12), who did a study of a population in the Kaskaskia River, its food consists of immatures of aquatic insects and small crustaceans. Spawning occurs in May in gravelly or coarse sand riffles. The details of spawning behavior are summarized in Winn (1958*a* and 1958*b*). Growth and population structure were discussed by Thomas (1970:12–16). The species is known to live for almost four years.

Distribution. — The blackside darter occurs in all parts of Illinois, but it is far more generally distributed in the eastern than in the western part of the state. Although still common in the eastern half of the state, it shows evidence of considerable decimation even there. It must have once been extremely abundant in the small, clear, meandering, prairie streams of Illinois.

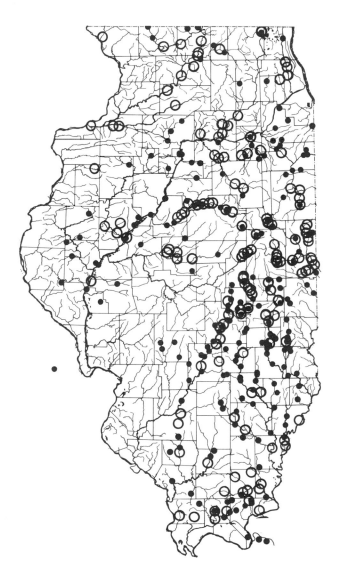

Distribution of the blackside darter in Illinois.

Slenderhead darter
Percina phoxocephala (Nelson)

Etheostoma phoxocephalum Nelson 1876:35 (type-locality: Illinois River and its tributaries, Illinois).

Alvordius phoxocephalus: Jordan 1878:39; O'Donnell 1935:488.

Hadropterus phoxocephalus: Forbes 1884:65; Large 1903:27; Forbes & Richardson 1908:285–286.

Percina phoxocephala: Smith 1965:10.

Diagnosis. — The slenderhead darter is a slender darter, tan or pale olive, with dim and irregular

Slenderhead darter

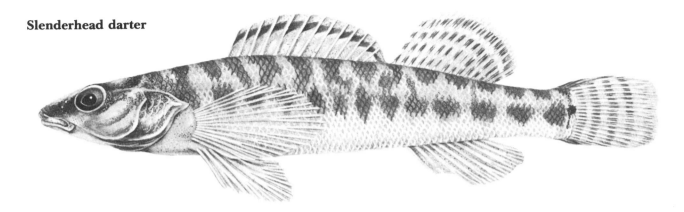

brown saddles well separated from 10–12 vague and more or less confluent blotches of greenish or brownish color along the sides, a prominent pre-orbital stripe but usually no teardrop, a discrete median caudal spot of black, a dark humeral spot, a submarginal row of orange spots in the first dorsal fin, a much-produced snout, the upper lip bound to the snout by a frenum, gill covers rather broadly connected at the isthmus, 60–70 lateral-line scales, 12 or 13 dorsal spines, and two anal spines. The breeding male becomes very dusky over the body and fins, and its dorsal rays are outlined with yellow. The pattern is intensified but except for the overall duskiness is not too different from that of the adult female. The body and head shape and the distinctive pattern set this species off from other Illinois darters, and even the small young is easily recognized. The species attains a length of about 100 mm (4 inches).

Variation.—No subspecies are recognized, and there is evidently little geographic variation in this species, which has a relatively small range. Specimens from southern Illinois occasionally have a weakly developed teardrop.

Ecology.—The preferred habitat is shallow raceways and riffles over sand-gravel bottoms in medium-sized to large rivers. The slenderhead darter occasionally occurs in primarily sand-bottomed raceways, but rarely can be found over silty bottoms. It generally avoids small streams but may be present there when water levels are low. Its food has been extensively studied in Illinois by Thomas (1970:8–12) and Page & Smith (1971) and is similar to that of other large darters. It spawns during a short time, usually in the first half of June, over fast gravelly raceways. Reproductive details and other aspects of its life history were studied by

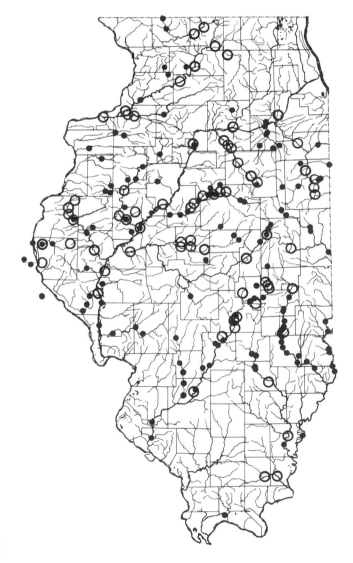

Distribution of the slenderhead darter in Illinois.

Page & Smith (1971). The species usually lives less than 3 years.

Distribution.—The slenderhead darter is statewide and generally distributed except in extreme southern and northern Illinois. It is locally common but has been extirpated from several streams in the state as a result of siltation or deterioration of water quality.

Dusky darter
Percina sciera (Swain)

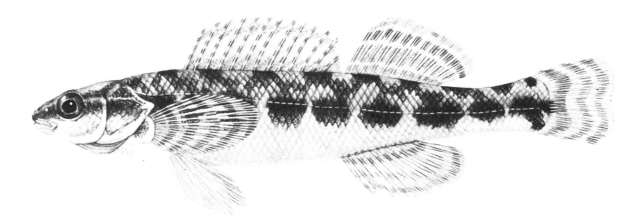

Hadropterus scierus Swain 1883:252 (type-locality: Bean Blossom Creek, Monroe County, Indiana); Large 1903:27 (recorded from Illinois); Forbes & Richardson 1908:289–290.
Serraria sciera: O'Donnell 1935:489.
Percina sciera: Smith 1965:10.

Diagnosis.—The dusky darter is a moderately slender darter, pale olive green or grayish-yellow above and whitish below, with 8–10 squarish black saddles well separated from 7–10 blackish lateral blotches; the terminal lateral blotch expanded downward and fused with the lowermost of three caudal spots, the median caudal spot not more intense than the spots above and below it; no teardrop; no blotches in the first dorsal fin; 13–15 dorsal spines; two anal spines; usually 57–70 lateral-line scales; the upper lip bound to the snout by a well-developed frenum; and gill covers moderately connected at the isthmus. The breeding male darkens overall, and the lateral blotches become broad lateral bands. In the breeding male a pale orange band is present on the distal margin of the first dorsal fin, and its posterior membranes develop a blackish blotch. The species most closely resembles the blackside darter but lacks the inky black, median caudal spot and teardrop and has moderately connected gill membranes and the distinctively expanded, terminal lateral blotch. The young is easily distinguished by the nature of the last lateral blotch. The species attains a length of about 110 mm (4½ inches).

Variation.—Studies of geographic variation in the species were published simultaneously by Hubbs & Black (1954) and Hubbs (1954), the latter recognizing the population in the Guadalupe River system of Texas as a distinct subspecies. The Illinois subspecies is *P. s. sciera.*

Ecology.—The dusky darter occupies deep raceways and riffles over a predominantly gravel bottom in medium-sized to large rivers. It is intolerant of turbidity, silt, and pollution, and is usually found only in channels with moderate to fast current. Its food consists primarily of midge and blackfly larvae but includes immature stages of other aquatic insects. Spawning occurs in late May and early June, when water levels are normal, over gravel in fast riffles and raceways. The feeding and reproductive habits as well as other aspects of the life history were studied in detail by Page & Smith (1970). Most individuals are sexually mature in their 2nd year, and although the species is known to live more than 4 years, most of them survive barely past their 3rd year.

Distribution.—The dusky darter is restricted to the Wabash-Ohio river drainage in Illinois and is common in only a few streams of the upper Wabash River system, most notably in the middle section of the Embarras River. While there is no distributional evidence of extensive decimation, the status of the dusky darter in Illinois is seriously threatened by proposed dams on the Embarras, Little Wabash, and Vermilion River (Middle Fork) systems.

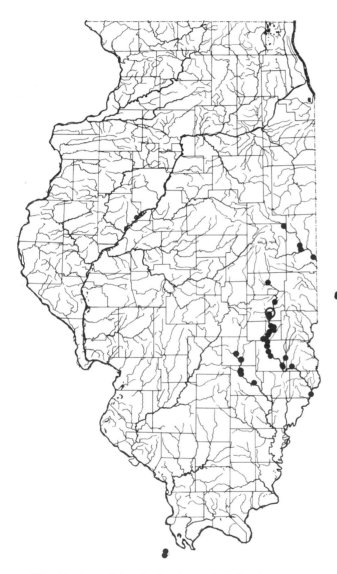

Distribution of the dusky darter in Illinois.

River darter
Percina shumardi (Girard)

Hadropterus shumardi Girard 1859*b*:100 (type-locality: Arkansas River near Fort Smith, Arkansas).
Imostoma shumardi: Jordan 1878:39 (recorded from Illinois); O'Donnell 1935:488.
Cottogaster shumardi: Forbes 1884:66; Large 1903: 27; Forbes & Richardson 1908:290–291.
Percina shumardi: Smith 1965:10.

Diagnosis.—The river darter is a rather slender darter, pale olivaceous above, with the dorsum inconspicuously mottled or with five or more dim saddles, 8–15 vertically elongate lateral blotches, anterior blotches usually much deeper than long, a prominent black anterior and posterior blotch in the first dorsal fin, a well-developed teardrop that projects slightly forward, the upper lip separated from the snout by a groove, the frenum absent or much reduced, gill membranes narrowly connected at the isthmus, scaled cheeks, 46–62 lateral-line scales, 9 or 10 dorsal spines, two anal spines, and the anal fin of male elongate (when depressed, its tip extending well behind the tip of the depressed second dorsal fin). The breeding male becomes darker and its pattern is intensified. The species is most closely related to the stargazing darter, which does not occur in Illinois, but differs in having all dorsal saddles, if present at all, equally developed; two distinct black blotches in the first dorsal fin; and vertically elongate, anterior blotches on the sides. From all other Illinois members of the genus that have a superficial resemblance, it can be distinguished by the groove separating the upper lip and snout and by the elongated anal fin of the male. The species attains a length of 65 mm (2½ inches).

Variation.—No subspecies are recognized even though the species has an extensive north-south distribution.

Ecology.—The river darter is typically a large-river species, usually found over gravel or mixed sand and gravel in fast-flowing water. It may be a species of deep channels, and hence its scarcity in collections. Occasionally it is encountered in clear, sand-bottomed canals that are not far removed from a large river, such as the Mississippi. Its food consists primarily of immatures of aquatic insects and microcrustaceans and was studied by Thomas (1970:8–12) in the lower Kaskaskia River. Its reproductive biology and other aspects of the life his-

River darter

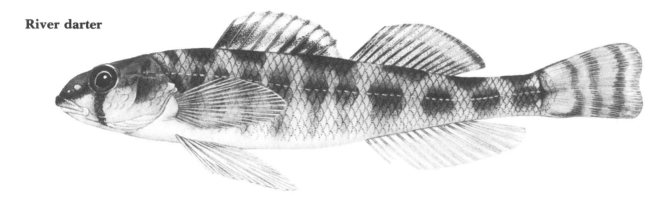

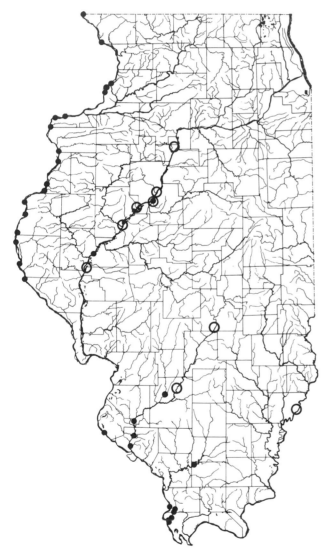

Distribution of the river darter in Illinois.

tory are almost unknown, except for some information on age and growth presented by Thomas (1970:15). The species may live as long as 4 years, but most individuals die at 3 years.

Distribution.—The river darter is restricted to the Mississippi River and the lower reaches of its major tributaries. It is generally distributed but not common in the Mississippi above the mouth of the Missouri. There is no evidence of change in its distribution or abundance, except that it probably has been extirpated from the lower Kaskaskia River, where it was once common, since the conversion of that part of the river into a barge canal in the late 1960's.

Stargazing darter*
Percina uranidea (Jordan & Gilbert)

Etheostoma (Cottogaster) uranidea Jordan & Gilbert *in* Gilbert 1887:48 (type-locality: Washita River at Arkadelphia, Arkansas).

Cottogaster uranidea: Large 1903:27 (known in Indiana but not Illinois).

Hadropterus ouachitae: Forbes & Richardson 1908: 288 (known from Wabash River of Indiana but not in Illinois).

Alvordius ouachitae: O'Donnell 1935:489 (known from Wabash River of Indiana but not in Illinois).

Percina uranidea: Smith 1965:12 (known from Wabash River in Knox and Posey counties, Indiana, but not Illinois).

Diagnosis.—The stargazing darter is a rather slender darter, russet above, with four widely separated distinct saddles much narrower than the interspaces and confluent with lateral blotches, lateral blotches rounded and more or less confluent

Stargazing darter

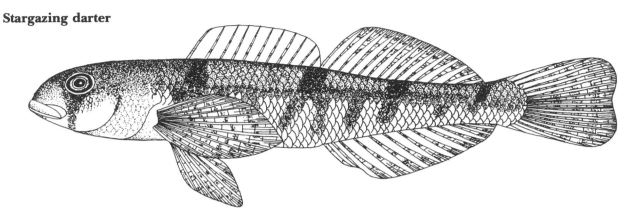

with each other, a teardrop that is vertical or directed slightly backward, many small brown flecks over the body, the upper lip separated from the snout by a shallow groove, the frenum absent or much reduced, gill membranes narrowly connected at the isthmus, scaled cheeks, 48–55 lateral-line scales, 10 or 11 dorsal spines, two anal spines, and the anal fin of the male elongate (when depressed, extending well behind the tip of the depressed second dorsal fin). The breeding male has the pattern more intensified. Of other Illinois darters, this species most closely resembles the river darter but lacks two intense black blotches in the first dorsal fin and has rounded lateral blotches, and has four dorsal saddles that are much more intense than the others. Superficially it resembles a johnny darter but differs in its generic characters, details of pattern, and longer anal fin. The species attains a length of about 65 mm (2½ inches).

Variation.—No studies of variation in this species have been published.

Ecology.—Thompson (1974) found that the food of the stargazing darter in Arkansas was almost exclusively snails and limpets. In the Wabash River of adjacent Indiana, the stargazing darter occurred in fast shoals over sand, gravel, and bedrock. Almost nothing is known of its reproductive habits.

Distribution.—The stargazing darter has never been reported from Illinois waters. It is included because it formerly occurred in the Wabash River and would have been expected to have been present on the Illinois side of the river as well as on the Indiana side.

Distribution of the stargazing darter in Illinois.

Ammocrypta Jordan

This eastern North American genus contains seven described species, including two which still occur in Illinois and another that occurred in the state before 1901. All species are well adapted to living over pure sand in small and large rivers, and all are pellucid fishes usually with incomplete squamation and well-separated dorsal fins. Another species in the genus (*A. vivax*) is known from adjacent Cape Girardeau County, Missouri (Pflieger 1971:547) but has seemingly not been able to get across the Mississippi River into Illinois.

KEY TO SPECIES

1. Tail fin distinctly forked; back crossed over by three to five broad dark saddles; 12–14 dorsal and anal rays .... *asprella**
   Tail fin not distinctly forked; back without broad dark saddles; dorsal and anal fins with fewer than 12 rays 2
2. Opercle with a needlelike backward-projecting spine; dots along lateral line, if present, irregular in outline and connected by a weak row of melanophores; a few rows of scales above the lateral line vaguely outlined with pigment .... *clara*
   Opercle without a needlelike backward-projecting spine; 12–19 sharply defined dots along lateral line, usually not connected by melanophores; several rows of scales above the lateral line sharply outlined with pigment .... *pellucida*

Crystal darter*
Ammocrypta asprella (Jordan)

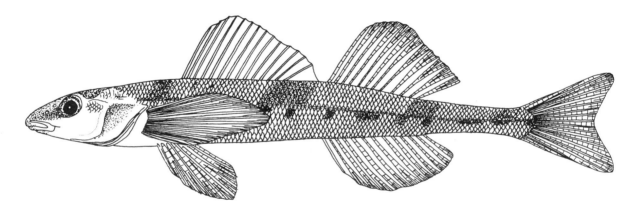

Pleurolepis asprellus Jordan 1878:38 (type-locality: rocky tributary, Mississippi River, Hancock County, Illinois).
Ammocrypta asprella: Forbes 1884:66; Smith 1965: 12 (extirpated, not collected since 1901).
Crystallaria asprella: Large 1903:28; Forbes & Richardson 1908:300–301; O'Donnell 1935:488.

Diagnosis.—The crystal darter is an extremely slender-bodied darter with three to five broad dusky saddles across the back, a distinctly forked tail, 80 or more lateral-line scales, the midline of belly naked but the rest of the body scaled, 12–14 dorsal rays, 12–14 anal rays, one anal spine, the dorsal fins rather close together, a pronounced snout, and a translucent (hyaline) body in life (opaque in preserved specimens). The species is highly distinctive both as an adult and as a juvenile, differing sharply from other sand darters in having a forked tail, almost complete squamation, and more dorsal and anal rays. It is somewhat similar to the stargazing darter, which does not occur in Illinois, but is more slender and fine scaled as well as fork tailed. The species attains a length of about 100 mm (4 inches).

Variation.—Some current workers believe that the crystal darter differs significantly enough from other sand darters to be placed in the monotypic genus *Crystallaria.* No subspecies are recognized, but Dr. J. D. Williams, who is studying geographic variation in sand darters, believes that the Ozark population differs substantially from that on the Gulf Coast (personal communication).

Ecology.—The crystal darter occupies rather deep and fast-flowing water over sand or gravel. It is evidently rare everywhere and seldom collected, partly because of its nocturnal habits. Its feeding and reproductive habits are almost completely unknown.

Distribution.—Extirpated in Illinois. The species was evidently always rare in Illinois. Besides the type-locality, the species has been recorded from the Rock River at Cleveland, Erie, and Milan; the Little Wabash River at Effingham; and the Wabash River near Vincennes and New Harmony, Indiana. All records are pre-1901, and the reasons for the extirpation of the species are difficult to pinpoint. It has been extirpated, or much decimated, in other parts of its range.

Distribution of the crystal darter in Illinois.

Western sand darter
Ammocrypta clara Jordan & Meek

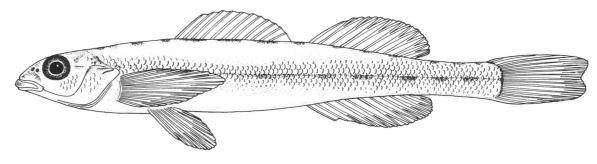

Ammocrypta clara Jordan & Meek 1885:8 (type-locality: Des Moines River opposite Ottumwa, Iowa); Smith 1965:10.
Pleurolepis pellucidus: Jordan 1878:38 (part., recorded from Illinois but not distinguished from eastern sand darter).
Ammocrypta pellucida: Large 1903:28 (part.); Forbes & Richardson 1908:301–303 (part.).
Vigil pellucidus: O'Donnell 1935:488 (part.).

Diagnosis.—The western sand darter is a terete and pellucid darter without pigment except for a few weakly developed dots along the lateral line connected by a line of melanophores, vague dusky outlining of the few scales above the lateral line, and an obscure dark marking on the snout. This species has a needlelike spine projecting backward from the opercle; a few rows of scales along the lateral line (the body is otherwise mostly naked); a pronounced snout; 8–10 dorsal spines; 8–10 anal rays; one anal spine; and widely separated dorsal fins. It is most like the eastern sand darter but is easily distinguished in both the adult and juvenile by the presence of the spine on the opercle and other key characters. The species attains a length of about 75 mm (3 inches).

Variation.—No subspecies are recognized, and no clinal variation trends are known in this species, which has a rather restricted range (Williams 1975: 14).

Ecology.—The western sand darter occurs in rivers and is restricted to a habitat of almost pure sand. The species is known to be nocturnal, and presumably it buries itself in the sand during daylight hours. Virtually nothing else is known about its ecology. It is assumed to be a summer spawner.

Distribution.—The western sand darter occurs in the Mississippi upstream from the mouth of the Missouri River, in the Sugar River in Winnebago County, and in the Kaskaskia River in Shelby and Fayette counties although the creation of the Carlyle and Shelbyville reservoirs in recent years may now have eliminated the Kaskaskia River populations. Formerly the species occurred sparingly over nearly all of the state except in the Wabash-Ohio drainage. It is rare and known from only a few localities and is thus a threatened species. Its decimation is probably the result of siltation. Strangely, there is no record of its ever having occurred in the middle Illinois River or in the Green and Kankakee rivers, where sand habitats are abundant.

Eastern sand darter
Ammocrypta pellucida (Putnam)

Pleurolepis pellucidus Putnam 1863:5 (type-locality not stated, but types are from Black River, below falls, near Elyria, Lorain County, Ohio); Nelson 1876:35 (recorded from Illinois); Jordan 1878: 38 (part.).

Ammocrypta pellucida: Forbes 1884:66; Large 1903: 28 (part.); Forbes & Richardson 1908:301–303 (part.); Smith 1965:10.

Vigil pellucidus: O'Donnell 1935:488 (part.).

Diagnosis.—The eastern sand darter is a terete and pellucid darter with a row of 9–13 discrete brown dots along the lateral line and a similar row along the dorsal ridge, paired dusky markings on the snout, pigment distinctly outlining the several rows of scales above the lateral line, a pronounced snout, 8–10 dorsal spines, 8–10 anal rays, one anal spine, and widely separated dorsal fins, and without a needlelike spine projecting backward from the opercle. It is similar to the western sand darter but has more scales and pigment and lacks the

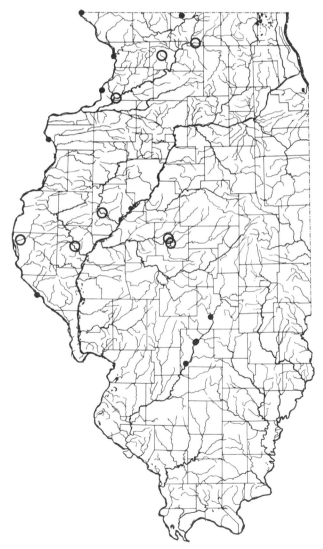

Distribution of the western sand darter in Illinois.

Eastern sand darter

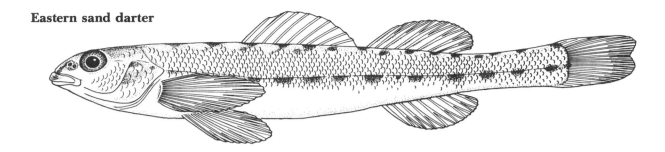

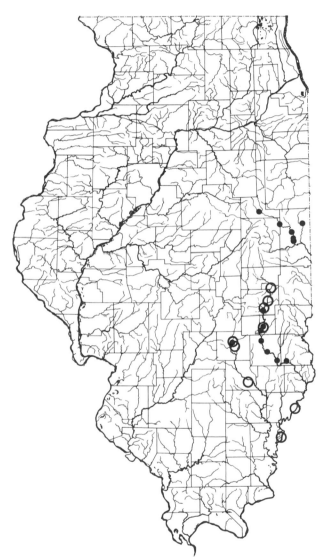

Distribution of the eastern sand darter in Illinois.

opercular spine. It attains a length of about 75 mm (3 inches).

Variation.—No subspecies are recognized, and no clinal variation trends have been noted (Williams 1975:19).

Ecology.—The eastern sand darter occurs in rivers of high water quality over beds of pure sand. It dives into the shifting sand and completely disappears for a time and then may stick only its head above the sand. Stomachs of specimens from the Embarras River contained midge and black fly larvae. Its reproductive habits have not been studied.

Distribution.—The eastern sand darter is restricted to streams in the upper Wabash River drainage and is common only in the middle Embarras River and Middle Fork of the Vermilion. It was formerly more general in occurrence in the Embarras, Little Wabash, and Wabash rivers and is decimated as a result of siltation, impoundments, and possibly deterioration of water quality. The Mississippi drainage records plotted in Forbes & Richardson's atlas of maps refer to the western sand darter, which they did not distinguish at that time.

Etheostoma Rafinesque

This large genus of darters contains 85 described species, mostly concentrated in the eastern United States, 16 of which occur in Illinois. As in most genera the species exhibit considerable diversity in habitat preferences, but unlike those of most genera, *Etheostoma* species also have diversified reproductive biologies. The male in nearly all species develops bright colors during the breeding season. The genus differs primarily from *Percina* in that the midventral row of enlarged and specialized scales is lacking in *Etheostoma* and usually the anal fin is appreciably smaller than the second dorsal fin. It differs from *Ammocrypta* in that the body of most Illinois species is well scaled and the dorsal fins in nearly all Illinois species are closely approximated. A few other species of *Etheostoma* occur in border counties of adjacent Kentucky and Missouri but not in Illinois. They include *E. smithi*, *E. stigmaeum*, *E. tetrazonum*, and an undescribed species of the subgenus *Ulocentra*, but the great rivers bordering Illinois are effective barriers to their dispersal into this state. All species in this genus are sexually mature at 1 year of age and live from 1½ to 4 years, depending upon the maximum size attained.

KEY TO SPECIES

1. Upper lip separated from snout by groove; anal spines, one or two; mouth horizontal 2

    Upper lip joined to snout medially by frenum; anal spines, two; mouth variable but usually oblique 5

2. Gill covers broadly joined medially by membrane across isthmus (Fig. 15a); sides of body with prominent V-shaped markings or large irregular blotches 3

    Gill membranes not broadly joined across isthmus (Fig. 15b); sides of body with many small flecks or X-shaped markings 4

3. Snout extremely short, snubbed, overhanging mouth; anterior half of maxillary fused with preorbital region; ventral fins without discrete markings .... *blennioides*

    Snout not short, snubbed, and overhanging mouth; maxillary separated from preorbital region by a groove; ventral fins with discrete brown markings .... *histrio*

4. Lateral line lacking on posterior part of body; cheeks scaled; dorsal fins widely separated; dark bridle continuing around front of snout; snout U-shaped in lateral profile .. .. *chlorosomum*

    Lateral line complete or almost so; cheeks usually naked; dorsal fins narrowly sepa-

Fig. 15. Key characters: a) underside of head, showing gill covers broadly connected; b) underside of head, showing gill covers not broadly connected.

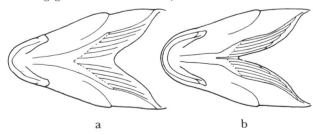

a   b

rated; dark bridle interrupted medially on snout; snout rather pointed in lateral profile .... *nigrum*

5. Lateral line absent or extremely short (fewer than eight anterior pored scales); dorsal spines, usually fewer than eight; pelvic fin of male angular, extending to or beyond anus; maximum size less than 50 mm (2 inches) 6

    Lateral line complete or incomplete but consisting of more than 10 pored scales; dorsal spines, eight or more (except in *E. kennicotti*); pelvic fin rounded and not extending to anus; maximum size more than 50 mm (2 inches) 7

6. Cheeks naked; lateral line usually with zero to two pores; dorsal spines, six or seven; mouth small, upper jaw barely reaching below front of eye; venter with evenly spaced black dots .... *microperca*

    Cheeks with imbedded scales; lateral line usually with three to seven anterior pores; dorsal spines, seven or eight; mouth large, upper jaw reaching behind front of eye; venter stippled with fine melanophores .... *proeliare*

7. Lateral line highly flexed upward to within three scale rows of base of first dorsal fin; body with bright green bars (in life); spinous dorsal fin with distal row of red dots .... *gracile*

    Lateral line not flexed upward to within three scale rows of dorsal fin base; color variable but not consisting of green body bars and red spots on distal portion of spinous dorsal fin 8

8. Spinous dorsal fin appreciably lower than soft dorsal; caudal fin boldly marbled with six or more black bands; dorsal spines of male usually with fleshy knobs at tips; conspicuous dark humeral spot above pectoral fin base 9

    Spinous dorsal fin not conspicuously lower than soft dorsal; caudal fin plain or indistinctly marbled and usually with fewer than six dusky bands; dorsal spines of male without knobs at tips; dark humeral spot present or absent 11

9. Nape scaled; opercles and breast with some scales; gill covers narrowly connected at isthmus so that juncture is V-shaped; caudal peduncle with three intense caudal spots; lateral line extending to rear of soft dorsal fin .... *squamiceps*

Nape, opercles, and breast scaleless; gill covers moderately to broadly joined at isthmus; caudal peduncle without three conspicuous caudal spots; lateral line extending only to front of soft dorsal fin 10

10. Lower jaw projecting beyond upper; scales in lateral line, more than 45; gill covers broadly connected at isthmus; sides usually with many longitudinal rows of dark dots .... *flabellare*

Lower jaw not projecting beyond upper; scales in lateral line, usually fewer than 45; gill covers slightly connected at isthmus; body without longitudinal rows of dark dots ... . *kennicotti*

11. Gill covers broadly joined at isthmus; mouth horizontal; sides of body with bright green bars (*E. histrio* green in winter, brown in summer) 12

Gill covers not broadly joined at isthmus; mouth oblique; sides of body without bright green bars 13

12. Nape, breast, opercles, and cheeks unscaled; underside of head, breast, and the fins with widely spaced, coarse black dots; pectoral fins enlarged, extending well behind tips of pelvic fins; spinous dorsal fin with anterior and posterior dark blotch .... *histrio*

Nape, breast, opercles, and cheeks scaled; underside of head, breast, and the fins without coarse black dots; pectoral and pelvic fins extending backward an equal distance; spinous dorsal fin without anterior and posterior dark blotch .... *zonale*

13. Lateral line complete; soft dorsal and caudal fins distinctly bordered by broad light band edged distally with dark pigment; sides with numerous thin longitudinal dark lines and scattered red dots; dorsal spines, 11 or 12 .... *camurum*

Lateral line not extending behind soft dorsal fin; soft dorsal and caudal fins not bordered by broad light band edged with dark pigment; sides with vertical bands or squarish blotches; dorsal spines, 8–11 14

14. Lateral line short, not extending to soft dorsal fin, highly arched; dorsal spines, eight or nine; body terete; sides with a series of quadrate dark blotches separated by red or orange patches; eye diameter greater than snout length .... *exile*

Lateral line extending to middle of soft dorsal fin, nearly straight; dorsal spines, 10 or 11; body somewhat compressed; sides with dark vertical bars; eye diameter less than snout length 15

15. Cheeks scaled; band at caudal base well developed and more prominent than other lateral bands; subdistal row of orange spots in spinous dorsal, below which the membranes are pale blue or gray; vertical bars on sides indistinct .... *asprigene*

Cheeks unscaled; band at caudal base no more prominent than other lateral bands; red band traversing middle of spinous dorsal fin, bordered above and below by blue-green bands; dark vertical bands on body usually distinct 16

16. Vertical bands on sides rather uniform and about equal to interspaces in width; male with red or orange spot in blue-green anal fin; sides of body without longitudinal rows of dark dots; pectoral fin rays, 13–15; gill covers slightly connected at isthmus .... *caeruleum*

Vertical dark bands on sides less uniform, narrower than interspaces and widened along lateral line; male without red or orange spot in blue-green anal fin; sides of body with some short longitudinal rows of dark dots; pectoral fin rays, 11 or 12; gill covers not connected at isthmus .... *spectabile*

Mud darter
Etheostoma asprigene (Forbes)

Poecilichthys asprigenis Forbes *in* Jordan 1878:41 (type-locality: small creek near Pekin, Illinois).

Etheostoma asprigene: Forbes 1884:64; Smith 1965: 10.

Etheostoma jessiae: Large 1903:29; Forbes & Richardson 1908:307–309.

Oligocephalus jessiae: O'Donnell 1935:489.

Diagnosis.—The mud darter is a somewhat compressed darter, brownish olive, with a small humeral spot, eight or nine dorsal blotches, six to eight indistinct vertical bars on the sides, a prominent bar on the caudal peduncle, a dark teardrop, a subdistal row of orange spots on the first dorsal fin, two anal spines, 10 or 11 dorsal fin spines, a scaled belly, fully scaled cheeks, 47–55 lateral-line scales, a relatively straight lateral line extending to below the middle of the second dorsal fin, first and second dorsal fins of nearly equal height, and the gill covers not united at the isthmus. The breeding male develops an orange belly, a bluish first dorsal

Mud darter

fin with intensified orange spots, rust-colored interspaces between the vertical bars on the sides, and a greenish cast to the pattern of blotches and bars. Among Illinois darters, the species most closely resembles the rainbow and orangethroat darters but differs from them, both in the adult and juvenile stages, in the scaled cheeks and prominent bar on the caudal peduncle. The species attains a length of about 65 mm (2½ inches).

Variation.—No subspecies are recognized. Wayne C. Starnes of the University of Tennessee is engaged in a study of the relationships of the species to *Etheostoma swaini* of the Gulf Coast and of trends in geographic variation in both species.

Ecology.—The mud darter occurs in sloughs, lakes, and low-gradient large rivers over a bottom of organic matter and debris. Forbes & Richardson (1908:309) reported that it feeds on mayflies and midges and spawns in April and May. Little else is known about its life history.

Distribution.—The mud darter is restricted to large rivers and adjacent bottomland lakes over most of the state but is absent in the northernmost counties. It is common in the Illinois, Kaskaskia, and Wabash rivers but rare in the Mississippi and Ohio, which have strong currents. Like many large-river species, it tends to occur in smaller streams in the southern part of Illinois. Forbes & Richardson (1908:308) reported it as "very abundant" and occurring in both large and small rivers. Since it is tolerant of silt and organic matter, its decimation over most of the state must be due to the presently smaller sizes of streams during drought periods.

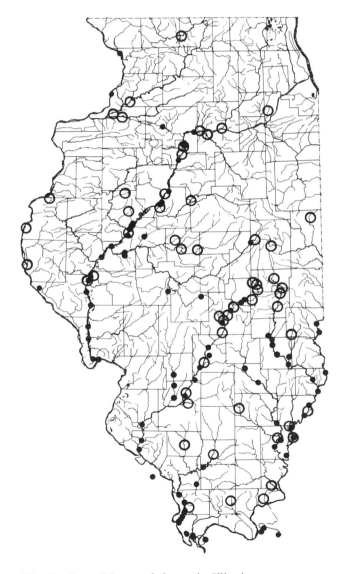

Distribution of the mud darter in Illinois.

Greenside darter
Etheostoma blennioides Rafinesque

Etheostoma blennioides Rafinesque 1819:419 (type-locality: Ohio River); Kennicott 1855:593 (recorded from Illinois); O'Donnell 1935:488; Smith 1965:10.

Diplesium blennioides: Jordan 1878:40; Forbes 1884:66.

Diplesion blennioides: Large 1903:27; Forbes & Richardson 1908:292–294.

Etheostoma blennioides pholidotum R. V. Miller 1968:26 (type-locality: Bean Creek, tributary of Middle Fork, 1 mile E of Potomac, Vermilion County, Illinois).

Diagnosis.—The greenside darter is a rather terete and extremely snubnosed darter, grayish or greenish, with five to eight V- or U-shaped dusky markings along the side, the back and upper sides tesselated with olive, and two dark suborbital bars. It is easily distinguished from other Illinois darters by the following combination of characters: the anterior half of the maxillary fused with the flesh of the preorbital region, a bulbous snout, eyes like a toad's, broadly connected gill membranes across the isthmus, and no visible frenum. The breeding female is yellowish green. The breeding male is a brilliant leaf green with many melanophores and small spots of orange over the body and upper sides; four to seven broad dark green bands on the sides; and bright green fins except the first dorsal, which has a basal band of red. The adult can be distinguished from other darters by the distinctive pattern, head shape, and green coloration. The banded and harlequin darters, which may also be green, lack the fused maxillary and preorbital and the V-shaped markings along the side. The young

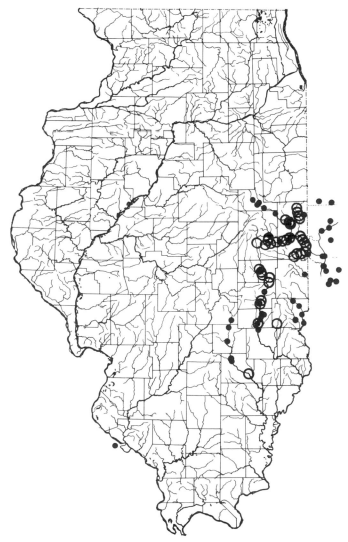

Distribution of the greenside darter in Illinois.

somewhat resembles the young johnny darter but has larger flecks along the sides and two anal spines rather than one. The species attains a length in Illinois of about 100 mm (4 inches).

Variation.—Miller (1968) analyzed geographic variation in the species and recognized four subspecies. That in Illinois is *E. b. pholidotum,* whose type-locality is Bean Creek in Vermilion County.

Ecology.—The greenside darter occupies fast, deep riffles and clear raceways of large creeks and rivers over coarse gravel and rocks, which often have growths of algae. It feeds primarily on insect larvae that live on rocks in the riffle habitat. Both sexes become green when the water becomes cold in late fall and remain so until spawning is completed in the spring. The life history of the species has been studied in several parts of its range. The

more detailed reports are by Fahy (1954) and Winn (1958*a* and 1958*b*). The males are strongly territorial and make aggressive displays to frighten competitors. The eggs are attached to algae or strands of other vegetation and require almost 3 weeks to hatch, since the water in the riffles is still cold in April.

Distribution.—The greenside darter is restricted in Illinois to streams in the upper Wabash River drainage of east-central Illinois. Except for the very old and questionable record for the Chicago area (Kennicott 1855), the species occupies the same range in the state that it always has, but it is much less generally distributed in the Vermilion River system than formerly. Stream impoundments, siltation, and pollution have destroyed many of the habitats once present in that part of the state.

Rainbow darter
Etheostoma caeruleum Storer

Etheostoma caerulea Storer 1845*a*:47 (type-locality: Fox River, Illinois).
Poecilichthys caeruleus: Nelson 1876:34.
Poecilichthys variatus: Jordan 1878:41.
Etheostoma coeruleum: Forbes 1884:64 (part.); Large 1903:29 (part.); Forbes & Richardson 1908: 309–311 (part.).
Oligocephalus coeruleus: O'Donnell 1935:489 (part.).
Etheostoma caeruleum: Smith 1965:10.

Diagnosis.—The rainbow darter is a compressed darter, brownish olive, with three prominent mid-dorsal bands; several vertical bars on the sides, each about the same width as the interspaces be-

tween them; preorbital and postorbital bars; a weakly developed teardrop; the first dorsal fin having horizontal bluish and reddish bands; two anal spines; usually 10 dorsal spines; naked cheeks; usually 40–50 lateral-line scales; a straight lateral line extending to the middle of the second dorsal fin; the gill covers slightly connected at the isthmus; 13–15 pectoral rays; and an uninterrupted suborbital canal. The breeding male is brilliantly colored with metallic blue-green bars that alternate with red-orange interspaces along the sides, an orange throat, a blue breast, bands of vivid blue and orange through the first dorsal fin, and a red-orange spot within the blue-green anal fin. The species is most like the allied orangethroat darter, differing from it by having more uniform vertical bands along the sides, 13 or more pectoral rays, and a complete suborbital canal, and by lacking longitudinal rows of dots along the sides. It attains a length of about 75 mm (3 inches).

Variation.—Dr. Leslie W. Knapp of the Smithsonian Institution conducted a study of geographic variation not yet published. He recognized three subspecies and several local races and commented upon the great amount of individual variation in the species. The subspecies in Illinois is *E. c. caeruleum*.

Ecology.—The rainbow darter lives in clear fast riffles over gravel and rock rubble in creeks and small rivers. It is often abundant in creeks referred to as "runs," which are margined by trees and too fast for silt to accumulate over the gravel or rocky bottoms. The food consists of immatures of aquatic insects and other invertebrates. Spawning occurs over gravel in riffles from late March through April. Winn (1958*a* and 1958*b*) described in detail the reproductive biology of a population in Michigan and summarized previously published studies in other parts of the species' range. Spawning grounds are partitioned into small territories and defended by the brilliantly colored males. Spawning is frenzied. The eggs are fertilized while the female is partially buried and the male is astride of her.

Distribution.—The rainbow darter occurs in high-gradient streams of the upper Wabash River drainage in east-central Illinois and northward to Wisconsin on the eastern side of the state. It does not occur in the northwestern, central, and western counties of Illinois and in southern Illinois is known only from Union, Pope, and Hardin counties. Between 1880 and 1930 authors did not distinguish it from the allied orangethroat darter, and no information is thus available on its former range and abundance. In view of its intolerance of silt, pollution, and impoundments, the species is undoubtedly decimated in Illinois, but where it still occurs it is common. In east-central Illinois entire populations are sometimes eliminated by the drying up of small water courses during drought periods.

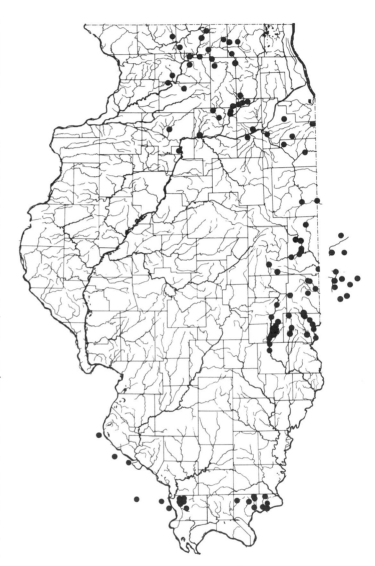

Distribution of the rainbow darter in Illinois.

Bluebreast darter
Etheostoma camurum (Cope)

Poecilichthys camurus Cope 1870a:265 (type-locality: headwaters of the Cumberland River, Tennessee).

Nothonotus camurus: O'Donnell 1935:489 (recorded from Illinois).

Etheostoma camurum: Smith 1965:10.

Diagnosis.—The bluebreast darter is a compressed and stout-bodied darter, olive-green, with dark pigment tending to form thin longitudinal lines, 8–10 poorly developed vertical bands along the sides, median fins and the belly dusky, a broad light-colored band edged with dark pigment on both the second dorsal and anal fins, two anal spines, 11 or 12 dorsal spines, a straight and complete lateral line, 50–60 lateral-line scales, a scaled belly and opercles, the nape and cheeks naked, the gill covers not connected at the isthmus, and a bluntly rounded snout. The breeding female is olive green with small brown spots irregularly arranged but tending to form longitudinal rows. The breeding male is also olive but has a bright blue breast, orange in the dorsal fins, and many small carmine spots that tend to be aligned in longitudinal rows. The young has the distinctive pattern of the adult female. No other Illinois darter has a broad light band edged with dark pigment on the second dorsal, anal, and caudal fins. The species attains a length of about 75 mm (3 inches).

Variation.—Zorach (1972) studied geographic variation in this species and its relatives. No subspecies are recognized for the bluebreast darter, but closely allied species occur in Kentucky and Tennessee.

Distribution of the bluebreast darter in Illinois.

Ecology.—The bluebreast darter is confined to large, very swift, boulder-strewn riffles in rivers of high water quality. Goodnight & Wright (1940) described the habitat as the "swiftest of waters" and noted that the darters were found beneath boulders of up to 600 mm (2 feet) in diameter. Its food has evidently not been reported. Spawning occurs in gravel near such boulders in May and June. The spawning behavior was described by Mount (1959), who found that the female is partially buried in gravel during the spawning act.

Distribution.—The bluebreast darter was reported from the Salt Fork of the Vermilion River near Oakwood in Vermilion County by Goodnight & Wright (1940). Numerous attempts to find the species at that site have been unsuccessful over the last 15 years, and it is assumed that the population has been extirpated, possibly the result of a local fish kill. The species still occurs at several sites in a short stretch of the Middle Fork between Collison and Kickapoo State Park in Vermilion County, but it will certainly be eliminated if the proposed Middlefork Reservoir is constructed (Smith 1968). No other Illinois stream provides the habitat required by this species. References to the species by several early authors were misidentifications or statements that the bluebreast darter had not yet been found in Illinois waters.

Bluntnose darter
Etheostoma chlorosomum (Hay)

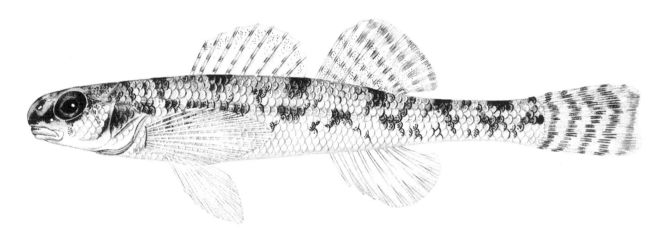

Vaillantia chlorosoma Hay 1881:495 (type-locality: tributary of Tuscumbia River, Corinth, Mississippi).
Boleosoma camura Forbes *in* Jordan 1878:40 (type-locality: Cache River and Clear Creek, Union County; Johnson County; Pekin [Illinois]).
Boleosoma camurum: Forbes 1884:66; Large 1903: 27–28; Forbes & Richardson 1908:298–300.
Vaillantia camura: O'Donnell 1935:488.
Etheostoma chlorosomum: Smith 1965:10.

Diagnosis.—The bluntnose darter is a terete and slender darter, pale yellow or whitish overall, with five or six small brown saddles, numerous brown flecks and small patches of pigment scattered over the sides, a distinct bridle-shaped marking surrounding the bluntly rounded snout, faint bars on the dorsal and caudal fins, one anal spine, a horizontal mouth, a straight but incomplete lateral line, scaled cheeks, a deep groove separating the upper lip from the snout, and distinctly separated dorsal fins. The breeding male is straw colored with melanophores intensifying the pattern on the body and fins. The species resembles the johnny darter somewhat but is readily separated from that species by the round snout, bridle-shaped marking, paler coloration, and more widely separated dorsal fins. The young is distinguishable by the same characters. The species attains a length of about 50 mm (2 inches).

Variation.—Dr. W. M. Howell of Samford University has studied geographic variation in the bluntnose darter. His study is as yet unpublished.

Ecology.—The bluntnose darter occurs in swamps, floodplain lakes, sloughs, and low-gradient creeks over substrates of mud, clay, or detritus. It is also known from large rivers, where it probably occupies backwaters. Females much distended with eggs have been found in late April, suggesting early May as the probable spawning time. Other information on the ecology of the species is lacking.

Distribution.—The bluntnose darter is generally distributed and rather common throughout the southern third of Illinois and in the middle and lower parts of the Illinois River. Formerly it was almost statewide in distribution, occurring everywhere except in the northern tiers of counties. The decimation of the species is rather surprising in view of its wide ecological tolerances and is likely due to the elimination of creek populations during drought periods when streams dry up. An old record for South Chicago in the Great Lakes drainage (Forbes & Richardson 1908: atlas of maps) may be valid, but the species no longer occurs in the area.

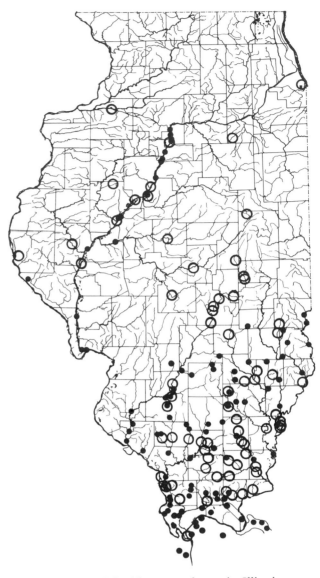

Distribution of the bluntnose darter in Illinois.

Iowa darter
Etheostoma exile (Girard)

Boleichthys exilis Girard 1859*b*:103 (type-locality: Little Muddy River, a tributary of the upper Missouri); Nelson 1876:34 (recorded from Illinois).

Boleichthys eos: Nelson 1876:34; Jordan 1878:42 (part.).
Etheostoma eos: Forbes 1884:64.

Etheostoma iowae: Large 1903:28–29 (part.); Forbes & Richardson 1908:306–307 (part.).
Boleichthys fusiformis: Forbes & Richardson 1908: 315–316 (part.).
Oligocephalus exilis: O'Donnell 1935:489 (part.).
Etheostoma exile: Smith 1965:10.

Diagnosis.—The Iowa darter is a terete and rather stout darter, brownish or olive, with 8–10 dorsal saddles, 10–14 squarish lateral blotches separated by reddish interspaces, a distinct teardrop and preorbital bar, barred fins, the lateral line highly flexed anteriorly and usually not extending as far as the second dorsal fin, eight or nine dorsal spines, usually two anal spines, 53–62 lateral-line scales, scaled cheeks, the eye diameter exceeding the snout length, the dorsal fins distinctly separated, the upper lip bound to the snout by a frenum, and slightly connected gill covers at the isthmus. The breeding male has a bluish dorsum and dark blue-green lateral blotches separated by rusty red interspaces, broad horizontal bands of blue and orange through the first dorsal fin, and a suffusion of orange along the lower sides. The species has been often confused with the slough darter, which has an even more highly flexed lateral line anteriorly (within three scale rows of the dorsal fin base) and green lateral bars (in life). The Iowa darter shares with the rainbow and orangethroat darters the blue- and orange-banded first dorsal fin and dark bars on the sides but differs from them in having scaly cheeks, a much larger eye, and more widely separated dorsal fins. The species attains a length of about 75 mm (3 inches).

Variation.—Such early authors as Jordan, Large, and Forbes hopelessly confused this species with members of the subgenus *Hololepis,* probably because of the great variability of the Iowa darter and because all species involved have a highly flexed lateral line anteriorly and similar habitat preferences. It was, of course, Hubbs (1926:64–68) who straightened out the confusion and assigned several names to the synonymy. The most thorough studies of variation are those of Gosline (1947) and Scott & Crossman (1973:783–784), neither recognizing subspecies but both commenting on the great variability of the species.

Ecology.—The Iowa darter occurs in clear well-vegetated lakes, sloughs, and low-gradient creeks. In streams it occurs in quiet pools over a mud or clay bottom with detritus and brush. Turner (1921) noted that the young fed on planktonic organisms and adults on aquatic insect immatures and amphipods. Spawning occurs in April in shallow water

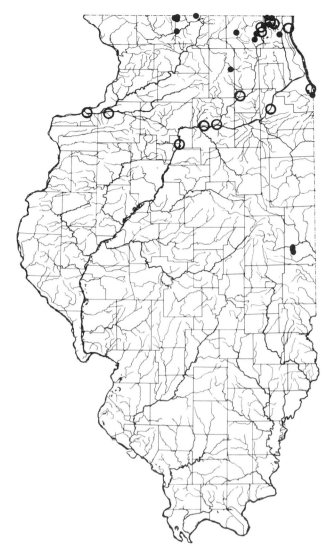

Distribution of the Iowa darter in Illinois.

over roots, vegetation or organic debris. Winn (1958a and 1958b) published detailed studies of the reproductive behavior in a Michigan population.

Distribution.—The Iowa darter is common in the glacial lakes of northeastern Illinois and is known from a few streams in extreme northern Illinois and in some deep and very old limestone quarries near Fairmount in Vermilion County. Formerly the species was rather generally distributed throughout the northern fourth of Illinois, including the upper Illinois River. Its extensive decimation in Illinois is probably the result of high turbidity and the draining of natural bodies of standing water. Records for southern Illinois of older authors were based on the slough darter, which they confused with the Iowa darter.

Fantail darter
Etheostoma flabellare Rafinesque

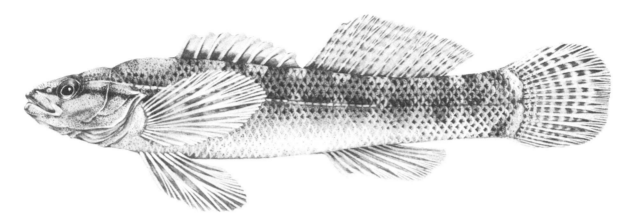

Etheostoma flabellaris Rafinesque 1819:419 (type-locality: tributaries of Ohio River).

Catonotus lineolatus Agassiz 1854:305 (type-locality: small creek near Quincy, Illinois).

Poecilichthys lineolatus: Nelson 1876:34.

Poecilichthys flabellatus: Nelson 1876:34.

Etheostoma flabellare: Jordan 1878:42; Forbes 1884: 64; Large 1903:29; Forbes & Richardson 1908: 313–314.

Etheostoma flabellare var. *lineolatum:* Jordan 1878: 42.

Etheostoma lineolatum: Forbes 1884:65.

Catonotus flabellaris: O'Donnell 1935:489.

Etheostoma flabellare Rafinesque subspecies: Smith 1965:10.

Diagnosis.—The fantail darter is a terete and rather slender darter, dark olive green or brownish both above and below, with the caudal fins boldly barred with black, a conspicuous humeral spot, many longitudinal rows of dusky dots that form horizontal lines along the sides (subspecies *lineolatum*) and/or 10–12 vertical bars (subspecies *flabellare* and young of both subspecies), a preorbital and postorbital stripe, the lower jaw projecting beyond the upper, a sharp snout, a naked head, the first dorsal fin appreciably lower than the second, usually eight dorsal spines tipped with fleshy margins (in the adult male), two anal spines, 45–60 lateral-line scales, the lateral line nearly straight and ending at the front of the second dorsal fin, the upper lip bound to the snout by a frenum, and gill covers broadly joined at the isthmus. The breeding male is dark olive green with intense black bars in the caudal fin, a prominently speckled

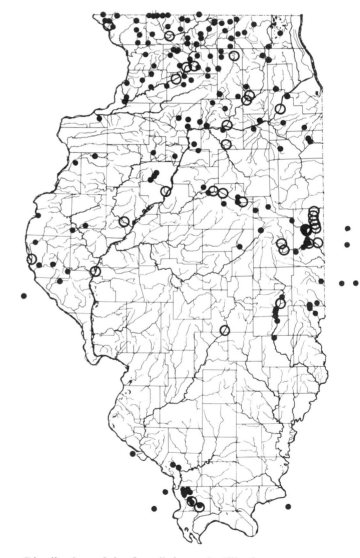

Distribution of the fantail darter in Illinois.

second dorsal fin, pale gold knobs tipping the dorsal spines, and a dusky distal margin on the first dorsal fin. Both sexes are firm bodied and slippery when alive. The young has most of the characters of the adult and is unique among Illinois darters in being very darkly pigmented above and below. The species attains a length of about 75 mm (3 inches).

Variation.—The fantail darter consists of three currently recognized subspecies, two of which occur in Illinois. The populations in the upper Wabash River drainage are *E. f. flabellare* or *E. f. flabellare* X *lineolatum* intergrades; those elsewhere in the state are *E. f. lineolatum*. The species may be a complex of several more undescribed subspecies and even species, and it is in need of a thorough study of geographic variation.

Ecology.—The fantail darter occurs in fast rocky riffles of rivulets, creeks, and small rivers, usually in shallow water. The male has well-developed knobs on the tips of the dorsal spines, and they are used to cleanse the site of egg deposition and also to clean the eggs after they have been laid. Spawn-

ing occurs in April and May in moderate current. Both sexes turn upside down during oviposition, and the female attaches the eggs to the underside of a rock. The complex reproductive behavior has been reported by several observers, the most recent of which was Winn (1958*a* and 1958*b*). The food consists of insect immatures and other aquatic arthropods (Karr 1964:278). Fecundity and growth were also studied by Karr.

Distribution.—The fantail darter occurs throughout most of the northern half of Illinois and is common in suitable habitats. It is much more general in occurrence toward the north but sporadic in central Illinois. An isolated population occurs in Jackson and Union counties in the Mississippi River drainage, but it does not occur elsewhere in southern Illinois. Although the habitat of the species has seemingly diminished in Illinois, there is no evidence of appreciable change in its distributional pattern and abundance except in the North Fork of the Vermilion River, where an impoundment eliminated upstream habitat, and in the West Branch of the Salt Fork, where pollution is chronic.

Slough darter
Etheostoma gracile (Girard)

Boleosoma gracile Girard 1859*b*:103 (type-locality: Rio Seco near Fort Inge, Texas).
Boleichthys eos: Jordan 1878:42 (part.).
Boleichthys elegans: Jordan 1878:43 (recorded from Illinois).
Etheostoma fusiforme: Forbes 1884:64.
Boleichthys fusiformis: Large 1903:29; Forbes & Richardson 1908:315–316 (part.).
Etheostoma iowae: Large 1903:29 (part.); Forbes & Richardson 1908:307 (part.).
Hololepis fusiformis: O'Donnell 1935:489–490 (part.).
Oligocephalus exilis: O'Donnell 1935:489 (part.).
Etheostoma gracile: Smith 1965:10.

Diagnosis.—The slough darter is a terete and rather slender darter, olivaceous in color, with 8–11 small and irregular brownish blotches alternating with bright green (in life) bars on the sides, a subdistal row of red dots or a red-orange stripe in the first dorsal fin, one or more small caudal spots, barred second dorsal and caudal fins, a preorbital and postorbital stripe, a weakly developed teardrop, the lateral line highly flexed upward anteriorly to within three scale rows of the first dorsal fin base, the lateral line usually ending at the front of the second dorsal fin, 42–55 lateral-line scales, scaled cheeks, 9 or 10 dorsal fin spines, two anal spines, the upper lip bound to the snout by a frenum, and the gill membranes narrowly connected at the isthmus. The breeding male has the green lateral bars and red markings in the first dorsal fin much intensified and many more melanophores over the entire body, and it develops intense blue-black pigment below the red dots of the first dorsal fin. Among Illinois species, the slough darter is unique in its very highly flexed lateral line, and even small specimens can be distinguished by this character because a groove is present even before the lateral-line pores develop. The upwardly flexed lateral line is also characteristic of the Iowa darter but less so, and there is otherwise little resemblance between them. Other Illinois darters with bright green lateral bars have broadly connected gill membranes at the isthmus. The species attains a length of a little more than 50 mm (2 inches).

Variation.—Geographic variation in the species has been studied at least twice, the more recent and more thorough study being that of Collette (1962). He found more individual variation within populations than between populations and recognized no subspecies.

Ecology.—The slough darter inhabits swamps, floodplain lakes, farm ponds, and low-gradient creeks, where it is most abundant in quiet pools over bottoms of detritus or clay. Its food (primarily insect larvae and plankton) and its reproductive habits were thoroughly studied by Braasch & Smith (1967), who described the highly complex breeding behavior. The highly colored male has pairs of nuptial tubercles on its chin, and these are used to stroke the snout of the female during courtship. In so doing, the male opens his mouth widely in a yawn and rubs the tubercles over the female's head. Spawning occurs in late May in pools, and eggs are attached individually to objects on the bottom.

Distribution.—The slough darter is widespread and common throughout the southern third of the state but somewhat less so toward the western side of Illinois. Evidently it has always been abundant in the same area, but its range has shrunk somewhat farther south than formerly, most likely because creek populations at the northern edge of the range are eliminated when streams dry up during periods of drought.

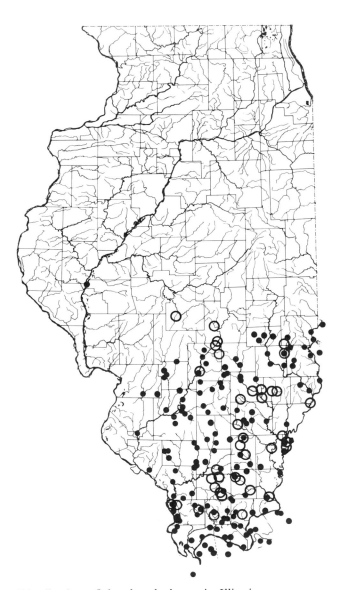

Distribution of the slough darter in Illinois.

Harlequin darter
Etheostoma histrio Jordan & Gilbert

Etheostoma (Ulocentra) histrio Jordan & Gilbert *in* Gilbert 1887:47 (type-locality: Poteau River near Hackett City, Arkansas; Saline River at Benton, Arkansas; and Washita River at Arkadelphia, Arkansas).

Etheostoma histrio: Smith 1965:10 (recorded from Illinois).

Diagnosis.—The harlequin darter is a rather stout darter, reddish tan, with five to seven dorsal saddles and seven or eight highly irregular vertical blotches that are brown in summer and bright green in winter (hence the common name harlequin darter), all fins prominently barred, a pair of large basicaudal blotches, vermiculate cheeks, widely spaced black dots on the breast, an anterior and a posterior blotch in the first dorsal fin, a large and expansive pectoral fin (the tip extending behind the pelvic fin tip), a naked breast and cheeks, a blunt snout and horizontal mouth, the gill covers broadly joined at the isthmus, the frenum reduced or absent, the lateral line straight and complete, 45–58 lateral-line scales, and usually two anal spines. Presumably the breeding male has the bright green markings that it had during winter and has melanophores scattered over the body and a distal red-orange band through the first dorsal fin. The species most closely resembles the banded darter but differs in having naked cheeks, two large basicaudal blotches, and a much reduced frenum. The young is as distinctive as the adult. No other Illinois darter has such large pectoral fins and the prominently barred pelvic fins. The species attains a length of slightly more than 50 mm (2 inches).

Distribution of the harlequin darter in Illinois.

Variation.—Tsai (1968) found "differences between populations so slight that no infraspecific categories need be recognized."

Ecology.—This darter, rare throughout most of its range, occurs in fast rather deep riffles over a bottom of mixed sand and gravel, especially those with some organic debris or roots on the bottom. Virtually nothing else is known about the species.

Distribution.—The harlequin darter is extremely rare and is restricted to a 20-mile stretch of the Embarras River in Cumberland and Jasper counties. The Illinois population, known from five sites, is the northernmost known for the species. Although the specimen is not available for reidentification, it is likely that the record from the Wabash River plotted by Forbes & Richardson (1908:305, atlas of maps) for the banded darter was the harlequin darter instead.

Stripetail darter
Etheostoma kennicotti (Putnam)

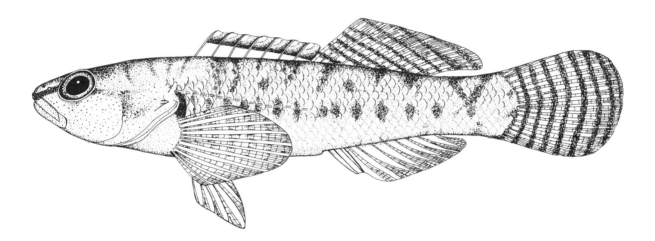

Catonotus kennicotti Putnam 1863:3 (type-locality: a rocky brook, Union County, Illinois—Page & Smith 1976:533).
Etheostoma obeyense: Large 1903:29; Forbes & Richardson 1908:311–312.
Oligocephalus obeyensis: O'Donnell 1935:489.
Etheostoma kennicotti: Smith 1965:10.

Diagnosis.—The stripetail darter is a slender and terete darter, grayish yellow, with six or seven brownish saddles and several highly variable and indistinct blotches along the sides, no teardrop, 9–11 distinct black bars in the caudal fin, a conspicuous humeral spot, a distal brown band on the first dorsal fin, usually seven or eight dorsal spines, the dorsal spines knobbed at the tip, the first dorsal fin much lower than the second, two anal spines, usually 38–44 lateral-line scales, the lateral line extending to the front of the second dorsal fin, naked cheeks and opercles, a frenum present, the gill covers moderately joined at the isthmus, and the lower jaw shorter than the upper. The breeding male is golden orange with dim vertical bands, or-

ange knobs on the tips of the dorsal spines, an intensified humeral spot, the second dorsal fin boldly marbled with jet black and white, and a strongly barred caudal fin. The species most closely resembles the fantail darter, differing in having larger scales, a much shorter lower jaw, slightly joined gill covers, and a distal stripe of brown in the first dorsal fin. The young somewhat resembles the spottail darter but lacks its three caudal spots and has the distinctive brown stripe on the first dorsal fin. The species attains a length of about 50 mm (2 inches).

Variation.—Page & Smith (1976) found clinal variation in several characters from east to west and recommended that *E. k. cumberlandicum* be synonymized, leaving the species without any recognized subspecies.

Ecology.—The life history of the species was studied by Page (1975), who found that the stripetail darter occurs in slab-rock pools in headwaters of rocky creeks. The food consists primarily of immatures of aquatic insects. Spawning occurs in late

April and, like the fantail darter, the spawning pair turn upside down and deposit eggs on the underside of a flat rock. The autecology of the species is discussed in detail by Page (1975).

Distribution.—The stripetail darter is abundant in rocky brooks and creeks in the Ohio River drainage of southeastern Illinois. Although many of the streams now dry up in late summer and autumn, many others continue to flow because of springs. Page & Smith (1976) explained the abundance of the stripetail darter on the grounds that no closely allied species occur with it in Illinois, whereas in most other parts of its range it is in competition with two or more other members of the same subgenus.

Distribution of the stripetail darter in Illinois.

Least darter
Etheostoma microperca
Jordan & Gilbert

Microperca punctulata Putnam 1863:4 (type-locality: various points in Michigan, Wisconsin, Illinois, and Alabama); Nelson 1876:34; Jordan 1878:43 (part.); Forbes 1884:64 (part.); Large 1903:29 (part.); Forbes & Richardson 1908:317–318 (part.); O'Donnell 1935:490 (part.).
Etheostoma microperca Jordan & Gilbert *in* Jordan 1888:134 (substitute name for preoccupied *punctulata*); Smith 1965:10.

Diagnosis.—The least darter is a tiny but robust darter, olive-brown above, with 8–12 small rectangular blotches along the lateral line, small vague saddles on the dorsum, a prominent teardrop and preorbital bar, barred caudal and second dorsal fins, many specks of brown pigment over the entire body, evenly spaced black dots on the venter, the lateral line completely absent or consisting of no more than two pored scales, 31–34 scales in lateral series, short and rounded dorsal fins, six or seven dorsal spines, two anal spines, angular pelvic fins, the pelvic fin of the male extending beyond the anus, the mouth small (the rear of the maxilla barely reaching the front of the eye), a bluntly rounded head, the gill covers moderately connected at the isthmus, the upper lip bound to the snout by a frenum, and naked cheeks. The breeding male is greenish brown with many melanophores scattered over the body and head, blackish blotches, a subdistal row of red dots in the first dorsal fin, and red-orange pelvic and anal fins. The species most closely resembles the cypress darter but differs in having naked cheeks, fewer pored lateral-line scales, fewer scales in lateral series, usually one less dorsal spine, a smaller mouth, and discrete dots on the venter. The specimen illustrated by Forbes & Richardson (1908:317) is an Iowa darter instead of a least darter. The species attains a length of about 40 mm (1½ inches).

Variation.—No subspecies are recognized, and no information is available on geographic variation in the species.

Ecology.—The least darter occurs in well-vegetated natural lakes and small shallow brooks with submerged vegetation. It is often found hiding in living or dead vegetation in the shallow margins of small streams. The food consists of small crustaceans and midge and mayfly immatures (Forbes &

Least darter

Richardson 1908:318). Spawning occurs in May in shallow water over vegetation. Eggs are deposited one at a time here and there on vegetation and debris. The spawning act is similar to that described for the slough darter except that the courtship is somewhat less elaborate. Several observations on the spawning behavior have been published and are summarized in Winn (1958*a* and 1958*b*).

Distribution.—The least darter occupies several counties in the northeastern corner of Illinois and is rather common but easily overlooked because of its small size. There is no clear-cut evidence of decimation, and it is now known from several areas where it had probably been missed by early investigators. The records for the southern half of the state cited by most of the early authors were based on the similar and related cypress darter, which was not then distinguished from the least darter.

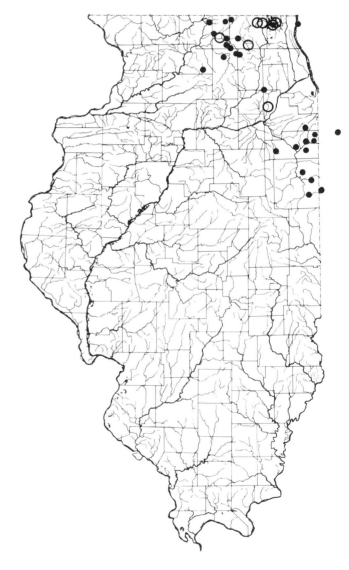

Distribution of the least darter in Illinois.

Johnny darter
Etheostoma nigrum Rafinesque

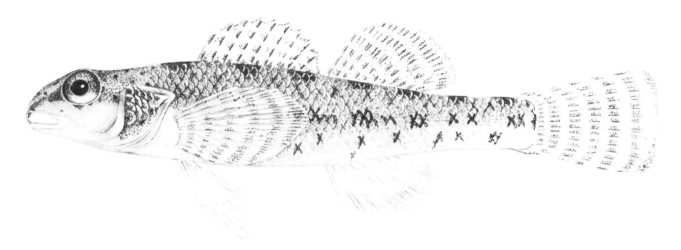

Etheostoma nigrum Rafinesque 1820*a*:37 (type-locality: Green River, Kentucky).

Boleosoma brevipinne: Nelson 1876:35 (recorded from Illinois).

Boleosoma olmstedi: Nelson 1876:35; Jordan 1878: 40.

Boleosoma maculatum: Jordan 1878:40.

Boleosoma nigrum: Forbes 1884:66; Large 1903:27; Forbes & Richardson 1908:294–298; O'Donnell 1935:488.

Etheostoma nigrum Rafinesque subspecies: Smith 1965:10.

Diagnosis.—The johnny darter is a slender and terete darter, pale tan or straw colored, with five or six quadrate brown saddles on the back, small W- or X-shaped markings on the sides that tend to be aligned along the lateral line, numerous minute flecks of brown scattered over the body, no teardrop, a preorbital stripe that ends at the snout tip, faintly speckled dorsal and caudal fins, a complete lateral line, 40–55 lateral-line scales, usually eight or nine dorsal spines, one anal spine, a rather pointed snout, the upper lip separated from the snout by a deep groove, a horizontal mouth, the gill covers narrowly joined at the isthmus, and the dorsal fins narrowly separated. The body and fins of the breeding male become blackish and almost unicolor except for four to eight vague vertical bands on the sides and a dark spot in the anterior rays of the first dorsal fin. The species most closely resembles the bluntnose darter but differs in having a complete lateral line, closely approximated dorsal fins, and a rather pointed snout without a dark bridle encircling it. The young superficially resembles the young greenside darter but has smaller patches of pigment along the sides and only one anal spine. The species attains a length of about 75 mm (3 inches).

Variation.—For several years the johnny darter was regarded as having a widespread subspecies in the Mississippi Valley and another restricted to the Driftless Area of Wisconsin and adjacent Minnesota and completely surrounded by the nominate form. The Driftless Area subspecies, *E. n. eulepis,* was said to differ in having a scaled breast, nape, and cheeks and to be more prone to occupy lakes and backwaters. Underhill (1963) analyzed populations throughout Minnesota and concluded that *E. n. eulepis* should not be recognized. It is structurally a different fish but does not fit the concept of subspecies. The squamation, it was suggested, may be determined by one or a few gene loci. In Illinois occasional specimens in the northern fourth of the state may have scaled napes, breasts, and cheeks, and the scaled nape appears even in some specimens from central Illinois. In all populations, however, there are some individuals that appear to be *E. n. nigrum*. Scaled cheeks occur less frequently in northern Illinois specimens than scaled breasts and napes. In view of the complexity of the variation, it is likely that other authors will regard the johnny darter as a highly variable species without subspecies.

Ecology.—The johnny darter is more tolerant of slow-moving water than are many other darters and reaches its greatest abundance in pools of creeks that have bottoms of mixed sand, silt, and gravel. Its food consists primarily of midges and other aquatic insects (Forbes & Richardson 1908:296). Several observations have been published on the reproductive habits of the species, some of which are summarized in Speare (1965), who also studied its reproductive habits. Spawning occurs in May on the undersides of rocks in a manner similar to that already described for the fantail and stripetail darters. As in those species, the male johnny darter has knobs at the tips of the dorsal fin spines.

Distribution.—The johnny darter occurs in all parts of Illinois and is abundant everywhere except in the low-gradient streams of the south-central and west-central parts of the state, where it is sporadic. Although it is presently widespread and common, it has probably been somewhat decimated by turbidity and siltation in many creeks that once had clear water and sandy bottoms.

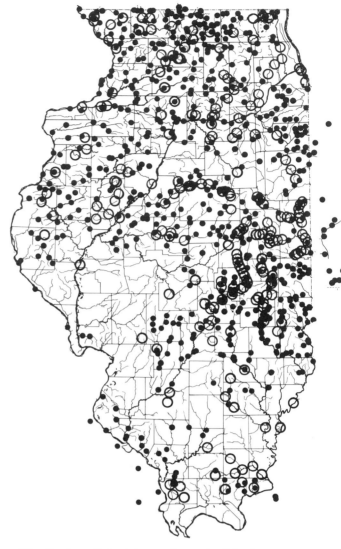

Distribution of the johnny darter in Illinois.

Cypress darter
Etheostoma proeliare (Hay)

Microperca proeliaris Hay 1881:496 (type-locality: small branch of Tuscumbia River at Corinth, Mississippi).
Microperca punctulata: Jordan 1878:43 (part., recorded from Illinois); Forbes 1884:64 (part.);

Large 1903:29 (part.); Forbes & Richardson 1908:317–318 (part.); O'Donnell 1935:490 (part.).
Etheostoma proeliare: Smith 1965:10.

Diagnosis.—The cypress darter is a tiny darter, olive-brown above, with 8–12 small rectangular blotches along each side, small vague saddles on the dorsum, a prominent teardrop and preorbital bar, barred caudal and second dorsal fins, the venter evenly stippled with fine melanophores, many specks of brown pigment over the entire body, the lateral line with two to eight anterior pores, 34–38 scales in lateral series, short and rounded dorsal fins, seven or eight dorsal spines, one or two anal spines, angular pelvic fins, the pelvic fin of male extending beyond the anus, the rear edge of the maxilla extending slightly behind the front of the eye, a bluntly rounded head, the gill covers moderately connected at the isthmus, the upper lip bound to the snout by a frenum, and cheeks with imbedded scales. The breeding male is brownish with the pattern intensified, many melanophores scattered over the head and body, and a subdistal row of red dots in the first dorsal fin. The species is similar to the least darter but differs in having imbedded scales on the cheeks, more lateral scales, more lateral-line pores, a larger mouth, and usually one more dorsal spine, and in lacking the widely spaced black dots on the venter. It attains a length of about 40 mm (1½ inches).

Variation.—No subspecies are recognized, and no information is as yet available on geographic variation in the species.

Ecology.—The cypress darter occurs in well-vegetated ditches and small streams, preferring shallow water over beds of rooted vegetation. Its feeding and reproductive habits are presumably similar to those of the least darter, but no information has been published about them.

Distribution.—The cypress darter is known from only a few localities in the extreme southern part of the state. It is, however, abundant in the well-vegetated canals across the Mississippi River in the bootheel of Missouri. It formerly occurred as far north as the Skillet Fork of Wayne County but was not distinguished from the related and very similar least darter by early authors.

Distribution of the cypress darter in Illinois.

Orangethroat darter
Etheostoma spectabile (Agassiz)

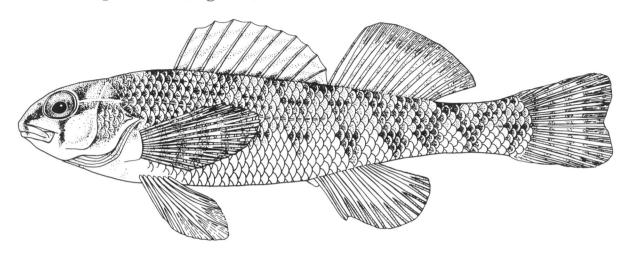

Poecilichthys spectabilis Agassiz 1854:304 (type-locality: Osage River, Missouri); Nelson 1876:34 (recorded from Illinois); Jordan 1878:41.
Etheostoma coeruleum: Forbes 1884:64 (part.); Large 1903:29 (part.); Forbes & Richardson 1908:309–311 (part.).
Oligocephalus coeruleus: O'Donnell 1935:489 (part.).
Etheostoma spectabile spectabile: Smith 1965:10.

Diagnosis.—The orangethroat darter is a compressed darter, brownish olive, with three prominent middorsal bands, several vertical bars on the sides narrower than the interspaces between them, numerous longitudinal rows of brown dots along the sides, preorbital and postorbital bars, a weakly developed teardrop, the first dorsal fin having bluish and reddish horizontal bands, two anal spines, usually 10 dorsal spines, naked cheeks, usually 40–50 lateral-line scales, a straight lateral line extending to the middle of the second dorsal fin, the gill covers not connected at the isthmus, 11 or 12 pectoral rays, and an interrupted suborbital canal. The breeding male is vividly colored with metallic blue-green bars alternating with red-orange interspaces along the sides, an orange throat, bright blue and red-orange bands through the first dorsal fin, and a bright blue-green anal fin. The species is most similar to the rainbow darter, differing from it in having narrower and less uniform vertical bands on the sides, 12 or fewer pectoral rays, an interrupted suborbital canal, longitudinal rows of dots along the sides, and a blue-green anal fin without a red spot in it. The species attains a length of about 75 mm (3 inches).

Variation.—A study of geographic variation in

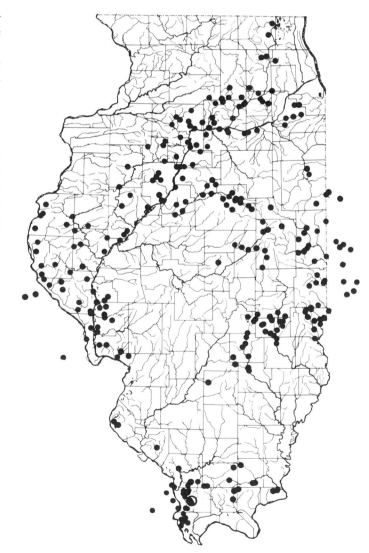

Distribution of the orangethroat darter in Illinois.

the species was done by Distler (1968), who recognized five subspecies. Only the nominate subspecies, *E. s. spectabile*, occurs in Illinois and other states east of the Mississippi River.

Ecology.—The orangethroat darter occupies riffles and pools of small creeks that have bottoms of mixed sand and gravel, and it is often abundant in prairie streams that have no marginal tree vegetation. It is a pioneering species that soon reoccupies formerly dry stream beds and ascends well into headwaters. Its food in Kansas consists of black fly larvae, bloodworms, caddisfly larvae, and other larval insects and fish eggs (Cross 1967:318). Spawning occurs in April in shallow gravel riffles. Spawning behavior has been described by Winn (1958*a* and 1958*b*) and Cross (1967:318). Spawning occurs in April in Illinois. The male sets up a territory on the spawning ground, which is a clear riffle with fine gravel. The male actively pursues the fe-male during courtship. When ready to lay her eggs, the female partially buries her body in the gravel, and the male takes a position just above her, fertilizing the eggs as they are laid. In nature the eggs hatch usually in about 1½ weeks. The young grow quickly and are almost adult size by fall.

Distribution.—The orangethroat darter is abundant where it occurs but is completely absent in several parts of the state for reasons not readily apparent. Since it was confused with the rainbow darter by most authors prior to Trautman (1930), no information on its former distribution and abundance is available. However, it is ecologically more tolerant than the rainbow darter and may have supplanted it in some areas following deforestation along creek banks and the deterioration of water quality in some streams.

Spottail darter
Etheostoma squamiceps Jordan

Etheostoma squamiceps Jordan 1877*b*:11 (type-locality: Russellville, Kentucky); Jordan 1878:42 (not in Illinois but in western Kentucky); Large 1903: 29 (recorded from Illinois); Forbes & Richardson 1908:312–313; Smith 1965:10.
Claricola squamiceps: O'Donnell 1935:489.

Diagnosis.—The spottail darter is a robust and terete darter, dark dusky olive and obscurely mottled, without a definite pattern on the sides but with three black caudal spots; boldly barred caudal and second dorsal fins; often pale gray saddles on the dorsum, sometimes confluent; a strong teardrop; the cheeks vermiculated with dusky pigment; a conspicuous humeral spot; the lateral line nearly straight and extending to the rear of the second dorsal fin; 48–54 lateral-line scales; the nape scaled; usually eight or nine dorsal spines; the dorsal spines tipped with small knobs in the adult male; the first dorsal fin appreciably lower than the second; two anal spines; the upper lip bound to the snout by a fleshy frenum; and the gill covers narrowly connected at the isthmus. The breeding male develops a thickened black head, seven or eight black vertical bars, and thickened and blackish fins (except the pectorals), and loses the typical mottling on the sides of the body. The young has a superficial resemblance to the young stripetail darter but is easily distinguished by the three caudal spots and the clear first dorsal fin. The species attains a length of about 75 mm (3 inches).

Distribution of the spottail darter in Illinois.

are laid within a few minutes, even though only one or two are deposited at a time. Other females may be courted so that the total number of eggs may be 1,500 side by side under the rock. Each egg is about 1.8 mm in diameter. The male guards the nest until the eggs hatch. Its life history was thoroughly studied by Page (1974).

Distribution.—The spottail darter is restricted to tributaries of the Ohio River in extreme southern Illinois and is generally distributed and common in creeks in southeastern counties. It formerly occurred as far north as Carmi in White County, and it still occurs in adjacent Posey County, Indiana. An old record for Robinson Creek in Shelby County (Forbes & Richardson 1908:313 and atlas of maps; O'Donnell 1935:489) was based on a misidentified specimen of the mud darter.

Variation.—No subspecies are recognized in this species with a rather small range, but undescribed and unnamed darters are known from Tennessee that may be closely related species.

Ecology.—The spottail darter occurs in slab-rock riffles and pools of creeks and gravelly headwaters of spring-fed streams. It feeds on a variety of aquatic invertebrates, mostly aquatic insects and crustaceans (Page 1974). It spawns in slab-rock riffles and pools from late March until early June and, like its relatives, deposits eggs on the underside of a large flat rock. The much larger male sets up a territory, which he vigorously defends while trying to entice females underneath the chosen rock. When ready, both male and female briefly invert with the male helping to hold the female in position with his body and fins. The 200–300 eggs

Banded darter
Etheostoma zonale (Cope)

Poecilichthys zonalis Cope 1868:212 (type-locality: North Fork, Holston River, Virginia).
Nanostoma zonale: Jordan 1878:41 (recorded from Illinois); O'Donnell 1935:489.
Nanostoma vinctipes Jordan 1880:236 (type-locality: tributary of Illinois River at Naperville, Illinois).
Etheostoma zonale: Forbes 1884:65; Large 1903:28; Forbes & Richardson 1908:304–306; Smith 1965:10.

Diagnosis.—The banded darter is a rather stout darter, yellowish or pale green, with 7–11 brown saddles on the dorsum and either 9–11 vertical and nearly confluent bars or a midlateral brown stripe that is coarsely serrate, 9–11 green vertical bars, a basal row of red dots in the first dorsal fin, well-scaled cheeks and breast, a blunt snout and an almost horizontal mouth, the gill covers broadly united at the isthmus, the lateral line straight and complete, 46–53 lateral-line scales, two anal spines, and the upper lip bound to the snout by a frenum. The breeding male has the colors intensified so that the lateral bands are bright green and the basal spots in the first dorsal fin are carmine with an anterior and a posterior blue blotch in the fin. The species most closely resembles the harlequin darter but differs in having the cheeks and breast scaled, smaller pectoral fins, and the venter and paired fins without spots or bars. It differs from the greenside darter in having a frenum and in having the maxilla free from the cheek as well as in

Banded darter

details of pattern. It differs from the green-colored slough darter in having a straight lateral line and in lacking a subdistal row of red dots in the first dorsal fin. The species attains a length of about 50 mm (2 inches).

Variation.—Tsai & Raney (1974) published a thorough study of geographic variation. They found numerous distinguishable subraces but concluded that only two subspecies were justified, one occurring above the Fall Line and the other below. The subspecies north of the Fall Line and in Illinois is *E. z. zonale*.

Ecology.—The banded darter is restricted to very fast, clear riffles over rocks or coarse gravel in high-gradient and well-aerated creeks and rivers. Often the rocks and gravel are covered with algae, and other submerged vegetation is present. The food consists mainly of larvae of small Diptera, and spawning is said to occur in late May and early June (Forbes & Richardson 1908:306). Its eggs are believed to be attached to algae or strands of moss. Virtually nothing else is known about the ecology of the species other than its intolerance for silt and pollution.

Distribution.—The species is sporadically distributed throughout the northern half of Illinois except in the more western counties. It is badly decimated, as might be expected, and has disappeared entirely from some stream systems. Where it still occurs, it is common in suitable habitat. As noted previously, the record for the Wabash River in southern Illinois (Forbes & Richardson 1908: 305 and atlas of maps) was probably the harlequin darter instead. The specimen is no longer available for re-examination.

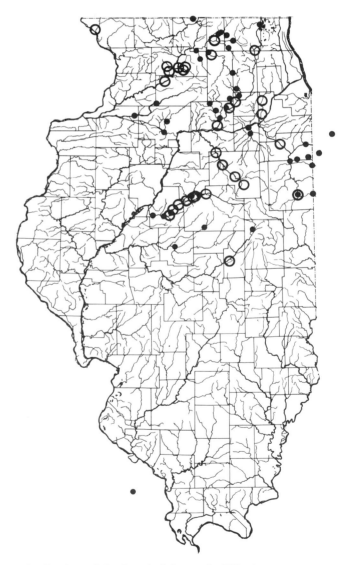

Distribution of the banded darter in Illinois.

Drums—Scaenidae

This large family contains many genera in the shallow seas off all of the continents. Only a few ascend into fresh waters in North America, and only one is restricted to fresh waters. It and many of the marine species are important commercial and sport fishes. The Illinois species is often caught on hook and line, using crayfish or doughballs as bait, but opinion varies on its desirability as a food fish. Because it attains large size, it is a popular sport fish usually referred to by fishermen as a perch rather than a drum.

Aplodinotus Rafinesque

This distinctive genus has numerous characters that make it unique among freshwater fishes. It contains only one species, which occurs in the interior of North America from Hudson Bay to Central America and which is widely distributed in Illinois.

Freshwater drum
Aplodinotus grunniens Rafinesque

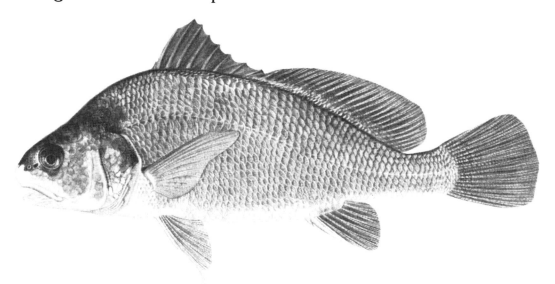

Aplodinotus grunniens Rafinesque 1819:88 (type-locality: Ohio River); Large 1903:30; Forbes & Richardson 1908:323–325; O'Donnell 1935: 490; Smith 1965:10.

Corvina oscula: Kennicott 1855:594 (recorded from Illinois).

Haploidonotus gruuniens: Nelson 1876:40 (misspelling).

Haploidonotus grunniens: Jordan 1878:50; Forbes 1884:62.

Diagnosis.—The freshwater drum is a much compressed and humpbacked fish, grayish white or silvery, with a conical snout, a horizontal mouth, conjoined spinous and soft dorsal fins, the base of the first dorsal fin only about half the length of the soft dorsal fin base, the first ray of the pelvic fin attenuated (in the adult), a small first and a much enlarged second anal spine, the caudal fin rounded or triangular, the lateral line continuing to the end of the caudal fin, ctenoid scales, and heavy and molariform pharyngeal teeth. The young is easily recognized by its head and body shape and the sharply triangular caudal fin. Superficially the drum resembles carpsuckers but differs in many important details, including the presence of dorsal spines and the absence of a forked tail. It differs from percichthyids and centrarchids in having only two anal spines, a short base on the first dorsal fin, and a rounded tail fin. The species attains a length of more than 1 meter (39 inches).

Variation.—Although wide ranging, the freshwater drum is remarkably stable in its characters, and no subspecies have been proposed. Krumholz & Cavanah (1968) found little difference between Kentucky and Wisconsin populations.

Ecology.—The drum is primarily a large-river fish, but it also occurs in large lakes and may ascend small rivers. It is a bottom-dwelling species, most abundant in turbid water over a bottom of mixed sand and silt. The young feeds on benthic insects and crustaceans; the adult, on molluscs, crayfishes, and fishes (Daiber 1952). Surprisingly little is known about the reproductive biology of the species, and it is assumed that the sound produced by the swim bladder may play a role in the spawning act. Daiber (1953) concluded that in Lake Erie spawning occurred in shallow water in July. The female produces an enormous number of eggs, which float at the surface and soon hatch. Growth is rapid in young but slower in adults, which live for many years.

Distribution.—The freshwater drum is extremely abundant in large rivers but sporadic in smaller streams. Recent records for all of northeastern Illinois are lacking, and the species has been extirpated in southern Lake Michigan. Otherwise, there is no real evidence that the species is decimated in the state, but it is likely that it was once more common in the medium-sized rivers when they did not fluctuate so greatly in size.

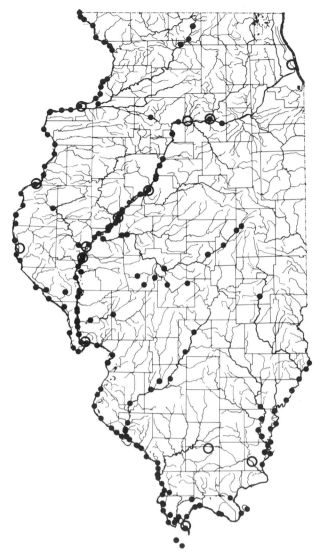

Distribution of the freshwater drum in Illinois.

LITERATURE CITED

Abbott, C. C. 1860. Descriptions of new species of American fresh-water fishes. Academy of Natural Sciences of Philadelphia Proceedings 12:325–328.

Agassiz, L. 1850. Lake Superior. Its physical character, vegetation, and animals, compared with those of other similar regions. Gould, Kendall, and Lincoln, Boston. x + 428 p.

———. 1854. Notice of a collection of fishes from the southern bend of the Tennessee River, in the state of Alabama. American Journal of Science and Arts, 2nd series, 17:297–308, 353–365.

———. 1855. Synopsis of the ichthyological fauna of the Pacific Slope of North America, chiefly from the collections made by the U.S. Expl. Exped. under the command of Capt. C. Wilkes, with recent additions and comparisons with eastern types. American Journal of Science and Arts, 2nd series, 19:71–99, 215–231.

Al-Rawi, A. H., and F. B. Cross. 1964. Variation in the plains minnow, *Hybognathus placitus* Girard. Kansas Academy of Science Transactions 69(1):154–168.

Applegate, V. C. 1950. Natural history of the sea lamprey, *Petromyzon marinus,* in Michigan. U.S. Department of the Interior, Fish and Wildlife Service Special Scientific Report (Fisheries) 55. xii + 237 p.

———, J. H. Howell, J. W. Moffett, B. J. H. Johnson, and M. A. Smith. 1961. Use of 3-trifluoromethyll-4-nitrophenol as a selective sea lamprey larvicide. Great Lakes Fishery Commission Technical Report 1. 35 p.

Bailey, R. M. 1954. Distribution of the American cyprinid fish *Hybognathus hankinsoni* with comments on its original description. Copeia 1954(4):289–291.

———. 1959. Distribution of the American cyprinid fish *Notropis anogenus.* Copeia 1959(2):119–123.

———, chairman. 1970. A list of the common and scientific names of fishes from the United States and Canada. 3rd ed. American Fisheries Society Special Publication 6. 149 p.

———, and M. O. Allum. 1962. Fishes of South Dakota. University of Michigan Museum of Zoology Miscellaneous Publication 119. 131 p.

———, and F. B. Cross. 1954. River sturgeons of the American genus *Scaphirhynchus:* characters, distribution, and synonymy. Michigan Academy of Science, Arts, and Letters Papers for 1953, 39:169–208.

———, and M. F. Dimick. 1949. *Cottus hubbsi,* a new cottid fish from the Columbia River system in Washington and Idaho. University of Michigan Museum of Zoology Occasional Paper 513. 18 p.

———, and C. L. Hubbs. 1949. The black basses (*Micropterus*) of Florida, with description of a new subspecies. University of Michigan Museum of Zoology Occasional Paper 516. 40 p.

———, and H. W. Robison. 1978. *Notropis hubbsi,* a new cyprinid fish from the Mississippi River basin, with comments on *Notropis welaka.* University of Michigan Museum of Zoology Occasional Paper 683. 21 p.

———, H. E. Winn, and C. L. Smith. 1954. Fishes from the Escambia River, Alabama and Florida, with ecologic and taxonomic notes. Academy of Natural Sciences of Philadelphia Proceedings 106:109–164.

Baird, S. F., and C. Girard. 1853a. Descriptions of new species of fishes collected by Mr. John H. Clark, on the U.S. and Mexican Boundary Survey, under Lt. Col. Jas. D. Graham. Academy of Natural Sciences of Philadelphia Proceedings 6:387–392.

———, and ———. 1853b. Description of new species of fishes, collected by Captains R. R. Marcy and Geo. B. M'Clellan, in Arkansas. Academy of Natural Sciences of Philadelphia Proceedings 7:390–392.

Barney, R. L., and B. J. Anson. 1920. Life history and ecology of *Elassoma zonatum.* Ecology 1:241–256.

———, and ———. 1923. Life history and ecology of the orange-spotted sunfish, *Lepomis humilis.* U.S. Commissioner of Fisheries Report for 1922, Document 938, Appendix 15. 16 p.

Barnickol, P. G., and W. C. Starrett. 1951. Commercial and sport fishes of the Mississippi River between Caruthersville, Missouri, and Dubuque, Iowa. Illinois Natural History Survey Bulletin 25(5):267–350.

Berg, L. S. 1964. Freshwater fishes of the USSR and adjacent countries. 4th ed. Vol. 2. Israel Program for Scientific Translations, Jerusalem. (Translation of Academy of Sciences of USSR Zoological Institute, 1949).

Bigelow, H. H., editor. 1963. Fishes of the western North Atlantic. Sears Foundation for Marine Research Memoir 1, Part III. xxi + 630 p.

———, editor. 1964. Fishes of the western North Atlantic. Sears Foundation for Marine Research Memoir 1, Part III. xxi + 630 p.

Black, J. D. 1945. Natural history of the northern mimic shiner, *Notropis volucellus volucellus* Cope. Indiana Department of Conservation, Division of Fish and Game, and Indiana University Department of Zoology, Indiana Lakes and Streams Investigations 2:449–469.

Bottrell, C. E., R. H. Ingersol, and R. W. Jones. 1964. Notes on the embryology, early development, and behavior of *Hybopsis aestivalis tetranemus* (Gilbert). American Microscopical Society Transactions 83(4):391–399.

Bowman, M. L. 1970. Life history of the black redhorse, *Moxostoma duquesnei* (Lesueur), in Missouri. American Fisheries Society Transactions 99(3):546–559.

Braasch, M. E., and P. W. Smith. 1965. Relationships of the topminnows *Fundulus notatus* and *Fundulus olivaceus* in the upper Mississippi River valley. Copeia 1965(1):46–53.

———, and ———. 1967 The life history of the slough darter, *Etheostoma gracile* (Pisces, Percidae). Illinois

301

Natural History Survey Biological Notes 58. 12 p.

Branson, B. A. 1963. The olfactory apparatus of *Hybopsis gelida* (Girard) and *Hybopsis aestivalis* (Girard) (Pisces: Cyprinidae). Journal of Morphology 113(2): 215–228.

Breder, C. M., Jr., and D. E. Rosen. 1966. Modes of reproduction in fishes. American Museum of Natural History, New York. xv + 941 p.

Brown, B. E., and J. S. Dendy. 1962. Observations on the food habits of the flathead and blue catfish in Alabama. Southeastern Association of Game and Fish Commissioners Proceedings for 1961, 15:219–222.

Brown, J. H., U. T. Hammer, and G. D. Kochinsky. 1970. Breeding biology of the lake chub, *Couesius plumbeus,* in Lac la Ronge, Saskatchewan. Fisheries Research Board of Canada Journal 27(6):1005–1015.

Buchholz, M. 1957. Age and growth of river carpsuckers in Des Moines River, Iowa. Iowa Academy of Science Proceedings 64:589–600.

Burr, B. M. 1974. A new intergeneric hybrid combination in nature: *Pomoxis annularis* X *Centrarchus macropterus.* Copeia 1974(1):269–271.

———. 1976. Distribution and taxonomic status of the stoneroller, *Campostoma anomalum,* in Illinois. Chicago Academy of Sciences Natural History Miscellanea 194. 8 p.

———. 1977. The bantam sunfish, *Lepomis symmetricus:* systematics and distribution, and life history in Wolf Lake, Illinois. Illinois Natural History Survey Bulletin 31(10):437–465.

———, and M. A. Morris. 1977. Spawning behavior of the shorthead redhorse, *Moxostoma macrolepidotum,* in Big Rock Creek, Illinois, American Fisheries Society Transactions 106(1):80–82.

———, and P. W. Smith. 1976. Status of the largescale stoneroller. Copeia 1976(3):521–532.

Cahn, A. R. 1927. An ecological study of southern Wisconsin fishes. The brook silversides (*Labidesthes sicculus*) and the cisco (*Leucicthys artedi*) in their relations to the region. Illinois Biological Monographs 11(1):1–151.

Calhoun, Alex, editor. 1966. Inland fisheries management. California Fish and Game Department [Sacramento]. vi + 546 p.

Carlander, K. D. 1969. Handbook of freshwater fishery biology. Vol. 1. Iowa State University Press, Ames. 752 p.

Carr, M. H. 1946. Notes on the breeding habits of the eastern stumpknocker, *Lepomis punctatus punctatus* (Cuvier). Florida Academy of Science Quarterly Journal 9(2):101–106.

Carranza, J., and H. E. Winn. 1954. Reproductive behavior of the blackstripe topminnow, *Fundulus notatus.* Copeia 1954(4):273–278.

Clinton, DeWitt. 1824. Description of a new species of fish from the Hudson River (*Clupea hudsonia*). Lyceum of Natural History of New York Annals 1: 49–50.

Coker, R. E. 1930. Studies of common fishes of the Mississippi River at Keokuk. U.S. Department of Commerce, Bureau of Fisheries Document 1072:141–225.

Collette, B. B. 1962. The swamp darters of the subgenus *Hololepis* (Pisces, Percidae). Tulane Studies in Zoology 9(4):115–211.

Conder, J. R., and R. Hoffarth. 1965. Growth of channel catfish, *Ictalurus punctatus,* and blue catfish, *Ictalurus furcatus,* in the Kentucky Lake portion of the Tennessee River in Tennessee. Southeastern Association of Game and Fish Commissioners Proceedings for 1964, 16:348–354.

Conley, J. M., and A. Witt, Jr. 1966. The origin and development of scales in the flier, *Centrarchus macropterus* (Lacépède). American Fisheries Society Transactions 95(4):433–434.

Cope, E. D. 1864. Partial catalogue of the cold-blooded Vertebrata of Michigan. Part 1. Academy of Natural Sciences of Philadelphia Proceedings 16:276–285.

———. 1865. Partial catalogue of the cold-blooded Vertebrata of Michigan. Part 2. Academy of Natural Sciences of Philadelphia Proceedings 17:78–88.

———. 1866. Synopsis of the Cyprinidae of Pennsylvania. American Philosophical Society Transactions 13:351–399.

———. 1867. On the genera of fresh-water fishes *Hypsilepis* Baird and *Photogenis* Cope, their species and distribution. Academy of Natural Sciences of Philadelphia Proceedings 19:156–166.

———. 1868. On the distribution of fresh-water fishes in the Allegheny Region of southwestern Virginia. Academy of Natural Sciences of Philadelphia Journal, Series 2, 6:207–247.

———. 1870a. On some etheostomine perch from Tennessee and North Carolina. American Philosophical Society Proceedings 11:261–270.

———. 1870b. A partial synopsis of the fishes of the fresh waters of North Carolina. American Philosophical Society Proceedings 11:448–495.

Copes, F. A. 1975. Ecology of the brassy minnow, *Hybognathus hankinsoni* (Cyprinidae). University of Wisconsin Stevens Point Museum of Natural History Reports on the Fauna and Flora of Wisconsin 10. Contributions to Ichthyology. Part III. 47–72.

Cross, F. B. 1953. Nomenclature in the Pimephalinae, with special reference to the bullhead minnow, *Pimephales vigilax perspicuus* (Girard). Kansas Academy of Science Transactions 56(1):92–96.

———. 1967. Handbook of fishes of Kansas. University of Kansas Museum of Natural History Miscellaneous Publication 45. 357 p.

Crossman, E. J. 1962. The grass pickerel *Esox americanus vermiculatus* LeSueur in Canada. Royal Ontario Museum, Life Sciences Division Contribution 55. 29 p.

———. 1966. A taxonomic study of *Esox americanus* and its subspecies in eastern North America. Copeia 1966(1):1–20.

Cuvier, G., and A. Valenciennes. 1829. Histoire naturelle des poissons. Paris. Vol. 3. 500 p.

———, and ———. 1831. Histoire naturelle des poissons. Paris. Vol. 7. 531 p.

———, and ———. 1840. Histoire naturelle des poissons. Paris. Vol. 15. 540 p.

————, and ————. 1842. Histoire naturelle des poissons. Paris. Vol. 16. 472 p.

————, and ————. 1844. Histoire naturelle des poissons. Paris. Vol. 17. 497 p.

Daiber, F. C. 1952. The food and feeding relationships of the freshwater drum, *Aplodinotus grunniens* Rafinesque, in western Lake Erie. Ohio Journal of Science 52(1):35–46.

————. 1953. Notes on the spawning population of the freshwater drum (*Aplodinotus grunniens* Rafinesque) in western Lake Erie. American Midland Naturalist 50(1):159–171.

De Kay, J. E. 1842. Natural history of New York. Zoology of New-York, or the New-York fauna . . . . Part IV. Fishes. W. & A. White & J. Visscher, Albany. xv + 415 p.

Distler, D. A. 1968. Distribution and variation of *Etheostoma spectabile* (Agassiz) (Percidae, Teleostei). University of Kansas Science Bulletin 48(5):143–208.

Dymond, J. R. 1943. The coregonine fishes of northwestern Canada. Royal Canadian Institute Transactions 24:171–231.

Eigenmann, C. H. 1887. Notes on the specific names of certain North American fishes. Academy of Natural Sciences of Philadelphia Proceedings 39:295–296.

————, and R. S. Eigenmann. 1893. Preliminary descriptions of new fishes from the Northwest. American Naturalist 27(314):151–154.

Evermann, B. W. 1892. A report upon investigations made in Texas in 1891. U.S. Fish Commission Bulletin for 1891, 11:61–90.

————. 1896. Description of a new species of shad (*Alosa alabamae*) from Alabama. U.S. Commission of Fisheries Report for 1895. 21:203–205.

Fahy, W. E. 1954. The life history of the northern greenside darter, *Etheostoma blennioides blennioides* Rafinesque. Elisha Mitchell Society Journal 70(2):139–205.

Fingerman, S. W., and R. D. Suttkus. 1961. Comparison of *Hybognathus hayi* Jordan and *Hybognathus nuchalis* Agassiz. Copeia 1961(4):462–467.

Forbes, S. A. 1881. A rare fish in Illinois. American Naturalist 15:232–233.

————. 1882. The blind cave fishes and their allies. American Naturalist 16(1):1–5.

————. 1884. A catalogue of the native fishes of Illinois. Report of the Illinois State Fish Commissioner for 1884:60–89.

————. 1885. Description of new Illinois fishes. Illinois State Laboratory of Natural History Bulletin 2(2):135–139.

————, and R. E. Richardson. 1905. On a new shovelnose sturgeon from the Mississippi River. Illinois State Laboratory of Natural History Bulletin 7(4):37–44.

————, and ————. [1908]. The fishes of Illinois. Illinois State Laboratory of Natural History. cxxxi + 357 p. plus separate atlas containing 102 maps.

————, and ————. 1920. The fishes of Illinois. 2nd ed.

Illinois Natural History Survey. cxxxvi + 357 p.

Forster, J. R. 1773. An account of some curious fishes, sent from Hudson's Bay. Royal Society of London Philosophical Transactions 63(1):149–160.

Gibbs, R. H., Jr. 1957a. Cyprinid fishes of the subgenus *Cyprinella* of *Notropis*. III. Variation and subspecies of *Notropis venustus* (Girard). Tulane Studies in Zoology 5(8):175–203.

————. 1957b. Cyprinid fishes of the subgenus *Cyprinella* of *Notropis*. II. Distribution and variation of *Notropis spilopterus*, with the description of a new subspecies. Lloydia 20(3):186–211.

————. 1963. Cyprinid fishes of the subgenus *Cyprinella* of *Notropis*. The *Notropis whipplei-analostanus-chloristius* complex. Copeia 1963(2):511–528.

Gilbert, C. H. 1884. A list of the fishes collected in the East Fork of White River, Indiana, with descriptions of two new species. U.S. National Museum Proceedings 7:199–205.

————. 1887. Descriptions of new and little known etheostomids. U.S. National Museum Proceedings 10:47–64.

Gilbert, C. R. 1961. Hybridization versus intergradation: an inquiry into the relationship of two cyprinid fishes. Copeia 1961(2):181–192.

————. 1964. The American cyprinid fishes of the subgenus *Luxilus* (genus *Notropis*). Florida State Museum of Biological Sciences Bulletin 8(2):95–194.

————, and R. M. Bailey. 1962. Synonymy, characters, and distribution of the American cyprinid fish, *Notropis shumardi*. Copeia 1962(4):807–819.

————, and ————. 1972. Systematics and zoogeography of the American cyprinid fish *Notropis (Opsopoeodus) emiliae*. University of Michigan Museum of Zoology Occasional Paper 664. 35 p.

Gill, T. N. 1861. Observations on the genus *Cottus*, and descriptions of two new species. Boston Society of Natural History Proceedings 8:40–42.

Gilliams, J. 1824. Description of a new species of fish of the Linnaean genus *Perca*. Academy of Natural Sciences of Philadelphia Journal 4:80–82.

Girard, C. F. 1850. A monograph of the freshwater *Cottus* of North America. American Association for the Advancement of Science Proceedings for 1849, 2:409–411.

————. 1856. Researches upon the cyprinoid fishes inhabiting the fresh waters of the United States of America, west of the Mississippi Valley, from specimens in the Museum of the Smithsonian Institution. Academy of Natural Sciences of Philadelphia Proceedings 8:165–213.

————. 1857. Notice upon new genera and new species of marine and fresh-water fishes from western North America. Academy of Natural Sciences of Philadelphia Proceedings 9:200–202.

————. 1858. Part IV. Fishes. *In* General report upon the zoology of the several Pacific railroad routes. U.S. House of Representatives, Washington, D.C. Vol. 10. xiv + 400 p.

————. 1859a. Ichthyological notices. Academy of Natural Sciences of Philadelphia Proceedings 11:56–68.

———. 1859*b*. Ichthyological notices. Academy of Natural Sciences of Philadelphia Proceedings 11:100–104.

Gmelin, J. F., editor. 1789. Caroli A Linne systema naturae (13th ed.) Tomus I. Pars III:1033–2224.

Goodnight, C. J., and B. A. Wright. 1940. Occurrence of the blue-breasted darter, *Nothonotus camurum* (Cope), in Illinois. Copeia 1940(3):175–176.

Gosline, W. A. 1947. Some meristic characters in a population of the fish *Poecilichthys exilis:* their variation and correlation. University of Michigan Museum of Zoology Occasional Paper 500. 23 p.

Greene, C. W. 1935. The distribution of Wisconsin fishes. Wisconsin Conservation Commission, Madison. 235 p.

Greer, J. K., and F. B. Cross. 1956. Fishes of El Dorado City Lake, Butler County, Kansas. Kansas Academy of Science Transactions 59:358–363.

Griffith, E. 1834. The animal Kingdom, class Pisces. Arranged in conformity with its organization, by the Baron Cuvier, with supplementary additions . . . . Vol. 10. London. viii + 680 p.

Griffith, R. W. 1974. Environmental and salinity tolerance in the genus *Fundulus*. Copeia 1974(2):319–331.

Gunning, G. E., and W. M. Lewis. 1955. The fish population of a spring-fed swamp in the Mississippi bottoms of southern Illinois. Ecology 36(4):552–558.

———, and ———. 1956*a*. Recent collections of some less common fishes in southern Illinois. Illinois State Academy of Science Transactions 48:23–26.

———, and ———. 1956*b*. The fish population of Sugar Creek, Illinois. Illinois State Academy of Science Transactions 49:21–24.

Günther, A. 1859. Catalogue of the fishes in the British Museum. Vol. 1. 524 p.

———. 1866 [On the fishes of the states of Central America, founded upon specimens collected in the fresh and marine waters of various parts of that country]. Zoological Society of London Proceedings for 1866:600–604.

Hall, G. E., and R. M. Jenkins. 1954. Notes on the age and growth of the pirateperch, *Aphredoderus sayanus*, in Oklahoma. Copeia 1954(1):69.

Hankinson, T. L. 1920 Report on investigations of the fish of the Galien River, Berrien County, Michigan. University of Michigan Museum of Zoology Occasional Paper 89. 14 p.

———. 1932. Observations on the breeding behavior and habits of fishes in southern Michigan. Michigan Academy of Science, Arts, and Letters Paper 15:411–425.

Hansen, D. F. 1939. Variation in the number of spines and rays in the fins of the brook stickleback. Illinois State Academy of Science Transactions 22(2):207–212.

———. 1951. Biology of the white crappie in Illinois. Illinois Natural History Survey Bulletin 25(4):211–265.

———. 1965. Further observations on nesting of the white crappie, *Pomoxis annularis*. American Fisheries Society Transactions 94(2):182–184.

Harkness, W. J. K., and J. R. Dymond. 1961. The lake sturgeon. The history of its fishery and problems of conservation. Ontario Department of Lands and Forests, Fish and Wildlife Branch. 121 p.

Harlan, J. R., and E. B. Speaker. 1951. Iowa fish and fishing. 2nd edition. Iowa State Conservation Commission [Ames]. 238 p.

———, and ———. 1956. Iowa fish and fishing. 3rd edition. Iowa State Conservation Commission [Ames]. 377 p.

Hay, O. P. 1881. On a collection of fishes from eastern Mississippi. U.S. National Museum Proceedings 3:488–515.

Heidinger, R. C. 1974. First record of the northern studfish, *Fundulus catenatus* (Cyprinidontidae, Pisces), in Illinois. Illinois State Academy of Science Transactions 67(3):364–365.

Helms, D. R. 1974. Age and growth of shovelnose sturgeon, *Scaphirhynchus platorhynchus* (Rafinesque), in the Mississippi River, Iowa Academy of Science Proceedings 81(2):73–75.

Hermann, J. 1804. Observationes zoologicae, quibus novae complures, aliaeque animalium species describuntur et illustrantur. IV. Pisces. Amandum Koenig, Paris. viii + 332 p.

Hile, R. 1936. Age and growth of the cisco, *Leucichthys artedi* (Le Sueur), in the lakes of the northeastern highland, Wisconsin. U.S. Bureau of Fisheries Bulletin 43:211–317.

Hill, L. G. 1969. Feeding and food habits of the spring cavefish, *Chologaster agassizi*. American Midland Naturalist 82(1):110–116.

House, R., and L. Wells. 1973. Age, growth, spawning season, and fecundity of the trout-perch (*Percopsis omiscomaycus*) in southeastern Lake Michigan. Fisheries Research Board of Canada Journal 30(8):1221–1225.

Hoy, P. R. 1872. Deep-water fauna of Lake Michigan. Wisconsin Academy of Science, Arts, and Letters Transactions for 1870–1872:98–101.

Hoyt, R. D. 1970. Food habits of the silverjaw minnow, *Ericymba buccata* Cope, in an intermittent stream in Kentucky. American Midland Naturalist 84(1):226–236.

———. 1971. The reproductive biology of the silverjaw minnow, *Ericymba buccata* Cope, in Kentucky. American Fisheries Society Transactions 100(3):510–519.

Hubbs, C. L. 1918. Geographical variation of *Notemigonus crysoleucas*—an American minnow. Illinois State Academy of Science Transactions 11:147–151.

———. 1920. Notes on hybrid sunfishes. Aquatic Life 5(9):101–103.

———. 1926. A check-list of the fishes of the Great Lakes and tributary waters, with nomenclatorial notes and analytical keys. University of Michigan Museum of Zoology Miscellaneous Publication 15. 77 p.

———.1930. Materials for a revision of the catostomid fishes of eastern North America. University of Michigan Museum of Zoology Miscellaneous Publication 20. 47 p.

———. 1945. Corrected distributional records for Minnesota fishes. Copeia 1945(1):13–22.

———. 1951. *Notropis amnis,* a new cyprinid fish of the Mississippi fauna, with two subspecies. University of Michigan Museum of Zoology Occasional Paper 530. 30 p.

———, and R. M. Bailey. 1940. A revision of the black basses (*Micropterus* and *Huro*) with descriptions of four new forms. University of Michigan Museum of Zoology Miscellaneous Publication 48. 31 p.

———, and ———. 1952. Identification of *Oxygeneum pulverulentum* Forbes, from Illinois, as a hybrid cyprinid fish. Michigan Academy of Science, Arts, and Letters Papers for 1951, 37:143–152.

———, and J. D. Black. 1947. Revision of *Ceratichthys,* a genus of American cyprinid fishes. University of Michigan Museum of Zoology Miscellaneous Publication 66. 56 p.

———, and ———. 1954. Status and synonymy of the American percid fish *Hadropterus scierus.* American Midland Naturalist 52(1):201–210.

———, and K. Bonham. 1951. New cyprinid fishes of the genus *Notropis* from Texas. Texas Journal of Science (1):91–110.

———, and G. P. Cooper. 1936. Minnows of Michigan. Cranbrook Institute of Science Bulletin 8. 95 p.

———, and W. R. Crowe. 1956. Preliminary analysis of the American cyprinid fishes, seven new, referred to the genus *Hybopsis,* subgenus *Erimystax.* University of Michigan Museum of Zoology Occasional Paper 578. 8 p.

———, and C. W. Greene. 1928. Further notes on the fishes of the Great Lakes and tributary waters. Michigan Academy of Science, Arts, and Letters Papers for 1927, 8:371–392.

———, and ———. 1935. Two new subspecies of fishes from Wisconsin. Wisconsin Academy of Science, Arts, and Letters Transactions 29:89–101.

———, and L. C. Hubbs. 1932. Experimental verification of natural hybridization between distinct genera of sunfishes. Michigan Academy of Science, Arts, and Letters Papers for 1931, 15:427–437.

———, and K. F. Lagler. 1941. Guide to the fishes of the Great Lakes and tributary waters. Cranbrook Institute of Science Bulletin 18. 100 p.

———, and ———. 1958. Fishes of the Great Lakes region. Cranbrook Institute of Science Bulletin 26. xiii + 213 p.

———, and T. E. B. Pope. 1937. The spread of the sea lamprey through the Great Lakes. American Fisheries Society Transactions 66:172–176.

———, and M. B. Trautman. 1937. A revision of the lamprey genus *Ichthyomyzon.* University of Michigan Museum of Zoology Miscellaneous Publication 35. 109 p.

Hubbs, Clark. 1954. A new Texas subspecies, *apristis,* of the darter *Hadropterus scierus,* with a discussion of variation within the species. American Midland Naturalist 52(1):211–220.

———, and K. Strawn. 1956. Interfertility between two sympatric fishes, *Notropis lutrensis* and *Notropis venustus.* Evolution 10(4):341–344.

Hunter, J. R. 1963. The reproductive behavior of the green sunfish, *Lepomis cyanellus.* Zoologica 48(1):13–24.

———, and W. J. Wisby. 1961. Utilization of the nests of green sunfish (*Lepomis cyanellus*) by the redfin shiner (*Notropis umbratilis cyanocephalus*). Copeia 1961(1):113–115.

Johnson, R. P. 1963. Studies on the life history and ecology of the bigmouth buffalo, *Ictiobus cyprinellus* (Valenciennes). Fisheries Research Board of Canada Journal 20(6):1397–1429.

Jordan, D. S. 1877a. A partial synopsis of the fishes of the upper Georgia. Lyceum of Natural History of New York Annals 11:307–377.

———. 1877b. Contributions to North American ichthyology based primarily on the collections of the United States National Museum. II. A.—Notes on Cottidae, Etheostomatidae, Percidae, Centrarchidae, Aphododeridae, Dorysomatidae, and Cyprinidae, with revisions of the genera and descriptions of new or little known species. U.S. National Museum Bulletin 1(10):1–68.

———. 1877c. On the fishes of northern Indiana. Academy of Natural Sciences of Philadelphia Proceedings 24:42–82.

———. 1878. A catalogue of the fishes of Illinois. Illinois State Laboratory of Natural History Bulletin 1(2):37–70.

———. 1880. Description of new species of North American fishes. U.S. National Museum Proceedings 2:235–241.

———. 1885a. Description of a new species of *Hybognathus* (*Hybognathus hayi*) from Mississippi. U.S. National Museum Proceedings 7(35):548–550.

———. 1885b. A catalogue of the fishes known to inhabit the waters of North America, north of the Tropic of Cancer, with notes on the species discovered in 1883 and 1884. U.S. Commission of Fish and Fisheries Document 94. 185 p.

———. 1886. Note on the scientific name of the yellow perch, the striped bass, and other North American fishes. U.S. National Museum Proceedings 8(5):72–73.

———. 1888. A manual of the vertebrate animals of the northern United States. 5th ed. A. C. McClurg and Company, Chicago. 375 p.

———. 1929. Manual of the vertebrate animals of the northeastern United States. 13th ed. World Book Company, Yonkers-on-Hudson, New York. xxxi + 446 p.

———, and B. W. Evermann. 1896. The fishes of North and Middle America. U.S. National Museum Bulletin 47. Part 1. lx + 1240 p.

———, and C. H. Gilbert. [1883]. Synopsis of the fishes of North America. U.S. National Museum Bulletin 16. lvi + 1018 p.

———, and ———. 1886. List of fishes collected in Arkansas, Indian Territory, and Texas, in September,

1884, with notes and descriptions. U.S. National Museum Proceedings 9:1–25.

————, and S. E. Meek. 1885. List of fishes collected in Iowa and Missouri in August, 1884, with descriptions of three new species. U.S. National Museum Proceedings 8:1–17.

Karr, J. R. 1964. Age, growth, fecundity and food habits of fantail darters in Boone County, Iowa. Iowa Academy of Science Proceedings 71:274–280.

Keast, A., and D. Webb. 1966. Mouth and body form relative to feeding ecology in the fish fauna of a small lake, Lake Opinicon, Ontario. Fisheries Research Board of Canada Journal 23(12):1845–1874.

Kennicott, R. 1855. Catalogue of animals observed in Cook County, Illinois. Illinois State Agricultural Society Transactions 1:577–595.

Kirtland, J. P. 1841a. Article III. Descriptions of four new species of fishes. Boston Journal of Natural History 3(1–2):273–277.

————. 1841b. Article X. Descriptions of the fishes of the Ohio River and its tributaries. Boston Journal of Natural History 3(3):338–352.

————. 1844. [Description of *Hybopsis storeriana*]. Boston Society of Natural History Proceedings 1:199–200.

Krumholz, L. A. 1948. Reproduction in the western mosquitofish, *Gambusia affinis affinis* (Baird and Girard), and its use in mosquito control. Ecological Monographs 18:1–43.

————, and H. S. Cavanah. 1968. Comparative morphometry of freshwater drum from two midwestern localities. American Fisheries Society Transactions 97(4):429–441.

Lacépède, B. G. E. 1802. Histoire naturelle des poissons. Vol. 4. 728 p. (Not seen)

————. 1803. Histoire naturelle des poissons. Vol. 5. 803 p. (Not seen)

Lachner, E. A. 1952. Studies of the biology of the cyprinid fishes of the chub genus *Nocomis* of northeastern United States. American Midland Naturalist 48(2):433–466.

————, and R. E. Jenkins. 1971. Systematics, distribution, and evolution of the *Nocomis biguttatus* species group (Family Cyprinidae: Pisces) with a description of a new species from the Ozark Upland. Smithsonian Contributions to Zoology 91. 28 p.

Large, T. [1903]. A list of the native fishes of Illinois, with keys. Appendix to Report of the State Board of Fish Commissioners for Sept. 30, 1900 to Oct. 1, 1902. 30 p.

Larimore, R. W. 1957. Ecological life history of the warmouth (Centrarchidae). Illinois Natural History Survey Bulletin 27(1):1–83.

————, and P. W. Smith. 1963. The fishes of Champaign County, Illinois, as affected by 60 years of stream changes. Illinois Natural History Survey Bulletin 28(2):299–382.

Laurence, G. C., and R. W. Yerger. 1967. Life history studies of the Alabama shad, in the Apalachicola River, Florida. Southeastern Association of Game and Fish Commissioners Proceedings 20:260–273.

Le Sueur, C. A. 1817a. A short description of five (sup-

posed) new species of the genus *Muraena*, discovered by Mr. Le Sueur, in the year 1816. Academy of Natural Sciences of Philadelphia Journal 1(5):81–83.

————. 1817b. A new genus of fishes, of the order Abdominales, proposed under the name of *Catostomus;* and the characters of this genus with its species, indicated. Academy of Natural Sciences of Philadelphia Journal 1(5):88–96, 102–111.

————. 1817c. Description of four new species, and two varieties, of the genus *Hydrargira*. Academy of Natural Sciences of Philadelphia Journal 1(6):126–134.

————. 1818. Descriptions of several new species of North American fishes. Academy of Natural Sciences of Philadelphia Journal 1:222–235, 359–368.

————. 1819. Notice de quelques poissons découverts dans les lacs du haut-Canada, durant l'été de 1816. Mémoires du Muséum d'Histoire Naturelle à Paris 55:148–161.

————. 1827. American ichthyology, or natural history of the fishes of North America. New Harmony, Indiana. (Not seen)

Lewis, R. M. 1957. Comparative study of populations of the striped bass. U.S. Department of the Interior, Fish and Wildlife Service Special Scientific Report (Fish) 204. 54 p.

Lewis, W. M. 1950. Growth of the white bass, *Lepibema chrysops* (Rafinesque), in Clear Lake, Iowa. Iowa State College Journal of Science 24(3):273–278.

————. 1955. The fish population of the main stream of the Big Muddy River. Illinois State Academy of Science Transactions 47:20–24.

————, and K. D. Carlander. 1948. Growth of the yellow bass, *Morone interrupta* Gill, in Clear Lake, Iowa. Iowa State College Journal of Science 22(2):185–195.

————, and D. Elder. 1953. The fish population of the headwaters of a spotted bass stream in southern Illinois. American Fisheries Society Transactions for 1952, 82:193–202.

————, and G. E. Gunning. 1959. Notes on the life history of the steelcolor shiner, *Notropis whipplei* (Girard). Illinois State Academy of Science Transactions 52(1–2):59–64.

Linnaeus, Carolus. 1758. Systema naturae. 10th ed. Vol. 1. Laurentii Salvii, Holmiae. 824 + iii p.

————. 1766. Systema naturae. 12th ed. Vol. 1. Laurentii Salvii, Holmiae. 532 p.

Lopinot, A. C., and P. W. Smith. 1973. Rare and endangered fish of Illinois. Illinois Department of Conservation Division of Fisheries. 53 p.

Luce, W. M. 1933. A survey of the fishery of the Kaskaskia River. Illinois Natural History Survey Bulletin 20(2):71–123.

Marshall, N. 1947. Studies on the life history and ecology of *Notropis chalybaeus* (Cope). Quarterly Journal of the Florida Academy of Science 9(3–4):163–188.

McAllister, D. E. 1963. A revision of the smelt family Osmeridae. National Museum of Canada Bulletin 191:1–53.

McPhail, J. D. 1963. Geographic variation in North

American ninespine sticklebacks, *Pungitius pungitius.* Fisheries Research Board of Canada Journal 29(1): 27–44.

———, and C. C. Lindsey. 1970. Freshwater fishes of northwestern Canada and Alaska. Fisheries Research Board of Canada Bulletin 173. 381 p.

McSwain, L. E., and R. M. Gennings. 1972. Spawning behavior of the spotted sucker, *Minytrema melanops* (Rafinesque). American Fisheries Society Transactions 101(4):738–740.

Meek, S. E. 1896. A list of fishes and mollusks collected in Arkansas and Indian Territory in 1894. U.S. Fish Commission Bulletin for 1895, 15:341–349.

———, and S. F. Hildebrand. 1910. A synoptic list of the fishes known to occur within 50 miles of Chicago. Field Museum of Natural History Zoological Series Publications 7(9):223–338.

Meyer, W. H. 1962. Life history of three species of redhorse (*Moxostoma*) in Des Moines River, Iowa. American Fisheries Society Transactions 91(4):412–419.

Miller, R. J. 1962. Reproductive behavior of the stoneroller minnow, *Campostoma anomalum pullum.* Copeia 1962(2):407–417.

———. 1968. Speciation in the common shiner: an alternate view. Copeia 1968(3):640–647.

Miller, R. R. 1950. A review of the American clupeid fishes of the genus *Dorosoma.* U.S. National Museum Proceedings 100(3267):387–410.

———. 1955. An annotated list of the American cyprinidontid fishes of the genus *Fundulus,* with the description of *Fundulus persimilis* from Yucatan. University of Michigan Museum of Zoology Occasional Paper 568. 25 p.

———. 1957. Origin and dispersal of the alewife, *Alosa pseudoharengus,* and the gizzard shad, *Dorosoma cepedianum,* in the Great Lakes. American Fisheries Society Transactions for 1956, 86:97–111.

———. 1960. Systematics and biology of the gizzard shad (*Dorosoma cepedianum*) and related fishes. U.S. Fish and Wildlife Service Fishery Bulletin 173:371–392.

Miller, R. V. 1968. A systematic study of the greenside darter, *Etheostoma blennioides* Rafinesque (Pisces: Percidae). Copeia 1968(1):1–40.

Minckley, W. L. 1959. Fishes of the Big Blue River basin, Kansas. University of Kansas Museum of Natural History Publication 11(7):401–442.

———, and L. A. Krumholz. 1960. Natural hybridization between the clupeid genera *Dorosoma* and *Signalosa,* with a report on the distribution of *S. petenensis.* Zoologica 44(4):171–180.

Mitchill, S. L. 1814. Report in part of Samuel L. Mitchill, M. D., on the fishes of New York. New York. 28 p. (Not seen)

———. 1815. The fishes of New York, described and arranged. Literary and Philosophical Society of New York Transactions 1(5):355–492.

———. 1817. Lyceum of natural history. Report on the ichthyology of the Walkill, from specimens of fishes presented to the Society . . . by Dr. B. Akerly . . . American Monthly Magazine and Critical Review 1(4):289–290.

———. 1818. Memoir on ichthyology. The fishes of New-York described and arranged. American Monthly Magazine and Critical Review 2(4):241–248, (5)321–328. (Not seen)

———. 1824. [The original description of the muskellunge, *Esox masquinongy,* according to DeKay 1842. Although subsequent authors have never been able to locate the article, they have accepted DeKay's word that it appeared in an 1824 issue of the *Mirror* (Crossman, personal communication)].

Moffett, J. W. 1957. Recent changes in the deep-water fish populations of Lake Michigan. American Fisheries Society Transactions for 1956, 86:393–408.

Mount, D. I. 1959. Spawning behavior of the bluebreast darter, *Etheostoma camurum* (Cope). Copeia 1959(3): 240–243.

Moyle, P. B. 1973. Ecological segregation among three species of minnows (Cyprinidae) in a Minnesota lake. American Fisheries Society Transactions 102(4): 794–805.

Nelson, E. W. 1876. A partial catalogue of the fishes of Illinois. Illinois Museum of Natural History Bulletin 1(1):33–52; also Illinois State Laboratory of Natural History Bulletin 1(1):33–52.

———. 1878. Fisheries of Chicago and vicinity. Pages 783–800 *in* Report of the U.S. Commissioner of Fish and Fisheries for 1875–1876, Part 4.

Nelson, J. S. 1968. Life history of the brook silverside, *Labidesthes sicculus,* in Crooked Lake, Indiana. American Fisheries Society Transactions 97(3):293–296.

———. 1969. Geographic variation in the brook stickleback, *Culaea inconstans,* and notes on nomenclature and distribution. Fisheries Research Board of Canada Journal 26(9):2431–2447.

———. 1971. Absence of pelvic complex in ninespine sticklebacks, *Pungitius pungitius,* collected in Ireland and Wood Buffalo National Park, Canada, with notes on meristic variation. Copeia 1971(4):707–717.

Netsch, N. F., and A. Witt, Jr. 1962. Contributions to the life history of the longnose gar, (*Lepisosteus osseus*) in Missouri. American Fisheries Society Transactions 91(3):251–262.

O'Donnell, D. J. 1935. Annotated list of the fishes of Illinois. Illinois Natural History Survey Bulletin 20(5):473–500.

Olund, L. J., and F. B. Cross. 1961. Geographic variation in the North American cyprinid fish, *Hybopsis gracilis.* University of Kansas Museum of Natural History Publications 13(7):323–348.

Page, L. M. 1974. The life history of the spottail darter, *Etheostoma squamiceps,* in Big Creek, Illinois, and Ferguson Creek, Kentucky. Illinois Natural History Survey Biological Notes 89. 20 p.

———. 1975. The life history of the stripetail darter, *Etheostoma kennicotti,* in Big Creek, Illinois. Illinois Natural History Survey Biological Notes 93. 15 p.

———, and P. W. Smith. 1970. The life history of the dusky darter, *Percina sciera,* in the Embarras River,

Illinois. Illinois Natural History Survey Biological Notes 69. 15 p.

———, and ———. 1971. The life history of the slenderhead darter, *Percina phoxocephala*, in the Embarras River, Illinois. Illinois Natural History Survey Biological Notes 74. 14 p.

———, and ———. 1976. Variation and systematics of the stripetail darter, *Etheostoma kennicotti*. Copeia 1976(3):532–541.

———, and R. L. Smith. 1970. Recent range adjustments and hybridization of *Notropis lutrensis* and *Notropis spilopterus* in Illinois. Illinois State Academy of Science Transactions 63(3):264–272.

Parker, H. L. 1964. Natural history of *Pimephales vigilax* (Cyprinidae). The Southwestern Naturalist 8(4):228–235.

Parsons, J. W. 1973. History of salmon in the Great Lakes. U.S. Bureau of Sport Fisheries and Wildlife Technical Paper 68. 80 p.

Pennant, T. 1784. Arctic zoology. Vol. 1. Henry Hughs, London. [viii] + [5] + 185 p.

Pfeiffer, R. A. 1955. Studies on the life history of the rosyface shiner, *Notropis rubellus*. Copeia 1955(2):95–104.

Pflieger, W. L. 1965. Reproductive behavior of the minnows, *Notropis spilopterus* and *Notropis whipplii*. Copeia 1965(1):1–8.

———. 1971. A distributional study of Missouri fishes. University of Kansas Museum of Natural History Publications 20(3):225–570.

———. 1975. The fishes of Missouri. Missouri Department of Conservation. viii + 343 p.

Phillips, G. L. 1969. Morphology and variation of the American cyprinid fishes *Chrosomus erythrogaster* and *Chrosomus eos*. Copeia 1969(3):501–509.

Poulson, T. L. 1963. Cave adaptation in amblyopsid fishes. American Midland Naturalist 70(2):257–290.

Purkett, C. A., Jr. 1961. Reproduction and early development in the paddlefish. American Fisheries Society Transactions 90(2):125–129.

Putnam, F. W. 1863. List of fishes sent by the museum to different institutions, in exchange for other specimens, with annotations. Harvard University Museum of Comparative Zoology Bulletin 1(1):2–16.

———. 1872. The blind fishes of Mammoth Cave and their allies. American Naturalist 6(1):6–30.

Rafinesque, C. S. 1817a. First decade of new North-American fishes. American Monthly Magazine and Critical Review 2(2):120–121.

———. 1817b. Additions to the observations on sturgeons of North America. American Monthly Magazine and Critical Review 1(4):288.

———. 1818a. Farther account of discoveries in natural history, in the western states. American Monthly Magazine and Critical Review 4(1):39–42.

———. 1818b. Description of three new genera of fluviatile fish, *Pomoxis, Sarchirus,* and *Exoglossum*. Academy of Natural Sciences of Philadelphia Journal 1:417–422.

———. 1818c. Description of new genera of North American fishes, *Opsanus* and *Notropis*. American Monthly Magazine and Critical Review 2(3):203–204.

———. 1818d. Discoveries in natural history, made during a journey through the western region of the United States. American Monthly Magazine and Critical Review 3(5):354–356.

———. 1819. Prodrome de 70 nouveaux genres d'animaux découverts dans l'intérieur des États-Unis d'Amérique, durant l'année 1818. Journal de Physique, de Chimie, d'Histoire Naturelle et des Arts 88:417–429.

———. 1820a. Ichthyologia Ohiensis, or natural history of the fishes inhabiting the River Ohio and its tributary streams, preceded by a physical description of the Ohio and its branches. Lexington, Kentucky. 90 p.

———. 1820b. Description of the Silures or catfishes of the river Ohio. Quarterly Journal of Science, Literature, and the Arts 9:48–52.

Raney, E. C. 1939. The breeding habits of the silvery minnow, *Hybognathus regius* Girard. American Midland Naturalist 21(3):674–680.

———. 1940. The breeding behavior of the common shiner, *Notropis cornutus* (Mitchill). Zoologica 25(1):1–14.

———. 1952. The life history of the striped bass, *Roccus saxatilis* (Walbaum). Bingham Oceanographic Collection Bulletin 14(1):5–97.

———, and E. A. Lachner. 1946. Age, growth, and habits of the hog sucker, *Hypentelium nigricans* (LeSueur), in New York. American Midland Naturalist 36(1):76–86.

———, and ———. 1947. *Hypentelium roanokense,* a new catostomid fish from the Roanoke River in Virginia. American Museum Novitates 1333. 15 p.

Reed, R. J. 1959. Age, growth, and food of the longnose dace, *Rhinichthys cataractae*, in northwestern Pennsylvania. Copeia 1959(2):160–162.

Reighard, J., and H. Cummins. 1916. Description of a new species of lamprey of the genus *Ichthyomyzon*. University of Michigan Museum of Zoology Occasional Paper 31. 12 p.

Richardson, J. 1836. Fauna Boreali-Americana; or the zoology of the northern parts of British America: Part third *The Fish*. Richard Bentley, London. 327 p. (Not seen)

Richardson, L. R. 1939. The spawning behavior of *Fundulus diaphanus* (LeSueur). Copeia 1939(3):165–167.

Rohde, F. C. 1977. First record of the least brook lamprey, *Okkelbergia aepyptera,* (Pisces: Petromyzonidae) from Illinois. Illinois State Academy of Science Transactions 69(3):313–314.

———, R. G. Arndt, and J. C. S. Wang. 1976. Life history of the freshwater lampreys, *Okkelbergia aepyptera* and *Lampetra lamottenii* (Pisces: Petromyzonidae), on the Delmarva Peninsula. Southern California Academy of Sciences Bulletin 75(2):99–111.

Savage, T. 1963. Reproductive behavior of the mottled sculpin, *Cottus bairdi* Girard. Copeia 1963(2):317–325.

Schultz, L. P. 1927. Temperature-controlled variation in the golden shiner, *Notemigonus crysoleucas*. Michigan Academy of Science, Arts, and Letters Papers for 1926, 6:417–432.

Scott, W. B., and E. J. Crossman. 1973. Freshwater fishes of Canada. Fisheries Research Board of Canada Bulletin 184. xi + 966 p.

Sigler, W. F. 1949. Life history of the white bass in Storm Lake, Iowa. Iowa State College Journal of Science 23(4):311–316.

———, and R. R. Miller. 1963. Fishes of Utah. Utah State Department of Fish and Game, Salt Lake City. 203 p.

Smith, B. G. 1908. The spawning habits of *Chrosomus erythrogaster* Rafinesque. Biological Bulletin 14(6): 9–18.

Smith, P. W. 1965. A preliminary annotated list of the lampreys and fishes of Illinois. Illinois Natural History Survey Biological Notes 54. 12 p.

———. 1968. An assessment of changes in the fish fauna of two Illinois rivers and its bearing on their future. Illinois State Academy of Science Transactions 61(1):31–45.

———. 1971. Illinois streams: A classification based on their fishes and an analysis of factors responsible for disappearance of native species. Illinois Natural History Survey Biological Notes 76. 14 p.

———, A. C. Lopinot, and W. L. Pflieger. 1971. A distributional atlas of upper Mississippi River fishes. Illinois Natural History Survey Biological Notes 73. 20 p.

———, and L. M. Page. 1969. The food of spotted bass in streams of the Wabash River drainage. American Fisheries Society Transactions 98(4):647–651.

Snelson, F. F., Jr. 1973. Systematics and distribution of the ribbon shiner, *Notropis fumeus* (Cyprinidae), from the central United States. American Midland Naturalist 89(1):166–191.

———, and W. L. Pflieger. 1975. Redescription of the redfin shiner, *Notropis umbratilis*, and its subspecies in the central Mississippi River basin. Copeia 1975(2):231–249.

Speare, E. P. 1965. Fecundity and egg survival of the central johnny darter (*Etheostoma nigrum nigrum*) in southern Michigan. Copeia 1965(3):308–314.

Starrett, W. C. 1950. Food relationships of the minnows of the Des Moines River, Iowa. Ecology 31(2):216–233.

———. 1951. Some factors affecting the abundance of minnows in the Des Moines River, Iowa. Ecology 31(1):13–27.

———, W. J. Harth, and P. W. Smith. 1960. Parasitic lampreys of the genus *Ichthyomyzon* in the rivers of Illinois. Copeia 1960(4):337–346.

Stegman, J. L., and W. L. Minckley. 1959. Occurrence of three species of fishes in interstices of gravel in an area of subsurface flow. Copeia 1959(4):341.

Storer, D. H. 1845*a*. [Original description of *Etheostoma caeruleum*]. Boston Society of Natural History Proceedings 2:47–49.

———. 1845*b*. [Original description of *Fundulus oliva-ceus*]. Boston Society of Natural History Proceedings 2:51.

———. 1846. A synopsis of the fishes of North America. American Academy of Arts and Science Memoirs 2:253–550.

Suckley, G. 1860. Report upon the fishes collected on the survey. Pages *in* Reports of explorations and surveys to ascertain the most practicable and economical route for a railroad from the Mississippi River to the Pacific Ocean. U.S. Senate, Washington, D.C. Vol. 12, Book 2, Part viii. 399 p.

Suttkus, R. D. 1958. Status of the nominal species *Moniana deliciosa* Girard and *Cyprinella texana* Girard. Copeia 1958(4):307–318.

Swain, J. 1883. A description of a new species of *Hadropterus* (*Hadropterus scierus*) from southern Indiana. U.S. National Museum Proceedings 6:252.

———, and G. B. Kalb. 1883. A review of the genus *Noturus*, with a description of a new species. U.S. National Museum Proceedings 5:638–644.

Tarter, D. C. 1970. Food and feeding habits of the western blacknose dace, *Rhinichthys atratulus meleagris* Agassiz, in Doe Run, Meade County, Kentucky. American Midland Naturalist 83(1):134–159.

Taylor, W. R. 1954. Records of fishes in the John N. Lowe collection from the Upper Peninsula of Michigan. University of Michigan Museum of Zoology Miscellaneous Publication 87. 50 p.

———. 1969. A revision of the catfish genus *Noturus* Rafinesque, with an analysis of higher groups in the Ictaluridae. U.S. National Museum Bulletin 282. vi + 315 p.

Thomas, D. L. 1970. An ecological study of four darters of the genus *Percina* (Percidae) in the Kaskaskia River, Illinois. Illinois Natural History Survey Biological Notes 70. 18 p.

Thomerson, J. E. 1966. A comparative biosystematic study of *Fundulus notatus* and *Fundulus olivaceus* (Pisces: Cyprinodontidae). Tulane Studies in Zoology 13(1):29–47.

———. 1969. Variation and relationships of the studfishes, *Fundulus catenatus* and *Fundulus stellifer* (Cyprinodontidae, Pisces). Tulane Studies in Zoology 16(1):1–21.

———. 1970. Food habits of allotopic and syntopic populations of the topminnows *Fundulus olivaceus* and *Fundulus notatus*. American Midland Naturalist 84(2):573–576.

———, T. B. Thorson, and R. L. Hempel. 1977. A record for the bull shark, *Carcharhinus leucas*, from the upper Mississippi River near Alton, Illinois. Copeia 1977(1):166–168.

Thompson, B. A. 1974. An analysis of sympatric populations of two closely related species of *Percina*, with notes on food habits of the subgenus *Imostoma*. Association of Southeastern Biologists Bulletin 21(2): 87.

Thompson, D. H. 1933. The finding of very young *Polyodon*. Copeia 1933(1):31–33.

———. 1935. Hybridization and racial differentiation among Illinois fishes. Illinois Natural History Survey Bulletin 20(5):492–494.

Trautman, M. B. 1930. The specific distinctness of *Poecilichthys coeruleus* (Storer) and *Poecilichthys spectabilis* Agassiz. Copeia 1930(1):12–13.

———. 1931. *Notropis volucellus wickliffi,* a new subspecies of cyprinid fish from the Ohio and upper Mississippi River. Ohio Journal of Science 31(6): 468–474.

———. 1956. *Carpiodes cyprinus hinei,* a new subspecies of carpsucker from the Ohio and upper Mississippi River systems. Ohio Journal of Science 56(1):33–40.

———. 1957. The fishes of Ohio. The Ohio State University Press, Columbus. xvii + 683 p.

Tsai, C. 1968. Distribution of the harlequin darter, *Etheostoma histrio.* Copeia 1968(1):178–181.

———, and E. C. Raney. 1974. Systematics of the banded darter, *Etheostoma zonale* (Pisces: Percidae). Copeia 1974(1):1–24.

Turner, C. L. 1921. Food of the common Ohio darters. Ohio Journal of Science 22(2):41–62.

Underhill, J. C. 1963. Distribution in Minnesota of the subspecies of the percid fish, *Etheostoma nigrum,* and of their intergrades. American Midland Naturalist 70(2):470–478.

Van Cleave, H. J., and H. C. Markus. 1929. Studies on the life history of the blunt-nosed minnow. American Naturalist 63:530–539.

Vanicek, D. 1961. Life history of the quillback and highfin carpsuckers in the Des Moines River. Iowa Academy of Science Proceedings 68:238–246.

Voightlander, C. W., and T. E. Wissing. 1974. Food habits of young and yearling white bass. American Fisheries Society Transactions 103(1):25–31.

Walbaum, J. J. 1792. Petri Artedi renovati, *i. e.* bibliotheca et philosophia ichthyologica. Ichthyologiae pars III . . . Grypeswaldiae. Ant. Ferdin, Roese. 723 p. (Not seen)

Wallace, D. C. 1973*a*. The distribution and dispersal of the silverjaw minnow, *Ericymba buccata* Cope. American Midland Naturalist 89(1):145–155.

———. 1973*b*. Reproduction of the silverjaw minnow, *Ericymba buccata* Cope. American Fisheries Society Transactions 102(4):786–793.

Weed, A. C. 1925. A review of the fishes of the genus *Signalosa.* Field Museum of Natural History Publications, Zoological Series 233, 12(11):137–146.

Weise, J. G. 1957. The spring cave-fish, *Chologaster papilliferus,* in Illinois. Ecology 38(2):195–204.

Wells, L. 1968. Seasonal depth distribution of fish in southeastern Lake Michigan. U.S. Bureau of Commercial Fisheries Fishery Bulletin 67(1):1–15.

———, and A. M. Beeton. 1963. Food of the bloater,

Coregonus hoyi, in Lake Michigan. American Fisheries Society Transactions 92(3):245–255.

Whitaker, J. O., Jr., and D. C. Wallace. 1973. Fishes of Vigo County, Indiana. Indiana Academy of Science Proceedings 82:448–464.

White, S. T., and D. C. Wallace. 1973. Diel changes in the feeding activity and food habits of the spotfin shiner, *Notropis spilopterus* (Cope). American Midland Naturalist 90(1):200–205.

Wigley, R. L. 1959. Life history of the sea lamprey of Cayuga Lake, New York. U.S. Fish and Wildlife Service Fishery Bulletin 59(154):561–617.

Wiley, E. O., III, and D. D. Hall. 1975. *Fundulus blairae,* a new species of the *Fundulus nottii* complex (Teleostei, Cyprinodontidae). American Museum Novitates 2577. 13 p.

Williams, J. D. 1975. Systematics of the percid fishes of the subgenus *Ammocrypta,* with descriptions of two new species. Alabama Museum of Natural History Bulletin 1:1–56.

———, and C. R. Robins. 1970. Variation in populations of the fish *Cottus carolinae* in the Alabama River system with description of a new subspecies from below the Fall Line. American Midland Naturalist 83(2): 368–381.

Wilson, A. [undated, *ca.* 1811]. *Clupea. In* Rees' New Cyclopedia 1:(no pagination). (Not seen)

Winchell, A. 1864. Description of a gar-pike, supposed to be new—*Lepidosteus (Cylindrosteus) oculatus.* Academy of Natural Sciences of Philadelphia Proceedings 16:183–185.

Winn, H. E. 1958*a*. Observations on the reproductive habits of darters (Pisces-Percidae). American Midland Naturalist 59(1):190–212.

———. 1958*b*. Comparative reproductive behavior and ecology of fourteen species of darters (Pisces-Percidae). Ecological Monographs 28:155–191.

———. 1960. Biology of the brook stickleback *Eucalia inconstans* (Kirtland). American Midland Naturalist 63(2):424–438.

Woods, L. P., and R. F. Inger. 1957. The cave, spring, and swamp fishes of the family Amblyopsidae of central and eastern United States. American Midland Naturalist 58(1):232–256.

Yokley, P., Jr. 1974. Habitat and reproductive behavior of the rosefin shiner, *Notropis ardens* (Cope), in Lauderdale County, Alabama (Osteichthyes, Cypriniformes, Cyprinidae). Association of Southeastern Biologists Bulletin 21(2):93.

Zorach, T. 1972. Systematics of the percid fishes, *Etheostoma camurum* and *E. chlorobranchium* new species, with a discussion of the subgenus *Nothonotus.* Copeia 1972(3):427–447.

INDEX TO COMMON AND SCIENTIFIC NAMES